KU-200-722

Conferences and Conventions

A Global Industry

Third edition

Tony Rogers

Routledge
Taylor & Francis Group

LONDON AND NEW YORK

385.479446dg   658.456 Rot
MAIN
Buks

First edition published 2003 by Butterworth-Heinemann
Second edition published 2008

Third edition published 2013
by Routledge
2 Park Square, Milton Park, Abingdon, Oxon OX14 4RN

Simultaneously published in the USA and Canada
by Routledge
711 Third Avenue, New York, NY 10017

Routledge is an imprint of the Taylor & Francis Group, an informa business

© 2013 Tony Rogers

The right of Tony Rogers to be identified as author of this work has been
asserted by him in accordance with sections 77 and 78 of the Copyright,
Designs and Patents Act 1988.

All rights reserved. No part of this book may be reprinted or reproduced
or utilised in any form or by any electronic, mechanical, or other means,
now known or hereafter invented, including photocopying and recording,
or in any information storage or retrieval system, without permission in
writing from the publishers.

Trademark notice: Product or corporate names may be trademarks or
registered trademarks, and are used only for identification and
explanation without intent to infringe.

British Library Cataloguing in Publication Data
A catalogue record for this book is available from the British Library

Library of Congress Cataloging in Publication Data
Rogers, Tony, 1945–
    Conferences and conventions: a global industry/Tony Rogers. — 3rd ed.
    p. cm.
    Includes bibliographical references and index.
    1. Congresses and conventions—Economic aspects. 2. Congresses and
    conventions—Management. 3. Convetion facilities. I. Title.
    AS6.R64 2012
    060—dc23
    2012027449

ISBN: 978-0-415-52668-5 (hbk)
ISBN: 978-0-415-52669-2 (pbk)
ISBN: 978-0-203-11940-2 (ebk)

Typeset in Helvetica Neue
by Florence Production Ltd, Stoodleigh, Devon, UK

MIX
Paper from
responsible sources
FSC® C004839

Printed by Bell & Bain Ltd., Glasgow

Conferences and Conventions

WITHDRAWN

Conferences and Conventions: A Global Industry provides a comprehensive introduction to the key elements of the global conference, convention and meetings industry. It examines the industry's origins, structure, economic, social and environmental impacts, education, training and career opportunities, and the industry's future development. It also explores its links with the wider tourism industry, and suggests that there should be a realignment of these links, putting a greater focus on designing, executing and measuring meeting and convention contents so that they have a purposeful impact on participants, thus creating greater value for stakeholders. It suggests that there should be greater emphasis on the role that meetings play in economic, professional and educational development, promoting the benefits they provide in knowledge exchange, scientific research, technology transfer, networking and motivation and showing clearly what such business events actually accomplish.

This revised third edition has been updated to reflect current trends and emerging topics and achieve a more international approach. This edition has also been updated with the following features:

- New content on social media, web-based marketing, the use of technology, experiential marketing and events, the role of trade shows in the conventions sector, issues of sustainability, and moves to create a profession for event management.
- Fully integrated and updated case studies to highlight current issues and demonstrate theory in practice. Also contains new case studies on the growth markets of Asia, Brazil and the Middle East.
- A detailed meetings and events industry lexicon.
- A companion website is available at www.routledge.com/cw/rogers and includes PowerPoint slides and additional case studies for lecturers, and Events Conference Scenarios and web and video links for students.

This book is written in an accessible and engaging style and structured logically with useful features throughout to aid students' learning and understanding. This book is an invaluable resource to students following Events Management, Hospitality and Tourism courses.

Tony Rogers is a consultant specialising in conferences, business tourism/business visits and events, and destination marketing and management. He is also Visiting Fellow at Leeds Metropolitan University's UK Centre for Events Management.

THE LEARNING CENTRE
EALING, HAMMERSMITH AND WEST LONDON COLLEGE
GLIDDON ROAD
LONDON W14 9BL

* 3 5 0 6 0 5 *

Books in the Events Management Series

Edited by
Glenn Bowdin, Leeds Metropolitan University, UK
Don Getz, University of Calgary, Canada
Conrad Lashley, Nottingham Trent University, UK

1. Management of Event Operations
   Julia Tum, Philippa Norton, J. Nevan Wright

2. Innovative Marketing Communications: Strategies for the Event Industry
   Guy Masterman, Emma H. Wood

3. Events Design and Experience
   Graham Berridge

4. Marketing Destinations and Venues for Conferences, Conventions
   and Business Events
   Tony Rogers, Rob Davidson

5. Human Resource Management for Events: Managing the Event Workforce
   Lynn Van der Wagen

6. Risk Management for Meetings and Events
   Julia Rutherford Silvers

7. Conferences and Conventions: A Global Industry, 2nd edn
   Tony Rogers

8. Events Feasibility and Development
   William O'Toole

9. Events Management, 3rd edn
   Glenn Bowdin, Johnny Allen, William O'Toole, Rob Harris, Ian McDonnell

10. Event Studies, 2nd edn
    Donald Getz

11. Conferences and Conventions: A Global Industry, 3rd edn
    Tony Rogers

Contents

List of illustrations   x
Preface   xiii
Foreword   xv

1 A GLOBAL INDUSTRY   **1**

Chapter objectives   1
Learning outcomes   2
Introduction   2
The origins of the conference industry   2
The foundations of a proper industry   5
CASE STUDY 1.1 Infrastructure investments in Sydney   8
The globalisation of the conference industry   12
Certain industry shortcomings   19
Industry parameters and definitions   24
Business tourism and leisure tourism   27
Benefits of conference and business tourism   28
Changing the perceptions and profile of conferences
    and business events   31
CASE STUDY 1.2 Qatar National Convention Centre   32
Summary   38
Review and discussion questions   39
References   39
Further reading   40

2 THE STRUCTURE OF THE CONFERENCE INDUSTRY   **41**

Chapter objectives   41
Learning outcomes   42

Introduction   42
The buyers   42
The suppliers   60
Agencies and intermediaries   64
Other important organisations   78
CASE STUDY 2.1 *Launch of Vauxhall Astra by experiential event*
agency TRO   81
CASE STUDY 2.2 *Oriflame Executive Conference 2012,*
Buenos Aires   84
CASE STUDY 2.3 *Conventa, the South East European exhibition for*
meetings, events and incentives   87
Summary   94
Review and discussion questions   95
References   95
Further reading   96

3 WINNING CONFERENCE BUSINESS: 1   **97**

Chapter objectives   97
Learning outcomes   98
Introduction   98
Marketing principles   98
Relationship marketing and customer relationship management   106
Branding   110
CASE STUDY 3.1 *Vilnius Convention Bureau branding   113*
The role of destination marketing organisations   119
Event agency marketing activity   127
CASE STUDY 3.2 *São Paulo Convention and Visitors Bureau, Brazil   130*
Summary   137
Review and discussion questions   138
References   138
Further reading   139

4 WINNING CONFERENCE BUSINESS: 2   **141**

Chapter objectives   141
Learning outcomes   142
Introduction   142
Web marketing   143
The use of social media   146
Familiarisation visits, workshops and showcases   148
CASE STUDY 4.1 *'Scotland Means Business'   149*

Conference ambassador programmes   *151*
Event bidding and tendering   *157*
Subvention and bid support practices   *160*
CASE STUDY 4.2 *Seoul Convention Bureau's three-step social media campaign in destination marketing*   *168*
CASE STUDY 4.3 *Congress of the World Federation of Societies of Intensive and Critical Care Medicine (WFSICCM)*   *172*
Summary   *175*
Review and discussion questions   *176*
References   *176*

5 PLANNING AND STAGING SUCCESSFUL CONFERENCES: AN ORGANISER'S PERSPECTIVE   177

Chapter objectives   *177*
Learning outcomes   *178*
Introduction   *178*
A general introduction to conference organising   *178*
Pre-conference planning and research   *180*
CASE STUDY 5.1 *Outsourcing to a PCO or event management agency*   *182*
Budgeting and financial management   *186*
Sourcing and selecting a venue   *192*
Negotiating with venues   *198*
Programme planning   *200*
Event marketing   *202*
CASE STUDY 5.2 *Using Twitter at 'The Future Is You' Conference*   *205*
Conference management and production   *206*
Event evaluation and measuring return on investment (ROI)   *208*
CASE STUDY 5.3 *The Kenes Group*   *214*
Social media blue paper   *218*
Summary   *226*
Review and discussion questions   *227*
References   *227*
Further reading   *228*

6 CONFERENCE MANAGEMENT: A VENUE PERSPECTIVE   229

Chapter objectives   *229*
Learning outcomes   *230*
Introduction   *230*
Professional inspection visits and showrounds   *230*

Yield management and 'REVPAR'   232
Negotiating with clients   235
Venue case studies   237
CASE STUDY 6.1 *China National Convention Center, Beijing, China*   237
CASE STUDY 6.2 *Highgate House, Northamptonshire, England*   242
CASE STUDY 6.3 *The Celtic Manor Resort, Newport, Wales*   246
Summary   250
Review and discussion questions   250
References   250
Further reading   250

7 THE ECONOMIC, SOCIAL AND ENVIRONMENTAL IMPACTS OF CONFERENCES AND CONVENTIONS

251

Chapter objectives   251
Learning outcomes   252
Introduction   252
Factors affecting conference sector demand   252
The economic impact of the conventions industry   255
Social impacts and legacies   263
Environmental impacts and sustainability issues   267
CASE STUDY 7.1 *The Conventa Exhibition's sustainability features*   274
CASE STUDY 7.2 *Vancouver Convention Centre, Canada*   276
Summary   282
Review and discussion questions   283
References   283

8 DEVELOPING THE INDUSTRY'S WORKFORCE: CREATING A PROFESSION

285

Chapter objectives   285
Learning outcomes   286
Introduction   286
Developing appropriate skills   286
Creating a profession   290
Education and learning, training and CPD opportunities   293
Careers in the conference industry   300
Salary levels   302
Career profiles of leading industry figures   304
Summary   320
Review and discussion questions   321
References   321

9 LEADING INDUSTRY ORGANISATIONS   323

Chapter objectives   323
Learning outcomes   324
Introduction   324
The roles of international organisations and associations   324
The roles of selected national trade associations   341
Online communities of industry professionals   349
An assessment of the conference industry's fragmentation   349
Summary   350
Review and discussion questions   350

10 THE FUTURE: TRENDS, CHALLENGES AND OPPORTUNITIES   351

Chapter objectives   351
Learning outcomes   352
Introduction   352
Understanding and promoting the value of the conference,
   meetings and business events industry   352
CASE STUDY 10.1 *29th International Congress of Ophthalmology*
                2002, Sydney   356
Technology applications and trends   356
CASE STUDY 10.2 *App keeps knee specialists on their toes   365*
Virtual, face-to-face or hybrid?   366
Corporate social responsibility   370
The future of meetings, conferences and conventions   373
In conclusion   385
Summary   386
Review and discussion questions   387
References   387
Further reading   389

Meetings and events industry lexicon   391
Index   417

Illustrations

Figures

1.1	Sydney Harbour	9
1.2	Qatar National Convention Centre	34
2.1	Analysis of the UK's conference venues by number and type	63
2.2	The growth of Conventa in terms of both buyers and suppliers	90
2.3	Conventa show floor showing apple crates instead of shell schemes	90
2.4	Conventa marketing activity	93
3.1	Four possible business philosophies	100
3.2	Vilnius Convention Bureau logo	113
3.3	View of Vilnius, capital city of Lithuania	114
3.4	Ponte Estaiada and the São Paulo skyline	131
3.5	SPCVB senior management team	133
3.6	São Paulo's 'DestinoSP' project and the 5-destinations map	135
4.1	'Scotland Means Business'	150
4.2	Forms of subvention available	161
4.3	The Glasgow Model	165
4.4	GCMB Team participating in Diabetes UK Fun Run	167
4.5	Seoul skyline	168
4.6	Seoul Sizzling Sweepstakes Campaign	169
5.1	Break-even illustration	190
5.2	Seating options	197
5.3	Meeting room checklist	198
5.4	Evaluation questionnaire	209
5.5	ROI pyramid	212
5.6	Kenes organigram	216
6.1	Conference capacity yield in a venue over a period of one week	234
6.2	China National Convention Centre	237
6.3	CNCC business mix	239

6.4   CNCC business share by sector   240
6.5   CNCC enquiry handling flowchart   240
6.6   Highgate House   243
6.7   Highgate House staff organisation chart   246
6.8   Celtic Manor Resort   247
7.1   Measurement of net economic impact from tourist expenditure through
       the application of the tourism multiplier concept   257
7.2   Vancouver, showing Vancouver Convention Centre   276
7.3   Vancouver Convention Centre living roof image   279
8.1   Linda H. DiMario   304
8.2   Duncan Reid   308
8.3   Leigh Jagger   311
8.4   Christian Mutschlechner   314
8.5   Paul Colston   317
10.1   The Meeting Architecture: the Manifesto   378

Tables

1.0   Formation of industry trade and professional associations   5
1.1   Investments in major Australian convention centres since the mid-1980s   6
1.2   Investments in major UK convention centres since 1990   7
1.3   ICCA rankings (number of international association meetings per country
       2009–11)   14
1.4   ICCA rankings (number of international association meetings per city
       2009–11)   15
1.5   ICCA rankings (number of meetings per region, in absolute figures and
       as a percentage)   16
1.6   UIA rankings: top international meeting countries in 2011   17
1.7   UIA rankings: top international meeting cities in 2011   18
1.8   'MICE' matrix (illustrating the segments which make up the business
       tourism sector)   26
2.1   Job titles   44
2.2   Main types of corporate meetings/events   45
2.3   Public perception's influence   47
2.4   Comparisons between corporate and association conferences   53
2.5   Summary of key findings from the British Meetings and Events Industry
       Survey 2011–12   54
2.6   Rotation patterns for international meetings   55
2.7   Bid document template   57
2.8   Typical portfolio of services offered by a professional conference organiser   66

2.9	Conventa exhibitors by country	89
2.10	Conventa hosted buyer applications	89
3.0	Destination Management Plan for Tourism in Brisbane 2008–11 – key goals and measures	101
3.1	QHotels total meeting packages	105
3.2	SPCVB bids	136
4.1	RFP example	158
5.1	Cashflow forecast form	189
5.2	Budget allocations for a typical corporate conference	191
7.1	Venues in Canada hosting events	260
7.2	Event expenditure in Canada	261
7.3	Legacies of business events	264
7.4	Conventa's sustainability metrics	275
8.1	LMU programmes	300
8.2	Salary levels	303

Case studies

1.1	Infrastructure investments in Sydney	8
1.2	Qatar National Convention Centre	32
2.1	Launch of Vauxhall Astra by experiential event agency TRO	81
2.2	Oriflame Executive Conference 2012, Buenos Aires	84
2.3	Conventa, the South East European exhibition for meetings, events and incentives	87
3.1	Vilnius Convention Bureau branding	113
3.2	São Paulo Convention and Visitors Bureau, Brazil	130
4.1	'Scotland Means Business'	149
4.2	Seoul Convention Bureau's three-step social media campaign in destination marketing	168
4.3	Congress of the World Federation of Societies of Intensive and Critical Care Medicine (WFSICCM)	172
5.1	Outsourcing to a PCO or event management agency	182
5.2	Using Twitter at 'The Future Is You' Conference	205
5.3	The Kenes Group	214
6.1	China National Convention Center, Beijing, China	237
6.2	Highgate House, Northamptonshire, England	242
6.3	The Celtic Manor Resort, Newport, Wales	247
7.1	The Conventa Exhibition's sustainability features	274
7.2	Vancouver Convention Centre, Canada	276
10.1	29th International Congress of Ophthalmology 2002, Sydney	356
10.2	App keeps knee specialists on their toes	365

Preface

I have been privileged to work for the past 23 years in the fascinating world of conferences and conventions. In that period there have been huge changes and developments in the way the industry is marketed, in the organisation and presentation of meetings and conferences, in the competition for a share of the lucrative economic 'cake' that conferences and conventions represent, and in a multitude of other ways. And yet the essence remains the same: it is about bringing people together to communicate by sharing information and ideas, to motivate and inspire, to launch new products and disseminate the latest research, to negotiate in order to reach a consensus on the different challenges facing our world.

This book attempts to describe the many facets of this global industry and to provide both an insight into how it is structured and a broader picture of an industry in its totality. It can be dipped into for discrete pieces of information on specific aspects of the industry, or read in its entirety by those wanting a better understanding of the parameters and characteristics of this true twenty-first-century industry. I hope very much that it will be of interest and practical use to students and lecturers, and to those working in the industry, as well as to those who may be looking to make a future career in the industry, to politicians (local and national), to journalists and consultants, and indeed to anyone seeking an overview of this dynamic, endearing, varied but still under-recognised sector of national and global economies.

The book would not have been possible without the unstinting help, advice and provision of data and material that I have received from literally hundreds of colleagues around the world. One of the delights of the conference industry, for me, is this very openness and willingness to share that I have experienced at every turn. To everyone who has helped in any way, I owe an enormous debt of gratitude. I trust they will understand if I do not mention them all individually. To do so would certainly take up several pages but I am very afraid of missing someone out and unwittingly giving offence. But please be assured that my appreciation is heartfelt – I just hope that they each feel that the book justifies the efforts and contributions they have made.

Third edition

This third edition of the book represents a very substantial rewriting. While the broad structure of the second edition remains, I have updated all of the factual and statistical information, replaced all of the case studies, and introduced a number of new topics (for example, experiential marketing and events; the applications of social media; the development of hybrid events; bidding best practice and subvention support; the social legacies of events; moves to create a profession for event management) which were not covered in the second edition or were only referred to briefly. I have also incorporated for the first time, with sincere thanks to event and communications agency Grass Roots, a detailed Industry Lexicon which will provide a very useful quick reference to the terminology in use in our sector. I hope, therefore, that it will prove to be a valuable resource both to new readers and to those who may have purchased previous editions.

Each chapter follows a similar pattern with chapter objectives, learning outcomes, introduction, main theme, summary, review and discussion questions, and references. Most chapters include case studies at the end of the chapter, giving more in-depth illustrations and elaboration of points made in the chapters. There are also mini case studies embedded in the main text of several chapters.

And, finally, I have used mainly UK terminology. I give below several common terms for which different words/phrases are used in North America and in certain other countries:

UK Terms	North American Equivalents
Accommodation	Housing
Exhibition	Exposition (sometimes just 'exhibit')
Professional conference/ congress organiser (PCO)	Independent meeting planner
Delegates	Attendees

Tony Rogers
June 2012

Foreword

The world needs great gathering places, and cities – indeed countries – aggressively compete to be selected by global companies, international associations and event organisers as the host destination. And once a location has been chosen, a fleet of professionals are required to ensure the undertaking's success.

If these were easy jobs, they'd easily be filled. Instead, they require the very best minds, the most innovative individuals and true professionals who breathe commitment every day. The field of convention organising is demanding. The expectations of those working on conferences – behind the scenes or at the podium – are high (and rising year over year).

Every aspect of tourism is touched by the conventions and conferences business – be that inter-country transportation or local transportation; the best restaurants or a catering company; electronics suppliers or retail outlets. Wherever people move and convene the entire economic infrastructure of the host property or community benefits through the immense economic spillover.

When I first encountered Tony Rogers's book, *Conferences and Conventions: A Global Industry*, it was in its first edition, long before this third iteration was contemplated. The importance of this work was apparent at a glance, and our organisation purchased two dozen copies to ensure that each member of our board of directors and our senior management team had it at hand. The scope of the content was rich (rare, even), and the depth of insight was refreshing.

Today's meeting industry is on the brink of change and challenge – but it seems to be ever thus. Adapting to change, rather than predicting it, is perhaps this book's most helpful attribute. But if one were to foreshadow the coming years of conferences and conventions, one might say:

Despite social media's ubiquitous ability to engage people in oblique ways, each of us cherishes the face-to-face reality of a conversation that can create decisions. We value live interactions that can lead to a handshake. And we will always want to learn with colleagues who become friends during the conference breaks. Let's meet.

Conventions are not novelties; they are the norm. Long has that been true, and long will it be so. International trade has followed explorers for decades, as surely as today's trade shows and exhibitions generate travel and tourism when people attend conferences. It is a cycle that appears to be endless, and an economic generator that requires care, attention and meaningful deliberations. The business of conference-making can never be taken for granted.

Our world's largest industries are furthered by the meetings industry. Being a part of making that happen is exhilarating and demanding. Anyone pursuing that endeavour would not want to be without the following 400 pages on top of their desk.

Rick Antonson
President and CEO
Tourism Vancouver
Canada

A global industry

CHAPTER OBJECTIVES

This chapter looks at:

- the origins of the conference industry
- the foundations of a proper industry
- the globalisation of the conference industry
- certain industry shortcomings
- industry parameters and definitions
- business tourism and leisure tourism
- the benefits of conference and business tourism
- changing the perceptions and profile of conferences and business events

It includes case studies on:

- infrastructure investments in Sydney, Australia
- the Qatar National Convention Centre

www.routledge.com/cw/rogers

LEARNING OUTCOMES

On completion of this chapter, you should be able to:

- explain why and how the conference industry developed in the way it did;
- understand the international dimensions of the industry and appreciate which are the most successful cities and countries;
- discuss the features of the industry which illustrate the steps still required to achieve full maturation;
- understand the key benefits afforded by conference and business tourism, and what distinguishes it from leisure tourism;
- argue the case for a potential realignment of conferences and business events in national economies.

Introduction

The conference industry is a young, dynamic industry which is growing and maturing at a rapid rate. From origins in Europe and North America, it is now a truly international industry witnessing huge investments across all continents. Its youthfulness, however, does mean that it lacks some of the necessary characteristics of more established industries, such as well defined terminology, adequate market intelligence, appropriate education and training structures and clear entry routes. Conferences have traditionally formed a part of the business tourism, or business events, sector, a major though often under-valued sector of the wider tourism industry, but it may be time to realign the sector and play down its association with tourism.

The origins of the conference industry

The world's political leaders gathering for the latest G8 summit, the British Small Animal Veterinary Association holding its annual conference in Birmingham, delegates attending the Asia-Pacific Federation of Coloproctology congress in Melbourne, shareholders of Microsoft or HSBC attending the company's annual general meeting, the sales force of GlaxoSmithKline coming together for a regular briefing or training event, or their high achievers jetting off for an incentive-cum-meeting trip to an exotic overseas destination – all these different events have one thing in common: they are all to do with bringing people together, both face-to-face and virtually, to exchange ideas and information, to discuss and in some cases negotiate, to build friendships and closer business relationships, to encourage better performance by individuals and organisations. They

are different facets of the same dynamic, international, economically vibrant conference industry. The terms used ('summit', 'meeting', 'conference', 'assembly', 'convention', 'congress', 'AGM', 'briefing', 'training', 'incentive') may vary, and the events themselves may have different formats and emphases, but the essential ingredients and objectives are the same.

Meetings, conferences and conventions are at the forefront of modern communications, whether this is for internal communications (sales meetings, training courses, board retreats, major annual congresses, for example) or as a vehicle for communicating with key audiences (such as press briefings, product launches, annual general meetings, some technical conferences). Meetings, conferences and conventions are generic terms to describe a diverse mix of communications events.

The phrase 'conference industry' is of very recent origin and is certainly not one that would have been heard until the second half of the twentieth century. Yet people's need to congregate and confer is one of the things that defines our humanity and, for a multitude of different reasons, meetings and gatherings of people have taken place since the early days of civilisation. Fenich (2012) says that:

> once humans developed permanent settlements, each town or village had a public meeting area, often called a town square, where residents could meet, talk and celebrate.

Shone (1998) traces the evolution of meetings since Roman times in Britain and Ireland, together with the development of meeting rooms and meeting places to accommodate such events, driven largely by the needs of trade and commerce.

An article in *Conference & Meetings World* magazine (Colston 2010) entitled 'History in the making' lists some of the most significant moments in world history which were decided, not on the battlefield, but in conference halls. The article references:

- the first Continental Congress (September/October 1774), held in Philadelphia, USA, to protest at the 'Intolerable Acts', passed by the British Government in response to the Boston Tea Party of 1774;
- the Quebec Conference (October 1864), held in Quebec City, Canada, leading to the creation of the Dominion of Canada;
- the Paris meeting (January 1919 to January 1920), Palace of Versailles, France, which led to the Treaty of Versailles and defined the structure of post-war Europe;
- the Yalta Conference (February 1945), in Livadia, Ukraine, the second of the two major wartime meetings between the 'Big Three': Churchill, Roosevelt and Stalin, following the Tehran conference of 1943.

One of the highest profile events in the past couple of hundred years, perhaps almost a launch event for our contemporary conference industry, was the Congress of Vienna held from September 1814 to June 1815. The Congress was called to re-establish the territorial divisions of Europe at the end of the Napoleonic Wars and representatives included all of the major world powers of the day (with the exception of Turkey). It is tempting to imagine what the 'delegate spend' must have been like, with delegates such as Alexander I, Emperor of Russia, Prince Karl August von Hardenberg from Prussia, and Viscount Castlereagh and the Duke of Wellington as the principal British representatives. Each representative would have been accompanied by a substantial delegation of support staff and partners, requiring accommodation, social programmes, lavish corporate entertainment, ground handling, not to mention state-of-the-art conference facilities. The Vienna Convention Bureau no doubt celebrated long and hard its success in attracting such a high-profile, high-spend event to the city!

As the nineteenth century progressed, universities increasingly provided facilities for the dissemination of information within academic circles, while the boom in spa towns and, in the UK, Victorian resorts with assembly rooms, began to make available larger public spaces for entertainment and meetings. At the same time, the development of the railway network was accompanied by the construction of railway hotels alongside major stations. Many of these hotels had substantial function rooms available for hire.

Shone (1998) contends that the dawn of the twentieth century was accompanied by a change in the demand for meetings:

> Though assemblies and congresses continued to be driven by trade and industry, there was a slow and gradual increase in activity which, rather than promoting products, or reporting a company's annual progress, looked to developing staff and sales. The precursors of the sales training meeting, the 'congress of commercials' (or commercial travellers) of the 1920s and 1930s, began to develop into something more modern and recognisable.

The situation was somewhat different in North America during the latter half of the nineteenth century, particularly across the eastern seaboard of the USA where various trade and professional associations, as well as religious groups, were being formed and, as they became more established, beginning to hold conventions for their memberships. Gartrell (1994) records that, in due course, a number of committees were also created to *lure the growing convention business from these expanding and thriving associations.* As more and more cities became aware of the value of convention business, Gartrell suggests that it was

> inevitable that the solicitation of these conventions would be assigned to a full-time salesperson; and, while this might have happened in any one of many major cities, history records that it first happened in Detroit, Michigan, when a group of businessmen decided to place a full-time salesperson on the road to invite conventions to their city. Thus, in 1896, the first convention bureau was formed, and an industry emerged.

Detroit was shortly followed by other US cities which established their own convention bureaux: Cleveland (1904), Atlantic City (1908), Denver and St Louis (1909), Louisville and Los Angeles (1910). Now many cities around the world have their own convention bureau, or convention and visitor bureau (CVB), also known as a destination marketing organisation (DMO), and similar entities have been created at a national level to promote an entire country as a meetings, convention and business event destination (see Chapter 3).

The foundations of a proper industry

While the origins of today's conference industry lie in the political and religious congresses of earlier centuries, followed by business meetings and, in the USA, trade and professional association conventions, the development and recognition of a proper 'industry' is a much more recent phenomenon, in Europe especially, effectively dating from the middle to latter part of the twentieth century.

The formation of trade associations is often a useful, objective way of marking the real formation of an industry. Some of the principal conference industry associations were founded as listed in Table 1.0.

Destination Marketing Association International (DMAI) (until 2005 known as the International Association of Convention and Visitor Bureaux – IACVB), on the other hand, with a predominantly North American membership, was founded as long ago as 1914.

Since the 1960s there has been a steadily increasing investment in the whole infrastructure that supports conferences, meetings and related events, an investment which

Table 1.0 Formation of industry trade and professional associations	
International Association of Exhibitions and Events (IAEE)	1928
Convention Industry Council	1949
Professional Convention Management Association (PCMA)	1957
Association Internationale des Palais de Congrès (AIPC)	1958
International Congress and Convention Association (ICCA)	1963
International Association of Professional Congress Organisers (IAPCO)	1968
Meeting Professionals International (MPI)	1972
Meetings & Events Australia (MEA) (originally Meetings Industry Association of Australia – MIAA)	1975
Joint Meetings Industry Council (JMIC)	1978
Association of British Professional Conference Organisers (ABPCO)	1981
Confederation of Latin American Congress Organizing Entities and Related Activities (COCAL)	1985
Southern African Association for the Conference Industry (SAACI)	1987
Meetings Industry Association (MIA) (UK)	1990
Eventia	2006

Table 1.1 Investments in major Australian convention centres since the mid-1980s

Name of Centre	Year of Opening/ New Developments	Cost (AU$m)
Adelaide Convention Centre	1987	38.7
	1990 – exhibition hall added	17.5
	2001 – extension	92.4
	2014 – first part of two-phase expansion adding 4,300 m² of space and meeting rooms	242
	2017 – second part proposes demolition of original building to be replaced by 3,000-seat plenary hall	108
Sydney Convention and Exhibition Centre	1988	230
	2016 – construction of the new Sydney International Convention, Exhibition and Entertainment Precinct	c.1,000
Canberra National Convention Centre	1989	Not available
	2007 – upgrade completed	30
	2011 – scoping study completed to establish a new centre – new centre completion c. 2017	1
		c. 350
Melbourne Exhibition and Convention Centre	1990 (1996 for Exhibition Centre)	254 (combined cost)
Melbourne Convention Centre	2009 – completion of a new 5,000-seat convention centre adjacent to existing facility	370
Brisbane Convention and Exhibition Centre	1994	200
	2012 – major 25,000 m² expansion of convention facilities adding 20 meeting rooms	140
Cairns Convention Centre	1996	50
	1999 – Convention Centre extension opened	30
	2005 – major refurbishment completed	11
	2012 – further refurbishment	6
Federation Concert Hall and Convention Centre – Hobart	2000	16
Alice Springs Convention Centre	2003	14.2
Perth Convention and Exhibition Centre	2004	220
Darwin Convention Centre	2008 – including a 1,500-seat main auditorium	Part of a 1 billion waterfront development project

Source: Tourism Australia and author's research

Table 1.2 Investments in major UK convention centres since 1990

Name of Centre	Year of Opening/ Additional Investments	Cost (£m)
International Convention Centre, Birmingham	1991	180
Plymouth Pavilions	1992	25
Cardiff International Arena	1993	25
Venue Cymru (formerly North Wales Conference Centre)	1994	6
Major expansion completed in 2007	2007	10.5
Edinburgh International Conference Centre – major expansion due for completion in 2013	1995 2013	38 30
Belfast Waterfront Hall (conference centre and concert hall)	1997	32
Extension to add 2,100 m² of exhibition space, banqueting for 750 and 5 breakout rooms each seating up to 200 people	2016	20
Clyde Auditorium at the Scottish Exhibition and Conference Centre	1997	38
Arena facility to be added	2013	80
ExCeL, London	2000	300
The exhibition centre added an international convention centre in 2010	2010	160
Manchester Central	2001	24
Re-development in 2010	2010	28
The International Centre, Telford – major re-development	2002	12
Hotel development on site	2004	10
Extension to International Centre	2011	10
New 200-bed hotel on site as part of £250 m Telford town centre development	2013–14	
Aberdeen Exhibition & Conference Centre – major re-development	2003	18
The Villa Marina, Isle of Man (major re-development)	2004	15
The Sage, Gateshead – arts and conference centre	2004	70
Wales Millennium Centre, Cardiff – arts centre and conference centre	2004	106
Bournemouth International Centre – major re-development	2005	22
Southport Theatre and Floral Hall complex – major re-development	2007	40
Arena and Convention Centre, Liverpool	2008	164
Development of new exhibition space planned for completion by 2014	2014	40
Harrogate International Centre extension	2011	13
Leeds Arena	2012	55

accelerated into a rapid growth during the 1990s. This investment has continued unabated in the new millennium. Tables 1.1 and 1.2 give details of newly built and redeveloped conference and convention facilities in just two countries, Australia and the United Kingdom, epitomising the huge scale of investment that has taken place over the past couple of decades. This list does not include other substantial investments in buildings which, though not purpose-built for the conventions industry, are capable of staging very large conferences, such as (in the UK) the Sheffield Arena (12,000 seats, £45 million), Birmingham's National Indoor Arena (13,000 seats, £51 million), Manchester's £42 million Bridgewater Hall and the 19,000-seat Nynex Arena and the Newcastle Arena (10,000 seats, £10.5 million) in Newcastle-upon-Tyne.

Case Study 1.1 summarises the huge investments being made by the city of Sydney, Australia, in the whole infrastructure that supports business events, investments which will total more than AU$7 billion in the period 2011–19.

CASE STUDY 1.1 Infrastructure investments in Sydney

In February 2011 Sydney, Australia, announced plans to spend over AU$7 billion on infrastructure investments. While not all of these investments are directly related to conference and business events facilities, it is anticipated that they will significantly enhance the attraction of Sydney as a business events destination, building on the strong base already established.

The developments are focused on Sydney's prime waterfront area and include the Sydney International Convention, Exhibition and Entertainment Precinct, Barangaroo and The Star.

Sydney international convention, exhibition and entertainment precinct

A new state-of-the-art, 12-hectare Sydney International Convention, Exhibition and Entertainment Precinct is due to open in 2016 at Darling Harbour, an investment of approximately AU$1 billion. The Precinct will combine world-class entertainment, sporting, leisure and convention facilities in Australia's first fully integrated facility, designed to 'cement Sydney as Australia's global city'. The new Sydney Convention and Exhibition Centre, which will complement the facilities at the existing Sydney Olympic Park venue, is expected to offer at least 40,000 m² of exhibition space and flexible plenary spaces with a combined capacity of 10,000 delegates.

(www.siceep.com)

Barangaroo

Located on the western edge of Sydney's Central Business District adjacent to Cockle Bay and Darling Harbour, Barangaroo is a 22-hectare former container port that is

FIGURE 1.1 Sydney Harbour

being transformed into a vital AU$6 billion extension to the harbour city. Lauded as one of the most ambitious and significant waterfront greening projects in the world, Barangaroo will include a new iconic landscaped Headland Park, spectacular public waterfront walks and parks, shops, cafes and restaurants, commercial office towers, a new hotel and apartments, all serviced by new and extended transport systems. The project is due for completion by 2019.

(www.bangaroo.com)

The Star

An AU$850 million facelift to transform Sydney's only casino and entertainment complex has been all but completed with the lifestyle property, The Star, officially opened in September 2011. Twenty new restaurants have opened throughout the property boasting some of the best local and international cuisine. The other highlight of the development is the new 12-floor, 171-room lifestyle hotel, The Darling, which will complement the existing 480-room hotel and apartment towers. Still under construction is a dedicated event space that will be housed within The Star complex, due for completion in 2013.

(www.star.com.au)

Other developments in Sydney include:

- The rejuvenation of Chinatown, which aims to make streets more pedestrian-friendly with reduced traffic, better lighting and paving, more trees and outdoor seating, and public art exhibits.
- The Green Square Urban Renewal is one of Australia's largest urban renewal projects. Encompassing 278 hectares of land between central Sydney, Sydney International Airport and Port Botany, the project will transform one of Sydney's oldest industrial areas into an attractive, vibrant and sustainable urban destination, with a diverse mix of housing, offices, retail and open space.
- The Concourse at Chatswood features a new concert hall, theatre, civic pavilion and studio to stage music, art, drama and dance, while new shops, restaurants and cafes and abundant open space will make it a popular meeting point for locals and visitors, day and night – the space is being promoted as a fresh alternative to the Central Business District and a vibrant setting for meetings, conferences and events on the north side of the harbour.

But it is not just in Europe, Australasia and North America that major investments are being made. In the past five to ten years, large-scale infrastructure projects have been undertaken throughout much of Asia and the Pacific rim, in the former East European countries such as Hungary and the Czech Republic, in the Middle East, and in a number of African countries, particularly South Africa, and in South America. Case Study 1.2 gives a detailed example of one such investment, the Qatar National Convention Centre, opened in December 2011.

There appear to be a number of reasons for these investments, many of which are paid for out of central or local government and other public sector funds:

- Such countries and destinations are probably already active in the leisure tourism sector and have developed much of the infrastructure for this sector which is the same (airports and other communications facilities, 3-star/4-star/5-star hotels, attractions, trained staff, for example) as that required to attract international conference business. And, although additional investment in purpose-built conference and exhibition facilities may be a not insignificant cost, it is likely to be a relatively small additional amount compared with the total infrastructure investments already made.
- Such destinations quite rightly see conference business as complementary to leisure tourism business, in the same way that the longer-established destinations do.
- Conference and business tourism, being at the high quality, high yield end of the tourism spectrum, brings major economic benefits for developing as well as for developed countries. Such benefits include year-round jobs and foreign exchange

earnings. There is also the potential for future inward investment from conference delegates who have liked and been impressed by what they have seen of a country while attending a conference there and return to set up a business operation, or persuade their own employers to do so.

- There is undoubted prestige in being selected to host a major international conference and some less developed countries would see this as a way of gaining credibility and acceptance on the international political stage. There is perhaps an element of conferences and conference centres being developed as status symbols, signs of having 'arrived' as destinations to be taken seriously.

Such huge infrastructure investments are driven by a number of demand factors, both economic and social (analysed in further detail in Chapter 7). The challenge for those planning major new purpose-built convention centres (usually local authorities or municipalities and public sector organisations) is to anticipate future demand accurately. Lead time from the initial idea for a convention centre until its opening can be as much as ten years. The process involves, inter alia, identification of a suitable site, design and planning stages, assembly of the funding package, construction of venue and related infrastructure, recruitment and training of staff, and advance promotion. In such a period, substantial changes in the wider marketplace may have occurred. The ultimate goal is to provide destination and venue appeal that will attract the buyer and contribute to the ongoing development of the destination, as summarised succinctly by Linda H. DiMario (2012), writing in *Convention Trends* e-magazine:

> *Each destination package is a unique composite of products and experiences. And each destination must weigh its strengths and weaknesses within the context of what meeting planners, event producers and other potential users might need, want and expect. From this type of pragmatic analysis, the model for each destination will be different. Convention centres, when they are conceived thoughtfully, built with optimal flexibility, supported by proportionate hotel inventory and surrounded by an appealing destination package, can spark a renaissance, resurrect a dormant tourism economy and fuel economic development.*

There is less of a risk for hotel and smaller venue developments, where the period between initial concept and completion is much shorter (typically 3 to 5 years), but the same principles apply. Many venues conceived, for example, in the boom times of the late 1980s found that they were opening in a very different market in the early 1990s, with the economy in full recession, and many of the venues struggled or foundered as a result. A similar economic cycle was experienced in the late 1990s and early years of the new millennium, and again from 2008 onwards.

The globalisation of the conference industry

Conferences, meetings and business events are closely aligned to the tourism industry, an industry which, in all its guises, is claimed to be the world's largest. Conferences and conventions are now a truly global industry, as evidenced by the examples of international investments described earlier in this chapter. But there is much other evidence to substantiate such a claim. Nowhere is its truth better demonstrated than in the evolution of one of the industry's major trade shows, IMEX, which is held in Frankfurt in May each year. The first IMEX was held in 2003 and, in that year, 119 countries were represented as exhibitors; by 2011 this number had increased to 160 countries. In 2003 there were 5,624 visitors to the show (including hosted buyers) drawn from 80 countries. In 2011 there were 8,944 visitors drawn from 86 countries. While just ten countries supplied 77 per cent of these visitors (Belgium, France, Germany, Italy, Netherlands, Russia, Spain, Switzerland, United Kingdom, USA), a further five countries supplied over 100 visitors each: Austria, Brazil, China, Poland and Sweden, clearly demonstrating the strength of the business events sector in globally dispersed destinations.

This claim can be further substantiated by the activity of one of IMEX's main competitors, Reed Travel Exhibitions. For some years Reed has organised 'EIBTM' (the 'European Incentive, Business Travel and Meetings Exhibition'), held in Barcelona in late November. This has now grown to include sister shows in the Middle East (GIBTM – The Gulf Incentive, Business Travel and Meetings – March), the USA (The Americas-AIBTM – June) and China (CIBTM – August/September). Reed Travel Exhibitions also manages the Asia-Pacific Incentives and Meetings Expo ('AIME' – held in Australia – February).

The global nature of the conference industry is also very well illustrated by figures produced annually by the International Congress and Convention Association (ICCA), from its headquarters in Amsterdam, and by the Union of International Associations (UIA), which is based in Brussels. Such figures record the staging of international conferences and conventions by country and city. They enable trends to be monitored and give an indication of which countries and cities are gaining market share and which may be losing it.

International Congress and Convention Association (ICCA) rankings

The International Congress and Convention Association (ICCA) began in 1972 to collect information on international association meetings. ICCA estimates that there are approximately 19,000 different international association meetings organised on a regular basis. The ICCA Association Database has collected information on approximately 80 per cent of these and holds in-depth profiles with information on the location and other characteristics of these international meetings, which have to conform to the following criteria for inclusion:

- be organised on a regular basis (one-time events are not included);
- rotate between at least three different countries;
- be attended by at least 50 participants.

Some of the key characteristics and trends of the international association conference market for the period 2001–10, as elicited by ICCA, are summarised in the section on international association conferences in Chapter 2.

The Database allows ICCA to provide rankings (by country and city) showing the market share achieved by individual countries and cities through securing and staging such international meetings. ICCA's figures for 2009–11, shown in Table 1.3, reveal market share for the top 40 countries by number of events in that three-year period (with rankings based on the country's performance in 2011). The table underlines the global nature of conferences, including as it does a number of countries which would not have appeared at all, even just a few years ago, such as Croatia and India.

Although international conferences and conventions are tracked by country as shown in Table 1.3, the events are actually won by individual destinations (normally cities) through a bidding process, and ICCA's record of where events were held on a city basis in 2009–11 (see Table 1.4) provides a challenging test to anyone's knowledge of world geography. As well as highlighting the strength of international competition for convention business, the rankings also confirm that Europe's historical pre-eminence remains but is being challenged by destinations in Asia (e.g. Singapore, Seoul, Beijing), Australia (e.g. Sydney, Melbourne) and South America (e.g. Buenos Aires, São Paulo, Santiago de Chile). Table 1.5 provides an analysis of the share of international association meetings secured by the main regions of the world over the three-year period 2008–10. ICCA offers the following comments on the regional breakdown:

- Generally speaking ICCA has identified more meetings for most regions over the years.
- Europe is still the most popular destination with 54 per cent of the meetings being held there in 2010. However, Europe's market share has been decreasing over the past ten years and so has the relative popularity of North America, due to an increase in attractiveness of Asia/Middle East and Latin America.
- Africa and Oceania have stayed rather stable over the years.

It should be noted that ICCA rankings are based purely on the *number* of meetings that meet the ICCA criteria, not their economic *value*. In other words, a destination would achieve a higher ranking than another destination because of a higher number of events held, even though such events might be considerably smaller in delegate numbers than a destination staging fewer events but with greater delegate numbers (and hence greater economic value).

Further information on ICCA statistics can be accessed at: www.iccaworld.com

Table 1.3 ICCA rankings (number of international association meetings per country 2009–11)			
	Country	Number of Meetings 2009	Number of Meetings 2010	Number of Meetings 2011
1	USA	727	623	759
2	Germany	524	542	577
3	Spain	385	451	463
4	United Kingdom	378	399	434
5	France	384	371	428
6	Italy	408	341	363
7	Brazil	297	275	304
8	China	284	282	302
9	Netherlands	271	219	291
10	Austria	241	212	267
11	Canada	230	229	255
12	Switzerland	227	244	240
13	Japan	278	305	233
14	Portugal	188	194	228
15	Republic of Korea	188	186	207
16	Australia	183	239	204
17	Sweden	207	192	195
18	Argentina	155	172	186
19	Belgium	154	164	179
20	Mexico	124	140	175
21	Poland	124	98	165
22	Finland	135	150	163
23	Turkey	132	160	159
24	Singapore	123	136	142
25	Denmark	167	136	140
26	Norway	134	125	138
27	Taiwan (Chinese Taipei)	102	138	131
28	Greece	128	119	127
29	Malaysia	108	119	126
30	Hungary	117	124	125
31	Czech Republic	114	103	122
32	Colombia	78	95	113
33=	India	101	100	105
33=	Ireland	80	83	105
35	Thailand	114	88	101
36	Chile	79	97	87
37	South Africa	102	86	84
38	Hong Kong	76	82	79
39	Croatia	42	50	72
40	Russia	58	48	69
	Total	**7,947**	**7,917**	**8,643**

Source: ICCA DATA (website: www.iccaworld.com)

Table 1.4 ICCA rankings (number of international association meetings per city 2009–11)			
	City	Number of Meetings 2009	Number of Meetings 2010	Number of Meetings 2011
1	Vienna	159	154	181
2	Paris	141	147	174
2	Barcelona	144	148	150
4	Berlin	135	138	147
5	Singapore	123	136	142
6	Madrid	92	114	130
7	London	114	92	115
8	Amsterdam	114	104	114
9	Istanbul	93	109	113
10	Beijing	114	98	111
11	Budapest	92	87	108
12	Lisbon	106	106	107
13	Seoul	97	91	99
14=	Copenhagen	114	92	98
14=	Prague	96	85	98
16	Buenos Aires	96	98	94
17=	Brussels	88	80	93
17=	Stockholm	111	89	93
19	Rome	89	72	92
20	Taipei	70	99	83
21	Kuala Lumpur	80	79	78
22	Hong Kong	76	82	77
23	Dublin	52	60	76
24	Shanghai	61	81	72
25	Helsinki	66	67	71
26	Bangkok	81	55	70
27	Rio de Janeiro	63	62	69
28	Warsaw	39	28	65
29=	Geneva	46	57	63
29=	Zurich	61	56	63
31	Melbourne	35	49	62
32	Oslo	60	49	61
33	São Paulo	78	75	60
34	Sydney	62	102	57
35=	Athens	69	69	55
35=	Munich	55	66	55
35=	Vancouver	47	58	55
38	Edinburgh	45	66	52
39=	Mexico City	37	43	51
39=	Washington DC	41	36	51
	Total	**3,342**	**3,379**	**3,605**

Source: ICCA statistics produced by ICCA DATA (website: www.iccaworld.com)

Table 1.5 ICCA rankings (number of meetings per region, in absolute figures and as a percentage)						
Region	2008		2009		2010	
	Number	Percentage	Number	Percentage	Number	Percentage
Europe	5,210	54.2	5,018	54.2	4,921	54.0
Asia/Middle East	1,755	18.3	1,664	18.0	1,737	19.0
North America	1,167	12.1	1,082	11.7	995	10.9
Latin America	881	9.2	920	9.9	913	10.0
Africa	334	3.5	352	3.8	283	3.1
Oceania	263	2.7	219	2.4	271	3.0
Totals	9,610	100	9,255	100	9,120	100

Source: ICCA Report 'The International Association Meetings Market – Worldwide 2001–2010'

Union of International Associations (UIA) statistics

Since 1949 the Union of International Associations (UIA) has published annual statistical studies on international meetings taking place worldwide (see UIA 2012). The statistics are based on information collected by the UIA Congress Department and selected according to very strict criteria. Meetings taken into consideration include those organised and/or sponsored by the international organisations (i.e. non-governmental organisations (NGOs) and intergovernmental organisations (IGOs)) which appear in the UIA's 'Yearbook of International Organisations' and 'International Congress Calendar' (the UIA database) and whose details are subject to systematic collection and updates on an annual basis by the UIA. Broadly these meetings comprise the 'sittings' of their principal organs (notably IGOs) and their congresses, conventions, symposia, and regional sessions grouping several countries. The meetings should have a minimum of 50 participants (or be of an unknown number of participants).

Other meetings of 'significant international character', especially those organised by national organisations and national branches of international associations, are included provided that they meet the following criteria:

- at least 40 per cent of the participants are from countries other than the host country and at least five nationalities are represented;
- the meetings last at least three days, or are of unknown duration;
- have at least 300 participants *or* a concurrent exhibition.

As at June 2012, the UIA held details of 376,581 qualifying meetings in its database. Of these, 317,440 took place in 2010 or earlier, 10,344 took place in 2011 and 5,545 are scheduled for 2012 or later.

Table 1.6 UIA rankings: top international meeting countries in 2011		
Country	Number of Meetings	Percentage of all Meetings
1 Singapore	919	9.0
2 USA	744	7.3
3 Japan	598	5.8
4 France	557	5.4
5 Belgium	533	5.2
6 Republic of Korea	469	4.6
7 Germany	421	4.1
8 Austria	390	3.8
9 Spain	386	3.8
10 Australia	329	3.2
11 Netherlands	299	2.9
12 United Kingdom	293	2.9
13 Italy	269	2.6
14 Hungary	221	2.2
15 Switzerland	219	2.1
16 China	200	1.9
17 Canada	186	1.8
18 Norway	169	1.6
19 Sweden	161	1.6
20 Portugal	160	1.6
21 Finland	159	1.6
22= Denmark	126	1.2
22= Thailand	126	1.2
24 Malaysia	125	1.2
25 Turkey	123	1.2
26 Poland	114	1.1
27= India	103	1.0
27= United Arab Emirates	103	1.0
29 South Africa	91	0.9
30 Mexico	83	0.8
31 Brazil	80	0.8
32 Greece	70	0.7
33 Czech Republic	65	0.6
34= Russia	54	0.5
34= Taiwan	54	0.5
36 Indonesia	53	0.5
37 Ireland	52	0.5
38 Argentina	47	0.5
39 Hong Kong	46	0.4
40 Philippines	39	0.4
Total	**9,236**	**90.0**

Source: Union of International Associations: statistics@uia.be – www.uia.org

Table 1.7 UIA rankings: top international meeting cities in 2011		
City	Number of Meetings	Percentage of all Meetings
1 Singapore	919	8.9
2 Brussels	464	4.5
3 Paris	336	3.3
4 Vienna	286	2.8
5 Seoul	232	2.3
6 Budapest	168	1.6
7 Tokyo	153	1.5
8 Barcelona	150	1.5
9 Berlin	149	1.4
10 Geneva	121	1.2
11 Amsterdam	118	1.1
12 Madrid	116	1.1
13 Stockholm	109	1.1
14= Copenhagen	105	1.0
14= London	105	1.0
16 Sydney	103	1.0
17 Melbourne	99	1.0
18 Lisbon	96	0.9
19 Istanbul	92	0.9
20 Beijing	90	0.9
21 Bangkok	88	0.9
22 Yokohama	84	0.8
23 Busan	82	0.8
24 Oslo	74	0.7
25 Dubai	73	0.7
26= Helsinki	70	0.7
26= Kuala Lumpur	70	0.7
28 Jeju	68	0.7
29 Montreal	60	0.6
30= Rome	59	0.6
30= Washington DC	59	0.6
32 Prague	54	0.5
33= Munich	49	0.5
33= New York	49	0.5
35= Kyoto	48	0.5
35= Lyon	48	0.5
37 Hong Kong	45	0.4
38 Valencia	44	0.4
39= San Francisco	43	0.4
39= The Hague	43	0.4
Total	5,221	50.9

Source: Union of International Associations: statistics@uia.be – www.uia.org

Excluded from the UIA database are:

- purely national meetings, as well as those of an exclusively religious, didactic, political, commercial or sporting nature;
- meetings with strictly limited participation, such as those of subsidiary (internal) statutory bodies, committees, groups of experts (held mainly at the headquarters of IGOs);
- corporate and incentive meetings.

The prime source of UIA data is international organisations themselves. The UIA's researchers work continuously throughout the year on the meetings database, adding or modifying records using information acquired from international organisations by mail and email and from other sources such as periodicals and the Internet.

The differences between the UIA and ICCA rankings are mainly accounted for by the different criteria used for inclusion i.e. ICCA only includes events which occur regularly, rotate between at least three countries, are organised by associations and attract at least 50 delegates. ICCA also collects information from a wider range of sources: from its member destinations and venues, from international associations themselves, and by conducting planned research.

The UIA figures for 2011 (published June 2012) include 10,344 meetings organised worldwide in over 183 countries and over 1,300 distinct cities or destinations. The UIA produces rankings by both country and city. Tables 1.6 and 1.7 provide more detailed analysis of these rankings, which continue to underline the strong positions held by Europe and the Asia-Pacific region. Among countries, 47.5 per cent of the top 40 countries are from Europe and 27.5 per cent from Asia-Pacific. Among cities, the percentages are even higher for Europe, which features 52.5 per cent of the top 40 cities, while 27.5 per cent are from Asia-Pacific. Further information on UIA statistics can be accessed at: www.uia.org/statistics.

Certain industry shortcomings

Limited market intelligence

It has been seen that, in comparison with many other industries, the conference industry is still a very young industry, barely 50 years of age in Europe and North America and even younger in most of the rest of the world. Although it is maturing at a very rapid rate, it is indisputable that one of the legacies of its relative immaturity is a lack of reliable statistics and regular research to provide a base of intelligence and information on trends and on the size and value of the industry (the ICCA and UIA statistics quoted in this chapter are something of an oasis in what has generally been a rather barren statistical landscape). This, in turn, has meant that governments have not taken the industry seriously as a major benefactor to national economies because it has been impossible to demonstrate clearly the economic impact that conferences can have – the exception to this being some of the so-called less developed countries which have very quickly realised its potential and invested accordingly.

However, new research activity and initiatives are now beginning which, over time, could contribute significantly to redressing the gaps in market intelligence. Among the most important is work to determine how a new statistical instrument, the Tourism Satellite Account (TSA), can be used to identify the economic contribution made by the conference and meetings industry. Davidson and Rogers (2006) describe the TSA as follows:

> *A Tourism Satellite Account (TSA) provides a means of separating and examining both tourism supply and tourism demand within the general framework of the System of National Accounts approved by the United Nations. The term 'Satellite Account' was developed by the United Nations to measure the size of economic activities that are not defined either as industries in national accounts or as a cluster of them. Tourism, for example, impacts heavily on industries such as transportation, accommodation, food and beverage services, recreation and entertainment and travel agencies.*

Jones and James (2005) state that:

> *Tourism is a unique phenomenon as it is defined by the consumer or the visitor. Visitors buy goods and services both tourism and non-tourism alike. The key from a measurement standpoint is associating their purchases to the total supply of these goods and services within a country. The TSA:*
>
> - *provides credible data on the impact of tourism and the associated employment*
> - *is a standard framework for organising statistical data on tourism*
> - *is a new international standard endorsed by the UN Statistical Commission*
> - *is a powerful instrument for designing economic policies related to tourism development*
> - *provides data on tourism's impact on a nation's balance of payments*
> - *provides information on tourism human resource characteristics.*

Agreement was reached in 2004 between the World Tourism Organisation (a specialised agency of the United Nations), the International Congress and Convention Association, Meeting Professionals International, and 'EIBTM' for the TSA to incorporate meeting

industry data for the first time, allowing studies to be made into the relationship between expenditure on meetings and other economic measures such as Gross Domestic Product and job creation.

A project team led by the Sustainable Tourism Cooperative Research Centre, based in Australia, was commissioned to make recommendations on how the economic impacts of meetings and conventions should be properly measured. Its report 'Measuring the Economic Importance of the Meetings Industry' (STCRC 2007) recommends a standard methodology for measuring the value of the meetings industry based on a TSA. It seeks to:

- identify the basic data units for collection of statistics;
- explore how these fit into existing TSA statistics;
- develop survey instruments to capture meetings-related expenditure and costs;
- identify the indicators/variables to be used for quarterly measurement of the performance of the meetings industry;
- create guidelines for the collection of statistics adapted to the functioning of the TSA;
- describe the roles of the stakeholders in the process to ensure credibility.

With support from the MPI Foundation, national economic impact studies for Canada, the USA and Mexico have been undertaken using the United Nations methodology (see Chapter 7), and other countries including the UK and France are adopting the same approach. These, together with other important research projects now well established in a number of countries (see examples in Chapter 7), do mean that overall market intelligence is improving, but there is undoubtedly still some way to go before industry practitioners will feel that they have the information resources that meet their needs and which accurately reflect the scope and importance of the industry.

Non-standardised terminology

One of the reasons for the limited statistics on the size and value of the industry is the lack of an accepted and properly defined terminology. At a macro level, arguments still rage over whether the term 'business tourism' is an accurate or appropriate one to describe a sector encompassing conferences, exhibitions and incentive travel. The link with 'tourism' is thought to be confusing and overlaid with a number of negative perceptions ('candy floss' jobs of a seasonal and poorly paid nature, for example, and dominant associations with holidays and leisure tourism). While business tourism is the phrase now widely in use in Europe as the accepted generic term, in Australia the industry has adopted the term 'business events' to describe its essential focus, a phrase also favoured by the author.

The acronym 'MICE' (for Meetings, Incentives, Conferences and Exhibitions, or Events) is also still in widespread use around the world, despite its somewhat unfortunate connotations! In Canada this is adjusted to MC&IT: meetings, conventions and incentive travel.

At the micro level, words such as 'conference', 'congress', 'convention', 'meeting' even, are often used synonymously or indiscriminately. Other words are also used with similar but more specialised connotations, such as 'symposium', 'colloquium', 'assembly', 'conclave', 'summit', though it is probably only the last of these for which it might be easy to reach a consensus on its precise meaning (namely, a conference of high level officials, such as heads of government).

A first attempt was made by a number of industry professionals in 1990 to produce a 'Meetings Industry Glossary'. A finished version of the Glossary was published in 1993 under the auspices of the Convention Liaison Council (now the Convention Industry Council – see Chapter 9) and the Joint Industry Council (now the Joint Meetings Industry Council – see Chapter 9) as the 'International Meetings Industry Glossary'. This has now evolved into an electronic glossary maintained by the Convention Industry Council as part of its Accepted Practices Exchange (APEX) initiative (www.conventionindustry.org/glossary). The glossary's definitions for several key industry terms, updated in 2011, are shown below:

Conference

1. Participatory meeting designed for discussion, fact finding, problem solving and consultation.
2. An event used by any organisation to meet and exchange views, convey a message, open a debate or give publicity to some area of opinion on a specific issue. No tradition, continuity or timing is required to convene a conference. Conferences are usually of short duration with specific objectives, and are generally on a smaller scale than congresses or conventions.

Congress

1. The regular coming together of large groups of individuals, generally to discuss a particular subject. A congress will often last several days and have several simultaneous sessions. The length of time between congresses is usually annual, although some are on a less frequent basis. Most international or world congresses are of the latter type; national congresses are more frequently held annually.
2. European term for convention.

Convention

Gathering of delegates, representatives, and members of a membership or industry organisation convened for a common purpose. Common features include educational sessions, committee meetings, social functions, and meetings to conduct the governance business of the organisation. Conventions are typically recurring events with specific, established timing.

Meeting

> An event where the primary activity of the participants is to attend educational sessions, participate in discussions, social functions, or attend other organised events. There is no exhibit (exhibition) component to this event.

The descriptions listed above help to shed some light on the nature of different kinds of 'communications' events, but it is perhaps not surprising that they have not as yet been adopted as succinct, easy-to-remember definitions in regular use within the twenty-first-century conference and convention industry.

It could be argued that the variety of available vocabulary is more a reflection of the rich diversity of the English language than a symptom of an industry with myriad events, each with its own distinct characteristics. At one level, it may not really matter whether an event is called a 'conference' or a 'convention', and certainly there are as many misuses of these terms as there are correct interpretations, if indeed such a thing as a correct interpretation really exists. Yet at another level, some of these terms do have a specific connotation in one part of the world, and a different connotation in another part, giving rise to potential confusion and misunderstanding. For example, the word 'conference' in the UK is used generically to describe events both large and small, whereas in the USA a 'conference' is essentially a 'meeting' and certainly implies an event with limited numbers of delegates/attendees. The word 'convention' is used to describe a large event in the UK and North America, whereas many countries in mainland Europe prefer the term 'congress' to describe a large 'conference'. An article in *Association Meetings International* magazine entitled 'Lost in the Atlantic', quotes Brian Riggs (2011) of AMC Association Headquarters, who felt that misunderstandings of terminology could be harming the industry:

> *It is a difference in dialogue but today's marketplace is truly global and individual meeting planners in the United States and around the world will miss out because we as a community are not using a language that is international. The disconnect will become more apparent as the world becomes more global. And remember every young person is already globally connected. It is in their DNA.*

Clearly it is vital that any potential confusion over terminology is minimised, enabling statistics and data to be collected and interpreted in a standardised way on a worldwide level, as befits a truly global industry. This will allow the real size and value of the conference industry to be established and monitored, and is critical to the national and international recognition and support which the industry now deserves and demands.

Incomplete educational and professional development frameworks

One of the other reasons for the lack of a standardised terminology is that, for many of those now working in the industry, it is their second or even third career. They have come into conference work from related disciplines such as hotel and catering, travel, sales and marketing, public administration, but also from what might appear superficially to be unrelated spheres of employment. Whereas many, if not most, other professions have a formal induction and training process for new entrants which provides opportunities for them to be educated in the use of the accepted, clearly defined terminology, such opportunities and structures have not existed within the conference industry, although this is now changing with the advent of university and college courses offering undergraduate and postgraduate programmes specific to the conference, conventions and events industry (see Chapter 8).

Professional qualifications for the industry have existed for some years in North America. Such qualifications are now emerging elsewhere (see Chapter 8) and it is likely that, within the next five to ten years, an appropriate range of continuing professional development (CPD) programmes and related qualifications will have been established at both national and international levels. Such a development will provide overdue support and recognition for what is a highly sophisticated industry but, nonetheless, one in which many conference organisers have received only minimal formal training, and lack recognised qualifications to prepare them for their event management responsibilities. It is also frequently the case that conference organising is only a small part of a person's job, undertaken for just a limited period of time (see Chapter 2). These are again factors which help to explain the problems sometimes experienced with semantics and the lack of a clear, well understood terminology.

Industry parameters and definitions

Business events

Even if precise definitions are not yet in regular use, it is important, at the beginning of a book on the conference industry, to set out certain parameters for the measurement of business events and the facilities which support and service them.

In the UK, trade body Eventia, organiser of the annual 'UK Events Market Trends Survey', together with the organisers of the first 'UK Economic Impact Study', agreed in 2012 to use the following definition in undertaking their surveys:

A Conference   An out-of-office meeting of at least four hours' duration involving a minimum of ten people.

This is the same definition used for the economic impact studies in Canada, the USA and Mexico (see Chapter 7).

Other research programmes use somewhat different definitions, while major conference hotel chains often base their own conference statistics on meetings involving two or more people. Clearly there would be benefits in agreeing and using a standard definition globally.

Conference venues

An early definition of a conference venue was: '*a conference venue must be able to seat 20 or more participants theatre-style*'. However, this is so hopelessly inadequate that it could even describe a large living room or den in a private house! In October 2002 leading industry bodies in the UK agreed to use the following definition of a conference venue: '*a conference venue must be an externally let facility (i.e. not a company's own meeting rooms), and have a minimum of three meeting/conference rooms with a minimum seating capacity of 50 theatre-style in its largest room*'. This is not perfect because it can exclude, for example, country house hotels with high standard facilities but only one or two meeting rooms, but it does offer a reasonable baseline for what can claim to be professional venues operating in a highly competitive marketplace.

Business tourism

The conference industry has traditionally formed one sector within 'business tourism', itself a sub-sector of the overall tourism industry which comprises both leisure tourism and business tourism. Apart from conferences, the other main components of business tourism are: exhibitions and trade fairs, incentive travel, corporate events or corporate hospitality and individual business travel (also referred to as 'corporate travel').

Table 1.8 provides a matrix of the main segments of business tourism and highlights some of their key characteristics.

Conferences, exhibitions and trade fairs, incentive travel and corporate events (sometimes referred to as corporate hospitality or corporate entertainment) are the four business tourism segments which are the prime focus of marketing activity by venues and destinations, because decisions about where the events take place are open to influence. The organisers of the event may have great flexibility in deciding where it is to be held, and are able to use their own judgement or discretion over choice of location. For this reason these four business tourism segments are sometimes described as 'discretionary'.

Individual business travel or corporate travel relates to those whose work regularly involves travel within their own country or overseas, such as a lorry driver or sales representative, as well as to people who may have to travel away from their normal place of employment from time to time (a management consultant, for example, or an engineer

Table 1.8 'MICE' matrix (illustrating the segments which make up the business tourism sector)

Segment	Corporate Organisation/ Corporation	National Association	International Association/ Intergovernmental Body	Public Sector/ Government
Meetings	An out-of-office meeting of at least 4 hours' duration involving a minimum of 10 people. Includes sales meetings, training, board meetings and retreats, AGMs.	Board meetings, regional meetings, training events, information events.	Limited number of board-level meetings, typically lasting 1–2 days maximum. Also international meetings hosted by national associations.	Mainly organising non-residential meetings of up to 1 day's duration. Also training courses which may last for several days, and information events.
Conferences	Typically of 1 or 2 days' duration with a formal programme that has been promoted in advance. Delegates are often compelled to attend.	Usually an annual conference/congress/ convention for members lasting 2–3 days.	An annual (or less frequent) congress or convention rotating around different countries or continents, with selection based on bids received from individual cities. Typically of 3–5 days' duration.	Mostly 1-day conferences (occasionally 2 days) attracting delegates from the local area or region.
Incentive Travel	A business tourism trip to motivate and reward employees and dealers, usually containing a conference element.	Not applicable.	Not applicable.	Not applicable.
Exhibitions	Product launches; attendance as an exhibitor at trade and consumer shows organised by specialist exhibition organisers or trade associations. Also attendance as a corporate visitor ('buyer') at trade shows.	May include the organisation of an exhibition to run alongside its own conference; also participation in other industry trade shows as an exhibitor. Trade associations are also primary exhibition organisers.	May include the organisation of an exhibition to run alongside its own conference; occasional participation in other industry trade shows as an exhibitor.	Information/regional trade events.
Corporate Events (also known as Corporate Hospitality)	Hosted entertainment at major sporting events, concerts, and other high profile functions, and/or participation in sporting or outdoor pursuits-type activities.	Not common, although some professional and trade associations may organise golf days or other sporting events for their members.	Not normally applicable.	Not applicable.

responsible for installing a new piece of equipment in a client's factory). In all such business travel, which represents a major portion of business tourism, the opportunities to influence where the individual travels to are minimal, and this segment is consequently referred to as 'non-discretionary'.

Business tourism and leisure tourism

Reference has already been made to the broad division of tourism into the two sectors of business tourism and leisure tourism, although these two sectors share much common ground. As Davidson (1994) points out:

> business tourism, in particular, can involve a substantial leisure element. Incentive travel, for example, may consist entirely of leisure, sport and entertainment. But, even for conference delegates, visitors to trade fairs and individual business travellers, excursions to local restaurants and places of entertainment, or sightseeing tours, can be a way of relaxing at the end of the working day. Socialising in this way can be an important part of the business tourism experience for groups, as it gives delegates or colleagues the opportunity to unwind together and get to know each other on a less formal basis.

This is why destinations, bidding to attract a major event, sell the concept of 'destination' and place great emphasis on everything from a destination's leisure, cultural and entertainment assets to shopping, sports and dining options.

Davidson also makes clear that:

> the distinction between the two categories of tourism is further blurred by the presence of 'accompanying persons' alongside many business tourism events. Incentive travel often includes the husbands or wives of those selected for such trips. But also, it is not uncommon for those travelling to exotic destinations for conferences or trade fairs and exhibitions to take their spouses along and make a short holiday out of the trip. In such cases, the couple may prolong their stay in order to have the time to tour around the destination after the business part of the trip is over.

The phrase 'leisure extenders' has emerged in the UK to describe this phenomenon, and much marketing spend is now devoted to increasing the number of leisure extenders. There is a useful paper on the website of the UK's Business Visits and Events Partnership (www.businessvisitsandeventspartnership.com) describing in more detail how to implement leisure extender practices. It is entitled 'Making the most of our business visitors' and is in the Publications section of the website.

Business tourism and leisure tourism rely on the same, or a very similar, infrastructure for their success. Both sectors need accommodation (hotels, guest houses), transport and communications (airports, railway stations, good road networks, coach and taxi services, modern telecommunications links), entertainment (shopping, bars and restaurants, night clubs/casinos, visitor attractions), as well as information and advisory services, emergency medical services and an attractive, welcoming, safe and secure environment.

But conference and business tourism has additional infrastructure needs, such as appropriate venues, specialist contractors (audio-visual suppliers, exhibition contractors, interpreters, for example), and, perhaps most importantly, staff who are trained to be aware of and to respond to the particular needs of conference organisers and delegates.

Benefits of conference and business tourism

Although business tourism and leisure tourism rely on a similar infrastructure, the former brings with it a number of significant extra benefits which makes it particularly attractive to destinations.

Greater profitability

Conference and business tourism caters for the high quality, high cost and, therefore, high yield end of the market. In 2011, for example, business and conference visitors to the United Kingdom from overseas spent on average 72 per cent more per day than leisure visitors (source: International Passenger Survey). The greater spending power of business tourists means increased economic benefits for the host destination and a greater return on its investment in infrastructure and marketing.

All-year-round activity

Conference and business tourism takes place throughout the year. Spring and autumn are the peak seasons of the year for conferences (with most of the larger, high profile association and political party conferences taking place at these times in the UK), but many smaller conferences and meetings are also held during the winter months. In the northern hemisphere, January, July and August are the months of least activity which, for many resort-type destinations, is an added benefit because it means that there is no clash between the demands of leisure and business tourism, but rather they are complementary.

The all-year-round nature of conference and business tourism also leads to the creation and sustenance of permanent jobs, as opposed to the seasonal, temporary jobs which are a frequent characteristic of the leisure tourism sector. This, in turn, ensures

that 'careers' rather than simply 'jobs' can be offered to new entrants, even though clearly defined structures and opportunities for career progression are not yet fully established.

Future inward investment

Those organising a conference or incentive travel trip will always be very keen to make sure that it is as successful as possible. One of the ways in which this can be achieved is by giving delegates and participants a pleasant, positive experience of the destination in which the event is being held. This usually means showing delegates the most attractive, scenic parts of the destination in the hope that, by creating a memorable experience for them, many will return.

Where this has been undertaken successfully, some delegates/participants return as leisure visitors, often bringing their partners and families for a holiday or short break. Some may have been so impressed that they may decide to relocate their business to the destination or look to set up a subsidiary operation there. As Davidson (1994) says:

> a business visitor who leaves with a good impression of the conference, trade fair or incentive destination becomes an unpaid ambassador for that place . . . these are often influential people, whose opinions of the destination will be instrumental in determining its image in the minds of others who have not visited it.

It could be argued that a single meeting of influential business executives can do more to increase a destination's exposure than years of promotion by economic development officials.

Professional development

Maple (2006), as president of the International Association of Congress Centres (AIPC) and general manager of the Vancouver Convention and Exhibition Centre, contended that:

> large events like conventions are designed to bring the best (people) in any given field together in an environment where information can be shared and progress identified. When this happens, it creates a big boost to local knowledge and skills in any imaginable discipline. Medical conferences are a great example. When the top researchers and practitioners get together, they are looking at the very latest results and procedures in their respective fields. They are deciding what advances are most important and which areas are the most promising for the future; in short, everything you would like the local medical community to have access to. Now multiply that possibility by any number of different professions, trades or business sectors, and you begin to get the idea of what having meetings, conventions and exhibitions can do to promote the professional skills in a community.

'Green' tourism

Conference and business tourism has fewer negative impacts on the environment than mass leisure tourism. It is concerned with smaller numbers, but much higher spend. It is characterised by the use of coach transfers and public transport (or Shanks' pony) within a destination, minimising traffic congestion and environmental pollution.

Conference delegates are together as a group, so that it is possible to inform and educate them about the local community in which their conference is being held in order to maximise the enjoyment of their stay but also to minimise any disruption and possible inconvenience to the local resident population. It is very much harder to manage, in the same way, the impact of individual leisure travellers on a destination.

However, it would be naïve to claim that business tourism does not have its negative impacts, especially on the physical environment. These are well summarised by Swarbrooke and Horner (2001):

> If we want to make business travel and tourism more sustainable, we have to recognise that there are characteristics of business tourism which make it particularly problematic in relation to the concept of sustainable tourism. First, most business tourists take more trips in a year than the average leisure tourist, thus making more demands on transport infrastructure and destination services. Business tourists tend to be very demanding and want high quality facilities, even in towns and cities in developing countries. While both of these are difficult to reconcile with the concept of sustainable tourism, the positive side of business tourism is the fact that business travellers tend to be higher spending than leisure tourists.

Green and sustainability issues and opportunities are examined in more detail in Chapter 7.

Improved quality of life

Convention centres and the kinds of activities they support play an important role in enhancing the overall quality of life in a community. Maple (2006) suggests that, to survive, communities need some kind of industrial activity, *preferably one that brings in money from outside the local economy*. But, she adds:

> a lot of these industries are less than completely benign, particularly from a community or environmental perspective. The convention business, on the other hand, does more than simply avoid damaging its host community. It actually thrives on the kind of qualities people typically want around them: things like an attractive environment and cultural attributes, and provides a sound economic reason to support and enhance these qualities to everyone's advantage.

Changing the perceptions and profile of conferences and business events

While the links between conferences and other business events with the tourism and leisure industries are important and undeniable, as described earlier in this chapter, it may be time to realign the sector more closely with other sectors of national economies, such as trade, investment, knowledge exchange, scientific research, and professional development. Reasons for this refocusing and realignment were set out by Rod Cameron (2010) of the Association Internationale des Palais de Congrès (AIPC), writing in *Conference & Meetings World* magazine, when he urged that, in order to promote a better understanding of the meetings and business events industry, a number of issues needed to be addressed:

- *Firstly, we need to emphasise the role that meetings play in economic, professional and educational development and downplay the leisure aspect. There has never been a greater opportunity for the industry, as the world continues to look at the course the recovery will take, and to search for any activities that can promise support in this regard. But to achieve this, we need to be taken more seriously*
- *Secondly, we need to enhance both the content and perceived value of meetings in order to give planners and delegates the arguments they need to justify their investment of time and resources*
- *In particular, we need to put more emphasis on the ability to demonstrate measurable outcomes that will resonate with increasing corporate concerns about return on investment (ROI).*

He concluded:

The fact is, nobody holds a meeting in order to fill hotel rooms, that's simply a by-product, and yet most of our current industry measures relate to what delegates spend, not what they actually accomplish. This trivialises meetings in the eyes of those who see them as engines for business and professional progress.

These points are reinforced by Leigh Harry (2010), President of the Joint Meetings Industry Council (JMIC – an international body representing the major international trade associations), Chief Executive of Melbourne Convention Exhibition Centre and President of the International Congress and Convention Association (ICCA), who said:

The most recent 'image crisis' was a direct result of our industry being seen by many as more closely related to leisure than economic and professional development. We are challenged by the fact that our greatest value is difficult to measure, that is, what meetings actually accomplish such as professional and technical advancement, new investment, innovation and technology transfer. These are the real reasons meetings and conventions take place.

He argued that the meetings and events industry should be thought of as a key component in the global knowledge economy, rather than as a branch of tourism.

Will Hutton, former UK *Observer* newspaper editor, speaking at the AIPC annual conference, held at the ACC Liverpool (July 2010), said that convention centres were now part of the emergent knowledge economy, and he described them as 'knowledge transfer institutions'. The key to their future success would be to form strategic alliances with knowledge businesses and sectors. Case Study 1.2, Qatar National Convention Centre, describes the Centre's focus on the global knowledge economy.

Hugo Slimbrouck (2011), Ovation Global DMC's Director of Strategic Partnerships, in an article entitled 'Keeping it real' (*Conference News*, December 2011), writes:

Those of you who think we are working in tourism or travel need to change your view. We are in the business of conceptualising and creating meaningful and inspiring meetings and events that meet specific business objectives to which our clients aspire. Events are critical to the development of business, research, the professions and technology – and also key factors in generating new investment and profile for the destinations that host them. All of us need to change the language we use with clients. We need to speak, think and breathe their language, not the business travel industry language. It will improve the image that our industry often has of being organisers of parties and change the perception of the business tools that our industry offers the world.

Appreciating the real value of meetings and conventions and gaining a better understanding of the benefits they deliver to business, to Government, and to the wider community are all key to the future success of the sector, a theme that will be further explored in Chapter 10.

CASE STUDY 1.2 Qatar National Convention Centre

Qatar: the country

Qatar, a former pearl-fishing centre and once one of the poorest Arabian Gulf states, is now one of the richest countries in the Middle East region, thanks to the exploitation of large oil and gas fields since the 1940s. Dominated by the Thani family for almost 150 years, the mainly desert country was a British protectorate until 1971, when it declared its independence, shortly after Bahrain had done, with both refusing to join

the United Arab Emirates. In 1995 Crown Prince Hamad bin Khalifa deposed his father to become emir and since then he has introduced some liberal reforms. Press freedom has been extended and the Qatari satellite TV station Al Jazeera has become one of the most important broadcasters in the Arab world. Elections in 1999 for a 29-member municipal council were the first in which Qatari women were allowed to vote and stand for office. The population is small (fewer than two million); foreigners, including labourers attracted by a construction boom, outnumber natives. Possessing more than 15 per cent of the world's proven gas reserves, Qatar has ambitions to become a global energy giant.

As part of its five-year plan, Qatar is investing US$17 billion in tourism infrastructure, including the construction of luxury hotels, resorts and meeting facilities. To meet forecasted demand, hotel capacity increased by 400 per cent to over 15,000 luxury rooms and apartments in the period up to 2012. Qatar will host the Football World Cup tournament in 2022.

Such growth and well-thought-out development provide a modern and sophisticated environment for business events. Doha, the capital, preserves its heritage and culture to complement the modernity of the developing city resulting in a truly authentic Arabian experience.

Qatar Foundation and Education City

Qatar Foundation is an independent, private, non-profit, chartered organisation founded in 1995 by decree of His Highness Sheikh Hamad Bin Khalifa Al-Thani, Emir of the State of Qatar, to support centres of excellence which develop people's abilities through investments in human capital, innovative technology, state-of-the-art facilities and partnerships with elite organisations, thus raising the competence of people and the quality of life.

Qatar Foundation's mission is to prepare the people of Qatar and the region to meet the challenges of an ever-changing world, and to make Qatar a leader in innovative education and research. To achieve this mission, Qatar Foundation supports a network of centres and partnerships with elite institutions, all committed to the principle that a nation's greatest natural resource is its people. Education City, Qatar Foundation's flagship project, is envisaged as a Centre of Excellence in education and research that will help transform Qatar into a knowledge-based society.

Qatar National Convention Centre (QNCC) is located within Education City to complement the eight international universities plus the research and technology communities within this vicinity including the Sidra Medical and Research Centre and Qatar Science and Technology Park. QNCC aims to be the focal point for a new global hub of ideas and innovation. With its futuristic metallic tree branches seeming to grow skywards from the ground, the Qatar National Convention Centre next to the main Qatar Foundation site is as unmistakable as it is unmissable.

Qatar National Convention Centre

The Qatar National Convention Centre (QNCC) was conceived from a vision: a vision to bring together the world's best minds under one roof. It was officially opened on 4 December 2011 (in conjunction with the 20th World Petroleum Congress). Built at a cost of QR4.2 billion (£730 million or US$1.2 billion), the QNCC today is one of the most sophisticated convention and exhibition centres in the world. The project was given the go-ahead in 2004, the construction team moved on site in May 2006 and the Centre opened after five and a half years of planning and construction.

The three-storey convention centre, designed by renowned Japanese architect Arata Isozaki, draws its inspiration from Qatar's iconic Sidra tree, the ancient meeting place for scholars and philosophers who gathered beneath its shady branches to share their knowledge. But the building also incorporates a wide range of twenty-first-century features that put it at the forefront of contemporary architecture, such as more than 3,500 m² of solar panels, electronically controlled walls and ceilings, and covered parking for 3,200 cars connected to the Centre by an air-conditioned moving walkway.

The 250 metre (820 feet) long curved steel tree structure forms the signature entrance to the QNCC reaching up to support the exterior canopy. The tree is a beacon of learning and comfort in the desert. It is treasured by the Bedouins, who used it for shelter and as a meeting place. Not only do the tree's branches provide shade, its fruit, flowers and leaves were and are still used for traditional medicine. QNCC is the new Sidra tree.

FIGURE 1.2 Qatar National Convention Centre

As part of Qatar Foundation's vision to attract and host major conferences and events, QNCC was built with the capacity and capability to host all types of events, not only regional and international conventions and exhibitions but also gala events, concerts, theatrical productions and corporate banquets. For instance, the conference hall can be used as a theatre-style hall with a seating capacity of more than 4,000 guests. By withdrawing the retractable seating, the same space can be converted to host a full banquet for more than 2,300 guests. The magnificent oyster chandeliers in the conference hall can be lowered and raised individually to alter the ceiling height and ambience and create a more intimate setting.

QNCC is the first of its kind built to the gold certification of the US Green Building Council's Leadership in Energy and Environment Design (LEED): the Centre's vast array of solar panels contribute an estimated 12.5 per cent of its electricity needs and there are water conservation, variable air-volume systems and energy efficiency measures in place too. It is also incredibly intelligent. For example, the exhibition hall ceiling consists of a series of gridded modules that can each be individually raised or lowered at the touch of a button all the way down to floor level, giving the building the flexibility to change its shape depending on the event that is being hosted.

QNCC capacity at a glance:

- 40,000 m^2 of exhibition space.
- Outdoor exhibition area of 3,100 m^2.
- 2,300-seat lyric style theatre.
- Conference hall for 4,000 delegates.
- Three-tiered auditoria, with 401, 290 and 495 seats respectively.
- A total of 52 meeting rooms.
- Six VIP lounges and seven hospitality lounges.

QNCC features:

- five-star international in-house catering;
- wireless conference management system;
- latest presentation technology and production capabilities;
- 35,000 m^2 of modular mobile rigging grids;
- 100 per cent fibre optic connections throughout;
- full pit and trench services system throughout the exhibition halls;
- wireless communication and digital voting systems throughout;
- radio frequency identification device (RFID) for tracking of delegates and building assets;
- covered parking for 3,200 vehicles connected by air-conditioned people mover (travelator).

Staffing

A crucial but sometimes overlooked element in the success of a convention centre is the staff who pull everything together and ensure the professional delivery of an event. From the very beginning, QNCC placed a very strong emphasis on building an experienced team with the passion and drive to make QNCC successful. A team of 392 full-time and 313 part-time staff (from 36 different countries) has been fully trained in their areas of responsibility.

QNCC departments include:

- human resources (including government affairs);
- business development (including sales, PR and communications);
- operations (including event planning, theatre, event operations, AV and production);
- information technology;
- food and beverage;
- kitchens (including chefs, stewarding);
- finance and administration (including quality assurance, purchasing);
- assets and building services (including housekeeping, health, safety and environment (HSSE), building services).

Market focus

As part of its soft opening and prior to its formal opening, QNCC hosted a major awards dinner (November 2011) recognising significant achievements in the fields of biomedical, energy, computing, environmental, arts, social science, humanities and Islamic Studies research. The dinner was the culmination of the Qatar Foundation Annual Research Forum that attracted 1,500 delegates and speakers from around the world. The three-day forum brought together Nobel laureates, international policy-makers, students, scientists, industry leaders, and top academic and research institutions to exchange knowledge and provide networking opportunities. QNCC General Manager, Adam Mather-Brown, said the venue was specifically targeting these types of conferences and exhibitions as Qatar realised its vision of moving from a carbon-based economy to one based on knowledge. He said:

> The Annual Research Forum is exactly the type of event that will help the country fulfil its ambitions. The QNCC is strategically located within the Qatar Foundation's Education City, an enclave of eight international universities including the Qatar Science and Technology Park and Sidra Medical and Research Centre. One of the reasons for locating the QNCC in Education City was for it to become the focal point for a new global hub of ideas and innovation. We are proud to be a world-class venue conceived to bring together the world's best minds under one roof. In addition to the local market, QNCC aims to be the intellectual nerve centre

and serve the education and research communities to host key regional and international events that shape the future of research and education in the twenty-first century and beyond.

Benefits to Qatar

Qatar is already a regional hub for conferences and exhibitions, with 95 per cent of visitors coming for business, whether as an individual traveller or to attend a conference, meeting, or exhibition. With the addition of new infrastructure like QNCC, the State is targeting a 20 per cent increase in the number of visitors in the five-year period to 2016.

QNCC is designed to attract high calibre events and be a catalyst for knowledge and business exchange, creating direct economic impact for the country. It aims to secure local, regional and international conferences and exhibitions and, through hosting such events, it is anticipated that the world's leading specialists and delegates from across many fields will visit Qatar.

Other benefits identified by QNCC include:

- It will create a positive economic impact on the destination. Based on reported data, each international conference delegate will spend an average of QR1,500 (£280) per day in Doha.
- It will increase the number of business travellers to Qatar and the Middle East.
- It will create jobs and wealth in the local market.
- It will enhance international media attention and recognition.
- It will help to promote Qatar as a world-class destination.
- It will create the opportunity for the improvement of facilities and infrastructure in Qatar.
- It will contribute to the skills development needs of the country.
- It will grow the tourism contribution to the country's GDP and increase the cumulative contribution to the national economy.

In the initial five-month period to the end of March 2012, QNCC hosted 52 events attracting more than 30,000 visitors, with an estimated economic impact from overseas visitors worth over QR41 million (US$11.2 million). Major international events scheduled for 2012 included the United Nations Conference on Trade and Development, the 25th Universal Postal Congress, and the United Nations Framework Convention on Climate Change (COP 18).

Conclusion

Qatar's goal is to achieve one of the most dynamic knowledge-based economies in the world, one that is dominated by information and technology, innovation and entrepreneurship. QNCC is a physical demonstration of this commitment and objective.

Mr Ahmed Al-Hajjaji, Chief Executive Officer of AMLAK, QNCC's holding company, is confident that the high-tech features incorporated in the building will send a clear message to people both in Qatar and from visiting countries. He said:

> QNCC will serve as a beacon to the rest of the world, demonstrating Qatar's ambition to push the boundaries of technology forward along with our own capabilities. It is a physical manifestation of Qatar Foundation's pursuit of excellence, reflecting the investment in research, design and technology and world-class education undertaken by QF. People visiting from the region and from further afield will understand the ethos of QF simply by seeing QNCC. At the same time, the quality of the facility will serve as inspiration to the new generations of engineers, architects and designers who will see what sort of projects they could be a part of if they work hard and take advantage of the educational opportunities they have here.

This case study was compiled with the assistance of Trevor McCartney, QNCC Director of Business Development, and Janet Leow, PR and Communications Manager (www.qatarconvention.com).

SUMMARY

- The USA was the first country to recognise the potential economic benefits of conference business for a city or local destination. Detroit was the first US city to establish a convention and visitor bureau in 1896, followed by a number of other US cities in the early years of the twentieth century. Europe did not follow suit until the latter half of the twentieth century, and it was at this time also that conferences and conventions came to be recognised as an industry in its own right.
- The final two decades of the twentieth century and the early years of the twenty-first century have witnessed spectacular investment in the infrastructure which supports both leisure and conference/business tourism. Such investments are taking place not only in the more established conference destinations of Western Europe and North America, but in every continent and region.
- The conference industry is now a truly global industry, with over two hundred countries vying for a share of the lucrative international conferences and meetings market. A greater market share is now being won by countries in Eastern Europe and in the Asia-Pacific region in particular.
- The conference industry is still young though maturing at a rapid rate. Symptomatic of the industry's youthfulness, yet contributing to its lack of proper recognition in commercial and political circles, is the lack of a comprehensive statistical base to

measure its true size and value, although improvements are now in sight. Its relative immaturity is also shown in its use and misuse of terminology.

- Conference/business tourism and leisure tourism are closely intertwined, relying on similar infrastructure and support services. However, conferences and business events also have a number of unique characteristics and advantages, which can bring additional benefits to those destinations successful in attracting conference business.
- There are a number of initiatives seeking to realign conferences, conventions and business events more closely with trade and investment, professional development and other business-focused sectors of national economies, and away from the leisure and hospitality industries.

REVIEW AND DISCUSSION QUESTIONS

1　Critically discuss the factors that have led to the development of the 'knowledge-based economy'; and discuss the role of conferences and conference venues as effective channels of knowledge transfer.

2　Discuss the relationship between conferences and the leisure tourism and hospitality sectors. Critically assess whether it is time to play down the existing links and, if so, how this might be best achieved.

3　Compare and contrast the conference industry with another young industry (for example, computing and information technology, the fitness and health food industry). Draw conclusions on which has progressed further, and give reasons why.

4　Review the principal issues and challenges regarding the terminology in use in the conference and business events sector. How could a more cohesive and standardised use of terminology be best achieved globally?

REFERENCES

Cameron, R. (2010) 'Time to Polish Our Image', *Conference & Meetings World* (June)

Colston, P. (2010) 'History in the Making', *Conference & Meetings World* (March)

Davidson, R. (1994) *Business Travel*, Addison Wesley Longman Limited

—— and Rogers, T. (2006) *Marketing Destinations and Venues for Conferences, Conventions and Business Events*, Elsevier Butterworth-Heinemann

DiMario, Linda H. (2012) 'Convention Centers: Creating the Ideal Balance', *Convention Trends 2012*, Association News/Sports Travel in conjunction with CSPI

Fenich, George (2012) *Meetings, Expositions, Events, and Conventions*, 3rd edn, Pearson Education

Gartrell, Richard B. (1994) *Destination Marketing for Convention and Visitor Bureaus*, 2nd edn, Dubuque, IA: Kendall Hunt Publishing Company, for International Association of Convention and Visitor Bureaus

Harry, L. (2010) 'Briefing Interview', IMEX-Frankfurt 2011 newsletter (July)

ICCA (2011) *ICCA Statistics Report 2001–2010: International Association Meetings Market,* International Congress and Convention Association

Jones, C. and James, D. (2005) 'The Tourism Satellite Account (TSA): A Vision, Challenge and Reality', *Tourism*, Issue 123, Quarter 2

Maple, B. (2006) 'More than Just Money', *Conference & Meetings World* (June)

Riggs, B. (2011) 'Lost in the Atlantic', *Association Meetings International* (November)

Shone, Anton (1998) *The Business of Conferences*, Butterworth-Heinemann

Slimbrouck, H. (2011) 'Keeping it Real', *Conference News* (December)

STCRC (2007) *Measuring the Economic Importance of the Meetings Industry,* Sustainable Tourism Cooperative Research Centre

Swarbrooke, J. and Horner, S. (2001) *Business Travel and Tourism*, Butterworth-Heinemann

UIA (2012) *International Meetings Statistics for the Year 2011*, Union of International Associations

FURTHER READING

Davidson, R. and Cope, B. (2002) *Business Travel*, Pearson Education

IAPCO (2009) *Dictionary of Meetings Industry Terminology*, 4th edn, available from the International Association of Professional Congress Organisers (www.iapco.org/dictionary.cfm?page_id = 130) (see Chapter 9)

The website of the Joint Meetings Industry Council (www.themeetingsindustry.org) contains a very useful listing of reports, papers and research studies

CHAPTER 2

The structure of the conference industry

www.routledge.com/cw/rogers

CHAPTER OBJECTIVES

This chapter looks at:

- the buyers (corporate, association, public sector, entrepreneurs/commercial conference organisers)
- the suppliers (venues, destinations, other suppliers)
- agencies and intermediaries
- other important organisations (trade associations, trade media, national tourism organisations, consultants, educational institutions)

It includes case studies on:

- the launch of the Vauxhall Astra by experiential event agency TRO
- Oriflame Executive Conference 2012, Buenos Aires, an incentive travel programme organised by event and communications agency Grass Roots
- 'Conventa' – the South East European Exhibition for Meetings, Events and Incentives

LEARNING OUTCOMES

On completion of this chapter, you should be able to:
- describe the overall structure of the conference industry;
- understand the characteristics of the different kinds of 'buyer';
- identify the myriad of organisations that make up the supply side of the conference industry;
- define the range of other organisations needed for the overall functioning and effectiveness of a twenty-first-century industry.

Introduction

The conference industry is highly complex, comprising of a multiplicity of buyer and supplier organisations and businesses. For many conference organisers and meeting planners ('the buyers'), the organisation of conferences and similar events is only a part of their job, and often one for which they have received little formal training and may only have a temporary responsibility. Suppliers include conference venues and destinations, agencies and specialist contractors, accommodation providers and transport companies. Both buyers and suppliers are welded together and supported by national bodies and associations, trade media and educational institutions, each contributing to the overall structure of this fast developing, global industry.

The buyers

In common with other industries, the conference industry comprises 'buyers' and 'suppliers'. The buyers in this case are conference organisers and meeting planners who buy or, more accurately, hire conference venues and related services in order to stage their events.

Most people working within the conference industry refer to two broad types of buyer: 'corporate' and 'association'. There are also 'public sector' buyers who may be regarded as a discrete group, rather than being subsumed within the 'association' category. There is also a category of risk-taking, entrepreneurial conference organiser who puts together a conference and hopes to be able to attract sufficient delegates for the event to be profitable. All of the above may also employ the services of various kinds of 'agency' or intermediary to assist them in the staging of their events.

The corporate buyer

Definitions

The term 'corporate' is used to describe conference organisers (often called meeting planners, especially in North America) who work for corporate organisations. Corporate organisations are companies established primarily to generate a profit and thus provide a financial return for their owners, whether these are the proprietors of a family-run business or the shareholders of a large publicly quoted company. They can be manufacturing or service companies.

Corporate organisations are to be found in all industry sectors. The sectors which have traditionally been prominent in generating corporate conference business include:

* oil, gas and petrochemicals;
* medical and pharmaceuticals;
* computing/IT and telecommunications;
* automotive manufacturing and other manufacturing;
* financial and professional services;
* food, drink and tobacco;
* travel and transport.

New industries and technologies expected to be important drivers of future meetings and conferences include:

* creative industries, art, architecture and design, marketing, media, film, photography, music and the arts, publishing;
* renewable energy;
* robotics;
* biotechnology and specialist sciences;
* electronic currency and finance;
* education, distance learning, virtual universities;
* security.

Identifying the corporate buyer

Not all companies have a dedicated conference or event management department. Indeed, during times of economic recession, this is often an area where many companies opt to make savings by closing down their event management departments and putting the work out to agencies on an outsourced contract basis. In some cases, such companies contract the employees from their former event management departments to continue to organise their events, but the staff now work on a freelance or self-employed basis and thus cease to be a direct overhead to the company.

Table 2.1 Job titles

Key Word in Job Title	Corporate Respondents	Association Respondents
Events	68	50
Marketing/communications/PR	73	40
PA/secretary/administration	31	65
CEO/MD/Board director	23	21
Sales/business development	23	3
Conference	6	17
Training and education	11	2
Project/programmes	5	4
Operations/logistics	3	5

Source: British Meetings & Events Industry Survey 2011–12 (Copyright CAT Publications Ltd 2012 – for further information visit: www.meetpie.com/bmeis)

The larger corporate organisations are, of course, multi-division entities located on a number of different sites, often in a number of different countries. Staff involved in organising meetings and conferences appear in a whole range of guises and job titles. Research carried out for the *British Meetings and Events Industry Survey 2011–12* (CAT 2011) found that less than a third of the conference organisers interviewed had job titles or responsibilities directly associated with 'conferences or events'. Table 2.1 gives further details of this research.

Principal job titles/responsibilities of staff engaged in conference organising

In broad terms, most corporate events fall within the ambit of the following departments: sales and marketing, training and personnel/human resources, central administration including the company secretarial activities.

Staff involvement in organising events often varies considerably. At one extreme, their task may simply be to obtain information on potential venues for an event, while at the other they can be given complete responsibility for planning and running the event. In the UK, the new breed of young event management students graduating from universities is beginning to have an impact on the levels of knowledge and professionalism but there are still many, more mature, corporate organisers who have received little formal training in conference and meeting planning. It may also be that such activities account for just a part of their overall responsibilities, and only be of a short-term nature. In the USA, the role of a meeting planner is more established, with better defined training and career structures.

Identifying the corporate buyer is, therefore, a major and continuous challenge for those organisations wishing to market their facilities and services to him. The transience

of some corporate conference organisers also makes it difficult to provide an effective education and training framework for them, and thus develop their expertise and increase their professionalism. It is only when such support systems are in place that the role of the corporate conference organiser will achieve full recognition and occupy its proper place at the centre of companies' communications strategies.

Corporate buying patterns

Decisions about the conference or meeting (choice of venue, budget, size of event, visiting speakers, programme content, and so forth) are taken by the corporate conference organiser or a line manager or the managing director, or by a group of such people in consultation. The decision-making process has traditionally been relatively straightforward and more-or-less immediate, although the influence of company procurement departments is having an impact, in some cases extending the time before a decision is made and pushing final decisions up to senior management levels.

Corporate events can be of many different types and sizes. The most common of these events are shown in Table 2.2.

Table 2.2 Main types of corporate meetings/events	
Annual General Meeting (AGM)	Product Launch
Board meeting/retreat	Sales conference
Corporate hospitality/entertainment	Training course/seminar
Exhibition/exposition	Technical conference
Incentive travel	Team-building event
Roadshow	Symposium

It is worth drawing the distinction between internal and external events. In the former case, the participants are employees of the company (typically sales conferences, general management conferences, rallies for the staff, etc.). External events are a vital part of Customer Relationship Management (CRM) strategies (see Chapter 3) with companies trying to build a long-term relationship with their key clients. One way of doing this is to invite these clients to be part of the company's development process through attending events: such events can include new product launches, or educational meetings explaining complex new products or upgrades (especially in the field of IT). Participation in these events enables account managers to get close to key clients over coffee breaks or in the bar. One of the benefits for companies in running these events is that they get real-time feedback and can measure the return on investment (ROI) in a way that is impossible with traditional internal sales conferences.

Venue preferences

The majority of corporate conferences and meetings are held in hotels. Some take place in purpose-built conference centres and management training centres, as well as unusual or unique venues (see later in this chapter for examples). Civic venues and town halls tend to attract relatively few corporate events because of a perception that they may be staid and 'basic', which is often far from the reality. Some corporate meetings are held in university and academic venues, especially where such venues have invested in dedicated conference facilities with high quality, en suite accommodation/housing (as, indeed, many have done).

Lead times and seasonality

Corporate events often have a fairly short 'lead time', especially compared with association conferences, with just a matter of weeks or a few months available to plan and stage them. The majority of these events involve relatively low delegate numbers (e.g. from 10 to 200).

Corporate conferences and events take place throughout the year, peaking in spring and autumn. In the northern hemisphere July and August are the months of least activity because of holidays, although the corporate hospitality sector is buoyant with its links to major sporting events such as tennis at Wimbledon or Paris, test match cricket, grand prix motor racing and international golf tournaments.

Budgets and the influence of public perception on events

The budget for corporate conferences, expressed in terms of expenditure per delegate, is generally higher than that for many 'association' conferences as it is the company which pays for delegate attendance, not the delegates themselves. The costs can be incorporated into a company's marketing or staff training budgets, for example, and the selection of an attractive, quality venue coupled with a professionally produced conference will reinforce the importance of the event in delegates' minds and contribute to the successful achievement of its objectives, whether these be motivational, information sharing, team building, or other.

However, the economic recession from 2008 onwards led to a much tighter control of costs and also, in some cases, strategic decisions to avoid using 5-star properties because of perceptions of luxury and extravagance. Companies did not want to be portrayed by the media as 'wasting' money on staging external events in expensive venues, and a certain trading down was experienced, with companies using 3-star instead of 4-star hotels, or 4-star instead of 5-star, and seeking to minimise the costs incurred. There are examples of meetings being booked into venues with event timings that meant lunch did not have to be provided for delegates, or delegates had to pay for their own lunches, in order to reduce the costs of the event. Table 2.3 summarises the

Table 2.3 Public perception's influence		
	Corporate (%)	Association (%)
Very important – venues and destinations must be seen to be appropriate	35.6	33.0
Quite important – although the venues and destinations must also suit delegates' needs	38.2	36.4
Neither important nor unimportant	13.3	15.7
Not really important	6.0	8.8
Not important at all – it's more important that the venues and destinations work logistically	6.9	6.1

Source: British Meetings & Event Industry Survey 2011–12 (Copyright CAT Publications – www.meetpie. com/bmeis)

influence of public perception on venue and destination decisions among both corporate and association buyers in the UK in 2011. It shows that 74 per cent of corporate buyers and 69 per cent of association buyers think public perceptions of their meetings venue and destination decisions are important, although they clearly see a balance between being seen to be appropriate and suiting delegates' needs.

Procurement and strategic meetings management

There is a clear case for changing and introducing more effective management systems to, indeed professionalising, the whole meeting venue booking or sourcing process, and there are unmistakable signs that this is happening through the influence of companies' central purchasing (or procurement) departments. The term 'strategic meetings management' is also coming to the fore, used to describe a comprehensive, strategic approach to the planning of meetings and the management of a complex set of relationships covering internal and external stakeholders. Strategic meetings management programmes (SMMP) are described more fully in Chapter 10.

Return on investment (ROI) and return on objectives (ROO)

Corporate conferences are now more intensive, business-related events than was the case during the 1980s and early 1990s, when they were often seen as something of a 'jolly'. Return on investment (ROI) and return on objectives (ROO) are two of the buzz phrases across the industry, emphasising the need to measure the effectiveness of all investments and activities, including those investments made in a company's workforce via its event programme. ROI and ROO are also covered more fully in Chapter 5.

Typical delegates

An earlier survey (the 'UK Conference Market Survey 2006') of 300 corporate organisations provided a useful insight into the typical delegate at a corporate event (the author has no reason to believe that this profile has changed significantly in recent years). The survey found that:

- the average age of a delegate attending a corporate event is 38;
- 64 per cent of corporate delegates are male, attending on average three events per year;
- at least 60 per cent of organisers categorise their delegates as senior or middle management, or sales and marketing professionals; 16 per cent are also organising events for accountants or accountancy-related positions, and 15 per cent for general administration.

In summary, therefore, the corporate sector of the conference industry is characterised by: events with fewer than 200 delegates, fairly short lead times, and higher spend (than associations) with costs being borne by the company. Conferences are one of the prime ways in which corporate organisations communicate with their employees and their customers, although the generic term 'conferences' may describe a variety of sizes and types of events. Conferences are a high profile communications vehicle conveying important messages about the company: it is vital, therefore, that conferences should be successful in meeting the objectives set for them.

The association buyer

Definitions

The term 'association' organiser or buyer covers those representing a wide range of organisations, including:

- professional or trade associations/institutions (whose members join because of their employment);
- voluntary associations and societies (whose members join primarily to further an interest or hobby);
- charities;
- religious organisations;
- political parties;
- trade unions.

The acronym 'SMERF' (social, military, educational, religious and fraternal) is sometimes used in North America to describe those types of organisations which are not work-related.

Associations are formed and operate at different levels. Many are purely national and restrict their memberships and their activities to one particular country. But, and perhaps increasingly in our global, shrinking world, these national associations are establishing

links and relationships at a continental level to form bodies with memberships and spheres of influence at this wider, regional level (e.g. the European Federation of . . . or the Asian Association of . . .). In other cases, truly international associations exist whose members are drawn from all corners of the world – these latter are described in more detail later in this chapter.

Very few, if any, associations are established mainly to generate a financial return. They are 'not-for-profit' organisations which exist to provide a service to their members and to the community at large. There is, however, an equal need for the conferences organised by associations, as with corporate conferences, to be run extremely professionally, not least because they are often in the public eye, through press and media exposure, in a way that corporate conferences are not. And, while the associations themselves may be 'not-for-profit', association conferences must cover their costs and, in some cases, be planned with the aim of generating a profit which can then be re-invested in the administrative and promotional costs of future conferences. Such profits also frequently become core income streams which assist in funding the general running of the association.

Association management companies (AMCs)

There are also specialist association management companies which make a living by providing a professional 'secretariat' for associations which do not have the resources or management expertise to run their association themselves. Association management companies are paid a fee to administer the association, and their role frequently includes the organisation of the association's meetings and conferences. Association management companies typically have a meeting planning department which, in essence, operates like a PCO (see below) on behalf of the organisations they represent.

Association delegate characteristics

Delegates attending association conferences share a number of common characteristics:

- They normally choose to attend the conference or other event run by the 'association', rather than being asked to attend by their employer. This is particularly true for professional associations which have an individual (rather than corporate) membership (i.e. it is the individual person who becomes the member, not their employing organisation).
- They may be required to pay their own expenses to attend, which means that the conference organiser must keep the costs as low as possible if it is important to maximise delegate attendance. In certain cases, particularly where the delegate is attending as a representative of a group of colleagues or fellow workers, as with trade union conferences, the delegate receives a daily allowance to cover his or her costs while attending the conference.

- A range of accommodation may be required, from guest house to 5-star hotel. At least one major association in the UK insists that a destination must have a caravan park before it can be considered to stage its conference!
- The number of delegates attending the main annual conference can be substantially higher than for corporate events. Indeed, association conferences can attract hundreds and sometimes thousands of delegates, and frequently receive high media attention.

These general characteristics may apply across the association sector, but they should not be allowed to hide some important differences between different types of associations. For example, delegates attending an annual surgeons' conference would expect to stay in accommodation of at least 3-star hotel standard (a 1,000-delegate conference with many delegates bringing spouses would require a destination with a substantial number of high quality hotels), whereas a charity or religious conference is likely to require more modest accommodation at the budget end of the spectrum.

Buying patterns

The association decision-making process is different from that in the corporate sector. Even though many of the larger associations have dedicated conference organisers and, in some cases, event organising units/departments, the decision on where the annual conference is to be held is normally taken by a committee elected by the membership. The conference organiser does much of the research and related groundwork, producing a shortlist of the most likely destinations and venues from which the committee will choose, and he or she may make recommendations. The selection committee scrutinises 'bid' proposals or tenders submitted by destinations or venues, in some cases compiled in conjunction with a professional conference organiser (PCO) or event management agency, outlining how they can help the association to stage a successful event (a similar form of bid document may also be provided to corporate buyers when seeking to attract corporate business).

Destination bid documents are likely to contain a formal invitation, often signed by the Mayor or other civic dignitary, a full description of the destination highlighting its attractions, access and communications details (e.g. road and rail links, the number of scheduled flights from the local airport), information on the support services available in the destination (transport operators, exhibition contractors, interpreters, audio-visual companies, and so on), a list of the services provided by the convention and visitor bureau or conference desk, details of hotel and other accommodation and, of course, full details of the venue being proposed to stage the conference (a more detailed example of the contents of a bid is given in the section below about international association conferences). The convention and visitor bureau/conference desk, acting on behalf of the destination, may be invited to make a formal presentation to the selection committee of

the association, in competition with other destinations similarly shortlisted. A representative from the main conference venue being proposed may also contribute to the presentation, perhaps with a recommended PCO, and this 'joined up' approach illustrating how the key players within a destination can work together in harmony conveys positive messages to the association about such a destination's ability to host its event successfully.

Bid proposals may also be put forward by host committees (i.e. local chapters of an association). Such host committees have an important influence on site selection. It should also be noted that internal 'politics' can also have a major influence e.g. the President or the Chairman's wife wants to meet in Florida!

Before the selection committee makes its final decision, it may undertake an inspection visit to the destination to assess at first hand its strengths and weaknesses. The whole decision-making process can, therefore, be very protracted, sometimes taking months to complete.

Lead times

Lead times for association events are much longer than for corporate events. It is not uncommon for associations organising a 1,000-delegate conference to have booked venues several years ahead. In part, this is because there is a much more limited choice of venue, in part because there is significantly more work involved in staging a 1,000-delegate conference than one for 100 delegates. Some of the larger, purpose-built conference/convention centres have provisional reservations ten years ahead from association conference organisers.

Rotations

National associations tend to follow one of several patterns or rotations in the staging of their main annual conference. The examples given below relate to the UK but similar rotations are likely to apply to most other countries with a significant 'national association' conference market:

- Some associations adopt an alternate north–south rotation, holding the conference in the north of England or in Scotland one year, and then in the south of England the next, returning to the north in year three.
- Some associations operate a three- or four-year rotation, moving to different regions of the country in order to be seen to be fair to their members who are probably drawn from most parts of the country.
- Other associations appear to be quite immobile, opting to use the same destination year after year.
- Finally, certain associations look for somewhere different each year, following no clear geographical pattern.

For those destinations and venues seeking to win their business, it is clearly important to have an understanding of which rotation pattern a particular association has adopted.

Partner programmes

Association conferences may have both delegates and their partners attending, a characteristic much less frequently found with corporate events, unless they include an incentive element. The partners do not normally attend the business sessions of the conference but they will be fully involved in the social events which form part of the conference programme. Partner programmes are designed to entertain partners while the conference is in progress. Destinations often work with the conference organiser to help in the planning of partner (or spouse) programmes, as well as in co-ordinating tours and activities both pre- and post-conference. Such pre- and post-conference tours, and the attendance by delegates' partners, add significantly to the economic benefits generated by the conference, encouraging many destinations to examine and adopt best practice in maximising their 'business extenders'.

Venue preferences

Association conferences, because of their larger size, are often held in purpose-built conference or convention centres. Hotels are also popular (particularly so in the USA where major resort hotels can cater for large conventions, all under one roof), while some associations use town hall and civic venues, and others book university and college venues. Where hotels are used, the event may well take place over a weekend because the hotel is offering cheaper rates than for weekday bookings. The peak seasons for association conferences are autumn and spring, but some conferences take place over the summer months and a limited number during the winter.

Table 2.4 summarises the similarities and differences between corporate and association conferences.

Table 2.5 summarises the key findings from the *British Meetings & Events Industry Survey 2011–12* (CAT 2011) based on interviews with 300 corporate conference organisers and 300 association conference organisers. The results for the previous year are shown in brackets.

International 'association' conferences

The above characteristics of national associations apply equally to those associations which are primarily international in nature, as well as to international governmental organisations and to academic bodies planning international scientific conferences. Destinations bidding to stage major international conferences have to be extremely professional in their approach and be prepared to begin working for such an event many years before it is due to take place. It is not unusual to find lead times of five years or

Table 2.4 Comparisons between corporate and association conferences	
Corporate Conferences	**Association Conferences**
Corporate buyers are employed by 'for profit' organisations	Association buyers are employed by 'not-for-profit' organisations
Corporate organisations are to be found in both the manufacturing and service sectors	Associations are to be found in the manufacturing, service and voluntary sectors
The event decision-making process is straightforward and more or less immediate	The event decision-making process is prolonged, often involving a committee
Events have a relatively short lead time (usually measured in weeks or months)	Major conferences have a relatively long lead time (often measured in years)
Corporate buyers may organise a wide range of events	Association buyers organise a more limited range of events
Delegate numbers are typically less than 200 (and frequently well under 100)	Delegate numbers are often several hundred and, for the larger associations, can be several thousands
Mainly held in hotels, purpose-built conference/convention centres and unusual venues	Mostly use purpose-built conference/convention centres, conference hotels, civic and academic venues
A higher budget per delegate, with the company paying	A lower budget per delegate, with the individual delegate sometimes paying. There are variations both by type of association and by country
Events are organised year-round	Major events primarily in the spring and autumn, with some in the summer
Events typically last between 0.5–1.5 days	Major conference typically lasts 2–3 days
Accommodation normally in hotels (3-star and upwards)	Wide range of accommodation may be required, dependent on the type of association and whether participants are paying out of their own pockets or whether their employers are paying
Delegates' partners rarely attend	Delegates' partners sometimes attend

more, necessitating a great deal of research by those destinations seeking to host the conference, particularly in their cost calculations. It could be all too easy to offer certain hotel rates and venue hire charges to the association which, because of the effects of inflation and other possible changes in the macro-economic climate, bear little relation to what should be being charged when the event actually takes place.

Rotations

International associations and international governmental organisations also operate rotational patterns or cycles in the staging of their events, often on a continental basis: for example, an international conference held in Europe one year may well not return to a European country for another five years. The Union of International Associations (UIA) and the International Congress and Convention Association (ICCA) both devote

Table 2.5 Summary of key findings from the British Meetings and Events Industry Survey 2011–12

	Corporate Sector	Association Sector
Mean number of events per organiser	30 (35)	26 (22)
Percentage expecting to organise more events in next twelve months	32 (32)	27 (25)
Percentage of residential events	30 (48)	21 (42)
Average number of delegates:		
– at main event	330 (345)	380 (418)
– other events	93 (129)	92 (119)
Average budgeted daily delegate rate	£54.50 (£59.80)	£42.50 (£47.40)
Average budgeted 24-hour delegate rate	£161.50 (£160.30)	£134.00 (£135.60)
Average annual budget for events	£216,300 (£187,700)	£108,900 (£129,500)
Reported percentage change in budget in last 12 months	+1.0%	+0.4%
Percentage change in budget anticipated in next 12 months	+0.8%	+0.6%
Percentage with procurement department involved in buying conference services	23.2 (25.4)	18 (17)
Mean percentage of event budget allocated to travel costs	14 (15)	11 (15)
Preferred venue incentive	Added value items	
Percentage of events with third party/ agency assistance	22.5 (21)	17.7 (13)
Technology most used for event organisation	Social media	
What contributes most to a successful event	Interesting content relevant to work/daily life	
Most important current issue	Delegates' increased expectations of events	

Source: British Meetings & Events Industry Survey 2011–12 (CAT 2011)

(Figures in parentheses relate to the previous year) (Copyright CAT Publications Ltd 2012 – for further information visit: www.meetpie.com/bmeis)

considerable resources to tracking where international conferences and congresses are held (see Chapter 1). In recent years there have been some moves by international associations to hold a greater proportion of their conferences in developing countries as a way of building up their memberships in such countries. ICCA reports in its 2011 survey that the proportion of international association meetings which rotate *worldwide* is decreasing and reached an all-time low in 2009. A greater proportion of meetings is rotating on a continental basis (especially Asia-Pacific, Latin America or Europe). The reasons for these changed patterns may include cost, travel time, a greater reluctance post '9/11' for delegates to be too far from home, or other factors. An analysis of the rotation areas of international meetings is shown in Table 2.6.

Table 2.6 Rotation patterns for international meetings										
Rotation Area	2001	2002	2003	2004	2005	2006	2007	2008	2009	2010
World/ International	2,733	3,166	3,152	3,754	3,840	4,064	4,153	4,447	4,229	4,208
Europe	1,440	1,688	1,823	2,111	2,234	2,494	2,665	2,895	2,793	2,713
Asia/Pacific	277	321	311	419	428	500	550	550	536	523
Latin America	162	160	203	229	283	299	323	342	342	354
Asia	150	169	164	234	238	284	315	330	302	296
Europe/North America	126	144	161	194	194	236	252	267	264	278
Interamerican	110	120	154	160	165	191	207	212	207	226
Nordic Countries	111	135	134	170	159	172	163	176	177	167
Ibero-America	93	110	115	130	136	150	156	167	167	154
Africa/Middle East	47	55	60	82	97	99	140	150	159	129
Totals	5,249	6,068	6,277	7,483	7,774	8,849	8,924	9,536	9,176	9,048

Source: ICCA Statistics Report 'The International Association Meetings Market – Worldwide 2001–2010' (www.iccaworld.com)

Bidding

Bids to host an international conference are often channelled through the national member representatives of that organisation. For example, a small group of Canadian or French members of an international association will form a committee to plan and present a bid to the selection committee. They are likely to get support and assistance from the destination (i.e. a Canadian city or a French city) which they are putting forward to stage the conference, while the national tourism organisation or national convention bureau may also play a part in helping to fund the bid and contributing to it in other material ways.

Those preparing to bid for an international association congress or convention must gain an understanding of the key factors which each association considers to be of particular importance when deciding on the destination for its event. These factors will vary to some extent between associations. For example, the International Congress and Convention Association (ICCA), whose annual Congress moves around all continents of the world, has set out the following as key questions and topics/issues to be answered by destinations when bidding for the ICCA Congress:

- *Value for money – ICCA perspective* How low is the 'package' price? What is the level of local sponsorship and reduced prices? This section should also state clearly any tax implications facing ICCA if the Congress is held in this country, and recommendations for the efficient handling of such matters.

- *Value for money – delegate perspective* What are the cost implications for delegates in addition to the package price e.g. airfare deals? Hotel rates? This section should include information regarding any visa costs facing delegates.
- *Accessibility – international and local* Provide objective data on access from worldwide; case studies of other large events hosted recently; transfer times on site and distance between key locations in host destination.
- *Capacity to attract delegates/destination appeal* What is unique or new about the destination? Why is '2015' a suitable year to hold the event in your destination? Marketing ideas?
- *Level of support/evidence of teamwork (ICCA members; local industry; political)* Vital that the bid is not reliant on one individual or organisation, and that there is strong support from ICCA members throughout the country. Successful bids inevitably have strong bidding teams.
- *Suitability/capacity/quality of meeting and exhibition venue(s)* Floor plans; capacities; track record, etc.
- *Quality and attractiveness of the social event venues* Give options and creative ideas which demonstrate the unique appeal of your destination.
- *Networking opportunities* Suitability of hotel(s) for this purpose; short transfer times; networking space available in venue.
- *ICCA development opportunities* Opportunities to recruit members in country/region; ideas for educating local meetings industry; whether ICCA has met in the country before; strategic changes that have occurred if proposing to return to a country where the Congress has been held previously.
- *Creativity* Each ICCA Congress is unique, with a strong local flavour. Creative ideas are needed each year to continuously improve the delegate experience, and can relate to any aspect of the Congress including marketing, formats and networking.
- *Environmental and corporate social responsibility* Each destination should highlight the key environmental and/or CSR factors that they wish the ICCA Board of Directors to take into account. This could include any 'green venues' included in the programme, local initiatives that will help to make the Congress more sustainable, suggestions for including local CSR speakers in the educational programme, etc.

Table 2.7 is an example of the Contents template for a bid document used to bid for an international association convention. More information on the bidding process and bid documentation used to attract conference and events business is given in Chapter 4.

Other characteristics of international association conferences and conventions, according to ICCA (2011), include:

- By far the majority of all international association meetings in the period 2001–10 were annual meetings. The relative number of biennial meetings (taking place every two years) is gradually diminishing. The numbers of meetings taking place less often

Table 2.7 Bid document template

1. **Invitation and Welcome** from appropriate, high-profile figures (e.g. Government minister(s), civic leader(s), destination head, senior figure(s) from the local host organisation and sector)

   a.   Welcome letter

   b.   Contact list for bid support team

   c.   Individual letters of welcome and support from key figures related to the sector

2. **Case for the bidding destination**

   a.   Information on convention bureau, convention centre, city council

   b.   Rationale for the bid – why this country? (Setting out the strengths, research expertise, pioneering initiatives, etc. currently visible in the bidding country in relation to the conference theme/topic)

   c.   Financial support and subvention available

   d.   Political support e.g. attendance by senior Government figure(s) at the conference

   e.   Dedicated destination support

       i.   Options on venues, accommodation and services for the event

       ii.   Tailored event-related site visits for National Bid Partners

       iii.   Assistance in negotiating with airlines and rail companies to secure preferred rates

       iv.   Promotional support and collateral designed to maximise delegate attendance (including attendance by bidding destination at the previous year's conference)

       v.   Options for pre- and post-conference delegate touring activity

       vi.   Options for partner programmes

       vii.   Advice on the planning and delivery of the event

       viii. Other assistance as required

   f.   Information on visa/Customs requirements and entry restrictions

   g.   Medical and security services and support

   h.   Proposed Local Organising Committee

3. **The Perfect Destination**

   a.   Destination overview

       i.   Summary of the region/county attractions

       ii.   Value for money

       iii.   Lifestyle

       iv.   Industry and economy

       v.   Accessibility and transport

       vi.   Culture and heritage

       vii.   Shopping

       viii. Food

       ix.   Festivals and events

       x.   Nightlife and entertainment

   b.   The convention city

       i.   Venue and accommodation listing

       ii.   Map of city or city centre

Table 2.7 Bid document template *(continued)*

    iii. Experience of staging successful conferences/events

    iv. Tailored site visit for an association representative or representatives

    v. Pre-event marketing support details

4. Your Event Solution

    a. A tailor-made solution for xxx national/international conference (name of conference and conference year)

    b. Proposed conference (and exhibition) venue

    c. Professional conference organisers and destination management support

5. Accessibility (expanding on the introductory information contained in 3a(v))

    a. Airport and railway station descriptions

    b. Future developments in air access

    c. Travel times from international destinations

    d. Lists of airlines and flights (direct and indirect) including frequency per week

    e. Accessibility within the destination for those with disabilities

6. Sustainability and the Environment

    a. The destination's sustainable and green credentials

    b. Minimising the event's negative impact on the environment

    c. Ensuring the event's social legacy (if appropriate)

    d. Green touring pre- and post-event

7. Experiences to Remember

    a. Suggestions for pre- and post-event touring

8. Supplementary Information

    a. Quick facts on the country/region/city

    b. Time zone differences

    c. Climate

    d. Taxes

    e. Tipping and gratuities

    f. Translating and interpreting services

    g. Travel and tourist information centres

    h. Medical and emergency services

    i. Banking hours and currency issues

    j. Shopping hours and key retail centres

    k. Driving licences

    l. Electricity

    m. Water

    n. Dates of public holidays

9. Appendix

    a. Letters of support

(e.g. every three or four years) are also decreasing, while the numbers taking place more frequently than once a year are increasing.

- The destination is chosen by the international organisation (the board, the general assembly, or a special committee). However, a growing minority of about 25–30 per cent of the decision-making processes no longer include an official bidding procedure. Instead the international association appoints a 'central initiator' who selects the location and venues based on pre-determined and strict criteria.
- Where a national association or local host committee is involved in submitting a bid they will, if successful, choose the venue and other suppliers, often drawing on the services of a professional conference organiser (PCO).
- Increasingly international associations are appointing a 'core PCO', who is contracted to organise the event no matter where it is being held. In the past, PCOs were appointed from within the country where the convention or congress was to take place, because of their local knowledge and expertise. The benefits from working with a core PCO include the PCO's understanding of the association and its specific requirements, built up over several years. Such understanding is deemed to be of greater value than the destination knowledge of a locally appointed PCO.
- The programme for the event is designed by a special programme committee, which can be part of the local organising committee or be a separate international body.
- The most popular period for organising international association meetings is the period from May to September, with September being the most popular month (1,434 international meetings in 2010), followed by June (1,290), October (1,205) and May (1,040). The month with the fewest international meetings was January, with 153.
- Throughout the period 2001–10 the average length in days of meetings gradually declined, replicating trends noted among corporate and national association events. The average in 2010 was 3.85 days, compared with 5.1 days in 2001.
- In 2010 the average number of participants reached its lowest point of the period 2001–10 with 571 participants per international meeting, compared to 696 in 2001.

The public sector buyer

The public sector (sometimes referred to as 'government') has much in common with the association sector (and, indeed, for research purposes is often subsumed within data for the association sector), covering organisations such as local authorities/municipalities, central government departments and agencies, educational bodies, and the health service. These organisations are all 'not-for-profit' organisations and are accountable for the ways in which they spend public funds. Although delegates from public sector organisations are not normally expected to pay their own expenses to participate in a conference, it is likely that the events will be run on fairly tight budgets, often using the less expensive venues such as civic facilities, universities and colleges, and hotels up to 3-star standard.

In the context of public sector and government organisations, it is worth noting the phrase 'per diem' (literally 'per day'). In the USA 'per diem' is a daily allowance which public sector employees can spend on food, accommodation and other expenses when attending a meeting or conference. The phrase may also be encountered outside the USA if hotels are dealing with US armed services or embassy personnel stationed overseas. In the USA some large hotel chains have a director of sales specialising in this area, assisting the group's hotels and also their government clients when quoting for conferences at which delegates are on this 'per diem' allowance.

The entrepreneurial buyer/commercial conference organiser

The fourth type of buyer is one whose role is essentially that of an entrepreneur operating within the conference sector. In other words, someone who identifies 'hot topics' in the business or academic world and then plans and produces a conference at which the topics can be presented, discussed and debated by high profile speakers and experts. The entrepreneur aims to sell places at the conference to anyone interested in paying to attend. The term 'commercial conference organiser' is often used to describe this role.

Clearly, as with any entrepreneurial activity, there is a financial risk to be borne as the entrepreneur incurs various costs (e.g. deposit payment on the venue hired, promotional costs, possibly cancellation charges to the venue and to speakers if the event does not go ahead) with no guarantee that he or she can run the conference successfully and make a profit. However, it is possible to make significant profits on such conferences with delegate fees for a one-day conference often being as much as £300–£500.

Entrepreneurial or commercial conferences are typically organised by publishing houses/media, trade associations, academic bodies, and independent conference producers/organisers. It can be seen from the brief description above that one of the pre-requisites for success in this area includes having a finger on the pulse of specific industrial and business sectors to understand what are the contemporary issues and challenges that might provide the material for a conference. It is also important to have access to quality databases of potential invitees to whom the conference can be promoted.

The suppliers

The suppliers are those who make available for external hire the venues, destinations and many other specialist services without which today's conferences could not take place.

Suppliers to the conference industry have grown in quantity and diversity in tandem with the overall growth of the industry over the past fifty years. Relatively few of these suppliers are dedicated exclusively to the conference industry, however.

This summary divides the supply side of the conference industry into three main categories:

- venues;
- destinations;
- others.

While the examples given relate mainly to the British Isles, most countries with a well-developed conference product have a similar base of suppliers, although the numbers and proportions vary from country to country.

Venues

Within the British Isles alone there are around 3,500 venues being promoted as suitable for conferences, meetings, and related business events. It is impossible to give a precise number because new venues are regularly becoming available for external hire, while other venues discover that their facilities no longer meet the requirements necessary for twenty-first-century conferences, and so they pull out of the market. A quality accreditation scheme for conference and meetings venues has been developed in the UK by the Meetings Industry Association: the scheme is known as AIM ('accredited in meetings') and it provides the opportunity for venues to be assessed and accredited at three different levels: entry level, silver and gold (for more details visit: www.mia-uk.org).

Hotels comprise over half of all conference venues, being particularly important to the corporate market sector. The main types of hotel active in the conference market are:

- city centre hotels;
- hotels adjacent to the national and international communications infrastructure (airports, motorways and highways especially);
- rural or country house hotels.

In addition to the conferences which they stage as venues in their own right, hotels located close to large convention centres also benefit as providers of delegate accommodation/housing when a major conference comes to town. Additionally, the bigger association conferences often choose one hotel as their 'headquarters' hotel, and there can be significant public relations benefits with the hotel being featured in national, and sometimes international, television and media coverage.

The larger hotel chains have invested very heavily in the design and equipping of their conference and meeting facilities, recognising that the standard multi-purpose function room is no longer adequate for the needs of the contemporary conference organiser. Many have also branded their conference product to assist in the promotion of these facilities and services, seeking to assure the buyer that he or she will receive the same level of service whichever hotel in the chain is used. Staff trained and dedicated to meeting the needs of conference organisers and delegates are to be found in all the major conference hotels.

Alongside hotels, other principal types of venue include:

- *Purpose-built centres (residential and non-residential)* Specifically designed to host meetings and conferences, whether they are the larger events for hundreds or even thousands of delegates (venues such as the International Convention Centre in Birmingham (England), the Orlando (Orange County) Convention Center in Florida, Hong Kong Convention and Exhibition Centre, Durban International Convention Centre in South Africa, Melbourne Convention and Exhibition Centre (Australia)) or smaller, day and residential, events (venues such as Chartridge Conference Centre, Buckinghamshire, England, and Belmont Square Conference Centre in Rondebosch, Cape Town, South Africa). In the USA, the term 'convention center' is used to describe a building with exhibition (referred to as 'exhibit') halls and convention/meeting rooms but no residential (sleeping) facilities. The term 'conference center' is used to describe a building with meeting rooms, bedrooms but no exhibition (or exhibit) space.
- *College, university and other academic venues* There are around 150 academic venues in the UK, many only available for residential conferences during student vacation periods (but still staging some non-residential meetings during term time). Germany has over 300 universities, such as Kiel and Karlsruhe, available for use as meeting and convention venues. An increasing number of academic venues have been investing in the construction of conference facilities which are available throughout the year, providing accommodation equivalent to a good 3-star hotel standard. In the UK the University of Warwick, Lancaster University and the University of Strathclyde are three very good examples of such investments. The East Midlands Conference Centre, located on the campus of the University of Nottingham, can seat up to 550 delegates in its main auditorium, complemented with exhibition/exposition or banqueting space and a range of syndicate rooms, and might equally be classed as a purpose-built conference centre.
- *Multi-purpose venues* Leisure centres, sports centres, council chambers and committee rooms, town halls and other civic facilities which are available for external hire e.g. Brisbane City Hall, Cardiff City Hall, and Bremen's Stadthalle are just three examples of such facilities.
- *Unusual venues* This is a somewhat ill-defined term to describe a very wide range of venues (sometimes described as 'unique' venues) which do not fit into the more common categories listed above. The attraction of unusual venues is that they can give an event a special appeal and can make it memorable for years afterwards. Some have very high quality meeting and conference facilities, others may be quite

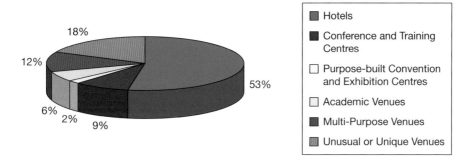

FIGURE 2.1 Analysis of the UK's conference venues by number and type

limited in this respect but the setting in which the event is being held compensates for such shortcomings in the eyes of the conference organiser (and, it is hoped, of the delegates). Unusual options include sporting venues (e.g. football and rugby stadia, racecourses, golf clubs), cultural and entertainment venues (museums, theatres, television studios, stately homes), tourist attractions (theme parks, historical sites, castles, heritage centres), transport venues (ferries, steam trains, canal barges), even a lighthouse or two! In the British Isles around one-fifth of the 3,500 venues being promoted to the conference market can be classified as unusual venues.

Figure 2.1 provides an analysis of the different types of conference venue in the UK.

Destinations

Conference organisers attach greater importance to 'location' than to any other single criterion when selecting their sites. Location may be expressed in terms of 'town', 'city', 'region of the country'. The widely accepted term to describe each of these is 'destination'. A destination may, of course, be an entire country (as a national destination), but within a country it is a discrete area with identifiable boundaries. Each conference destination should contain a range of venues, facilities, attractions, support services and appropriate infrastructure to help it to attract conference business.

Within the British Isles, an analysis of the leading destinations active in serving the conference industry reveals the following:

cities	23
towns	15
counties/regions	20
islands	3
countries	4

Destination marketing organisations (DMOs), often trading as 'convention and visitor bureaux (CVBs)' or 'conference desks' (see Chapter 3), bring the destination to the marketplace, offering a 'one-stop-shop' enquiry point to the conference and event organiser. Their role is to promote the destination, highlighting all its strengths and facilities, generating and converting enquiries into confirmed business. They are also involved in product development: for example, identifying gaps in venue provision and in general infrastructure, or enhancing industry knowledge and skills among destination staff through training.

Other suppliers

The conference industry has to draw upon the services of many different supplier organisations in order to offer a complete service to its buyers. Those suppliers who fulfil a 'buying' role on behalf of corporate or association clients are described in the next section (agencies). Examples of other key suppliers include the following:

- audio-visual contractors (supply and operation of specialist audio-visual equipment);
- telecommunications companies (videoconferencing/teleconferencing/satellite conferencing);
- transport operators (airlines, coach and rail companies, car hire, taxi firms, ferry companies);
- interpreters and translators (for international conferences);
- after-dinner speakers, entertainers, corporate events companies (e.g. companies running 'Murder Mystery' events, sporting and outdoor activities);
- speciality caterers (banquets, receptions, buffets);
- floral contractors (flower displays for conference platforms, registration areas, exhibition/exposition stands);
- exhibition/exposition contractors;
- companies which develop specialist computer software (e.g venue-finding and event management programmes).

Agencies and intermediaries

'Agencies' is a generic term used to describe a range of different organisations which are both suppliers and buyers. They undertake a buying role on behalf of their clients, who may be companies or associations, while at the same time supplying a service to them. They act as intermediaries or 'middle-men', and can be contracted to assist in the planning and running of a conference or similar business event.

Agencies come in a number of forms, and the nomenclature can be somewhat confusing, but below are listed the principal kinds of intermediaries operating within the conference and business events industry.

The professional conference organiser (PCO)

The professional conference organiser, sometimes professional congress organiser, is often referred to simply as a PCO. In the USA the term PCO is not widely used and reference is more likely to be to an independent meeting planner, while a destination management company (DMC) may also fulfil some of this role (see description of a DMC below). Multi-management firm is another term used in the USA with a similar connotation i.e. a company offering complete turnkey organisational support for a meeting, including administration and meeting management services.

Employed to assist in the organisation of a conference, the PCO's role can include researching and recommending a suitable venue, helping to plan the conference programme including the social programme, marketing the conference and handling delegate registrations, booking accommodation/housing for delegates, planning an exhibition to run concurrently with the conference, producing a budget and handling all of the conference finances. The PCO is normally paid a management fee by the client organisation, calculated on the basis of a registration fee per delegate (with a guaranteed minimum number of delegates) or on the estimated staff costs required to manage the event (number of staff needed × number of days × amount per day). PCOs may also charge a commission to the conference venue (usually 8 per cent to 10 per cent of the value of the conference to the venue itself), as well as a commission on accommodation bookings and on other services provided, although the trend is for greater use of a management fee and less reliance on commissions.

Table 2.8 shows a typical portfolio of services offered by a professional conference organiser. Further insights into the work of a PCO are given in Chapter 5.

Venue finding agency

As their name implies, such agencies offer a more limited service, restricted to researching and recommending a suitable venue for an event (sometimes described as 'venue sourcing or procurement'). Venue finding agencies typically put forward a shortlist of three potential venues to their client (or in some cases just one venue initially) and expect to receive a commission (paid to them by the venue chosen for the conference) of 8 per cent to 10 per cent of the value of the booking to the venue. Venue finding agencies may also get involved in booking accommodation for delegates, and again would expect to charge commission to the hotels and other accommodation providers. The agency's services to the client are usually provided free of charge.

However, in the UK at least, many of the most successful venue finding agencies have expanded into the field of event management in order to develop a longer-term relationship with their clients. They have introduced client management team structures within the company, comprising an account manager, a venue finder, and an event planner, who often manage a handful of major accounts. This approach is attractive to

Table 2.8 Typical portfolio of services offered by a professional conference organiser

- Venue selection, booking and liaison
- Reservation and management of delegate accommodation
- Event marketing, including the design of conference programmes and promotional materials, PR and media co-ordination, presentations to committees and boards
- Programme planning, including speaker selection and briefing
- Event administration, provision of an administrative secretariat, handling delegate registrations, recruitment and briefing of conference staff, co-ordinating delegates' travel arrangements
- Organisation of exhibitions/expositions, including sales and marketing functions
- Advising on and co-ordinating audio-visual services and the production of the event, including the provision of multilingual interpretation and translation services
- Planning the catering for an event, liaising with chefs, conference and banqueting staff, and independent catering companies
- Arranging social events, tour programmes and technical visits
- Arranging security cover and advising on health and safety issues, risk management and insurance issues
- Recording, transcribing and producing the proceedings of meetings for publication, arranging poster sessions, processing of abstracts
- Preparation of budgets, managing event income and expenditure, generating revenue through sponsorship, exhibitions/expositions and satellite meetings, and handling VAT issues
- Preparation of contracts with venues and other suppliers

Source: Association of British Professional Conference Organisers (www.abpco.org)

large corporations and pharmaceutical companies who are constantly looking to obtain benefits from the economies of scale that the big agencies claim to deliver.

Conference production company

Such companies specialise in the actual staging of the conference: designing and building conference sets, providing lighting, sound systems, presentation technology (e.g. video/DVD, data projection, rear projection, overhead projection, satellite conferencing, webcasts), audience response systems and special effects. Their expertise lies in audio-visual and communications technology, which they are required to match to the needs of different clients. They also need creative and theatrical skills, recognising that conferences have to be professionally stage-managed and should be a memorable, striking experience for the delegates.

The technology is developing at such a rapid rate that it is highly likely that new equipment and presentation systems will be in use in three or four years' time which have not even been heard of at the time this text is being written (spring 2012). Chapters 5 and 10 give further information on the technology in use by conference organisers and conference production companies.

Event management companies and experiential marketing agencies

There is considerable overlap between the roles of an event management company and a professional conference organiser (PCO). The key distinction would probably be in the scope of work undertaken, with event management companies getting more involved with a broader range of events rather than mainly meetings and conferences, for example product launches, awards dinners, motivational events, sporting events. It is also more likely that their clients will be from the corporate (i.e. for profit) sector, whereas PCOs are more typically employed by associations and academic bodies (the not-for-profit sector). Event management companies are skilled in the management of all types of events, for employees, business and consumer audiences. Their role could perhaps be summarised as 'providing business solutions through the use of events'.

Within the overall group of event management companies, there is a specialist niche of experiential marketing and communications agencies which use live (and virtual) events to enable customers and potential customers to experience and interact with a particular brand or product. *FaceTime* (2012) magazine in an article entitled 'Reasons to Use Experiential Marketing' quotes Columbia Business School guru Bernd H. Schmitt, who wrote:

> *Today, customers take product quality and a positive brand image as a given. What they want are products, communications and marketing campaigns that dazzle their senses, touch their hearts and stimulate their minds – that deliver an experience.*

The article continues:

> *Experiential is the marketing world's answer to this call. The term 'experiential' reflects the use and integration of emotions, logic and general thought processes to connect with the consumer. By taking a sensory-based approach to marketing, you inspire consumers to connect with your brand, products and services by actually experiencing it.*

Live events, often combined with digital campaigns, have proved to be an extremely effective way of giving customers an experience of a product or brand, not least because they can employ all five senses which heavily influence our behaviour and attitudes towards a brand, creating memories and a lasting impression.

A new experiential marketing code of conduct was launched in the UK in February 2012, designed to further strengthen the protections for consumers and marketers offered by the UK's advertising self-regulatory system. Further details are available from Eventia (www.eventia.org.uk).

Case Study 2.1 illustrates how experiential marketing agency TRO created a series of event experiences for consumers and dealers as part of the launch of the Vauxhall Astra in 2010.

Incentive travel and performance improvement agencies

All-expenses-paid travel, often to overseas destinations, is still regarded as one of the best incentives a company can use to motivate and reward its employees, distributors, and retailers. Two separate benchmarking studies were conducted in 1990 and 1995 by P&MM, the UK incentive travel specialists, surveying over 800 corporate buyers of incentives to rank the effectiveness of different types of non-cash incentive. In both studies 'group travel' came top with 'individual travel' second. 'Incentive travel', as the group travel product has come to be known, was developed in the USA in the second half of the twentieth century and is now an important event industry segment in its own right. The official definition, according to Site (the Society of Incentive and Travel Executives), is as follows:

> Incentive Travel is a global management tool that uses an exceptional travel experience to motivate and/or recognise participants for increased levels of performance in support of organisational goals.

Site suggests that 'the highest levels of workplace performance are reached by individuals and teams that are highly motivated. Motivational experiences are a powerful business tool to reward and unlock human potential to achieve corporate objectives.'

A 2011 study into the impact of motivational events on the business environment carried out by Staples USA and reported in 'Meetings:review' (5 December 2011) found that incentive programmes promote a 'competitive and reward-oriented culture' and that motivational events, when implemented in a creative and efficient way, can boost company morale and improve financial performance. The study showed that 85 per cent of employees feel valued when an incentive programme is introduced, 70 per cent said they felt more motivated, and 65 per cent more loyal to their employer.

A study by the Incentive Research Foundation (IRF 2011) reported that today's highly educated workforce responds to more tailored, non-cash incentive plans that celebrate creativity and promote best practice. It suggested that personalised recognition based on personal performance, innovation and mastery of skill are key to capturing the intellectual and emotional commitment of employees. The study underlined that, while salary remains the primary pact between employer and employee, the personalisation of rewards is crucial to individual effort and motivation.

However, a questioning of the value of incentive travel programmes was voiced by David Baker, founder of performance improvement agency DBMT, and quoted on

www.meetpie.com (22 March 2012), as he felt that such schemes only work for 10–15 per cent of the sales force. He said:

> These are the top performers who are already motivated and they seek the recognition that winning a travel programme provides. What concerns me is the 85 per cent of the sales force who fail to be motivated by the travel campaign. It's often obvious who's going to win before the programme has started, as they are previous winners and are known within the sales force for their achievements. If that's the case, those average participants might say 'Why should I bother?'

David Baker goes on to argue for a greater understanding of motivation by senior management:

> Motivation takes place long before you talk about travel trips; it's about company culture and people skills. Incentives, marketing, training and communication should all form part of a long-term engagement programme, implemented from top down. There are too many people who have just come into the incentive market who really don't know it, just selling travel and vouchers to make a quick buck. For the industry that's wrong.

John Fisher of FMI Group, incentive travel specialist and writer, contends (in a personal communication) that the truth is more complex than this. He says:

> Most incentive schemes involve a wide cross-section of the target audience and are multi-layered in terms of reward. So it is not unusual to have a group incentive travel event at the top of the incentive pyramid aimed at the high fliers with weekend domestic events as secondary prizes, supported by retail vouchers or electronic gift cards for middle-ranking achievers who have reached the first rung of exceptional achievement. The idea is that the rewards budget should be targeted at different but achieving sections of the audience to encourage more than just the very best to 'win something'. Incentive travel sits at the top because it is the most attractive reward. But the downside is that it costs relatively more per head than other rewards. So with a generally fixed budget there are going to be less travel winners than there are gift card winners, for example.

Incentive travel programmes should be tailored to the needs of each client company and its specific profile. What works for a luxury car manufacturer is not going to work for a downmarket retailer. But there is no such thing as an 'off-the-shelf' product or programme. Even if the destination is the same, e.g. Paris, there are many variants to the ground programme which need to reflect both the lifestyle and expectations of the group profile. An 'off-the-shelf' incentive programme is really a contradiction in terms. Incentive travel has been described as an '*extraordinary reward for extraordinary performance*' (Paul Flackett, Site member and Managing Director, IMEX Ltd). Incentive travel programmes are, therefore, designed to create an allure or dream which will make people want to produce that extra effort, achieve that exceptional performance, and strive to be the winners within a corporate organisation. From the company's perspective, it is also about strengthening the loyalty of its best employees or distributors, making them want to be associated with the organisation, and giving them reasons to perform even better in the future.

Incentive travel programmes sometimes have an educational element for the participants. This can involve visits to factories and businesses in the same industry sector as that of the award winners, team-building programmes and a conference-type session with an award presentation ceremony and announcements of corporate plans, designed to encourage the incentive winners to reach future performance targets. A 2011 report by the Incentive Research Foundation (IRF 2011) also noted that organisers of incentive travel and performance improvement programmes were increasingly introducing a corporate social responsibility (CSR) element into their programmes. This is partly to offset the perception of incentive travel as being too lavish but also to fall in line with the genuine needs of many organisations to be seen to be thinking about their environment and their communities rather than just spending money.

Incentive travel is probably more susceptible to the ups and downs of national and global economies than most other segments of the business events sector, simply because it can be perceived to be an expensive reward option. In 2009, there was huge media coverage of what came to be known as the 'AIG effect', doing considerable damage to the incentive travel and performance improvement sector. Media and politicians heavily criticised AIG (an insurance company) and banks and other financial services companies, in particular, for what were portrayed as lavish and inappropriate expenditures on incentive trips during a period of recession and redundancy. Writing in *Meetings and Incentive Travel* magazine, David Hackett (2011), an expert on incentive travel programmes, said:

> The words 'incentive travel' may still be unacceptable in some quarters but the principles remain the same: whether to drive performance or to create a positive environment to communicate business messages, travel works. It is unique, desirable and aspirational. So clients are using it to support and achieve business objectives.

The beauty of incentive schemes is that they can be mostly self-funding, with the travel award being paid for by the success of the incentive travel programme, if the rules are constructed in an appropriate way. If no one meets their sales targets, no one wins and so the loss is restricted to the promotional materials and planning time. It is, therefore, one of the most effective promotional techniques available as the ROI can easily be calculated beforehand and the rules set in such a way that no rewards are paid out until the performance is created.

John Fisher explains (in a personal communication):

Choice of destination for incentive travel is a factor of the available budget per head, the accessibility by air from the sponsor's country, the perceived image of the destination and to some extent the destination's ability to promote itself effectively. There are many wonderful places in the world but, if there is no air access on scheduled flights from the departing country, it is unlikely the budget will be able to stretch to a private air charter as the only alternative means of transport. Equally for the destination to work as a promotional incentive, potential participants need to have some prior knowledge of the destination and want to go there. Destinations such as Monte Carlo and Rio de Janeiro sell themselves but how about Sardinia or Quito? That said, 'new' destinations are always being introduced to the market and, thanks to some investment in promotion and industry exhibition appearances, new places can capture a significant part of the market if they promote heavily enough. Scottsdale, Arizona springs to mind as a good example of somewhere ordinary folk would not recognise but, due to heavy business to business promotion, it is certainly one of the choices whenever a buyer asks about options in the USA for an upmarket incentive travel event. Dubai is a similar example of a destination buying its way into the market. It has been hugely successful from a standing start but there has been significant Government money and infrastructure planning to make it viable.

Together with economic factors in the health of this business segment is the national/international political situation. The Gulf War in 1990, for example, virtually wiped out the American incentive travel market, even to Europe. Similarly, the events of 11 September 2001 (9/11) in the USA caused a steep fall, particularly in American incentive travel business. The more recent 'Arab Spring' has caused a great deal of uncertainty in North Africa and the Middle East in general with regard to group travel and, although Dubai had forced its way into the top five incentive travel destinations in the first decade of the twenty-first century (see above), the general upheaval has caused many corporates to withdraw from the entire area. No one should die as a result of a marketing programme, to put it bluntly. Company directors would never knowingly want to put their best employees or distributors on an aeroplane and risk losing them all (in fact, as standard policy, they would normally use several different flights to transport award winners to their incentive destination to minimise such risks). Incentive planners rate the safety and security of a destination as very important in destination choice and will consult widely before recommending a new or unknown global destination.

The specialised nature of the incentive travel sector, combining travel knowledge with marketing skills, has led to the growth of performance improvement agencies (sometimes referred to as 'incentive houses' or 'motivation agencies') which now incorporate incentive travel as a key product/service. It is also common to find that event management companies (see above) often have specialist incentive divisions or departments focused on this particular overseas travel segment. Such agencies generally charge a time-based fee to their clients for the work they undertake on their behalf, although contingency fees are sometimes levied if the numbers of travellers are not known at the outset of the programme.

It is debatable whether incentive travel as a market segment will ever hit the dizzy heights of the 1990s when groups of 300–400 participants were not unusual, especially within the financial services sector. In these more austere times the average group size is nearer 40–50 participants. But the enduring appeal of group, hosted travel as an incentive suggests that this particular service will continue within certain niche markets and be serviced by specialist operators for many years to come.

Case Study 2.2 describes an incentive travel programme for Oriflame (cosmetics company) organised by event and communications agency Grass Roots.

Site has published (Celuch and Davidson 2011) a very useful handbook of incentive travel case studies entitled *Better Business Results through Motivational Experiences and Incentive Travel*, authored by Krzysztof Celuch (Vistula University, Warsaw) and Rob Davidson (University of Greenwich). The Site website is a useful source of research reports on the sector: www.siteglobal.com/Foundation/Research.aspx

Destination management companies (DMCs)

Destination management companies (or DMCs) are specialist ground operators in the incentive travel field (who may also provide services to conference organisers, especially where a conference is being organised overseas). The definition of a DMC, given by Site (www.siteglobal.com), is as follows:

> A DMC is a local service organisation that provides consulting services, creative events and exemplary management of logistics based on an in-depth knowledge of the destination and the needs of the incentive and motivation markets.

By comparison, ground operators have a more limited role:

> A ground operator provides transportation in a locale i.e. coaches, rental cars, rail, etc.

DMCs, therefore, have detailed knowledge and expertise of a specific destination, be this a city, an island or other discrete region, and sometimes even a whole country. They also have access to unusual venues such as private houses and stately homes which are not normally open to the general public. They have considerable buying power which makes them very useful to incentive travel and performance improvement agencies based in countries other than the one in which the incentive travel award is to be taken.

When a company knows that it wants to hold an incentive event (or conference) in a particular destination, it can employ the services of a DMC to locate a venue, handle delegate accommodation, assist with transport arrangements, and put together itineraries and social programmes (for example, special interest visits, theme parties, unusual activities), even to provide 'pillow gifts' for award winners. DMCs are expected to develop tailor-made programmes within budget for their clients. They need to be creative and innovative and provide an experience which will give the participants an insight into a country or region which will be beyond the reach of the normal visitor or holidaymaker.

In terms of charging for their services, Harry Fine, a specialist on the DMC segment (www.harryfine.com), explains (in a personal communication):

> Normally DMCs earn their money by marking up each of the line items they include in their proposal. Whilst a more professional approach would be to pass on net all the charges from their local suppliers and then add a fee for their services, this would actually be very difficult to implement. The reason for this is that, currently, the major clients of DMCs tend to be event management companies or conference/incentive agencies who usually will charge their client (the end user) a fee for their service. End users do not easily understand the justification for two sets of fees which then would need to be endorsed by the end user's procurement department. The challenges of such a process are obvious, hence the popularity of the current method of DMC charging.

It can be seen that there is significant overlap between the work of a PCO and that of a DMC, as well as the work of a convention and visitor bureau. Nowadays a DMC has to have some PCO, or at least venue finding, expertise.

Incentive travel agencies and DMCs work very closely together. However, their relationship can sometimes be fraught, often centering upon the definition of 'creativity' or the requirement to meet extremely tight deadlines and even tighter budgets. Incentive travel agencies demand more and more creativity, wanting things that have never been tried before for their clients, but the budget or time available to achieve this may be insufficient, putting the DMC under great pressure to meet and satisfy such objectives.

An article by Padraic Gilligan (of Ireland-based Ovation Global) in *Meetings & Incentive Travel* magazine (Gilligan 2011) entitled 'Love on the Rocks' succinctly describes some of the stresses in the incentive agency/DMC relationship:

> Back in the day, destination-based destination management companies (DMCs) were briefed by incentive houses and the two worked together with distinct yet complementary roles to create and deliver the customer's dream. The incentive house knew the customer and their business, the DMC knew the destination and its secrets. It was the perfect marriage, the offspring or progeny of which was, usually, a perfectly formed and smiling motivational experience. Most of us – both incentive houses and

DMCs – still believe in the sanctity of this marriage and yearn nostalgically for the old values of commitment and loyalty which underpinned it.

He goes on to describe the threats to this relationship posed by the Internet and by company procurement departments, with DMCs and incentive agencies both venturing into each other's space. But he concludes the article by stating that the marriage can survive through a changing relationship and different ways of working:

Event/incentive agencies tasked by customers to execute Strategic Meetings Management Programmes [see Chapter 10 for further details of these] across multiple destinations where they have no local presence themselves could consult with their DMCs and pay a fee to them for their destination knowledge. This shifts the emphasis onto the key, unique dimension to the DMC value proposition and places a financial value on it – good news for DMCs who have often been obliged to live on line item mark-ups.

The following website gives details of DMCs around the world: www.GMIportal.com – see DMC Finder section of the site. Recommendations of good DMCs can normally be made by the hotels of a particular destination as they will enjoy close working links and will have experience of those providing the most professional services.

Corporate events and corporate hospitality

Corporate events (also known as 'corporate hospitality' and 'corporate entertainment') is one of the discrete segments of the business events industry which, while being separate from the conference sector, is often closely aligned to it. Corporate hospitality and corporate entertainment frequently involve the exploitation of major sporting and cultural events to strengthen the links between an organisation, usually a corporate organisation, and its clients or potential clients: for example, inviting clients to spend a day watching an international golf tournament, or being wined and dined at grand prix races at Monza or Montreal. Alternatively, activities may be arranged specifically for a client company, and typically involve drinks receptions, dinners and banquets, dances and discos. Wherever possible, such activities include a formal presentation or short speech to ensure that the company 'gets its message across'.

Specialist corporate hospitality/entertainment companies are usually hired to organise these events and programmes for their clients. Others may act in an entrepreneurial fashion (rather similar to conference entrepreneurs described earlier in this chapter), putting together corporate hospitality packages around major sporting or cultural events for sale to interested parties.

Corporate hospitality/events companies are also involved in corporate team building exercises and activities, aimed at clients and/or employees. These activities include golf

days, clay pigeon shooting, off-road driving, go-karting, 'paint ball', and many, many more. In recent years there has been a noticeable trend towards the active, participatory kinds of corporate events, rather than the more traditional, passive, spectator type of hospitality.

An article by Ted Walker (from specialist UK corporate hospitality provider Keith Prowse) in 'Meetings:review' (Walker 2010) describes the importance of food in the hospitality experience:

> One thing that has not changed is the core of a successful hospitality product – the dining experience enjoyed by guests. The Keith Prowse Customer Survey conducted with key buyers showed that food is still the most important factor when choosing a hospitality product. Some 98 per cent of those quizzed cited the quality of food as 'important' or 'very important' to their company when purchasing corporate hospitality.

He also describes the emergence of the experiential package which could:

> single-handedly change the face of our industry over coming years. An exclusive opportunity to ask sports stars questions face-to-face after a match, such as in our Players' Lounge at Twickenham (English rugby stadium), has put guests in the shoes of the media in an age when the average sports fan is extremely knowledgeable. Customers want their clients to be able to embrace the spirit of an event rather than be shut off from it.

Travel management company/business travel agency

This is a form of travel agency, but one which seeks particularly to cater for the needs of business customers rather than the general public and which will not normally have a presence on the local High Street. The main thrust of their work is usually business travel: booking air, rail, coach, and ferry tickets, as well as making hotel reservations, to meet the needs of people travelling nationally and internationally for business purposes. But many of the larger business travel agencies also get involved in sourcing venues for conferences and similar business events, and may contribute in other ways to the planning and organisation of such events.

Some of the larger travel management companies have staff physically located in the offices of their major corporate clients. Such arrangements are referred to as 'agency implants'.

Exhibition organiser

Exhibitions are, of course, a major business events segment in their own right, but any clear divide between exhibitions and conferences which may have existed in the past has now been greatly eroded, especially as far as business-to-business (B2B) exhibitions are concerned (less so for consumer exhibitions catering for the general public – B2C). Many exhibitions have a conference programme running alongside as a way of adding value to the exhibition and making it even more worthwhile for business people to visit. Similarly, many of the larger conferences and conventions have an exhibition running in parallel: for the exhibitors, the conference delegates are seen as important customers or potential customers, and for the conference organiser the exhibition is an important source of revenue which helps to offset the costs of the conference.

Despite technology innovations and the explosion of social media, exhibitions and trade shows remain relevant and powerful as the only marketing channel to offer a flexible, face-to-face buying experience. They are a prime example of experiential marketing activity, with exhibitors able to design stands and product offerings which can appeal to all of a visitor's five senses. Yet exhibitions must harness the latest technology to ensure their continued relevance and to deliver outstanding experiences for visitors and exhibitors – for example, utilising technology and personal portable devices to complement the event offering will be a key success driver.

Exhibitions do more than just sell: they build product branding, strengthen existing customer relationships, produce high quality leads, educate, have applications for market research, generate media coverage and are often used to launch new products. Exhibitions play a vital role in the marketing mix offering a wide range of benefits.

Exhibitions provide a cost-effective competitive platform for small and medium-sized enterprises (SMEs) to promote and sell their products and services, enabling many SMEs to establish themselves in the marketplace and, through international visitor attendance at exhibitions, often providing SMEs with their first openings to export markets.

In terms of seasonality, the peak seasons for trade exhibitions are February to June and September to November, but when public exhibitions are also taken into account exhibitions become essentially a year-round activity.

While some conference organisers undertake the organisation of their exhibition themselves, others prefer to employ the services of a specialist exhibition organising company. In the UK there are approximately 100 exhibition organising companies represented by the Association of Event Organisers (AEO).

When contracting a specialist exhibition organiser, conference planners either pay them a management fee for their work or negotiate a payment based on the size of the exhibition itself (e.g. the net exhibition area in square metres, where 'net' means the floor coverage taken up by stands alone, thus excluding aisle space and other space in the exhibition area). A further alternative is for the exhibition to be contracted out for a set period to an exhibition organiser in return for a fee paid to the owner of the exhibition (i.e. the conference organiser).

Agreements or contracts may well include incentives or bonuses linked to the sale of space or cost savings achieved by the exhibition organiser, although this latter approach could encourage the cutting of corners and result in an exhibition of unacceptable quality.

The larger exhibition organising companies can bring added value to an event through their own network of contacts or simply via bulk purchasing power which would not be accessible to a conference organiser working independently. Exhibition organisers may already have links with airlines, hotel groups, stand and electrical contractors, carpet and furniture suppliers, as well as knowledge of the exhibition venue and specialist technical expertise. The services of such trade contacts can be made available to their conference organiser client at preferential rates, while first-hand knowledge and experience can be another invaluable asset.

There is a very broad spectrum of relationships possible between conference and exhibition organiser, from just buying into certain specialist expertise to handling specific aspects of the exhibition (e.g. visitor badging and registrations, stand erection), right through to contracting out the organisation of an exhibition in its entirety. The reasons for such variations on the part of the conference organiser include: in-house staff resources (numbers of staff available and their experience and expertise), the need for a guaranteed financial return from the exhibition (minimise risk by opting for a known income, even if this is less than it might have been possible to achieve), the overall profile of the event and the need to ensure its success, the benefits of having a well-known exhibition organiser working alongside thus giving confidence to potential exhibitors that the exhibition will be well organised and successful.

The economic impact of exhibitions

A report by Oxford Economics (2012), *The Economic Impact of the UK Exhibitions Industry*, found that:

- UK exhibitions attracted over 13 million visitors in 2010 to almost 1,600 events across a range of sectors for both trade and public (consumer) audiences;
- over 265,000 exhibitors participated in events, with 20 per cent coming from outside the UK. Exhibitors spent almost £2.7 billion on goods and services to demonstrate at events in 2010;
- exhibition visitors spent over £1.4 billion on accommodation, travel and other purchases;
- event venues, organisers, exhibitors and visitors directly generated around £2.6 billion in value added (GDP – Gross Domestic Product) for the UK economy in 2010 and directly supported over 76,300 jobs;
- the purchases made by the exhibitions sector and its supply chains generated £3.8 billion in additional output for UK suppliers, indirectly contributing an additional £1.8 billion to UK value added through its supply chain and supporting another 41,900 jobs in 2010;
- the spending of employees in the sector and its supply chains supports further, induced economic activity, which helped to support a further £1.2 billion of value added and 30,300 UK jobs in 2010;

- overall the UK exhibitions sector generated £11 billion in spending and contributed £5.6 billion in value added to the UK economy in 2010, equivalent to 0.4 per cent of UK GDP. This activity supported 148,500 jobs in the UK, equivalent to total employment in the city of Milton Keynes and 0.5 per cent of total employment in the UK.

Further explanations of direct, indirect and induced impacts are given in Chapter 7.

Case Study 2.3 examines the development of the Conventa exhibition in Slovenia, first launched in 2009, and now firmly established as a prime business event in South East Europe.

Some useful websites for additional information on the exhibition sector include:

- www.iaem.org (International Association of Exhibitions and Events);
- www.ufi.org (UFI – The Global Association of the Exhibition Industry) (the initials UFI stand for Union des Foires Internationales, although the full name is no longer used);
- www.ceir.org (Center for Exhibition Industry Research);
- www.eventsindustryalliance.com (the marketing arm of the UK-based Association of Event Organisers – AEO, Association of Event Venues – AEV, and the Event Supplier and Services Association – ESSA);
- www.eeaa.com.au (the Exhibition and Event Association of Australasia).

Other agencies

There are other companies who undertake at least part of a conference organising role for their clients, although this is not usually the main focus of their work. They include: public relations and advertising consultancies (who will organise conferences and seminars, press briefings, product launches, for example), management consultancies (organising 'retreats', meetings, training events) and training companies (running training, motivational, team-building events).

Other important organisations

As an industry emerges and matures it requires other bodies and structures to help it to function professionally, to establish standards and codes of practice, to represent the industry to other industrial/business sectors as well as to government departments and public agencies. Within the conference industry, such bodies include, inter alia:

- trade and professional associations;
- trade media;
- national tourism organisations;

- consultants;
- educational institutions.

Trade and professional associations

Trade and professional associations are formed to serve the interests of their members. Their activities usually include lobbying and representation, establishing codes of practice, marketing and promotion, education and training, research and information.

Within the conference industry, some such associations are international in the composition of their membership, others are strictly national. Among the leading international associations are:

- Association Internationale des Palais de Congrès (AIPC) (International Association of Congress Centres);
- Destination Marketing Association International (DMAI);
- European Cities Marketing;
- International Association of Professional Congress Organisers (IAPCO);
- International Congress & Convention Association (ICCA);
- Meeting Professionals International (MPI);
- Professional Convention Management Association (PCMA);
- Site (Society of Incentive and Travel Executives).

Further details of the services and activities of these and other international associations, as well as those of leading national associations, are given in Chapter 9.

Trade media

Traditionally the conference industry trade media have been glossy magazines published on a monthly, bi-monthly or quarterly basis. Increasingly electronic media are being developed in the form of conference/events industry websites and e-newsletters (or e-zines), which can be updated on a continuous basis providing the latest news, topics and issues for debate.

Both the paper-based and electronic media contain articles on new facilities and infrastructure developments, topical issues, how to stage successful events, destination reports, personnel changes, summaries of new books and reports, a correspondence section, and so on. They fulfil a very important role in keeping the industry abreast of the constant changes and developments taking place. Through their circulation to buyers, they also provide an important advertising and PR medium for suppliers wishing to promote their facilities/services to potential clients. Some of the magazines and media are international in content, emphasising once again the global nature of the conference industry.

National tourism organisations

Most countries in the world now have some form of national tourism organisation, publicly funded, established for promotional activities to the international tourism industry. These bodies are primarily concerned with marketing, but some may also fulfil training, product development, and lobbying and representational roles. Within the conference sector of the tourism industry, a number of countries have established a national convention bureau specifically to market to this sector. There is no standard format for such national convention bureaux – indeed, it would be difficult to find two which operate in the same way with similar levels of funding and resources and providing the same kind of services. Examples of the roles of national tourism/conference organisations are given in Chapter 3.

Some countries also have voluntary bodies established to provide a forum for networking, lobbying, and joint working on key initiatives. These bodies play a vital role in furthering the interests of the business events sector. Examples include the UK's Business Visits and Events Partnership (www.businessvisitsandeventspartnership.com) and Australia's Business Events Council (www.businesseventscouncil.org.au).

Consultants

Consultants play an important role in undertaking projects on a fee-paying basis for clients who are normally operating on the supply side of the conference industry. Typically, consultancy covers:

- the potential market for a proposed new conference centre;
- the specification for a new conference centre or for a major refurbishment of an existing venue;
- advice on marketing strategies for a destination or venue;
- a feasibility study to establish and run a new convention and visitor bureau;
- research projects analysing the value, volume and key trends aspects of the sector.

Consultancy can, however, cover any aspect of the industry. Consultancy is carried out either by specialist staff within the larger management consultancies (e.g. KPMG, Deloitte, PriceWaterhouseCoopers, Pannell Kerr Forster) or by one of the smaller consultancies catering specifically for the tourism, hospitality and business events sectors.

Educational institutions

The education and training of the conference industry's future workforce is vitally important in ensuring the continued growth and development of the industry. College

and university institutions are now giving serious attention to conference and meetings and event management in their course programmes and syllabuses. A number of trade associations have developed educational programmes and certificated courses available to both members and, sometimes, non-members. Other training programmes within the wider tourism industry, such as 'Welcome Host' and 'Investors in People', also contribute significantly to the improvement of skills and expertise for those already working in the industry.

Further details of education, training and professional development opportunities are given in Chapter 8.

CASE STUDY 2.1 Launch of Vauxhall Astra by experiential event agency TRO

Background and brief

At the end of 2009, experiential agency TRO was challenged by automotive manufacturer Vauxhall to create the live launch of the all-new Astra in the UK. The series of live events would include a conference and a corporate hospitality event in November and December, preceded by a consumer roadshow which started in October, and continued into January 2010, visiting 10 key city locations. The conference and roadshow were highly interactive, incorporating innovative film technology and social networking to attract the car's prime target market.

The conference was primarily a training event, introducing the new car to Vauxhall's 275-strong UK dealer network. Given the tough trading climate of 2009, the event needed to be highly motivational as well as educational – to provide not just the key information, but also the enthusiasm to return to the dealerships and persuasively sell the new car.

In addition, over 2,500 existing and potential Astra customers, drawn from the earlier roadshow and a Vauxhall web-based hand-raiser campaign, were also invited for four days to the Millbrook (Bedfordshire) event.

As the final element of its experiential activity, Vauxhall wished to invite many of its fleet customers to experience the educational programme.

Objectives for TRO

- Devise a creative concept that would complement the Astra TV campaign, which was to roll out from Boxing Day 2009 (26 December).
- Produce a live event solution that would appeal to Astra's technologically savvy target market.
- Introduce the product to the retail network in the UK. Also to selected customer prospects.

- Create powerful experiences in keeping with Astra's brand personality, that would turn every delegate and customer prospect into a passionate brand advocate for the new car.

Solution

Roadshow

The consumer roadshow took place in popular shopping centres at 10 city locations, siting the activity in areas of high footfall. TRO was inspired by the car's television advertising theme to create the environment and experiences that would attract consumer traffic.

In the TV ad, the Astra appeared as the star of a film sequence. The film theming was brought to life through two high-tech interactive brand experiences incorporating film technology.

Gadgetry, social networking and, above all, interactivity are prime motivators for Astra's target market, so a high-tech approach was needed to engage with the consumer audience. The two interactive experiences devised by TRO both incorporated cutting edge film technology.

For the first of these experiences, members of the public were photographed taken in various star poses in a customised photo pod. On exiting the pod they were given a film poster in postcard format, which promoted the première of the *All New Astra* and pictured the individual in the starring role. After 48 hours, a 90-second Astra film trailer with the subject's own picture incorporated as the film's co-star, was emailed to the individual who was then able to upload their own personalised trailer onto their Facebook page. In this way footage was marketed virally by the consumers themselves.

For the second experience, consumers sat in the driving seat of a cut-away Astra car, wearing wraparound 360-degree goggles. Through the goggles they viewed a specially filmed driving sequence taking place around the Astra film set. To create this, a professional stunt driver had driven the Millbrook track with the camera positioned in front of his face, so that the film of his driving experience became the consumer's eye-view. As well as producing the sensation of being the stunt driver, this had the effect of placing the subject inside the film itself – as an 'actor' on the Astra film set.

Dealer launch event and conference

Millbrook Proving Ground provided the obvious venue for the dealer launch. In addition to being Europe's leading vehicle testing facility offering both hill and flat driving terrain, Millbrook features regularly in BBC's *Top Gear* television programme and also made a guest appearance in the James Bond film *Casino Royale*. Most importantly, Millbrook's meetings facility offered a vast flexible space with high

ceilings, which permitted the construction of raked seating – a key element of the event's design.

The conference was named the *UK Astra Première* and was cinematically themed throughout. TRO created a cinema with a 6.5 metre-wide projection screen, raked seating and surround sound. The big screen atmosphere was enhanced by usherettes serving ice creams on trays. Delegates could also help themselves to popcorn, hot dogs and nachos. Short film trailers were played as part of the presentation, including one which asked delegates to switch off their phones. The film sequence used in the TV advertising was dramatised on arrival by a cinema lightbox featuring the UK Astra Première.

Rather than delivering traditional PowerPoint presentations, TRO assisted presenters in using keynote graphics on the big screen. They were rehearsed until they were word-perfect, and their presentations were rendered all the more dynamic by images of the vehicle. A car was positioned on a rotating platform for the product presentation so details of the design could be demonstrated by interacting with the vehicle instead of trying to read series of bullet points on-screen.

Aside from the training sessions and test drives at the Proving Ground, delegates enjoyed the same high-tech interactive experiences incorporating film technology that had been used in the consumer roadshow.

TRO devised the creative concept and was responsible for logistics, branding and the interactive technology film experiences.

Corporate event

A final activity was also devised for Vauxhall fleet customers: 75 of the company's top corporate customers enjoyed a VIP weekend with their partners in Bath. After their Millbrook product familiarisation they drove to Bath for a weekend of high quality hospitality and test driving on scenic routes.

Results

- The photo pod and the virtual test drive films were enormously popular with the techno-savvy consumer audience and generated word of mouth and viral marketing – all leading to increased visits to Vauxhall showrooms by the general public.
- The post-conference evaluation yielded high delegate satisfaction scores, including the following:

    Q: 'Are you enthusiastic about the new　　　Score: 9.63 out of 10
    Astra launch?'

    Q: 'Do you have the right tools you need to　　Score: 9.46 out of 10
    successfully launch the new Astra?'

Sales consultants gave the launch one of   9.41 out of 10
Vauxhall's strongest ever scores:

Overall satisfaction score: 8.76 out of 10
                                        deemed a high score
                                        for this audience

- The Astra Vauxhall Interactive Trailer won a Gold Award at the 2010 IVCA (International Visual Communication Association) Awards.
- In delivering the required number of hand-raisers – pre-qualified customer prospects who were in-market within a three-month purchase window – the experiential campaign exceeded its target by 71 per cent.

Summing up the activity, Keith Michaels, Head of Marketing Operations Vauxhall Motors, said:

> Astra is Vauxhall's most established brand and has been our best-selling vehicle since its original launch 30 years ago. This has been a major launch at the end of a challenging year. We are delighted with the experiential activities supporting the launch of the All New Astra – a very powerful and integrated combination of events which will greatly contribute in strengthening our marketing strategy. The Vauxhall brand continues to move forward with great new product design – and so does its experiential marketing, thanks to innovations like these interactive technologies.

- To view the film trailer, visit: www.youtube.com/user/VauxhallVideo#p/u/6/NgMaqZX88O0
- For more information on TRO visit: www.tro-group.co.uk

CASE STUDY 2.2 Oriflame Executive Conference 2012, Buenos Aires, organised by event and communications agency Grass Roots

Client brief

Oriflame Cosmetics specialises in selling high quality natural skincare and cosmetics through home demonstrations and catalogues. Their sales force of approximately 3.5 million independent consultants spans 60 countries and the Executive Conference is an incentive travel programme to recognise and reward the top 350 sales consultants.

Key objectives included:

- delivery of an incentive trip to Buenos Aires, Argentina with a focus on 'money can't buy' experiences;

- provision of a highly valued, experiential ground programme to a multi-cultural audience;
- paying particular attention to the Top 15 Sales Consultants;
- clearly demonstrating Grass Roots' value adds experience, including cost negotiation.

Solution

Oriflame typically contract directly with, and manage, the DMC relationship for all event logistics so partnering with an agency was a new and unusual concept to them. Grass Roots were able to successfully demonstrate an intuitive understanding of the client, their brand and to translate this through to Grass Roots' partner in Buenos Aires.

The initial site inspection took place 18 months in advance of the programme and, due to the experience and research by Grass Roots, a bespoke programme was suggested offering a true flavour of all aspects of Argentinian life. Grass Roots worked closely with Oriflame to ensure the programme met the requirements of their multi-cultural audience. This programme was so strong that it did not change at all from its initial conception and the results speak for themselves.

On arrival in Buenos Aires, group accommodation was provided at the 5-star Hilton Hotel located in the newest area of the city, Puerto Madero. On the first night an informal welcome buffet was available throughout the evening for consultants to meet with colleagues in a casual environment and, more importantly, in their own time, considering some guests had travelled for up to 36 hours from countries such as Mongolia and Indonesia.

Day two was the business update, providing Oriflame's CEO and COO the opportunity to share key messages to the Top 50 Oriflame Consultants. That evening guests were immersed in the dance of tango. Grass Roots negotiated the exclusive use of the famous Esquina Carlos Gardel Tango House for the formal Welcome Dinner, where guests enjoyed a sumptuous meal, which of course included the famous Argentinian beef and red wine. The evening entertainment included a spectacular show of tango, telling the story of its progression through the years.

On day three guests were at leisure with the option to relax in the hotel, explore the city independently or to book into one of the nine available tours ranging from city, shopping or bike tours to tango lessons, Evita Tour, La Boca Football Stadium, wine tasting or venturing out of the city to the Tigre Delta.

Day four, for most, was considered the highlight of the trip! A full day excursion to a family-run Estancia where they were welcomed with true Argentinian hospitality by owners Pancho and Florencia. Guests enjoyed a morning polo game and were lucky enough to have four of Pancho and Florencia's nine children, who are professional polo players, join the game and interact with the guests! On conclusion of the polo match which, of course, the Oriflame team won, the gauchos entered the field displaying their impressive traditional gaucho horsemanship skills, including a challenge where the gaucho gallops as fast as possible and spears a wedding ring on the end of their joust and presents it to a lady in the audience! Very impressive!

This morning of activities was followed by a barbecue lunch in the gorgeous and relaxing grounds of the Estancia, while guests were further entertained by traditional folklore music and dancing. The remainder of the afternoon was left free to explore the grounds either on foot or by horse and carriage and to just relax in the sun and converse with the family! A truly memorable, 'money can't buy' experience.

Delivering a fitting finale to this spectacular programme was a challenge but Grass Roots, along with their Buenos Aires partner, succeeded with the fascinating El Zanjón tunnels. El Zanjón was discovered during a housing renovation where the owner accidently unearthed city ruins including the old foundations, old walls, floors, water wells and most significantly the tunnels of San Telmo. After 25 years of meticulous restoration, elegant new steel and glass elevators transport visitors to and from the illuminated depths of El Zanjón offering an unusual glimpse into five centuries of urban archaeology. This site is now considered one of the most important archaeological locations in Buenos Aires, while the venue itself has had no expense spared and provides a stunning, high-tech events space. Finding entertainment to match this spectacular venue that would translate to a multi-cultural audience was an interesting prospect. However, Grass Roots delivered with a Circus Extravaganza. The scene was set with a mysterious ring master before jugglers and acrobats burst onto the scene, quickly followed by an urban street dancing crew displaying an impressive array of tricks. Next the music slowed down for a dynamic display of strength by four artistes suspended high into the ceiling on rings. The captivating finale was a terrifying display of gymnasts on silks to the haunting rendition of 'Roxanne'. The evening concluded with high energy music where all the acts took to the floor with the guests and danced the night away.

Results

Feedback from Oriflame Consultants was a resounding success! They were delighted by how much of Buenos Aires they were able to experience while still achieving that feeling of relaxation; all in such a short space of time too. Equally important to Grass Roots was the feedback from the Oriflame Conference Team, who have had experience of their Executive Conference for numerous years. This feedback was overwhelmingly positive. The Conference Team were truly appreciative of the professionalism and level of detail provided by Grass Roots, making each of their allocated tasks much smoother to manage and allowing them more time for networking with their consultants.

From the stakeholder client

Comments from the stakeholder client included:

Grass Roots performed very professionally during preparation and execution of the Oriflame Executive Conference in Buenos Aires. The Grass Roots team was very cooperative and supportive. We highly appreciated their flexibility and quick reaction to our last minute changes. They were always several steps ahead, and had stuff ready in advance – which facilitated Oriflame team's work a lot, and gave Oriflame team possibility to concentrate on other tasks, such as solving the more individual requests of the participants.

With Grass Roots' thorough preparation, great support before and during the events and excellent execution turned the programme into a memorable event. In Grass Roots you will find a partner that is reliable and pleasant to work with. We hope for future cooperation with Grass Roots.

From a delegate's perspective

Delegate feedback included:

The Leaders were happy to attend the conference – they liked the city of Buenos Aires, the events programme, the gifts and the Hilton hotel. They commented on the Buenos Aires conference/incentive as one of the best ever experienced.

This case study was compiled by Aileen Reuter, Practice Lead Creative Communications, Grass Roots (www.grassroots-events.co.uk).

CASE STUDY 2.3 Conventa, the South East European exhibition for meetings, events and incentives

First staged in 2009, Conventa is the principal trade exhibition for business events in South East Europe, held each January at Ljubljana Exhibition and Convention Centre – GR in Slovenia. It is organised by the Slovenian Convention Bureau with sponsorship from the Slovenian Tourist Board and Ljubljana Tourism, and seeks to promote the meeting and incentive destinations of South East Europe to an audience of global meeting planners. Such destinations include: Slovenia, Croatia, Serbia, Montenegro, Bosnia and Herzegovina, Macedonia, Romania, Bulgaria and Albania, many of which are still perceived internationally to be new or emerging destinations. While the main Conventa trade show takes place at the Ljubljana Exhibition and Convention Centre – GR, the educational programme and social events are held in various venues in Ljubljana.

A business-to-business (B2B) trade show such as Conventa is considered by the Organisers to be one of the best sales and marketing tools, enabling face-to-face communication between providers of meeting services and clients and creating relationships based on trust.

This case study traces the growth of Conventa and examines its unique and distinctive features.

The growth of Conventa

Conventa exhibitors range from convention bureaux, tourist boards, PCOs and DMCs to congress centres, convention hotels, special venues, event agencies, airline companies and more. Exhibiting companies can present their meetings industry services to carefully selected buyers at the pre-scheduled one-to-one meetings as well as at the various social functions.

The number of South East European countries exhibiting at Conventa has increased steadily year-on-year: from 7 in 2010, to 9 in 2011 and 10 in 2012. Table 2.9 provides a breakdown of the number of exhibitors by country and shows the growth over the three-year period 2010–12.

Conventa is a B2B trade show open only to specific target groups. It welcomes selected hosted buyers from throughout Europe who undertake scheduled appointments with exhibitors. It also invites a limited number of trade visitors (meeting industry professionals who attend to network with their colleagues and business partners), media representatives, together with guests such as political, economic and diplomatic representatives with influence over the strategic development of the meeting industry, the tourism sector and/or the wider economy.

In total 819 individual visitors registered to attend Conventa 2012 of whom 34 per cent were exhibitors, 32.5 per cent hosted buyers, 22 per cent guests, 7 per cent media representatives, 3 per cent organisers and assistants and 1 per cent trade visitors. This compares with a total of 393 in 2009, the first year of the show (when 47.1 per cent were exhibitors, 40.9 per cent hosted buyers, 10.9 per cent guests and 1 per cent trade visitors).

Hosted buyers are carefully selected meeting planners from associations, corporations and event agencies. They organise, influence or make budgetary decisions for international meetings, incentive travel, conferences, product launches, staff training initiatives and events. The hosted buyers commit to attend a daily minimum of ten appointments with exhibitors. Aware that the success of the event depends on the quality of meetings planners, the Conventa Organisers focus on attracting hosted buyers with real buying power and a confirmed interest in the region of South East Europe, giving Conventa a strategic advantage over other industry events. Table 2.10 shows the ratio of applications to acceptances for hosted buyers for both 2011 and 2012 – 155 meeting planners from 25 countries visited Conventa 2012.

Table 2.9 Conventa exhibitors by country

Country	Year 2010	Index 2011/ 2010*	Year 2011	Index 2012/ 2011	Year 2012
Slovenia	49	126.5	62	93.5	58
Croatia	30	106.7	32	100.0	32
Montenegro	5	100.0	5	120.0	6
Albania	0	200.0	1	100.0	1
Serbia	4	150.0	6	116.7	7
Bulgaria	2	150.0	3	33.3	1
Bosnia and Herzegovina	1	100.0	1	200.0	2
Neighbouring region Friuli Venezia Gulia, Italy	0	200.0	1	100.0	1
Neighbouring regions Styria and Carinthia, Austria	0	1000.0	9	77.8	7
Romania	0	0.0	0	200.0	1
Macedonia	2	−100.0	0	0.0	0
Number of SEE countries	7	128.6	9	111.1	10
Total meeting providers	93	129.0	120	96.7	116
Total media exhibiting	8	125.0	10	100.0	10
Total other providers exhibiting	14	64.3	9	177.8	16
Total	115		139		142

* Index numbers characterise the magnitude of changes in the number of exhibitors per country of origin over time. The index between years 2012/2011 shows how the volume of exhibitors per country of origin changed between the year 2011 and 2012.

Table 2.10 Conventa hosted buyer applications

Status	Year 2011	Year 2012
Number of international applicants	332	469
Confirmed international hosted buyers	146	155
Selection per cent (of those who applied to be hosted buyers)	44%	33%

The majority of international hosted buyers come from Belgium, France, Germany, Italy, the Russian Federation, the Netherlands and the United Kingdom. In 2012, the highest proportion of hosted buyers came from the United Kingdom and the Russian Federation (16 per cent respectively), followed by Belgium, the Netherlands, Germany, France and Poland.

In addition to international hosted buyers, the Organisers strive to attract Slovenian meeting planners to visit Conventa.

Figure 2.2 summarises the growth of Conventa in terms of both buyers and suppliers.

22-23 January 2009	21-22 January 2010	19-20 January 2011	18-19 January 2012
7 SEE destinations	7 SEE destinations	9 SEE destinations	10 SEE destinations
82 Exhibitors	115 Exhibitors	139 Exhibitors	142 Exhibitors
157 Hosted buyers	266 Hosted buyers	271 Hosted buyers	266 Hosted buyers

FIGURE 2.2 The growth of Conventa in terms of both buyers and suppliers

Future growth plans

The Conventa Organisers foresee a modest increase in the show's size for both the number of hosted buyers and exhibitors, and a greater focus on quality, specifically to attract high quality hosted buyers with a real potential to place business in South East Europe. The meeting industry destinations of South East Europe have different levels of market maturity and market organisation, and Conventa will aim to accelerate their development across all South East European countries as well as attract the main meeting industry providers from these countries.

Unique features of Conventa

Apple crates instead of shell schemes

FIGURE 2.3 Conventa show floor showing apple crates instead of shell schemes

Apple crates present one of the sustainable measures implemented to reduce the negative environmental impacts of the trade show. Paul Colston, a media visitor, commented (*Conference & Meetings World* magazine, February 2011):

> *There was no shell scheme to be seen on the show floor and only one custom-build stand. Instead the Organisers pulled off a brave eco experiment by way of a uniform stand design made out of traditional apple crates. This simple idea could have looked cheap, but fruit and flower garlands on the basic wooden crate structures brought a very green and democratic idea to life and provided a good talking point for delegates and visitors.*
>
> Conventa 2011

Further details of Conventa's sustainable features are to be found in Chapter 7.

Education programme 'Conventa Academy'

Conventa offers opportunities to gain in-depth knowledge and best practice examples in subjects as diverse as meetings management and destination marketing. The guiding principle is to share knowledge and experience that have been developed through years of tradition and professional practice with those who will be shaping the future of the meeting industry. Conventa participants can learn about the latest developments in the global meetings industry.

Conventa Academy awards

To inspire meeting professionals to go above and beyond what is expected of them and thus further develop the meetings industry in South East Europe, Conventa acknowledges innovative achievements and outstanding individuals. The Conventa Hall of Fame recognises individual meeting professionals for their outstanding and invaluable services to the regional meetings industry.

Pre-scheduled appointments

Face-to-face business development is acknowledged to be the most successful form of selling and of building a personal and direct relationship with meetings industry clients. Conventa participants are entitled to an online diary of prescheduled one-to-one meetings with hosted buyers. In the first stage, appointments are buyer-driven and hosted buyers select which exhibitors they would like to meet. In the second phase, exhibitors are encouraged to make a targeted selection of the hosted buyers and request individual appointments with them.

Levels of hospitality offered to visitors

The Conventa programme is designed to provide a business-friendly environment where exhibitors and hosted buyers enjoy a range of services enabling them to focus on building a network of potential partners. The Conventa show offers these services to all participants which creates an *equal* basis for forming business partnerships. Conventa participants have acknowledged the rich programme and warm welcome and hospitality.

The hosted buyer programme includes a complimentary economy return air ticket from selected destinations within Europe to Ljubljana on Adria Airways flights, overnight accommodation, airport and other transfers, meals, networking opportunities, personal itinerary of appointments, fam trips and the services of the Conventa support team before and during the show.

The exhibitor packages include access to online meetings between exhibitors and buyers, inclusion in the show catalogue and *Meet in SEE* directory as well as access to contact details of participating buyers. The stand packages include an equipped exhibition stand as well as attendance with buyers at social and networking events and catering throughout the trade show.

Another distinctive feature of the Conventa trade show is equal exhibition stands where the exhibitors hold their one-to-one appointments. While providers at other global meeting industry trade shows are presented on stands of different size and equipment, Conventa exhibition stands are of equal dimensions and outlook. This means that all exhibitors are presented equally, showcasing the region as a destination of equally important meeting industry providers.

TV studio broadcasting live from the show floor

While the trade show is open only to selected publics, key parts of the programme are broadcast via Conventa TV to the international community of meeting professionals. Conventa TV, powered by *Kongres Magazine*, is available online before, during and after the trade show. Viewers are able to watch the highlights from Conventa with daily updated videos and live streaming of interviews with meeting industry professionals and much more.

Attendance by politicians at the show party

Conventa aims to increase recognition of the meeting industry as a benefactor to tourism and the wider economy by inviting political, economic and diplomatic representatives to visit Conventa and become familiar with the latest developments and research in the meeting industry. By learning more about the economic, cultural and tourism impacts of the meeting industry, these political and economic delegates can make informed decisions about the strategic development of the meeting industry in South East Europe.

Partnership thinking

Conventa is built on a partnership model of creating synergies with official, regional, international and media partners. Their engagement plays a crucial role in the success

and development of the trade show and consequently also in the development of the meeting industry in South East Europe. By searching for synergies with 15 official partners, 20 regional and 16 media partners, Conventa moves boundaries, establishing competitive cooperation among meeting industry professionals of South East Europe.

Conventa Marketing Activity

In line with its sustainability commitments, Conventa's marketing platform is based on digital communication. A summary of Conventa's marketing activities is shown in Figure 2.4.

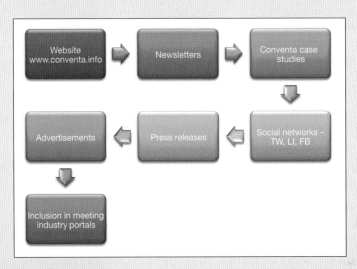

FIGURE 2.4 Conventa marketing activity

Conventa distinguishes between communication with hosted buyers, exhibitors and guests. The marketing platform for communication with exhibitors is based on personal sales, followed by telemarketing, emailings, direct mailings and participation at various trade shows and events. Personal sales are the driving force for attracting meeting industry providers from South East Europe to exhibit at the Conventa show.

The marketing platform for communication with the hosted buyers is based on partnership with group leaders and international associations who invite meeting planners to Conventa through their channels of communication. However, Conventa also communicates independently with meeting planners through emails, direct mail, advertisements and participation at global events and trade shows.

Visitor feedback

I first heard about Conventa in September 2011, when I joined HelmsBriscoe. I applied for hosted buyer status because it is really important for me to increase my network with hoteliers but also to have a better view of the market and the destinations. I am not at all familiar with the region. I've never travelled to South East Europe. At Conventa I will try to get more information about the hotels in the South East European region, what they have to offer to my clients, what are the capacities for groups. I cannot sell them properly if I don't know them. I will also be attending the fam trip to Dubrovnik. Overall I hope to extend my knowledge about the South East European region and be able to propose those destinations to my clients.

HelmsBriscoe, Belgium

This case study was compiled by Maruša Rosulnik, early stage researcher at GoMice, technical organiser of Conventa, and Miha Kovačič, Director of the Slovenian Convention Bureau and organiser of Conventa (www.conventa.info).

SUMMARY

- The buying side of the conference industry includes corporate organisations, associations and government/public sector agencies, and conference entrepreneurs.
- Corporate organisations plan a wide variety of conferences, meetings and other events. Staff involved in the organisation of these activities have many different job titles. For the most part, corporate events attract fewer than 200 delegates and have comparatively short lead times. They have a higher average per capita expenditure than association conferences, with costs being borne by the companies themselves.
- The term 'association' is used to describe a sector of the industry which encompasses professional and trade bodies, voluntary organisations, charities, political parties and other non-corporate entities. Association conferences are different in many respects from those held in the corporate sector, especially in their average size, duration, types of venues used, and accommodation/housing required. International association and inter-governmental conventions form a major segment of the 'association' market in their own right.
- Government/public sector organisations have many similar buying characteristics to associations, although delegate expectations are rising and some comparisons with the corporate sector may be drawn, particularly in respect of the types of venues used.
- Conference entrepreneurs (commercial conference organisers) develop conferences in response to an identified demand as a purely commercial activity.
- The supply side of the conference industry comprises venues, destinations, and myriad other companies offering specialist services, from audio-visual equipment supply to contract catering, from interpreting to coach hire.

- The industry also features an important group of intermediary agencies which provide services ranging from conference management to venue finding, and from incentive travel planning to exhibition organising.
- This complex industry is reliant on a range of other institutions to enable it to operate professionally and develop in a structured way. Such institutions include trade associations, trade media, national tourism organisations, consultants and educational bodies.

REVIEW AND DISCUSSION QUESTIONS

1 Assess the benefits and disadvantages, for a corporate organisation, of maintaining its own, in-house event department. Include an analysis of the pros and cons, for the company, of employing a business travel agency as an 'implant'.

2 Identify and give reasons for the most appropriate types of conference/events business for the following venues:

   a a 4-star city-centre hotel with 250 bedrooms and conference facilities seating up to 400 delegates. Choose a city which has an important manufacturing or service industry base;

   b a multi-purpose heritage building in a resort location with a seating capacity of 1,500;

   c a residential conference centre with six conference rooms (the largest seating 80), accommodation of 3-star standard, situated in a rural location.

3 Critically review the role of exhibitions (both live and virtual) as a sales and marketing tool in the digital age.

REFERENCES

CAT (2011) *British Meetings and Events Industry 2011–12*, CAT Publications Ltd, available at www.meetpie.com/bmeis (accessed 11 August 2012)

Celuch, K. and Davidson, R. (2011) *Better Business Results through Motivational Experiences and Incentive Travel*, available at www.siteglobal.com/Resources/BetterBusinessBook.aspx (accessed 2 September 2012)

Conventa (2011) 'Conventa Comes of Age', *Conference & Meeting World* magazine (February)

FaceTime (2012) 'Reasons to Use Experiential Marketing', *FaceTime* (February), available at http://view.digipage.net/?userpath=00000745/00016035/00074157/&page=45 (accessed 7 September 2012)

Gilligan, P. (2011) 'Love on the Rocks', *Meetings & Incentive Travel* magazine (September), available at www.meetpie.com

Hackett, D. (2011) 'Where Is the Wow?', *Meetings & Incentive Travel* magazine (April), available at www.meetpie.com

ICCA (2011) *The International Association Meetings Market: Worldwide 2001–2010,* International Congress and Convention Association, available at www.iccaworld.com (accessed 11 August 2012)

IRF (2011) *Motivating Today's Workforce: The Future of Incentive and Recognition Program Design,* Incentive Research Foundation

Oxford Economics (2012) *The Economic Impact of the UK Exhibition Industry,* Oxford Economics

Walker, T. (2010) 'Inside the Corporate Hospitality Market', available at www.meetingsreview.com (accessed 2 November 2010)

FURTHER READING

Fisher, J. (2003) *Sales Rewards and Incentives,* John Wiley & Sons

—— (2008) *How to Run Successful Employee Incentive Schemes*, 3rd edn, Kogan Page

SIF/ITC (2012) *Incentive Travel: The Participant's Viewpoint,* Site International Foundation and the Incentive Travel Council

CHAPTER 3

Winning conference business: 1

CHAPTER OBJECTIVES

This chapter looks at:

- marketing principles (customer focus, marketing planning, market segmentation, and the marketing mix)
- relationship marketing and customer relationship management
- branding, including destination and venue branding and promotion
- the role of destination marketing organisations (both local and national)
- event agency marketing activity

It includes case studies on:

- Vilnius Convention Bureau branding, Lithuania
- São Paulo Convention and Visitors Bureau, Brazil

www.routledge.com/cw/rogers

THE LEARNING CENTRE
EALING, HAMMERSMITH AND WEST LONDON COLLEGE
GLIDDON ROAD
LONDON W14 9BL

LEARNING OUTCOMES

On completion of this chapter, you should be able to:

- describe the key principles of marketing and illustrate their application to the conference industry;
- explain how customer relationship management and branding have been embraced by the industry;
- define the roles of different types of destination marketing organisation;
- appreciate how conference venues approach the market, both individually and collectively (as part of marketing consortia);
- understand the tactics and tools used by event agencies to secure and retain business.

Introduction

Securing new and repeat business is essential for any business operation. Winning business in the conference industry requires a range of strategies and tactics and the ability to keep abreast of a changing and evolving marketplace. The topic is such a large one that two chapters of this book will be devoted to exploring a range of approaches and examples of best practice. This chapter will examine general marketing principles with specific reference to the conference, convention and business events sector. It will also look at the branding and promotional activities of destinations, venues and event agencies. Chapter 4 looks at some of the 'newer' marketing tools, such as web marketing and social media, together with other important activities including bidding and conference ambassador programmes.

Marketing principles

There are many benefits from staging conferences and meetings, both to the delegates and attendees who participate in such events but also to the destinations, venues, agencies and other suppliers which are reliant on the economic, social and promotional benefits that conference business generates. However, in what is now a global marketplace, competition for such business is intense and grows fiercer year on year. It is, therefore, vital that those locations and organisations which are competing for their share of this lucrative market adopt professional practices and identify the right sales and marketing strategies, tactics and tools to ensure their success.

Before looking at a range of strategies and tools in use in the twenty-first-century conference and business events industry, it will be useful to summarise some of the general principles of marketing and how they apply to the sector.

Customer focus

There are many definitions of marketing. One of the more straightforward ones is that adopted by the (British) Chartered Institute of Marketing, which defines marketing as:

> *The management process responsible for identifying, anticipating and satisfying customers' requirements efficiently and profitably.*

This focus on customers' needs is the key to all successful marketing activity. There are alternative philosophies which are well described by Cooper *et al.* (1993) and reproduced in Figure 3.1.

> *Examples 1 and 2 [in Figure 3.1] can be ineffective due to problems encountered in having the wrong product for the market, and therefore having to devote more resources to promotion and selling in order to achieve sales. In these examples it is normal to find companies which believe their products are acceptable, and all that is required for sales to occur is the identification of prime markets and methods of selling.*

The emphasis is on the product, and in tourist promotional literature it is often characterised by photographs of empty bedrooms or conference rooms, of buildings and views of the destination. It is selling 'features' rather than the 'benefits' the consumer is seeking, and fails to show pictures of tourists and delegates enjoying themselves and receiving good service.

On the other hand, examples 3 and 4 in Figure 3.1

> *offer the ideal approach to organising business in today's tourism marketplace. They are driven by research which creates an understanding of the consumer, the business and the marketplace. The tourism industry is spending vast sums of money on developing new attractions, improving products, building hotels and investing in technology. The only way for the risk level to be kept to a minimum is through adoption of a marketing philosophy which provides products related to the needs of consumers.*

The establishment of a customer orientation which permeates through every department of a conference venue, agency or conference marketing organisation is essential to its success. This provides the basic building blocks upon which marketing strategies can

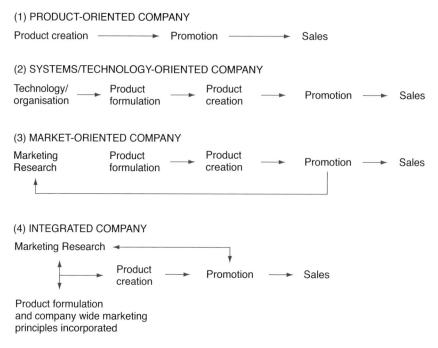

FIGURE 3.1 Four possible business philosophies

be constructed. It will ensure that the physical product or service is suited to market needs: it will confirm, for example, that the multi-purpose hotel function room is less and less able to meet the increasingly sophisticated needs of today's conference planners. It will also ensure that the people servicing a venue have a proper understanding of the specific needs of the conference organiser and his or her delegates, and that they are equipped with the personal and technical skills to meet such needs in ways which will encourage the customer to return again and again.

Marketing planning

The practical steps involved in preparing to approach the marketplace include development of a marketing plan or strategy, against which performance can be measured, and future marketing programmes fine-tuned in the light of experience. While there is no definitive standard of what should constitute a marketing plan, it is likely to contain most or all of the following sections:

- introduction setting out the organisation's vision and mission and overall objectives;
- an overview of the current market, highlighting opportunities and threats specific to the organisation;
- an assessment of the organisation's strengths and weaknesses, in the form of a product audit, identifying specific competitive advantages;

| Table 3.0 Destination Management Plan for Tourism in Brisbane 2008–11 – key goals and measures ||
Goal	Measure
Increase awareness, preference and intention in key target markets	• Growth in number of Brisbane preferences and intenders from target markets
	• Growth in positive associations with brand attributes
Increase visitor expenditure	• Growth in visitor expenditure and average length of stay in Brisbane
Increase number of tourism jobs	• Growth in employment in the Brisbane destination's tourism and hospitality industry
Increase tourism investment and infrastructure in the Brisbane destination	• Growth in appropriate tourism investment as outlined in the Destination Management Plan
Ensure sustainable development of the destination's tourism product	• Stakeholder support and consideration of content of the DMP through references to the document in their strategic planning
	• Development of new product suited to the needs of the target market
	• Increase in international ready product

- details of the marketing strategies to be implemented, outlining the markets to be reached, tactics and work programmes to achieve the strategies, with specific and measurable targets and timescales;
- a comprehensive marketing calendar which summarises the key items from section 4 into a month-by-month activity plan, also showing where the lead responsibility for each activity lies;
- a detailed budget.

The plan may also include a PEST analysis, looking at the political, economic, social and technological changes which could affect the organisation and the market.

Tourism Queensland published the *Destination Management Plan for Tourism in Brisbane 2008–11*, covering both leisure and business tourism/events, which sets out the following as its vision: Brisbane is recognised amongst the world's most desirable destinations for leisure, business and lifestyle. It is a youthful and progressive Australian city offering access to diverse and rewarding tourism experiences. Table 3.0 describes key goals and measures and all of these are explained and detailed much more fully in the plan document. The substantive chapters in the plan for Brisbane are entitled:

- Vision for the Destination;
- Key Strategic Priorities;

- Strategies to Achieve the Vision;
- Strategic Overview;
- Implementation, Monitoring and Evaluation.

The plan has objectives for '*increasing business events, including potential meetings, conventions and exhibition visitation in the key interstate target markets of Sydney and Melbourne*', and '*increase meetings, conventions and exhibition visitation in the key international markets*'. To view the full plan, visit: www.tq.com.au

Writing and implementing a marketing plan, while important, are never sufficient. There also needs to be a regular and rigorous evaluation of the effectiveness of the plan, measuring actual performance against the objectives and targets detailed in the plan. This evaluation will, almost certainly, lead to some revision and re-writing of the plan for the following year(s), as lessons are learnt and adjustments are made in the light of experience in putting the plan into practice – the Brisbane Plan described above was to be '*reviewed and refreshed every three years*'. It is also likely that, at some point, a major review of the Plan will be carried out, leading to the drafting of a new marketing strategy.

The Daytona Beach Area Convention and Visitors Bureau (Florida, USA), in its 2011–12 destination marketing plan for the Halifax area, sets out the different approach required when marketing the destination for 'meetings, convention and sports sales' rather than to the leisure consumer market:

> *While traditional advertising works well on the leisure side of business, professional selling often requires a detailed process which includes one-on-one networking, relationship building, site visits, familiarisation tours, negotiating, and a highly co-ordinated effort between CVB, area hotels, and meeting facilities such as the Ocean Center. A destination team approach is required in order to be both competitive and successful in this area. Often the selling process with these travel professionals takes years, however the pay-off can be substantial. These bookings allow destinations to sell large numbers of rooms; engage support partners such as restaurants and attractions; and improve Average Daily Rates (ADR) and Occupancy (OCC) during needed time frames. All these elements work to provide our area with a well-rounded tourism industry that also increases employment opportunities and new infrastructure investments.*

Market segmentation

An important part of the marketing planning process is the identification of appropriate market segments from which it is anticipated that business can be won. In broad terms, the conference and conventions sector (as we have seen in Chapter 2) is typically divided into the following segments:

- corporate meetings, conferences and events;
- national association meetings and conventions;
- government and public sector meetings and events;
- international association conventions and congresses.

These broad categories can then be subjected to further segmentation in a variety of ways. For example, by industry sector, with the following sectors being particularly important:

- oil, gas and petrochemicals;
- medical and pharmaceutical;
- computing/IT and telecommunications;
- automotive manufacturing and other manufacturing;
- financial and professional services;
- food, drink and tobacco;
- travel and transport.

Another important type of segmentation is that done by size of event: a venue might decide, for example, that it will target corporate meetings and conferences of between 50–100 delegates, even though it might have a room with a capacity of 200, because it lacks sufficient syndicate rooms for a 200-delegate conference to break down into five or six smaller groups. Similarly, there is probably little point in a destination with a 2,000-capacity convention centre targeting events of this size if the destination's overall infrastructure does not have enough bedrooms of the right quality to accommodate a residential 2,000-delegate convention.

Segmentation can also be done by source or location of potential clients. It may be that very good transport links exist with particular cities or countries, facilitating travel to the destination from these areas. Such a criterion will be more relevant to corporate meetings and conferences where delegates may be travelling from only one or just a limited number of starting points. It will be less important within the association segment as delegates are normally travelling from a much wider range of locations to attend the convention or congress.

The Daytona Beach Area Convention and Visitors Bureau Marketing Plan 2011–12 referenced above identifies the following key target market segments:

- SMERF (see Chapter 2);
- associations;
- sports;
- government;
- corporate.

For further details visit: http://daytonabeachcvb.org/marketing_plan1

Research can be carried out for all market segments in order to identify the opportunities for marketing activity. Clearly, research must also be undertaken by a destination or venue into its own 'product' in order to build a comprehensive picture of its strengths and weaknesses so that appropriate target markets match the strengths of the destination or venue. Similarly an event agency will need to identify the market niches for which its knowledge, experience and skills are especially suited e.g. pharmaceutical and healthcare sector events; incentive and performance improvement programmes; association conferences in the financial services sector, etc.

Marketing mix strategy

Once market research has been completed and target markets of current and potential customers have been identified, an appropriate marketing mix strategy can be developed.

The marketing mix is frequently defined as comprising the four Ps: product, price, promotion and place (distribution). Other marketing gurus would extend these traditional four points to eight, to include packaging, planning, the prospect and post-sale. The following terms, for example, have significance in the marketing of a conference destination or venue:

- *Product* is the destination/venue and its facilities and resources. To conference organisers and meeting planners, it means a destination/venue which can handle the convention, meeting or exhibition requirements. It covers such issues as service, quality, branding, and those unique features which differentiate it from competitors (USPs or unique selling propositions).
- *Price* may cover a variety of issues including conference centre/venue hire charges and delegate rates, hotel or guest house accommodation costs, and transport costs. Pricing policies must take account of many factors including projected future demand and any seasonal fluctuations expected; the need to maximise yield (see Chapter 6); the perishable nature of the product – it is something that cannot be stored for future use, like a conference room that is unused on a particular day and brings in no revenue and that potential revenue is lost forever; the psychological impact on clients of raising or lowering prices; the activities of competitors; and the wider economic situation.
- *Packaging* relates to the way in which the product and price are offered in the market. Special delegate packages may be offered in conjunction with local tourist attractions or between conference venues and hotels. Most venues, both residential and non-residential, promote their own delegate packages: QHotels in the UK offer standardised 'eight-hour' and '24-hour' delegate packages (see Table 3.1) across the group of hotels. Some convention centres make available their meeting rooms rent-free to certain types of not-for-profit organisations whose events meet specific economic benefit criteria. In October 2011 Brussels launched 'The Brussels Fund for Scientific Conferences', designed to attract more international delegates to the destination.

Table 3.1 QHotels total meeting packages

Eight-Hour Total Meetings Package (2012) includes:
- Hire of main meeting room
- LCD projector, screen, flip chart
- Free Internet access for all delegates for the duration of their stay
- Constant refreshments throughout the day
- Flexible lunch options to choose from: restaurant lunch, networking lunch, in your meeting room or in a breakout area or choose a working lunch
- Dedicated Event Manager on the day

24-Hour Total Meetings Package includes all aspects of Eight-Hour Total Meetings Package PLUS:
- Accommodation
- Restaurant dinner
- Use of leisure facilities where available
- Full English/Scottish breakfast

Source: www.qconferences.co.uk/total-meeting-package

The Fund, a form of subvention, is funded by the Brussels-Capital Region and the City of Brussels and managed by the convention bureau VisitBrussels and will be used to pay for congress pre-financing and subsidies. Various rules and criteria apply but the maximum amount of pre-financing available is EUR 50,000 per congress and the maximum subsidy, for congresses of fewer than 200 delegates, is EUR 10,000. See also Chapter 4 for further information on bidding and subvention activity.

- *Place (or distribution)* focuses on the activities used by an agency, destination or venue to make its product/service available and accessible to prospective clients. Such distribution channels include websites, trade shows, company brochures and destination or venue guides and brochures, and videos/DVDs.

- *Planning* is the strategic process of analysing markets, assessing the competition, identifying programmes, and selecting appropriate marketing strategies.

- *Promotion* communicates information about the agency or the destination/venue and its products to prospective clients. There is a need to inform and persuade current customers to remain loyal, potential future customers to experience the product, and also journalists and other key people (leading figures in the local community and politicians, for example) who may in some way influence business activity levels. Advertising, public relations, e-marketing, selling, special events and familiarisation visits are some of the promotional activities undertaken.

- *Prospect (or client/customer)* is the sole reason for, and the object of, all the organisation's marketing endeavours. The Body Shop retail company expressed the importance of the customer in its mission statement as follows:

    A customer is the most important visitor on our premises. She is not dependent on us. We are dependent on her. She is not an interruption to our work. She is the purpose of it. She is not an outsider in our business. She is part of it. We are not doing her a favour by serving her. She is doing us a favour by giving us the opportunity to do so.

It is this same customer orientation which is crucial to the success of organisations seeking to attract and win conference business.

- *Post-sale* processes address the continuing need to provide service to, and for, prospects and to ensure that the sense of expectation generated at the sales meeting is not just met but exceeded in the run-up to an event and, indeed, in the provision of service during and after it. Client retention is not always possible within the conference industry because of the buying patterns of certain organisations, especially within the association sector, but keeping satisfied clients is a much more cost-effective way of maintaining and building market share than having constantly to find and attract new clients. Recommendations by colleagues/peers of venues and destinations is frequently found to be a key way in which these are sourced, as a satisfied customer becomes an unpaid ambassador (or 'distribution channel') whose value should never be under-estimated.

Other marketers suggest further Ps be added to the marketing mix, such as *People* – those who are between the product and the prospect, delivering the product/services to the client including convention bureau staff, venue personnel, destination management companies, professional conference organisers, event management companies, restaurateurs, and retail and visitor attraction staff.

There is clearly some overlap between these different marketing mix tools, but in total they provide the essential ingredients for bringing a conference agency, venue or destination to the marketplace in a way that is professionally planned and likely to enjoy the greatest success.

Relationship marketing and customer relationship management

One of the key features of conference venue and destination marketing is the forging of relationships between suppliers and buyers, the building of trust between those offering facilities and services and those looking to make use of them to stage events. Gartrell (1991), writing about the role of convention bureaux, suggests that:

though a convention bureau is a sales organisation, its premise of operation is the development of a relationship with planners that cultivates understanding and trust. Though such a relationship may not initially appear mutually supportive, the reality is that the bureau and planner have common goals and in essence need one another.

The meeting planner or conference organiser needs, for example, to carry out familiarisation or inspection visits to a destination and its venues, to assess their appropriateness for specific events. The convention and visitor bureau is the ideal vehicle for the organisation of such visits because it can provide a comprehensive overview, pull together all the necessary information, arrange a schedule of visits to venues and attractions and usually escort them as well, and then advise on the availability and accessibility of all the other components of a given conference package. DMCs and, to a lesser extent PCOs, may also be involved in this process in a similar way. For the individual conference organiser to plan such a visit using his or her own resources, possibly from hundreds or thousands of miles away, would require a huge investment in time and resources.

Trust and understanding are also of critical importance between the venue which is to stage the conference and the conference organiser. A chain of relationships is formed, initially between the venue sales manager and the conference organiser and then between the conference and banqueting manager/event co-ordinator and the organiser. All need to have confidence in each other: the conference organiser needs to trust the venue staff to deliver what has been promised within agreed budgets, and the venue staff need to feel comfortable that their client will keep his or her side of the deal (for example, in actual numbers of delegates attending, in the administration of the conference programme, and in the implementation of any specially planned arrangements). When such strong and trusting relationships exist, there is a much greater prospect of successful events and of future repeat business. When relationships are less strong, often because of high staff turnover in the venue, poor communications between client and venue, or because of insufficient planning time allocated by the conference organiser, problems are much more likely to occur.

It goes without saying that, for event agencies and PCOs, the establishment of client relationships built on trust and mutual respect is also crucial in the profitable development of their business. Much time and money is invested in bidding for and winning client contracts (see section on Bidding in Chapter 4) and it is important that, wherever possible, the successful securing of a new piece of business should lead to an ongoing relationship with that client which will lead to future event management opportunities with the same client. The event agency will be keen to position itself as an integral part of the strategic management team for the client company. Their ability to forge close and trusting relationships of this kind with clients, understanding and contributing to the ethos, philosophy and strategic business objectives of client companies, is likely to become one of the ultimate tests of their success as an intermediary agency.

In the author's experience, one of the real attractions of the conference industry is the many opportunities it affords for the development of relationships between buyers and suppliers, between buyers and buyers, and between suppliers and suppliers. It is very much a people industry and, while there may be fierce competition for business, this generally takes the form of friendly rivalry rather than cut-throat aggression. Formal and informal networks are established, and it is quite common for one destination to pass on information about a client or an event to the destination which will play host to them next. Similarly, buyers exchange their experiences of venues and destinations and peer recommendation is one of the most important ways in which future venues are sourced.

Relationship marketing and customer relationship management (and also key account management) are the terms used to describe the establishment and nurturing of relationships with clients. Relationship marketing focuses on the initial identification and building of contacts with potential clients, while customer relationship management concentrates on the fostering and strengthening of such relationships.

The key to successful marketing lies in the ability to put oneself in the shoes of one's potential consumers or customers. In fact, marketing starts and finishes with the customer or target market. There is little point in developing a product unless there is a potential market for it. Similarly, there is no point in creating a great product unless potential customers can be informed effectively about it.

The customer (or consumer or client) is, in the words of Cris Canning (www.Hospitality Ink.com), CMP, Adjunct Professor at the University of Nevada (Las Vegas) and the University of California (San Diego):

> the number one asset of a company – nothing happens until a sale is made. But a close second is the valuable information collected about those customers: knowledge is power. Enter the world of customer relationship management, or CRM. CRM is not about technology any more than hospitality is about throwing out a welcome mat. Rather it is a philosophy that should mobilise an entire organisation toward serving the customer better. It is the 'architecture' behind a successful relationship management programme that puts the customer first. This creates loyal customers who purchase more, cost less to sell to and who will refer at least five other customers over a lifetime. To be successful in using CRM, a venue or destination must already have a good sales process in place. If the processes, culture and skills are not in place, automating something that does not work will not enhance results.

Canning maintains that CRM is not a new principle:

> the corner grocer of 100 years ago could remember all his customers and their buying habits. Now, with the aid of technology, greater quantities of that kind of information can be stored and sorted in very sophisticated ways. Modern CRM systems are designed to focus on integrating sales, customer service and marketing systems into one collaborative unit. Key features include:
>
> * basic demographic and contact information;
> * a single customer view combining all business and buying;
> * connectivity to include mobile phones and pdas;

- *lead management;*
- *campaign management;*
- *data import/export;*
- *third party support; and (sometimes)*
- *geographic information systems (GIS) tying geographic maps with data.*

Canning distinguishes between two levels of CRM: operational and analytical. Operational CRM creates a database of customers and the activities they have with the destination or venue. It represents the destination or venue's relationship with the customer and can be categorised by leads, potential clients, referrals, etc. Operational CRM systems can hold a wealth of information that can improve relationships and support customers. But, she suggests, this type of system alone will struggle to provide the deeper customer understanding required to add value to every interaction with each customer.

The sheer volume of customer information and increasingly complex interactions with customers have propelled 'data mining' to the forefront for making customer relationships profitable. Data mining uses a variety of data analysis and modelling techniques to discover patterns and relationships that may be used to make accurate predictions. The data mining process involves capture of data, 'scrubbing' it, pulling scattered entries into a single record and keeping it updated. Scrubbing data is the standardisation of crucial fields to ensure usability (otherwise an entry for 'IBM' would not synchronise with one that said 'I.B.M.'). Some types of strategic concepts seem universal in the analytics of data mining:

- *Customer recognition (e.g. at a hotel it would include a customer's choice of room type and details of his other preferences).*
- *Data capture and maintenance (by each employee or department that touches the customer).*
- *Channel integration and consistency (each hotel property within a chain as well as the national sales office, for example, must contribute).*
- *Ranking and discrimination (which customers are A, B or C clients).*
- *Two-way personalised dialogues (so that no matter how the destination or venue contacts the client, or vice versa, this information is ready).*

One of the growing challenges facing CRM is the impact of data protection legislation which can restrict the amount of personal information to be kept on clients and, perhaps even more importantly, the uses to which such data may be put. It seems likely that this type of legislation will only increase in the future in order to protect the rights and the privacy of the individual. In the UK, for example, at the time of writing, the Data Protection Registrar (a government agency) requires that those employed by a company/organisation (as opposed to the private individual) have to be given the opportunity to 'opt out' of having their contact details held within a database. It is quite conceivable that this could change at some point to an 'opt in' regime i.e. such business contacts would have to give their assent to their contact details being stored in a database. Such a change would undoubtedly reduce the size of CRM databases and, depending upon the stringency of other aspects of any new legislation, have a potentially negative impact on CRM activity.

Branding

The branding of consumer products (cars, washing machines, for example) has played a major part in their promotion for many years. More recently, branding theory has been applied to the practice of marketing destinations and is now seen as a key component or tool in any successful promotion of cities, regions and countries. The city of Glasgow (winner of the ICCA 'Best Marketing Award 2006' for the launch of the 'Glasgow: Scotland with Style' brand) claims that:

> a positive and unique image is the primary reason why visitors choose a city for a short break, the overriding reason why a convention organiser selects one destination over another and the impetus behind an investor believing in the lifestyle values Glasgow offers. The management of that image, effectively positioning the city in a coherent, consistent way, is fundamental to ensuring future economic success (GCMB 2006).

The classical definition of a 'brand' is: 'A name, term, sign or design, or a combination of them, which is intended to identify the goods or services of one seller or group of sellers and to differentiate them from their competitors' (De Chernatony and McDonald 1998).

However, this is very much a supply-side perspective – it is also necessary to consider the consumer's role in branding and to take account of the messages the consumer receives. A more modern definition of a brand which acknowledges this two-way process is the following:

> A brand is a simple thing: it is in effect a trademark which, through careful management, skilful promotion and wide use, comes into the minds of consumers, to embrace a particular and appealing set of values and attributes, both tangible and intangible (Interbrand 1990).

> A brand is a 'product or service made distinctive by its personality and its positioning. Its personality is a unique combination of tangible/physical attributes (i.e. what do I get?) and intangible/symbolic attributes (how do I feel?). Its positioning defines the

point of reference with respect to the competitive set, and occupies a unique space in the consumer's mind (Hankinson 2001).

Brands work by:

facilitating and making the customer's choice process more effective. The objective of branding is to provoke a positive action in customers by facilitating the decision-making process. The development of a name, logo and the presentation of an attractive and (both physically and emotionally) feasible proposition for the brand validated by consumers and deliverers are basic branding procedures (Doyle 1989).

To achieve really successful destination branding, the brand must come alive for visitors and delegates. Marketers must:

be in the business of delivering impactful experiences, not merely constructing a clever brand indentity on paper with slick slogans and brand logos (Morgan, Pritchard and Pride 2002).

Today many destinations have (or at least claim to have!) superb venues and hotels, easy accessibility, diverse visitor attractions, and a unique cultural heritage. But their future success in attracting visitors will depend on their ability to create a unique identity for themselves, to differentiate themselves from their competitors.

In this marketplace, what persuades potential tourists to visit (and revisit) one place instead of another is whether they have empathy with the destination and its values. The battle for customers in tomorrow's destination marketplace will be fought not over price but over hearts and minds – and this is where we move into the realm of branding (Morgan, Pritchard and Pride 2002).

George Whitfield (2006) describes the importance of place branding in the following terms:

Branding is all about making the experience of a place as positive, memorable, different and exceptional as it can possibly be. A brand is a promise. To mean anything, a brand must be delivered and kept. The promise is not that visitors will find features of the destination physically present but that they will enjoy the experience of those physical attributes in a way that far exceeds their expectations. It is the experience, not the physical attributes and features, that fulfils a brand's promise. However spectacular the scenery, however famous the culture, however grand the built environment, the most important measure of any destination remains the reality of how visitors are treated and how they are made to feel. The most beautiful landscape in the world will not compensate for an inability to make a visitor or guest feel wanted, welcome and delighted.

Murdaugh (2005) recommends that, from a destination perspective, the destination marketing organisation (DMO) or convention and visitor bureau (CVB):

should craft a brand development programme that supports the destination through a fully co-ordinated and effective marketing communications plan. Branding steps should include the following, guided by research. First, define the unique selling points that separate your destination from the competition. Then produce and prioritise a series of crisp and clear motivational messages for consumers that address the positive visitor characteristics of the community. Next, craft a market 'positioning statement' that describes the destination and separates it from other competitors in the eyes of the potential customer. Finally, consider creating a new theme line and graphic logo for the destination that supports the recently created positioning statement.

Whitfield (2006) reinforces this point:

Ultimately, it is always the people that assume the responsibility for delivering the brand promise and who are consequently essential to the brand's development. Physical attributes like great scenery, renowned culture, iconic monuments and the dramas of history all play a part but cannot, in and of themselves, present the real experience of a place. However stunning their vistas, mountains don't smile back and it is how the visitor is treated that defines and differentiates one city, region or country most powerfully from the next.

And, of course, to this list he might have added 'venue'.

The life-cycle of a brand is such that it becomes fashionable after a successful launch, achieves peak sales as it becomes famous, but suffers from diminished appeal as it becomes too friendly. At this point, or just before it, the brand needs a revised image or the marketing of the brand needs re-inventing to keep the appeal of the brand fresh rather than over-familiar.

There is not space here to explore fully the theory and practice of destination branding, but it is worth emphasising that:

whatever branding proposition is used, it must have the potential to last, to grow old and to evolve in a long-term branding campaign, so it is essential to get it right. However, the point of differentiation must reflect a promise which can be delivered and which matches expectations. Good destination branding is, therefore, original and different but its originality and difference needs to be sustainable, believable and relevant (Morgan, Pritchard and Pride 2002).

Case Study 3.1 describes the key elements of a new brand identity for Vilnius Convention Bureau, in Lithuania's capital city, launched in 2012.

CASE STUDY 3.1 Vilnius Convention Bureau branding

Vilnius Convention Bureau's new and first-ever brand under the title 'Vilnius Open' was launched at the beginning of 2012. The aim of the new promotional identity is to promote Vilnius as a meeting and incentive destination more efficiently and to improve the competitiveness of Vilnius among Northern and Eastern European cities.

FIGURE 3.2 Vilnius Convention Bureau logo

It is important to note that 'Vilnius Open' is only an institutional brand, *not* a city (or destination) brand. Vilnius is still in the process of creating a common city brand which can be used to attract investments and talented people and to increase tourism to the city.

The need for a discrete Vilnius Convention Bureau brand grew steadily and became paramount as the Bureau started to develop its services and take on a more proactive marketing role. Being the main official body responsible for promoting Vilnius as a meeting destination, the Bureau recognised that it would not be sufficient simply to create a 'nice logo' for the institution. It needed to incorporate the right, easy-to-remember message that would be suitable for promoting Vilnius.

Vilnius Convention Bureau is a part of the Vilnius Tourist Information Centre and Convention Bureau – it does not act as a separate institution. The existing brand of Vilnius Tourism was, therefore, a good background for the new image of Vilnius Convention Bureau:

- *The brand message* – Vilnius is not just another capital city with good infrastructure and facilities for meetings. It is a city which has maintained its unique, small town feel and rich cultural identity that gives unforgettable positive emotions for all.
- *Image idea* – Since ancient times Vilnius has always been known as an open city for different nationalities, cultures and religions. Nowadays Vilnius is not only a hospitable and tolerant city. It is a modern and dynamic city always open to new ideas and experiences, new developments and business. With a strong academic community and smart, young and well-educated people (there are 14 universities in Vilnius for a population of 550,000), Vilnius is known as a city of advanced

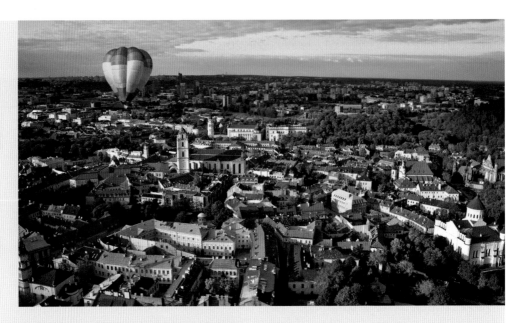

FIGURE 3.3 View of Vilnius, capital city of Lithuania

technologies and innovations. Modern Vilnius provides excellent opportunities and open platforms for knowledge interchange.

- *Open Vilnius* is not an aspiration: it is the reality of which the Bureau is proud and wishes to share with the world.
- *Image colours* – Using the same colours in Vilnius Open and in the logo of Vilnius Tourism, the city's character is communicated cohesively. Four colours symbolise the multiplicity and cultural flamboyance of Vilnius, the capital of Lithuania:
  - purple symbolises the royal origin of the city and its rich cultural heritage;
  - violet reflects the city's identity full of legends, mysteries and magic;
  - light green denotes the welcoming aura and green policy of the city;
  - orange signifies the dynamics and drive of the city.
- *Graphics* – The essence of the new image is both business-like and creative. The title 'Vilnius Convention Bureau' represents the institution itself. The dynamic and colourful letters O P E N express a lively and friendly city. Such a composition makes for a well-balanced whole.

The new promotional identity of Vilnius Convention Bureau has become an efficient marketing tool to highlight Vilnius as a meeting destination. All promotional material now carries the new branding. The Convention Bureau's website (www.vilinius-convention.lt) has also been completely redesigned to enhance its usability and navigability for clients.

This case study was compiled by Vita Žilinskaitė (Chief Convention Manager) and Jolanta Beniuliene (Director of Vilnius Tourist Information Centre and Convention Bureau).

Davidson and Rogers (2006) describe a variation on the theme of destination branding in the form of the BestCities Global Alliance (www.bestcities.net), a global collaboration comprising the convention bureaux of ten cities: Berlin, Cape Town, Copenhagen, Dubai, Edinburgh, Houston, Melbourne, San Juan, Singapore and Vancouver. The Alliance was launched with the notion that convention bureaux could learn from strategies successfully practised in other industries: the airline industry, financial institutions and automotive manufacturing all provide examples of the formation of global alliances which have become an essential business strategy for the long term. The Vision for BestCities is *'to be recognised globally for being innovative and setting and delivering the world's best convention bureau practices for the meetings industry'*. The BestCities Mission Statement says that it *'will deliver the world's best service experience for meeting planners and will help its partners earn more business as a result'*.

An alternative model of global partnership and branding is The Energy Cities Alliance, formed in 2007 and comprising four member destinations: Aberdeen, Abu Dhabi, Calgary and Perth (Australia). It is a partnership of organisations from the business events industry, all with a common focus on ensuring conferences and exhibitions held in their destinations are successful. The common factor is, of course, 'energy', which describes the oil and gas industries that thrive in these destinations. However, according to the Alliance website, energy *'also portrays the images of light, life and excitement that are the heart and soul of the cities'*. The Alliance is a partnership of some of the world's most dynamic and economically booming cities in the oil and gas and mining resources industries. The Alliance is aimed at supporting meeting planners who are looking to host successful world-class conferences. Recognising that these cities are global leaders in trade and investment, the Energy Cities Alliance is about sharing this success with associations and corporations involved with meetings and conventions. Further details at: www.energycitiesalliance.com

Other examples of global destination partnerships include:

- Future Convention Cities Initiative (Abu Dhabi, Durban, London, San Francisco, Seoul, Sydney and Toronto) – launched in 2011;
- Science Alliance (Adelaide, Daejeon, Hyderabad and Toulouse) – launched in 2012.

It is very difficult for an individual conference venue to market itself effectively by operating on its own (unless they are part of a major hotel chain, such as Marriott, Hilton or Radisson, where marketing is undertaken corporately to promote the brand – see below). Venues seeking to establish a market presence must contend with factors such as the scale of the competition (possibly several thousand other venues in the same country and many more worldwide), the substantial costs of marketing (both in human and financial resources), and the predisposition of buyers to buy location first. It is for these reasons that most venues work in partnership with the destination in which they are located to generate awareness and enquiries from potential clients. The venues build links with the appropriate destination marketing organisation, be this a convention and visitor bureau or conference office, an area or regional tourist board, and/or a national tourism organisation. Many venues are also members of marketing consortia (groupings of similar properties interested in the same types of clients) which give them a higher market profile and through which they engage in collaborative marketing activities. Consortia can also provide tangible business benefits such as bulk purchasing discounts, networking, benchmarking and training. Belonging to a consortium can also give a venue credibility in the eyes of the buyer. Examples of major consortia operating in the conference industry include:

- *Unique Venues* is a grouping of several thousand non-traditional meeting facilities and function rooms in the USA, Canada and the United Kingdom: colleges, universities, museums, mansions, cinemas or movie theatres, conference centres, entertainment venues, cruise ships, restaurants, business centres and others. In this case, the common theme is the individuality or uniqueness of the venues involved, with a particular focus on their ambiance, memorability, flexibility, technology and affordability. Unique Venues has administrative offices in Colorado, Pennsylvania, South Carolina (USA) and British Columbia (Canada). Further details: www.uniquevenues.com

- *Conference Centres of Excellence* is the UK's largest consortium of dedicated, specialist conference and training venues, with over 40 such venues in membership (as at March 2012). It was formed in 1992, with objectives to:

  - undertake joint marketing through pooling marketing resources;
  - share PR activity designed to enhance the image of management centres in membership;
  - investigate opportunities to market the centres in mainland Europe;
  - share information and expertise.

  One of the main aims of Conference Centres of Excellence has been to promote and market the unique benefits of conference venues that offer first-class facilities and professional standards (making comparison with other venues that do not dedicate staff or facilities to the business conference, meeting or training sector). Members are required to meet certain minimum criteria, which include '*actively seeking to attract conference, meeting or training events as their main Monday–Friday source of business*'. Criteria are also laid down to cover the standard of conference rooms, bedrooms and other facilities provided. Members are also expected to participate in the Consortium's booking referral system and to promote its hotline 'One Call'. Would-be member venues are required to submit to inspection by the Conference Centres of Excellence's membership committee before being accepted into membership. While users of the Conference Centres of Excellence venues are guaranteed to receive excellent service in quality surroundings, the individual nature

of the member properties offers contrasting atmospheres ranging from country houses in beautiful settings to purpose-built centres often attached to academia. Further information: www.cceonline.co.uk

- *The Westminster Collection* is unusual in being a grouping of venues located in one specific geographical location (the city of London). The Westminster Collection was formed in 2004 and is supported by Westminster City Council and London and Partners (the destination marketing organisation). At September 2011 the collective had 54 members representing the *'very best conference, meeting, exhibition and banqueting venues in Westminster'*, a London borough which attracts £10 billion of visitor expenditure per annum, 32 per cent of which can be attributed to business tourism. By forming a high-integrity, not-for-profit marketing collective that pro-actively promotes its members and services, 'brand Westminster' and each one of The Westminster Collection's members within it become stronger. Further information: www.thewestminstercollection.co.uk

Other examples of venue consortia include: Historic Conference Centres of Europe (www.hcce.com) and Leading Hotels of the World (www.lhw.com).

Branding of hotel venues

In the early 1990s Forte Hotels (now broken up and sold off among other hotel groups) pioneered a branded conference product when it launched 'Venue Guarantee' as a standard package available at conference hotels across the Forte Group. Subsequently most, if not all, the major hotel chains introduced their own conference brand, examples being: 'The Academy' (Holiday Inn), 'meeting@Novotel' (Accor) and 'Meeting Plan' (Thistle). However, the trend now seems to be for hotels to undertake promotions for the overall hotel brand rather than for a specific conference product.

Davidson and Rogers (2006) suggest that hotel chains' use of branding has

> brought them a considerable measure of brand equity in the form of the four major assets described by Aaker's (1991) model of consumer-based brand equity, as explored in Pike (2004):
>
> - Brand loyalty – repeat and referral custom, arising from the desire for a reduced risk of an unsatisfactory experience.
> - Brand awareness – the foundation of all sales activity. Awareness represents the strength of the brand's presence in the mind of the target. There is general agreement that planners' familiarity with hotels' meetings facilities brands has increased through repeated exposure and strong associations.
> - Perceived quality – there is little point in branding any product that is of poor or variable quality.

- *Brand associations – a brand association is anything 'linked' in memory to a brand. These associations are a combination of functional and affective attributes, of which some will represent key buying criteria. 'What is most critical is that brand associations are strong, favorable and unique, in that order' (Keller 2003, quoted in Pike 2004).*

In an article entitled 'Emotional Intelligence' (*Conference & Incentive Travel* magazine), Michael Wale (2006), Starwood Hotels' senior vice-president and regional director of operations for North West Europe, wrote:

To continue to grow and develop, Starwood must create differentiated world class hotel brands. We have moved away from price-based competition and bed wars and are focusing instead on emotionally relevant branding. Therefore, we have clearly defined each of our eight brands with meaningful positionings, to clarify to our guests, our suppliers and our associates (staff) what it feels like to be a Sheraton guest, what experience is part of the W Hotels ethos, etc. To create memorable and meaningful brands, guest service is the most powerful differentiator we have: we must sell on experience not a price point. We need to make the connection between branding and bonding with our guests, connecting with them and having an intellectual and emotional impact on them.

A key objective behind branding is, therefore, to convey to clients that they can expect ethical practices and quality service and facilities at the same high standards, no matter whether the hotel is in Belfast or Bombay, Jakarta or Buenos Aires. Having staged a successful conference at one hotel within the group, they can expect a similar outcome by using other hotels in the group. Branding is about building customer loyalty and increasing business retention because customers will have the confidence to keep their conferences and meetings within that particular group. Their own success is assured by the branded service and product which those hotels guarantee.

This approach has many strengths and, as all major chains have adopted branding, it seems to justify in financial returns the substantial investments required in venue and staff development. For customers it also has many attractions, yet it has one drawback: the very sameness of product can serve as a disincentive to its use. Conference organisers are constantly looking for somewhere new, somewhere a little different to make their event live long in the memory of their delegates. If delegates find that their surroundings and the type of service received are more or less identical at each conference, regardless of where it is being held, delegate perceptions of the event may not always be as favourable as the organiser would have wished.

Research among meeting planners and conference organisers in the UK often seems to show that, when they are selecting venues, they do not rank buying into a hotel or venue brand as being as important as good service, knowledgeable staff, dedicated

facilities, good quality food, good accommodation and good value. However, Nigel Cooper (2011), Divisional Managing Director of Motivcom Plc, writing in the *British Meetings and Events Industry Survey 2011–12*, says:

> If two venues are close by, of similar size and similar price, but one has a higher brand profile or position, I am inclined to believe that most buyers will go for the better brand. Ask yourself if you would buy own label beans if they were the same price as Heinz – some would, but a great many would not. I totally agree that price and location are the dominant factors (in venue selection), but I also think that brand might just be a little bit more influential than it appears (in the survey). I'm sure the owners of Four Seasons, Ritz-Carlton, Mercedes Benz and BMW would tell you not to underestimate the power of a good brand – even if they do have to discount occasionally.

In the author's experience, it is always important for an organiser to inspect a conference venue before booking because it is indeed the quality of staff and their service standards which is always one of the most decisive factors in venue selection and re-selection. No matter how strong the branding, and how good the staff training, the cloning of conference sales managers and banqueting co-ordinators has not yet been achieved (fortunately!). Individual personality and friendliness are often the crucial unique selling propositions (USPs), and these must be experienced at first hand.

The role of destination marketing organisations

'Location, location and location' is a commonly heard expression within the conference industry. When it comes to choosing a conference venue, the most important initial consideration for many event organisers is its location. This factor has often assumed greater importance than factors such as price, type of venue, quality of facilities, and proximity to tourist attractions. Buyers purchase location first and foremost.

Location can mean a number of different things: a town, a city, a county, a region, an island, a rural area, a city centre, even a country in the context of high profile international conventions. In some cases an organiser will express location in terms of *'proximity to an international airport'*, *'within a 20-mile radius of a certain town'*, *'somewhere between two named motorways'*.

Where the reference is to a discrete area, the term most frequently and aptly used to describe this area is 'a destination'. Gartrell (1994) defines destinations as follows:

> From the perspective of the consumer, destinations are perceived as those geographic areas that have attributes, features, attractions, and services that appeal to the prospective user. How the consumer defines a geographic area varies greatly and may or may not include specific geographic boundaries.

The key phrase here is 'areas . . . that appeal to the prospective user'. The marketing of conference venues and destinations must be driven by what makes sense to the consumer, in this case the conference organiser and the delegates he or she is seeking to attract. It cannot be undertaken successfully by the artificial 'destinations' which are sometimes created to satisfy bureaucratic or political whims.

Destination or 'place' marketing is undertaken at both a local level (city or county or even a region, for example) and a national level (by a national tourism organisation). This next section looks at a number of models of destination marketing organisations at both levels.

Local destination marketing

Reference has already been made to the role of convention and visitor bureaux in the formation of the conference industry (Chapter 1) and in the provision of services to that industry (Chapter 2).

In structure, conference or convention bureaux (variations on the name are to be found) are usually formed and financed as partnerships between public and private sector bodies. In the UK this can include local authorities/councils, chambers of commerce, local enterprise companies/agencies, hotels, venues, and other private sector suppliers. The bureaux are established as not-for-profit organisations, controlled by a management board, to fulfil a strategic marketing role and to be the 'official' voice of the destination they represent. In most cases the bureau is established at arm's length from the local authority or authorities which it represents, but in others (Telford and Shropshire Conferences or Conference Leeds, for example) the bureau remains an integral part of the local authority/local municipality structure.

Funding is derived from public sector contributions (usually the largest single source), private sector membership fees (members including venues of all kinds, accommodation providers, PCOs/DMCs, transport operators, audio-visual companies, and other kinds of suppliers), sponsorship, joint commercial activities with members, and, in some cases, commission which is charged to venue members on business placed. Some bureaux prefer to have a high membership fee which covers a full package of benefits and services to their members (with no or few hidden or extra charges). Other bureaux opt for a much lower membership fee which provides a core of benefits and then invite their members to buy into additional activities and services on a partnership basis. Both models have their strengths and weaknesses:

- *High Membership Fee* – For the bureau, the high membership fee, which can amount to as much as £5,000 per annum for large hotels, enables longer term planning to be undertaken with greater confidence, provided of course that the bureau can also achieve a high retention level amongst its membership. The bureau knows that it should receive a certain membership income in ensuing years and can plan its

activities and expenditure accordingly. The high membership fee model also means that the bureau is not having to go back to its members on a regular basis to seek their financial support for particular activities during the year, which can be time-consuming for the bureau and a cause of irritation to its members. The weakness, or perhaps more accurately the challenge, of this funding model is the need to guarantee significant returns to members for their high investment in the bureau.

- *Lower Membership Fee* – This would typically be a membership fee of several hundred pounds (£500–£1,000 is the normal range). For the bureau this can make it easier to 'sell' bureau membership to potential members because the initial outlay for them is much smaller. For bureau members there is greater flexibility in buying into those activities of the bureau (a stand at a trade exhibition or an entry in a piece of promotional print, for example) which are of most interest to them and which match their budgets. They do not have to buy into a full package of benefits, some of which they may not require. On the downside, there are significantly higher administrative costs with this model. It can also be argued with some justification that those members paying a lower membership fee may be less committed to the bureau than those who have paid a high fee and need to see the bureau succeed to justify their investment.

There is no right or wrong model. Each destination and the suppliers within it must agree what is appropriate for themselves and then develop and fine-tune the model in the light of experience. Bureaux are dynamic entities which must continue to evolve in the light of local circumstances, changes in market trends, the demands of clients and a multitude of other factors.

In the British Isles there are around 40 conference bureaux. Bureau is a generic term which, as has been seen, disguises a variety of models in terms of their staffing, funding and operations, although all share the same fundamental mission which, in the words of Gartrell (1994), is to:

> solicit and service conventions and other related group business and to engage in visitor promotions which generate overnight stays for a destination, thereby enhancing and developing the economic fabric of the community.

The concept of a convention and visitor bureau (CVB) is now widely adopted around the world. In the USA there is a longer tradition of CVBs (even relatively small towns have a CVB), with the world's first visitor and convention bureau, Detroit (or Metropolitan Detroit Convention and Visitor Bureau as it is now known) being established in 1896. In the USA bureaux are also funded differently, principally through a system of *hotel transient occupancy tax* (or bed tax) which means that hotel guests pay a tax which goes to the local city or town council, and can be added to the resources available to market the destination. In North America CVBs also play a prominent role at the centre of community life, being involved in a wide spectrum of community development issues which may impact on the future prosperity of the visitor industry.

Linda H. DiMario (2012), in an article entitled 'What do meeting planners really want?', provides some valuable insights into how DMOs and CVBs should address often unconsidered factors if they are to be successful in attracting meeting planners and conference organisers to their destination. She writes:

> So, while you must certainly focus on the identified 'decision-making factors', remember that there are three, often unspoken, emotional and psychological decision-making factors in play. Manage these factors as well as you manage the identified decision-making factors and you will improve the quality of your relationships, build credibility and polish your reputation and that of your destination. Addressing these factors will go a long way to help you make your case beyond hotel inventory, convention centre capacity or air lift. And you may just find that, delivering on these three meeting planner mantras, will sometimes trump the hard decision-making factors when all else is equal.

- *Make me look good.* I am only human. I want to do good work and be recognised for it. I want my boss, employees and attendees to think I am the master of what I do. I want them to appreciate the 'miracles' I pull off and the great deals I negotiate. I want you to respect me and the value of the business I am bringing to you. I want you to appreciate what I do. I want you to help me look good.
- *Make it easy.* I have too much to do and too little time. I need easy! Help me get my job done by minimising the number of contacts and contracts. Help me manage the destination's moving parts. Improve communication to decrease the potential for things to go wrong. Maximise services, connections, networks, and opportunities. Turn the destination on for me. Don't give me lists. Give me options.
- *Make it the right decision.* If I trust you and bring my meeting to your destination, you have to come through for me. Don't let me down. Be there when I need you. Be in a position to guarantee that what you promised can and will be delivered. Take responsibility to assure that everyone I need to perform is available, responsive and doing what they said they would do. Recognise us when we are in your city. Pull out all the stops to impress us.

Convention and visitor bureaux provide a range of services, many free of charge, to conference organisers and meeting planners. They aim to offer a 'one-stop' enquiry point for their destination, with impartial advice and assistance (although there is increasing debate over whether their role should now be focused on steering customers towards the suppliers best able to meet their needs, rather than seeking to represent all of their suppliers in a comprehensive, unbiased way). Such CVB services are likely to include some or all of the following:

Pre-booking the event

- Literature and website information.
- Venue location and selection advice.
- Availability checks.
- Rate negotiation.
- Provisional booking service.
- Familiarisation/inspection visits.
- Preparation of bid documents.
- Assistance with bid presentations to a selection committee/board.
- Assistance with civic hospitality and subvention requests.

Preparing for the event

- Block accommodation booking service for delegates.
- Co-ordination of the full range of support services including transportation, registration, translation, office support. In some cases these will be provided in conjunction with a professional conference organiser (PCO) or destination management company (DMC).
- Promotional and PR support to maximise delegate numbers and increase awareness of the event in the host destination.
- Supply of delegate information.
- Planning partner programmes, social programmes, and pre- and post-conference tours.
- Arranging contact with local conference service companies and event organisers.

During the event

- Provision of 'Welcome Desks' for delegates at major points of entry.
- Civic welcome and recognition, and possible financial or in-kind support and subvention.
- PR support.
- Provision of tourist information.

After the event

- Post-event evaluation and follow-up research.
- Consultancy support to the destination which will next host the conference.

Case Study 3.2 summarises the structure, objectives and activities of the São Paulo Convention and Visitors Bureau, Brazil, established in 1983.

National destination marketing

The role of national conference destination marketing is undertaken by a variety of bodies which differ from country to country. In some cases these bodies equate to a national convention bureau – and frequently contain the words 'convention bureau' in their name – and have many features in common with the city convention bureaux described earlier in this chapter. In other cases they are fully public sector organisations funded and administered within the central government structure.

Several examples of such national entities follow, highlighting their objectives and the marketing activities which they undertake to secure more conference and events business for their countries.

England: VisitEngland

VisitEngland is the national tourism organisation for England and incorporates a dedicated business visits and events team. The team, comprising three staff in London and an international network of ten staff (three offices in Europe, one in North America and one in India) is responsible for promoting England's corporate events, incentive and large convention product around the world. Strong support is also provided from the London head office's PR, marketing partnerships, international operations and research teams.

VisitEngland does not operate as a full service national convention bureau, but rather generates enquiries via its sales team which are disseminated to destinations across England for fulfilment. VisitEngland also provides sales and marketing platforms, such as exhibition presences (e.g. at IMEX-Frankfurt, EIBTM and IMEX-America) and outgoing missions, enabling English destinations and venues to promote themselves under an England umbrella. VisitEngland's role also includes the provision of updated news through its website and the dissemination of quarterly newsletters for buyers, and the chairing of several working groups looking to establish and share best practice in the winning and hosting of business events.

The geographical focus of marketing activity in the period up to 2012 was Western Europe and North America, but VisitEngland is extending its future reach to the BRIC countries (Brazil, Russia, India and China). The sector focus embraces agencies, corporates and associations – this includes the organisation of two to three England buyer events (usually dinners) each year for association buyers, including a very popular event in Brussels. Similar events have also been held in Geneva and Paris. Key economic sectors have been identified as:

- life sciences;
- energy;
- advanced engineering;
- creative industries;
- IT and telecommunications;
- environmental technologies.

VisitEngland does not operate a national conference ambassador programme but works closely with English cities to support their local ambassador programmes, wherever possible. However, at the time of writing (April 2012), more national ambassador events were being planned in order to harness the expertise available in England at a national level.

www.visitengland.com

Germany: German Convention Bureau

The German Convention Bureau (GCB) markets Germany as a destination for conventions, meetings, events and incentives both on a national and international level. The GCB was founded in 1973. It is a not-for-profit organisation and has around 200 members which include leading hotels, convention centres and destinations, car hire firms, event agencies and service providers to the German meetings and convention industry.

The GCB is an interface between organisers of meetings and conventions and suppliers from the German meetings and conference market. It offers advice and support for planning and organising events, and provides contacts and addresses. The GCB was established to market Germany as a conference location and to provide impartial advice and suggestions to meeting planners concerning facilities, sites, accommodation, and programmes in Germany. It is based in Frankfurt with 13 staff and also has an overseas office in New York.

The GCB arranges conference services in Germany for clients around the world. It also works in close co-operation with German representatives of international associations and organisations and with meeting planners of associations, agencies and companies from abroad. Its website features an online search facility for meeting venues, a newsletter, a Germany guide and more.

The GCB is also the strategic partner with IMEX, the '*worldwide exhibition for incentive travel, meetings and events*', held in Frankfurt each spring.

Contact details: German Convention Bureau e.V., Münchener Strasse 48, 60329 Frankfurt/Main, Germany. Telephone: +49 (0)69 24 29 30 0; fax: +49 (0)69 24 29 30 26; email: info@gcb.de; website: www.germany-meetings.com

Malaysia: Malaysia Convention and Exhibition Bureau

The Malaysia Convention and Exhibition Bureau (MyCEB) was established by the Ministry of Tourism Malaysia to further strengthen the country's business events brand and to position the country as one of the world's leading international meetings, incentives, conventions and exhibitions (MICE) destinations. A non-profit organisation, MyCEB serves as a one-stop centre to assist meeting and event planners to bid for and to stage regional and international business events in Malaysia and to act as a conduit for national product development. MyCEB works closely with Tourism Malaysia offices worldwide to extend its services globally.

In June 2011 MyCEB launched a specialist unit known as the International Events Unit (IEU) which focuses on identifying and supporting international event bids including sports, art and culture and lifestyle events. Besides identifying and supporting bids by Malaysian event organisers to secure events for Malaysia, the IEU is responsible for evaluating and assisting home-grown and hosted events to maximise the potential for international publicity and attendances through strategic alliances. This includes identifying and supporting 'cluster' events designed to strengthen the global appeal of existing major events. A specific set of criteria has been set up to evaluate a proposed event on its direct and indirect economic value and the level of support required in order to maximise overall economic value. The criteria include:

- number of international participants;
- length of stay;
- publicity value;
- other qualitative factors including opportunities to package and promote extended stays and benefits for the business and local community.

The IEU will collaborate with various private and government entities including the Ministry of Tourism, Ministry of Youth and Sports, and Ministry of Culture, Arts and Heritage to attract and develop international events in Malaysia.

www.myceb.com.my

Thailand: Thailand Convention and Exhibition Bureau

In October 2011 a marketing campaign was launched by the Thailand Convention and Exhibition Bureau (TCEB) as part of a five-year strategic marketing and events plan with the aim of raising the standard and number of trade shows in the country. Entitled 'The Next Best Shows' initiative, the plan sought to achieve a 60 per cent increase in overseas visitors and generate revenues of 14,000 million baht by the time the campaign ended in 2014. The Next Best Shows aimed to retain existing international trade fairs held in Thailand, as well as to elevate the standard of fairs to become competitive at the ASEAN Economic Community level. TCEB had a budget of 85 million baht (approximately £1.75 million) to support the three-year project by subsidising trade fairs that meet the required criteria. To be eligible for the benefits that the campaign provided, an applying trade fair was required to meet the following criteria:

- be held three times consecutively in Thailand and committed to continue in Thailand for the next three editions;

- foreign visitors should represent at least 5 per cent of total visitors;
- occupy at least 4,000 m² of exhibition space;
- implement an international registration system in accordance with global exhibition association UFI's instructions.

www.tceb.or.th

Event agency marketing activity

Corporate and association clients are spoilt for choice when it comes to selecting an event management agency, and, depending on their own culture they may select from a range that spans large multi-discipline companies to niche independents.

At one time, agency–client relationships were built on mutual trust and tended to remain loyal for years on end, until one of the personalities in the partnership left the business and changed the dynamics of that relationship. But from the late nineties onwards, the larger corporate organisations have progressively relied upon their internal Procurement departments to control the purchasing of marketing services – including those of event management agencies.

Today, agencies have to go through rigorous pitch processes to be admitted onto a 'preferred supplier' roster, and even then there is no guarantee that work will be forthcoming. In many cases agencies will be required to re-pitch for individual projects, rather than assume that the client account belongs exclusively to them.

So how do agencies reach the hallowed status of preferred supplier? What must they do to attract the attention of client prospects and earn the opportunity to pitch for their business?

Public relations

Corporate clients are pretty much impervious to cold calling, and agencies must rely on the more subtle tactics of marketing to reach the consciousness of their client prospects. It will almost certainly be their reputation – as a creative business with a sound track record and solid financial base – that will earn them that vital RFP (request for proposal).

Public relations is, therefore, the principal route to gaining that reputation, and most if not all event management agencies will at some time issue press releases, case studies and comment for inclusion in the relevant media. The larger agencies generally retain external PR consultancies because few of them have their own in-house marketing departments. There are a few early exceptions to this and as the consolidation trend grows – with small agencies being acquired by larger groups – it is likely that the bigger players will progressively develop their own in-house resource.

Word-of-mouth recommendation is surprisingly important in the events industry. Business can be won through pre-existing personal connections: executives from client organisations may leave to work for 'new' companies and recommend their agency to their Procurement department. It is also not unknown for agency staff to leave and take jobs in the corporate sector, again becoming overnight client prospects in their own right. The smarter agencies therefore take great pains to maintain friendly relationships with *anyone* who could potentially recommend them to a client prospect.

Awards entry

A specialised form of PR, entry to industry awards can yield phenomenal benefits – for those agencies that win. In addition to third-party endorsement by a jury of their peers (and potential clients!), the winners are able to publicise their success on their website, on email signatures, as part of ongoing PR activity and within 'creds' presentations – that initial part of the pitch process for which the agency is required to sell themselves to the client prospect. All of the leading agencies take awards entry very seriously indeed, and commit substantial resource to preparing their entries to the highest possible standard.

Sponsorship

Agencies hardly ever advertise – those that do are invariably large companies with a one-off tactical message to convey – such as a rebranding exercise, or a merger. Occasionally trade magazines are successful in persuading agencies to buy advertising space as part of an 'advertorial' package, but the decision to purchase tends to be reluctant rather than strategic.

One way to combine the benefits of advertising and PR, however, is for a company to invest in sponsorship. This may be via the purchase of an awards package: the agency sponsors a category at an awards dinner and gains the benefit of printed recognition in the programme, tickets to attend the event as well as a spot-lit and photographed personal appearance on-stage. While this represents an expensive outlay, those agencies that have invested in it generally consider it a good return on their investment.

Many agencies also sponsor charitable activity of one kind or another – and enjoy the spin-off marketing benefit of the ensuing media coverage.

Exhibitions

Agencies have a wary relationship with trade exhibitions – knowing that they are more likely to be sold *to* by their own suppliers while they strive to catch the attention of a rare passing client prospect. Some have tried exhibiting at trade shows once or twice, but few are regular participants. There is, however, an alternative exhibition format that

promises a richer client-facing experience. Broad-spectrum marketing 'forums' are held on-board cruise ships or similar luxury locations. Here the invited client guests are literally a captive audience and agencies have a two-day window of opportunity to set out their stall in the absence of either suppliers or competitors. These are fiendishly expensive exercises, however, and are taken up by only a small minority of wealthy agencies.

Electronic communications

Until recently, many agencies toyed with the publication of newsletters, which were distributed to their client (and client prospect) database. These still exist in some quarters, and over the last five to ten years have been transferred to the electronic medium of e-newsletters. However, the frenetic and unpredictable lifestyle of the average events agency, coupled with the scarcity of dedicated marketing staff, has rendered these difficult to maintain on a regular basis. The ascendancy of social media has also introduced a more flexible and immediate way of communicating company news.

Online marketing

At the time of writing (June 2012), the events industry is reaching a tipping point in terms of social media marketing. For the business-to-business sector, Facebook and Twitter are still treated with an element of suspicion, although those agencies that began carefully using these media for staff recruitment or supplier research are gaining confidence and thinking carefully about how to use social media as a serious communication tool. Many agencies are managing their corporate identity and those of their staff on LinkedIn. Meanwhile, the meteoric advance of YouTube and Pinterest, the content sharing service for images, videos and other objects, has provided welcome outlets for agencies to showcase their work.

The shape of marketing to come

Marketing will continue to transfer online, and agencies will seize the opportunity to blog, tweet and post details of their activities, with the primary objective of achieving visibility and talkability in a highly dynamic space. Their secondary objective will be to drive visitors to their websites – which themselves will become increasingly interactive and content-rich. Those in the vanguard of this revolution are seeing the benefits of a virtuous circle, in which online communications are picked up, tracked and passed on by influencers, to ultimately reach the notice of those coveted client prospects.

The text above on event agency marketing activity was written by Sarah Webster, of Webster Wright Marketing Communications (www.wwmc.biz), a specialist PR and communications consultancy operating in the business events sector.

Marketing consortia are not restricted to destinations and venues. There are also examples of PCO consortia, such as:

- *INCON* is a dynamic partnership of leading companies providing conference and event management by combining global presence and local expertise. Each of the INCON Partners is a prominent professional conference organiser and destination management company with expertise in their own country. In March 2012 INCON had ten Partner companies operating in 150 destinations and employing 3,000 staff. Clients are increasingly setting global standards with local delivery and that is what INCON seeks to offer. INCON has substantial purchasing power and organises around 10,000 projects annually, serves three million delegates, procures five million hotel bednights, and manages budgets in excess of one billion euros (www.incon-pco.com).
- *The World PCO Alliance* had 15 PCO companies in membership (June 2011) covering all six continents. The Alliance was created to help associations organise effective meetings throughout the globe by capitalising on the efficiency of consolidating conference and event services within one network (www.worldpco.org).

CASE STUDY 3.2 São Paulo Convention and Visitors Bureau, Brazil

São Paulo: the destination

The city of São Paulo is also capital of the Brazilian State of São Paulo, a state with an Atlantic Ocean coastline of over 600 kilometres and a myriad of beautiful beaches. Around one hour's travel inland from the coast, São Paulo the city is the largest industrial hub in Brazil and is also recognised worldwide as the financial capital of Latin America. Home to some of the leading educational, technology and research centres in Latin America, São Paulo is also home to eight of the ten largest technology companies in the country. The University of São Paulo is the largest in Brazil and the third largest in Latin America.

The 'city that never stops' hosts over 90,000 events a year, attracts more than 12 million visitors spending R$8 billion per year (approximately £3 billion or US$5 billion). It can offer well located and equipped convention centres, world-class hotels (in total there are some 450 hotels and 42,000 bedrooms), excellent gastronomy, first-world infrastructure, lots of culture, musicals and shows and attractions for all budgets and tastes.

An article in *Travel and Tourism World* magazine (November 2011) describes São Paulo as:

> a truly cosmopolitan city. It is a centre of art and culture dotted with museums, cultural complexes, ancient churches, splendid monuments, exhibition halls, etc.

FIGURE 3.4 Ponte Estaiada and the São Paulo skyline (photographer Andre Stefano; photograph courtesy of SPCVB)

If you are a nature lover, you will enjoy yourself thoroughly as you explore the waterfalls, rivers, hills, mineral water springs, natural parks, caves, rainforests and beaches of São Paulo.

In convention terms, the city has ten major convention centres, although it can still be challenging to accommodate a large congress of, say, 3,000 participants due to high occupancy by exhibitions and trade fairs. São Paulo stages 75 per cent of all the exhibitions taking place in Brazil, including major events such as: 'Salão do Auto-móvel' (Motor Show) attracting an estimated 750,000 visitors; 'Francal' (59,000 visitors) and 'Couromoda' (90,000) (both of these shows are related to leather products, shoes and bags); 'Hospitalar' (90,000, hospital equipment). The ideal size of convention, because of such high demand factors, is up to 1,000 delegates, allowing major event hotels to be used as well as purpose-built centres.

São Paulo Convention and Visitors Bureau (SPCVB)

São Paulo Convention and Visitors Bureau (SPCVB) was founded in 1983 and is one of 120 convention and visitor bureaux in Brazil. It is a not-for-profit organisation, financed by the private sector, and established within the destination marketing organisation Visit São Paulo (Visite São Paulo in Portuguese). Its mission is to promote, attract and generate events in order to increase the flow of visitors to São Paulo and to its 25 partner destinations which include Barueri, ABC region, Brotas, Guarulhos, Ilhabela, Itapecerica da Serra, Itu, Mogi das Cruzes, Osasco and São Roque, São Sebastião and more.

SPCVB objectives, membership, funding and services

The main objectives of SPCVB are:

- to expand the number of visitors and the time they spend in São Paulo;
- to increase business and consumer markets through tourism activity, not only generating more events for the city but also helping to improve service quality levels for visitors (for example, through training programmes);
- to promote, attract and support events that take place in São Paulo city and nearby destinations.

It can be seen from the above that, while the main focus for SPCVB is on destination marketing, it also has an involvement in destination management, seeking ways of continually improving the destination product and thus enhancing the visitor experience.

The SPCVB has approximately 600 members, covering every segment of the tourism industry ensuring that companies, tourists and events are always welcome. Hotels are the key partners followed by PCOs and travel agencies.

The SPCVB does not charge for the services it provides. Funding for the SPCVB comes from its members, through a monthly membership fee and an optional hotel room tax. The room tax payments made by hotel guests are reinvested back into SPCVB, a practice used in hundreds of cities worldwide. SPCVB is a not-for-profit entity, legally termed Fundaçao 25 de Janeiro, financed by its private sector members. Some of the members pay a fixed monthly membership fee, but hotels do not pay a membership fee nor do certain not-for-profit associations or public bodies. However, the major part of SPCVB's income (around 90 per cent) comes from an optional room tax, collected by hotels from guest contributions and charged at 1 per cent of the bedroom rate. Due to the challenge of charging an optional tax, SPCVB has created other sources of revenue through partnerships with private companies and the provision of advertising opportunities on the SPCVB website. The annual operational budget is US$3 million.

Of about 2,000 major events taking place in the city each year (the 2011 total of 1,978 registered events represented an increase of 13.5 per cent compared with 2010), SPCVB has an involvement in approximately 30 per cent (510 such events in 2011). Such involvement includes event bidding, event marketing (to maximise attendance), consultancy advice on venue selection, social programme activities and similar, and the provision of delegate materials.

SPCVB structure and management

SPCVB is managed by an Executive Board which is chaired by an elected President and is comprised of 11 board members each representing a specific segment of the business events industry. None of them are paid for their time and contributions. The Board membership includes a representative from Embratur, Brazil's national tourism organisation.

The staff comprises a CEO – Toni Sando – five managers (National Events Manager, International Events Manager, Relationship Manager, Market Relations Manager, and Administrative-Financial Manager), and approximately 20 other employees. A staff structure covering senior roles is shown at Figure 3.5.

On an annual basis, managers meet to review how successful they have been in achieving the objectives of the past year and to share their objectives for the year

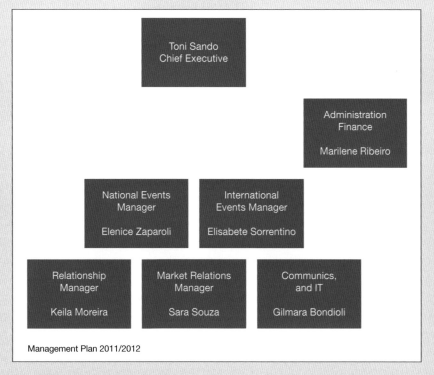

FIGURE 3.5 SPCVB senior management team

ahead. The objectives consist of five goals relevant to each manager's specific job responsibilities. Once these objectives have been approved by the Senior Management Team, each Department works to meet them and a review meeting is held every three months to update colleagues on the progress made.

SPCVB's relationship with the city municipality and key stakeholders

SPCVB collaborates with the official São Paulo Tourist Office (www.spturis.com) through a form of public–private partnership arrangement. They work together in partnership on several projects without reliance on government funds, and share certain costs (e.g. the cost of stands at trade exhibitions, or the production of marketing materials which can be used in both the business and leisure markets).

The official Tourist Office is responsible for sporting and other big events taking place in the city, such as Formula 1 motor racing, Indy, and the Gay Parade. It also develops and oversees public tourism policies.

SPCVB is mainly focused on attracting association conferences and events, and is in charge of the production of bid documentation for such events. SPCVB participates in international trade fairs dedicated to the business events sector, and the city Tourism Office is invited to attend with them, always exhibiting as part of the Embratur stand.

The 'DestinoSP' Project

An innovative feature of São Paulo's destination management activity is based around The 'DestinoSP' Project, in which São Paulo has been divided into five geographical areas (or mini-destinations) to create five discrete and largely self-contained exhibition, convention and hotel zones. This was initially driven by Berrini, a relatively new financial area in the south of the city which enjoys a strong concentration of multinational companies, laboratories and banks, attracting many hotels including some international brands such as Hilton, Hyatt and WTC. The hotels formed a committee to discuss ways of promoting themselves and the Berrini area. With assistance and advice from SPCVB, marketing collateral was produced to promote the hotels with conference and event space, and to include details of all the other hotels in Berrini as well as a schedule of the main events taking place in the zone. This proved so successful that other hotels in other parts of the city wanted to create similar geographic marketing entities. One of the outcomes has been the production of a map of the São Paulo conurbation clearly demarcating the five zones. The map has been complemented by an electronic search tool, developed by SPTURIS, for use by meeting planners based on this strategic geographic division (www.cidadesaopaulo. com/mice). The 'DestinoSP' Project is an excellent example of public and private sector partnership leading to innovative solutions for clients and customers, as well

FIGURE 3.6 São Paulo's 'DestinoSP' Project and the 5-destinations map

as satisfying the varying, and sometimes conflicting, needs of suppliers. Figure 3.6 shows the launch of São Paulo's unique 5-destinations map.

Part of this consolidation strategy also includes the regular three-monthly publication, in printed and digital formats, of an event schedule giving details of events taking place in the city during the year, designed to help organisers and meeting planners find the best locations and dates for organising their own events.

Target markets, marketing activity and staff development programmes

São Paulo is the largest business centre in Brazil and Latin America. The city attracts the most important trade fairs and congresses, in addition to major sporting and cultural events.

The business sectors generating most congress activity in 2011 were medicine (26 per cent); technical-scientific (20.3 per cent – this group includes engineering, marketing, human resources, economics and law); and science, technology and communication (17.9 per cent – this covers communications and sound, audio-visual, logistics, industry, telecommunications, informatics, physical sciences, mathematics, construction, equipment and materials, telecommunications and technology).

Table 3.2 illustrates the number of major association congress bid documents compiled and sent to clients in 2011, both for national events and for international events. It also provides an indication of the economic impact of such events in 2011, showing the number of participants and the number of bednights generated for São Paulo's hotels. During 2011, SPCVB's National and International Events Departments contacted more than 600 associations which had the potential to bring future events to the city.

Table 3.2 SPCVB bids					
Bids for National Events	Participants at National Events	Bednights Generated by National Events	Bids for International Events	Participants at International Events	Bednights Generated by International Events
23	3,909,828	263,432	25	27,974	37,792

Source: SPCVB

SPCVB invests 60 per cent of its budget in specialist professionals working intensively on research, bidding processes, monitoring and supporting events. Added to this, the resources offered by the Municipal Council of Tourism, through the City Hall, help to promote the city at international trade fairs, printing or producing promotional materials (folders, banners, videos, etc.) and other activities that are carried out in a public–private partnership.

This resource has also facilitated the development of a series of training programmes, known as 'Programa Bem Receber' (a 'Welcome Programme') focused on employees of associated companies to develop their skills in welcoming visitors to the city. This hospitality programme has trained over four thousand professionals to improve the city's services to visitors.

The strategy for 2012 and 2013 is based on three pillars: attracting events, marketing and management, with integration between the areas, working in technical (internal) committees, more participation in trade events and the consolidation of partnerships with other cities in the State of São Paulo, along with SPCVB's associates and partners.

Conference ambassador programme

São Paulo has developed an interesting approach to conference ambassador programmes. The International Events Manager at SPCVB recruited students at the University of São Paulo to track ICCA events that had taken place at the University itself (after it was realised that a number of international events had been held there without any external promotion). The students' role was broadened to inform all of the University's 135 departments (on the main campus) of the role of SPCVB and its support for bringing international events to the city. The research team found that it was possible to obtain a list of lecturers' overseas trips to attend international events, and these lecturers could be contacted about bidding to bring these events to São Paulo. While SPCVB no longer works in this way with students, the project did lead to the production of a written account of the project (known as 'Projeto Jovens Embaixadores' or 'Young Ambassadors Project – September/December 2008), and it offers a potential alternative model for ambassador programme development to other destinations.

In 2012 the information gathered from the initial University research project was still being used to maintain contact with key individuals identified in the original project. Discussions are also underway with Tourism Faculty lecturers at the University to find ways of incorporating the ambassador programme as a current course study topic.

Marketing awards

The marketing achievements of SPCVB have been recognised by prestigious awarding bodies, with accolades including: 'Best Marketing Award' and 'Top Marketing Award'. Both of these were awarded for its marketing strategy entitled 'Integration and Mobilisation', based around the three integrated themes of 'capture, empower and communicate' (in Portuguese the three words start with 'C': captar, capacitar e comunicar), involving the whole production chain.

This case study was compiled with the assistance of Elisabete Sorrentino, SPCVB International Events Manager (www.visitesaopaulo.com).

SUMMARY

- A focus on the needs of customers should drive all marketing activity, which has to be planned through the specific application of marketing principles and strategy to the conference and business events sector.
- The identification, recruitment and building of productive relationships with customers and clients is an essential factor in the success of all conference businesses, and needs to be undertaken continually and professionally.
- An understanding of branding principles underpins many aspects of marketing activity, for destinations, for event venues, and for intermediaries and event agencies.
- Destination marketing is undertaken by convention bureaux and conference offices/ desks which involve the public and private sectors in collaborative partnerships. The structures, funding and activities of such organisations vary from destination to destination, although two basic models are apparent.
- The activities of city or local area convention bureaux are complemented in many countries by national tourism and conference organisations.
- Some conference venues join marketing consortia, which comprise venues with similar characteristics, in order to develop a stronger profile in the marketplace.
- Event management agencies use a range of marketing tools (sponsorship, awards, online, etc.) to develop and retain their client base, but are also required to go through rigorous tendering procedures and gain a place on 'preferred supplier rosters' if they are to be successful in persuading procurement departments to contract them for their events.

REVIEW AND DISCUSSION QUESTIONS

1 Undertake a 'SWOT' analysis of two conference destinations, summarising the strengths, weaknesses, opportunities and threats for each. Use the analysis to propose the most suitable target markets for both destinations.

2 Critically review the reasons for branding any kind of product and discuss how and why conference destinations are increasingly being branded, including an analysis of the role of convention bureaux in the branding process.

3 Convention bureaux constantly need to demonstrate that they add measurable value to their many stakeholders. Discuss the methods most commonly used by them to show that they are working effectively in their local communities.

4 Analyse the current economic, technological, demographic and socio-cultural changes in the marketing environment to which conference venues must adapt in order to market themselves successfully.

5 Assess the impacts of procurement departments on the bidding and tendering process for conferences. What benefits are brought to the process by procurement professionals, and what are the dis-benefits? Review also how this has affected event management agencies and their relationships with their clients.

REFERENCES

Aaker, D. (1991) *Managing Brand Equity*, Free Press

Cooper, C., Fletcher, J., Gilbert, D. and Wanhill, S. (1993) *Tourism Principles and Practice*, Longman

Cooper, N. (2011) 'No brand awareness? I don't believe it', in CAT, *British Meetings and Events Industry Survey 2011–12*, CAT Publications, available at www.meetpie.com

Davidson, R. and Rogers, T. (2006) *Marketing Destinations and Venues for Conferences, Conventions and Business Events*, Butterworth-Heinemann/Routledge

De Chernatony, L. and McDonald, M. (1998) *Creating Powerful Brands*, Butterworth-Heinemann

DiMario, L. H. (2012) 'What Do Meeting Planners Really Want?', in her own e-newsletter (May), available at www.dimarioandassociates.com

Doyle, P. (1989) 'Building Successful Brands: The Strategic Options', *Journal of Marketing Management*, 5 (1)

Gartrell, R. (1991) 'Strategic Partnerships for Convention Planning: The Role of Convention and Visitor Bureaus in Convention Management', *International Journal of Hospitality Management*, 10 (2)

—— (1994) *Destination Marketing for Convention and Visitor Bureaus*, Kendall Hunt

GCMB (2006) 'Glasgow: Scotland with Style – The City Brand', brochure, Glasgow City Marketing Bureau

Hankinson, G. (2001) 'Location Branding: A Study of the Branding Practices of 12 English Cities', *Journal of Brand Management*, 9 (2) 127–142; doi:10.1057/palgrave.bm.2540060 (accessed 12 September 2012)

Interbrand (1990) *Brands: An International Review*, Mercury Books

Morgan, R., Pritchard, A. and Pride, R. (2002) *Destination Branding*, Butterworth-Heinemann

Murdaugh, M. (2005) *Fundamentals of Destination Management and Marketing*, Educational Institute of the American Hotel and Lodging Association/International Association of Convention and Visitor Bureaus

Pike, S. (2004) *Destination Marketing Organizations*, Elsevier

Wale, M. (2006) 'Emotional Intelligence', *Conference & Incentive Travel* magazine (October), available at www.citmagazine.com

Whitfield, G. (2006) Series of articles on branding (various titles), in *DMO World*, available at www.frontlinecommunication.co.uk/dmoworld

FURTHER READING

Ford, R. and Peeper, W. (2008) *Managing Destination Marketing Organizations: The Tasks, Roles and Responsibilities of the Convention and Visitors Bureau*, ForPer Publications

ADME (2011) *Best Practice in Destination Management*, Association of Destination Management Executives

CHAPTER

4

Winning conference business: 2

This chapter looks at:

- web marketing
- the use of social media
- familiarisation visits, workshops and showcases
- conference ambassador programmes
- event bidding and tendering
- subvention and bid support practices

It includes case studies on:

- 'Scotland Means Business' event
- Seoul Convention Bureau's three-step social media campaign in destination marketing
- the tendering and selection process for the congress of the World Federation of Societies of Intensive and Critical Care Medicine

www.routledge.com/cw/rogers

LEARNING OUTCOMES

On completion of this chapter, you should be able to:

*   appreciate the factors underpinning successful website design and web marketing;
*   understand the relevance and importance of social media to conventions and business events;
*   describe the creative and resource investments needed to attract buyers to familiarisation visits and destination/venue showcases and the returns that can be achieved;
*   explain the role of conference ambassador programmes in securing new association conference business and enhancing destination partnerships;
*   understand the critical importance of the tendering and bidding process in securing conference business and the need for the highest levels of professionalism in compiling and presenting event bids;
*   assess the role and range of subvention practices in winning association conference business.

Introduction

Chapter 3 explored the key marketing principles and practices which should guide organisations in the conference industry as they seek to develop their businesses, retain customers and increase their market share. This chapter looks in detail at some of the key technology tools available for winning more business, especially the Internet and the opportunities afforded by social media. It also examines a number of innovative approaches to marketing activities such as re-styled familiarisation visits and showcases, and conference ambassador programmes. It concludes with an in-depth appraisal of event bidding and tendering practices and the growing importance of subvention.

Historically, the various players in the conference industry have relied heavily on many of the more traditional sales and marketing tools to secure new business and to retain existing business. Davidson and Rogers (2006) describe the use of both above-the-line and below-the-line promotional tools, ranging from printed and electronic guides, printed and e-newsletters, public relations, advertising, to exhibiting, running 'educationals', using e-blasts, and others. Many of these tools still have an important role to play. However, the explosion in Internet and social media usage has driven many new approaches and initiatives. At the same time, ever more creativity is needed in the promotion and organisation of familiarisation trips (educationals) in order to persuade the hard-pressed

buyer to leave his or her desk. The first decade of the twenty-first century also witnessed a growing recognition of the value of conference ambassador programmes as a vehicle for securing more national and international association conventions and congresses. Yet, however good and innovative these new tools and approaches may be, they are often doomed to fail if, at the final hurdle, the bid or proposal to host and/or manage a conference is not assembled attractively and delivered professionally – and it may also need the carrot of subvention support to ensure its success.

This chapter will, therefore, focus on these newer approaches and highlight examples of best practice from event agencies, event venues and event destinations, as they seek to compete effectively and win their share of the conference and meetings market.

Web marketing

The Internet is now well established as a prime source of information and services for conference organisers and meeting planners. It is, therefore, vital for destinations, venues and other service suppliers within the sector to ensure that they have a winning website. The ideas and tips for achieving this, set out below, are supplied by two specialists in Internet marketing: Philip Cooke, The Destination Marketing Group (www.thedmg.co.uk) and Lesley Pritchard, Frontline Communication (www.frontlinecommunication.co.uk).

Site design/structure

The graphic design element of a website should be kept relatively clean and uncluttered. This does not mean that a site has to look plain or boring, but ensures that the focus is enabling users to find information, and the design should not overshadow structure or content. Good quality photography of a venue or destination, perhaps including a virtual tour, can also assist an organiser to assess suitability, while event agencies could include quality images of successful events staged to impress potential clients.

There are many established and emerging technologies, including JavaScript, Flash, movie files, html5, etc. that can be used to enhance a website's design but it is important to remember that the site must cater for visitors who will be using a broad range of different browsers and devices.

It should also be recognised that, increasingly, visitors to websites will be using 'untethered' devices i.e. Blackberries and iPhones, etc. and so the site's design and user-friendliness should also work on smartphones and other small screen devices. Large size header graphics and images look great on a large screen, but not so good on small screens, so consider creating a dedicated mobile website to run in parallel with the main site.

Good sites are built to W3C (World Wide Web Consortium) standards and all pages should validate – see http://validator.w3.org/ for more information. CSS (Cascading Style

Sheets) should also be used to provide a uniform look and feel throughout the site and also to enhance search engine visibility and user accessibility.

Site architecture/navigation

Finding key information on a site should not be an intellectual or time-consuming challenge. It is important to have a consistent header and navigation system throughout the site and, for larger sites, a 'breadcrumb navigation' can be used to ensure that visitors can always tell which content tier they are on.

First level navigation should readily identify the major sections of the site and ensure users know where to find the information they require. As a basic rule, the user should be able to get where they want to be within 'two clicks'.

Site content

Content should be uppermost in any site. If the site is to promote a conference venue, all of the key features of the venue should be included, such as:

- venue name and geographical location;
- room details, dimensions and capacities;
- where appropriate, overnight accommodation capacities and options;
- additional services: catering, technical, concierge services, security;
- technical specifications and floor plans in a downloadable format;
- contact details, including formal quotation form(s) or request for proposal (RFP) documentation.

Other useful content could include case studies providing independent testimonials from satisfied customers; event planning tools; destination information such as how to get there (with suitable maps in printable formats), and links to local hotels, restaurants and recreational facilities.

Site copy

One of the most frequently overlooked and badly executed features of a website is the text. Copywriting for the web is a different discipline from print copywriting. Years of research and experience have shown that website surfers generally do not read lengthy copy. In fact, they 'scan' the page looking for relevant information.

The copy should be purpose-written, with short words, short sentences and short paragraphs. Avoid large blocks of text and use plenty of bullet points and dialogue boxes, etc.

The tone should be appropriate to the business and understood by the target market. Jargon should be avoided, and the main copy should focus on what the venue or destination or supplier can do for conference organisers and clients.

Search engine visibility is greatly enhanced by using 'key-word rich' copy and by ensuring that the text includes the same words and industry terms that a prospect would enter into Google etc. and the site's own search engine. There are a number of free online tools available, including one by Google, which reveal the most popular search terms currently being used and assess the level of competition i.e. how many other websites are also using these key words in their content.

It is also important that any key search terms that are included appear both within the page content and are also hidden within the page code i.e. metadata.

Content weighting

Many sites contain a wealth of useful information but unfortunately the site is not 'weighted'. The most important content in the site should be ranked accordingly. The site is, after all, about selling a venue or destination's or supplier's services and facilities.

A clear hierarchy of headings should be used throughout the text to ensure that the most important content appears closer to the top of each page. This is also a useful way of ensuring accurate search engine indexing.

Domain choice

A good choice of domain name can make a big difference. A simple and intuitive domain ensures that prospective clients can find the site without too much trouble, be that in a search engine or simply by recollection from promotional literature. In particular, a well-chosen domain name containing keywords that should be found if used in a search will dramatically impact on the site's search engine ranking. Domain names are relatively inexpensive and making multiple domain name purchases can prove beneficial when used as part of a specific promotional campaign.

Watch out, too, for the use of new types of top level domains such as .travel, etc.

Search engine optimisation (SEO)

Search engine optimisation (often abbreviated to SEO) should be a key criterion for any web development brief. The site should be optimised for key words, be registered with all major search engines and directories and be open to search engine spiders:

- Spiders, also known as 'bots', are the automated programs that search engines use to crawl the web and index its content. For example, Google's spider (or bot) is known as Googlebot (www.google.com/support/webmasters/bin/topic.py?topic=8843) and it is the program used by Google to look at billions of pages on the web and automatically retrieve their content before adding Google's search index for use by the public.

Attempting to establish or enhance a ranking retrospectively is much harder. A good statistics package, such as Google Analytics, will provide profile information on a site's visitors and highlight any areas that need adjusting – for instance, the choice of key words, the success, or otherwise, of specific campaign landing pages, navigation routes around the site, etc.

Social media

Many organisations now use social media to enhance their web presence and drive traffic to their website. Content on Facebook, Twitter, YouTube and Flickr, for instance, can provide new opportunities for sharing content and news, building communities of followers, responding to customers and enhancing CRM. (See also further information on social media later in this chapter and in Chapter 5.)

However, management of these new channels requires a firm commitment of resources from an organisation if they are to be a successful part of any web marketing strategy.

Multilingual

Consideration should be given to offering multilingual options on the site. These could be in the form of translated introductions or downloadable PDFs. Additionally, a translation tool can be added to the site, such as Google Translate – although not 100 per cent accurate, these can provide a useful guide for visitors.

The use of social media

Our ways of communicating are changing. Today there are powerful communication tools at our disposal which make it possible to reach an audience greater than we can ever imagine. Thanks to social media, the world is getting smaller and it is easier than ever to spread a message, share thoughts and make meaningful connections. The description of social media applications below is drawn from an article entitled 'Social Media: Joining the Conversation' written by Basak Gurbuz of Turkey-based PCO, Serenas Group (2011), and reproduced with permission.

What is social media?

The meaning of the term 'social media' can be derived by examining each of the words which constitute it. 'Media' generally refers to an instrument of communication. 'Social'

implies the interaction of individuals within a group or community. Social media is part of the Web 2.0 revolution, the use of web-based channels and mobile technologies to turn communication into interactive dialogue. We are all part of this dialogue and so it is important to learn how, what and where to communicate.

Why do we need social media?

While social media is fast, interactive and accessible, it is also a cost effective way to communicate directly with a target audience. Social media tools help distribute content in ways that print media can never achieve. Social media platforms including Facebook, Twitter and LinkedIn help organisations to distribute their message, promote their brand and create awareness of events.

The power of social media

Social media makes it easier to access information, people, brands, companies, events, etc. Social media tools allow us to contribute the content and make it more relevant and meaningful. Who we are and what we say is more important than ever. The key differentiation from traditional marketing is that companies now need to be part of the conversation as opposed to simply broadcasting their message with no feedback or interaction.

How to use social media

A successful social media strategy includes the following actions:

- *Define your objectives/goals* – Why do you think you should be on social media? What do you want to say? What do you expect to achieve? Defining goals is one of the fundamental steps in implementing a social media strategy.
- *Define your target audience* – Who do you want to reach? Where are they? Understanding your target audience and how they use social media is key.
- *Use the right tools* – Today people have many ways to discover, share and tell others what they think. Analyse your options and choose the most effective and appropriate way to communicate with your audience.
- *Value your content* – Obsolete, outdated conversation has no place on your Facebook page or Twitter account. What you say is as important as when you say it. Conversation must be alive, current and up-to-date. You must be prepared to add value.
- *Measure your results* – Whichever social media tools you adopt, it is important to monitor their effectiveness against pre-defined goals and adapt your activity accordingly. There is no 'one size fits all' solution to social media analytics but in order to manage it you have to measure it.

Social media and the meetings industry

Social media shares the same goal as conferences and events: gathering people around a certain topic. Social media has the potential to impact greatly on the life-cycle of an event. Associations are creating Facebook pages around conferences to promote awareness and generate community before the event starts. Social media tools enable information sharing and networking during the event. And once it has concluded, the conversation continues.

INCON research found that Facebook and LinkedIn are the platforms which most meeting and event companies are using to concentrate their social media efforts. To download the full article visit: www.incon-pco.com

Chapter 5 will look in more detail at the use of social media around conferences and events, as a tool for organisers to maximise and enrich the delegate experience. Case Study 4.2 looks at how one destination, Seoul, exploited social media as a marketing tool to create increased awareness of Seoul as a meeting and business events destination.

From a conference or meeting venue perspective, a useful paper reviewing the impacts and opportunities afforded by social media was published in 2012 by the International Association of Conference Centres, entitled *A Guide to Social Media 2012* (IACC 2012).

Familiarisation visits, workshops and showcases

Familiarisation visits organised by destinations and venues have long been an important marketing tool in seeking to secure new conference and convention business. However, the days when it was simply enough for a destination to put together a one-day or two-day programme of venue visits, hospitality and activities are largely gone. Now, with time pressures on buyers, it is essential that such programmes are highly tailored to the needs of individual buyers and also extremely creative in the ways in which the time is spent in order to maximise the networking, site inspection and educational opportunities afforded.

Similarly from a supplier perspective, the expectations are that such visits will not only allow them to showcase their venues and services, but also provide quality time and opportunity to meet buyers on a one-to-one, personal level. Their expectations will also be that buyers are carefully researched and qualified to make sure that the business they have to place is genuine and appropriate to the destination and venues that they will be visiting. The history of the conference industry is littered with many examples of bogus buyers and timewasters who have managed to inveigle their way on to familiarisation visits, or, perhaps more disappointingly, have often been invited to participate because the research into their buying credentials has been inadequate.

Alternatives to actual familiarisation visits, such as virtual fam trips, are now in existence (e.g. www.virtualfamtrip.uk.com) and, while these may offer access to useful data when compiling tenders for business, it is unclear how they could or should replace the 'real thing'.

Case Study 4.1, the 'Scotland Means Business' workshop, organised by Visit Scotland's Business Tourism Unit, is an example of the highly professional way in which familiarisation visits, showcases and workshops now need to be organised if they are to be worthwhile and successful. It demonstrates considerable creativity and detailed attention to meeting the needs of both buyers and suppliers.

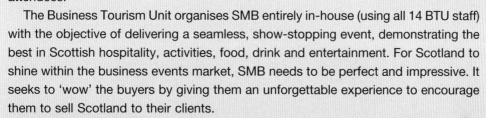

CASE STUDY 4.1 'Scotland Means Business'

VisitScotland's Business Tourism Unit (BTU) organises a biannual event for business events buyers known as 'Scotland Means Business' (SMB), designed to provide an opportunity for buyers to meet a range of Scottish venues and suppliers. Each SMB is completely unique and organised from scratch with different venues, suppliers and attendees.

The Business Tourism Unit organises SMB entirely in-house (using all 14 BTU staff) with the objective of delivering a seamless, show-stopping event, demonstrating the best in Scottish hospitality, activities, food, drink and entertainment. For Scotland to shine within the business events market, SMB needs to be perfect and impressive. It seeks to 'wow' the buyers by giving them an unforgettable experience to encourage them to sell Scotland to their clients.

'Scotland Means Business' objectives

The objectives of SMB are to:

- create measurable economic benefit through generating new leads;
- attract high quality purchasers with high propensity to buy;
- raise the profile and awareness of the Scottish business tourism product.

Operations, marketing and sponsorship

- Working six months in advance, clear roles and responsibilities are allocated to each team member with one overall event manager.
- In-kind support is negotiated by team members – some sponsorship of flights, free or discounted accommodation, meals and activities.
- Highly targeted promotion – direct invitations to Scottish suppliers; buyers approached through BTU's own databases or via agents. All attendees are vetted by BTU to ensure high quality and the correct business mix of suppliers and buyers.

- Personalised itineraries are issued well in advance. A package of information and contact details on suppliers and buyers is circulated in advance. Appointments are carefully tailored and scheduled in advance to increase the effectiveness of participation.
- Digital marketing is undertaken through website features and dedicated SMB site, direct emails and Twitter.
- Press releases are issued to the UK and international trade press as well as the Scottish business press.
- Relationship building is maximised through proactively maintaining contact, supporting and hosting reunions at international events.

'Scotland Means Business' November 2011

The November 2011 event attracted 46 international meeting and event organisers (drawn from nine countries) for the two-day event held in Glasgow (each event is staged in a different part of the country). There were also representatives from the

FIGURE 4.1 'Scotland Means Business'

trade media in attendance. The Day One programme began with short welcome presentations, followed by a series of six 15-minute scheduled appointments between buyers and suppliers, based on preferences selected by the buyers via a dedicated 'Scotland Means Business' website (see Figure 4.1). This was followed by a buffet lunch with an international twist, featuring different food stations including *A Taste of Scotland*, *Fragrant Indian Flavours*, and an *Around the World Dessert Station*. Lunch was followed by a further seven scheduled appointments. All in all, 500 appointments took place during the workshop, which included a presentation by politician Fergus Ewing, Minister for Tourism in the Scottish Parliament, who underlined Scotland's dedication to business tourism and to delivering world-class events.

For the evening entertainment, guests transferred to the new Riverside Museum for a drinks reception and further networking against the backdrop of an imitation Glasgow street from the 1900s, and were offered tours of the transport museum. This was followed by an evening of seasonal Scottish produce at the Kelvingrove Museum and Art Gallery, and of course no Scottish gala dinner would have been complete without the address to the haggis and some ceilidh dancing!

Day two consisted of a fast-paced and informative treasure hunt of Glasgow. Guests and Scottish suppliers headed into Glasgow city to visit a number of local businesses, tasked with such challenges as sourcing some vegetarian haggis, taking a photo of a team member playing the bagpipes, and finding out which hotel hosted the world's first television transmission. The treasure hunt was the perfect opportunity to allow the delegates to discover Glasgow city and also an excellent way for the groups to get to know each other and to provide further valuable networking opportunities.

In order for guests to make the most of their brief visit to Scotland, the event was surrounded by a series of familiarisation visits throughout the country. In total, 66 Scottish venues were visited in the run-up to, and after, the 'Scotland Means Business' workshop.

The November 2010 Scotland Means Business event, held at Turnberry, Ayrshire, achieved over £3 million of confirmed business, a return on investment of 56:1.

Conference ambassador programmes

Conference ambassador programmes (also known as local host programmes) are primarily based around the identification, recruitment, training and support of key individuals in the local community (university academics, hospital professional staff, leading industrialists, members of the business community, trade unionists) as 'ambassadors' for the destination, assisting them to bid for and attract the annual conference of the professional institution or trade union to which they belong. Other variations of ambassador programmes aim to recognise and publicly acknowledge particular initiatives undertaken by companies and organisations designed to attract more conference and events business to the destination.

How to identify and recruit conference ambassadors

The ICCA paper *Congress Ambassador Programmes* (ICCA 2010) suggests that the key trait that all ambassadors should have in common is a '*positive emotional bond to the destination and/or the aspirations of that destination*'. It states that, apart from this, the most successful programmes are very flexible in terms of other requirements and it lists the following types of ambassadors:

Ambassador connections

- born in destination;
- lives in destination;
- studied or studies in destination;
- created something in destination (e.g. work of art; building);
- long-term family ties to destination;
- passionate supporter of historic figure linked to destination;
- fan of destination or some characteristic of destination.

Ambassador backgrounds

- business leaders;
- senior medical practitioners;
- senior medical administrators;
- scientists (non-academic);
- academic leaders (all fields);
- postgraduates and graduates;
- political and social leaders and opinion formers;
- writers or commentators;
- celebrities.

Useful ambassador traits or skills

- natural communicator;
- internationalist;
- passionate about destination;
- strong 'presence';
- leadership skills/influential figure;
- recognised expert;

- groundbreaking researcher;
- 'rising star';
- strong reputation/ethical.

Useful reference and information sources for identifying and recruiting potential ambassadors include

- university websites;
- university staff newsletters;
- universities' own departmental research groups/sessions;
- training and induction packs/programmes produced by universities for new academic staff;
- alumni and university communications with alumni;
- university inaugural lectures;
- university conference offices;
- research institutes;
- local press and media;
- science festivals/special events;
- referrals and word of mouth;
- LinkedIn has an advanced search facility e.g. 'who is the conference manager at . . .?';
- www.specialistinfo.com – for information on the specialisms of UK doctors and consultants. An annual subscription is required to access the data;
- chambers of commerce;
- city council inward investment and economic development teams.

Research undertaken by Fire Circle Ltd and Tony Rogers Conference and Event Services in summer 2010 among UK and Ireland and worldwide destinations ascertained that, on average:

- universities and colleges provide 54 per cent of ambassadors in the UK and Ireland, but only 35 per cent elsewhere in the world. However, the range in the UK and Ireland was from 19 per cent to 90 per cent;
- hospitals generate 29 per cent of ambassadors in the UK and Ireland, but 38 per cent elsewhere;
- the corporate sector provides 10 per cent of ambassadors in the UK and Ireland, and 12 per cent elsewhere.

Benefits of being an ambassador

By being a conference ambassador and helping to bring their conference to their home destination, ambassadors:

- increase the profile and recognition of their specialist field and department nationally and internationally;
- benefit personally and professionally from their association with a successful event;
- bring the world's experts from their sector to their home destination;
- achieve in 2–3 days the networking benefits which might, otherwise, take months to realise;
- enjoy the prestige and sense of civic pride from seeing the conference in their home destination and the benefits it brings to the economy of the region;
- generate potential funding, research and investment opportunities;
- enjoy VIP access to events and entertainment in their home destination;
- attend exclusive ambassador networking events with peers and with the wider business and academic communities in the area;
- tap into the full range of support available from the convention bureau and/or PCO/DMC in bidding for, organising and staging their conference in their home city.

Thomas Reiser (2010), Director of Interel Association Management, describing his experiences of conference ambassador programmes run by destinations said:

> The most important aspect, in my opinion, is that an ambassador or a local host programme focuses on why the respective destination would be good for the overall success of the association. Meetings nowadays need to be increasingly focused on having the appropriate impact on the profession/trade/sector/industry (particularly healthcare). A meeting can no longer be seen one at a time but needs to become part of an overall strategy, which may – in the interest of the association and its stakeholders – mean that one destination would not be ideal from a pure business point of view one year but may be two years later. This kind of understanding, and also to become an ambassador not only for a destination but for the respective local community for a more sustained and sustainable involvement in an organisation, is most impactful. To illustrate this – for nephrology – the Japanese society was greatly interested in hosting the world congress. Over several years, they built their membership from under 500 to over 1,000 to demonstrate their willingness and interest to be part of the global kidney community. Ultimately, they did not get the meeting (because the facilities did not fit) but, instead of abandoning ship, they continued their strong involvement and have since then had two of the smaller meetings placed in Japan and will likely continue to get meetings rewarded.

While securing association congresses has been, and continues to be, the prime target for destinations, venues and event agencies via Conference Ambassador Programmes, initiatives are underway to extend such marketing activity to the corporate meetings and conference sector.

Club Melbourne and the Cardiff Ambassador Programme and Corporate Champions Initiative are two examples of contemporary Ambassador Programmes, with similar objectives but slightly differing approaches. Both are summarised below.

Club Melbourne

The Club Melbourne ambassadors programme is a collaborative strategy supported by the Melbourne Convention and Exhibition Centre, the Melbourne Convention and Visitors Bureau and the State Government of Victoria.

The programme brings together medical, scientific and industry leaders who assist in the ongoing attraction of business events to Melbourne. Members include former Nobel Prize winner Professor Peter Doherty; founder of the first drug for type two diabetes, Professor Paul Zimmet; and the creator of the first intelligent software agent to fly a space mission on NASA's space shuttle, Professor Michael Georgeff. A strong list of women are represented such as Professor Jenny Graves, leader in the Australian and international cell biology genetics and genomics communities; Professor Nadia Rosenthal, regenerative medicine specialist and Founding Director of the Australian Regenerative Medicine Institute; and Professor Helen Herrman, Director of the World Heath Organization Collaborating Centre in Mental Health.

The programme, which started in 2005 with 20 influential Melburnians, now boasts a membership of 134. These people work and live in Melbourne, they are passionate about their city and they are committed to keeping Victoria's expertise 'top of mind' around the world.

Ambassadors promote Melbourne as an innovative 'thinking city' and a leading destination for science, medicine and business. International conventions provide them with the opportunity to:

- raise their profile nationally and internationally;
- showcase Australian innovation;
- gain exposure for their company, organisation, university and research teams in the international marketplace;
- maximise the economic benefits that flow from major international conventions for the city and state.

Club Melbourne ambassadors have been involved in securing 58 international events (as at May 2012) for Melbourne bringing over 75,000 delegates to the city. Further information: www.clubmelbourne.com/au/the-program

Cardiff ambassador programme and corporate champions initiative

Cardiff (via Cardiff & Co – its destination marketing organisation) operates both an ambassador programme and a corporate champions initiative.

The Cardiff Ambassador Programme has led to the appointment of some 475 business and academic individuals as ambassadors for the city – approximately 65 per cent of these are 'business ambassadors' and 35 per cent are 'academic ambassadors'. Their role is to be '*powerful advocates for the Cardiff city-region, enhancing its reputation as a place to invest, do business and host valuable conferences and events*'. Conference enquiries generated via the ambassador programme in the three-year period from April 2009 to March 2012 were estimated to be worth almost £2 million for Cardiff.

The Cardiff Corporate Champions Initiative is an:

> *opportunity for businesses in the Cardiff city-region to join the strong coalition already in place to promote the area as a world-class destination to do business, live, work, visit and study. Champions will understand how being part of such a coalition can add value to their own company's Corporate Social Responsibility agenda.*

The initiative offers companies the opportunity to invest and contribute to the efforts to promote the Cardiff city-region. Becoming a Cardiff Corporate Champion will '*result in widespread recognition of your company's investment in the promotion of Wales' capital city which will, in turn, help raise your profile in a positive way*'. Sectors of the business community identified as potentially appropriate include:

- property (commercial and residential);
- recruitment;
- education/training;
- transport;
- legal;
- financial services;
- retail;
- accountancy (business services);
- independent suppliers within media;
- sports/cultural partners.

All Cardiff Corporate Champions receive a full pack of relevant collateral including publications promoting Cardiff as an investment location and a business and leisure destination. In addition, Cardiff Corporate Champions have access to the Cardiff promotional DVD, plus Cardiff & Co image library and other materials. Champions are also able to use the *Cardiff Corporate Champion* logo – 'Proud to be a Cardiff Corporate Champion' – on all their marketing materials. The Cardiff city-region:

enjoys a first-class reputation for business, learning and a distinct quality of life which continues to attract people and investment. Cardiff needs to build on this reputation and this is where a unified approach to the marketing of the city will enable the city to compete more effectively in the future. By encouraging businesses in the city to invest in championing Cardiff, the Cardiff Corporate Champions initiative aims to strengthen the resources available to market the city and thus develop a more prosperous city that will benefit all involved.

Gold and Silver Corporate Champions initiative packages are available. The packages are detailed in full via the following link: http://whycardiff.com/Cardiff-Corporate-Champions.html. Further information on the Cardiff Ambassador Programme is available at: www.whycardiff.com

Event bidding and tendering

Event agencies and PCOs, destinations and venues invest substantial resources in winning new clients and new client business. Compiling a bid tender in response to a client's Request for Proposal (RFP) demands high level creativity and ingenuity. It also requires: time to be spent in researching event options; assessments to be made of staff time, staff numbers and staff experience in order to deliver the client event successfully; budgets to be devised and fee levels calculated. All of the information needs to be assembled into an effective event bid document which must be submitted before the client's deadline (usually measured in just a few days or weeks). This investment of time and ideas has, of course, no guarantee of being successful and may cost the tendering entity thousands of pounds to compile.

Table 4.1 reproduces an RFP circulated to UK event agencies in 2011 to invite tenders for the organisation of a high level global conference in the IT sector.

Bidding process, bid writing and production

Every conference and event bid is different but the following are typically the main steps involved in bidding for an association congress – the tips are to be found on the Business Events Sydney website: www.businesseventssydney.com.au. It should be noted that, while these steps apply particularly when bidding for international events, a very similar process will also apply when bidding for national events:

• *Plan the conference bidding strategy* – Before launching into the bid process, it is important to assess the association's criteria for the event, and analyse its previous events. Strategy planning and research also mean undertaking a review of the destination's bidding competitors, as well as taking into account political agendas that may influence the final decision.

Table 4.1 RFP example

The information below is an example of the actual details supplied to event management agencies for a high profile, CEO-level global customer conference in the IT sector, inviting tenders or proposals for management of the event. The RFP was received in June 2011, with the event taking place in May 2012. Location for the event was Europe, with good weather and good access also being requirements.

PREFERRED DATES

- May 2012. Any Tuesday–Friday pattern in May
- 2–3 days for set-up of meeting space (pre-event: Saturday/Sunday to Monday)
- 4 days for the event (Tuesday to Friday)
- 1 day de-rig day (Saturday)

MEETING SPACE

- Plenary room   1100 pax (delegates) theatre/auditorium style with staging and back projection
- Offices   4–5 offices for up to 20 pax each

FOOD AND BEVERAGE SPACE

- Night 1: Welcome reception   Cocktail reception and sit-down or buffet dinner – 1000 attendees (rolling so maximum capacity of 700)
- Night 2: Dine-arounds   Restaurants within close proximity of hotels to accommodate 1100 for dinner
- Night 3: Party   Offsite/onsite venue for informal party for 1000

Breakfast and lunch   Hotel space to accommodate 1100 delegates

NB: Will be considering both onsite and offsite venues for dine-arounds and gala party.

ACCOMMODATION

- Night 1 (set up)   50 double rooms for single occupancy
- Night 2 (set up)   150 double rooms for single occupancy
- Night 3 (set up)   150 double rooms for single occupancy
- Night 4 (peak night)   500 double rooms for double occupancy
                            150 double rooms for single occupancy
- Night 5 (peak night)   500 double rooms for double occupancy
                            150 double rooms for single occupancy
- Night 6 (peak night)   500 double rooms for double occupancy
                            150 double rooms for single occupancy
- Night 7 (tear down)   150 double rooms for single occupancy

Note: 550 in 5-star properties, the remaining 150 could overflow into 4-star venues for crew

EVENT REQUIREMENTS/CRITERIA

- Theatre-style auditorium or meeting room with a ceiling height of at least 4 metres (at lowest point)
- Internet access required for all offices with Wi-Fi preferred, but can be set up if not readily available
- Exclusivity of venue preferred
- No IT competitors in house
- Overall capacity/traffic/location/infrastructure
- High quality food and service
- Wide range of 'traditional' and exciting activities
- Please quote commissionable rates
- Please detail any add-ons (i.e. complimentary rooms, upgrades, etc.)

- *Prepare the conference bid document* – The bid document provides the host organisation with the destination information upon which the final decision or choice of location is made. It must clearly assess the association's criteria, emphasise the advantages of hosting the event in 'x' destination, and detail the support available to the association if it brings its event to this destination.
- *Lobby for event bid votes* – Part of lobbying for bid votes is to analyse the voting process. It is important to know who will vote, and the best way to convey your message to decision-makers. The goal is to ensure that the message crafted will motivate the association to bring its event to your destination.
- *Conduct a destination site inspection* – During the bid process, it is common for the bidding destination to invite the association's international committee to visit and take a tour of the destination's congress infrastructure, to ensure that the city and its venues meet the association's requirements. This will normally entail covering all of the committee's expenses while staying in the destination.
- *Make the final bid presentation* – Often a final presentation is made to the association's international board, or to association delegates from each country. Less formal lobbying also frequently takes place among delegates and participants at this time.
- *Manage the post-bid relationship* – The work does not stop after a bid has been won. The successful destination should continue to guide the association as it plans the event. Depending on the scale of the event, the CVB/DMO may help the association to appoint a Professional Conference Organiser (PCO), assist with marketing activities and collateral, and promote the event in the media.

If the bid has not been successful, it may still be appropriate to work with the association or organisation to research other conference possibilities. Persistence in continuing to maintain relationships can often mean that winning bids can be mounted within a few years of losing the first bid.

In an attempt to support its major venues and to provide a more consistent and standardised response to clients, the city of Birmingham (England) has developed a digital bidding system. It has been developed via Marketing Birmingham, the city's strategic marketing partnership, which operates the city's leisure tourism programme (Visit Birmingham) and business tourism programme (Meet Birmingham – www.meet birmingham.com), as well as the city's inward investment programme (Business Birmingham). The digital bidding system has been designed to facilitate a more joined-up approach to attracting events to the city and region, and is being used by other partners such as The NEC (National Exhibition Centre) Group and Edgbaston County Cricket Ground. It provides templates and a consistent package of information about the city and region, but also allows the generic content to be tailored to specific event tenders. The tender is then delivered electronically to the client, who is sent log-in details to access and to download and print a copy, if required. Bids can contain copy, images, film, audio and interactive flash files, such as interactive floor plans of conference rooms. The digital bid system was used successfully to secure the annual conference of the Association of Colleges for Birmingham in 2011, 2012 and 2013.

The Convention Industry Council's Accepted Practices Exchange (APEX) released a new RFP Workbook in August 2011, to *'offer planners a way to create and organise the most common RFPs associated with a meeting, convention, exhibition or event'*. The Workbook takes a streamlined approach, removing as much unnecessary or duplicative information as possible, and providing simple, drop-down menus and auto-populating fields where possible. It is designed to offer the following benefits to meeting professionals:

- save time by reducing retyping of basic event information;
- quickly create RFPs using drop-down menus and automatic calculations;
- produce clean, professional documents;
- stay organised with all major RFPs in one place;
- free to use.

To download a copy, visit: www.conventionindustry.org/StandardsPractices/APEX/RFPWorkbook.aspx

The International Association of Professional Congress Organisers (IAPCO) publishes the following guidelines pertinent to RFPs and bidding:

- request for proposal (RfPs) for the appointment of a PCO for international meetings;
- request for proposal (RfPs) for the appointment of a PCO for national meetings;
- bidding for a congress.

They are available for free download from: www.iapco.org. An example of a detailed bid document template for an international association congress is shown in Chapter 2.

Case Study 4.3 describes the congress of the World Federation of Societies of Intensive and Critical Care Medicine (WFSICCM) and the criteria used to assess the destinations and venues seeking to bid for this event. It also outlines the steps involved in the selection process.

Subvention and bid support practices

Subvention (defined by the *Oxford Dictionary of English* as a *'grant of money, especially from a government'*), seems increasingly to be a requisite component in bids to secure international (and often national) conference and events business. It can take a variety of forms of monetary and in-kind support. It has been suggested that *'subvention is recognised nationally and internationally as the single most important factor for attracting many types of conferences, in particular those affiliated to international associations'* (BVEP 2011).

The key objectives and uses for subvention include:

- to attract high yield, high spend international conferences linked to a country's areas of expertise in industry, commerce or science and medicine; to boost the economy and benefit inward investment;
- to enable a country's cities and destinations to be competitive within the international conference market;
- to attract additional international conferences that may not be attracted without subvention.

Figure 4.2 shows the different forms and levels of subvention available, comparing the UK with overseas destinations/countries.

In comparison to their UK counterparts, international destinations are more frequently providing welcome receptions at the town hall, banners in the town, welcome desks at airports/rail stations and public transport for delegates, all free to the conference. Loans to associations or funding of the association's marketing activity prior to registration funds being received by associations are increasingly popular. These enable funding allocations to be recouped by the city and help both parties – association and city – to attract more attendees through increased marketing.

Subvention and the need for it is not showing any signs of decline, despite many in the industry disliking it as a practice. In fact, the opposite seems to be the case: 86 per cent of international destinations and 41 per cent of UK destinations contributing to the BVEP (2011) report said that subvention requests from international associations are on the increase. The average annual subvention budget in 2011 among international

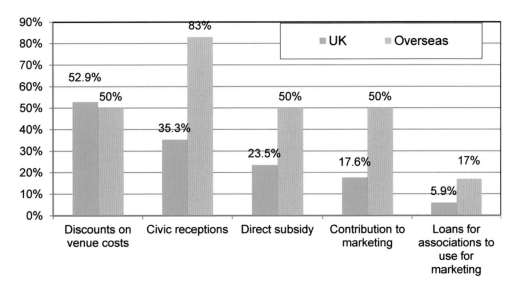

Figure 4.2 Forms of subvention available

destinations was found to be €358,109, all provided by individual cities or municipal governments' budgets.

Destinations which provide subvention evaluate the qualification of associations applying through analysis of the economic benefits generated by the conference. This can include the room nights, total spend value, and other values such as PR, marketing or profile gained as a result of the conference taking place. Many require accommodation for attending delegates to be booked through the DMO's own booking services in order to quantify and justify the subvention provided. Other evaluation criteria include the synergy of the conference content with the specific strengths of the local destination economy and with the ambassadors recruited to assist in the bidding process. Some destinations link subvention to the booking of their destination for more than one year by the association. The return on investment (ROI) of subvention funding averages in the region of 12.5:1, according to the BVEP research.

The full BVEP (2011) subvention report can be downloaded free of charge from: www.businessvisitsandeventspartnership.com. Some examples of subvention support schemes are given below.

Holland's 'Pre-Financing and Guarantee Fund'

Initiating and organising an international conference is like starting up a new enterprise, whilst knowing that its lifespan is limited. Such an enterprise usually requires starting capital to pay the initial costs. Insurance to cover possible risks due to unexpected reduced attendance may also be needed.

The Pre-Financing and Guarantee Fund was set up by the Netherlands Board of Tourism and Conventions (NBTC) and the Dutch Convention Industry Association, in cooperation with the Ministry of Economic Affairs, to meet these needs.

The Pre-Financing and Guarantee Fund offers two facilities:

- An interest-free loan to finance the initial costs of an international conference – the maximum amount of the loan is €90,000, and this must be repaid in full before the start of the conference. The organiser must provide '25 per cent coverage of the amount guaranteed, while the Fund grants a maximum guarantee of 75 per cent'.
- Insurance (non-commercial rate) against possible financial risks due to unexpected reduced attendance.

These two facilities may be used both separately and in combination.

Associations that are planning to organise an international convention (minimum duration is two days) in Holland can apply to NBTC for an interest-free loan or for a guarantee. NBTC is their intermediary for requests for pre-financing or guarantees under the Pre-Financing and Guarantee Fund. Whether a request will actually be granted depends on 'the soundness of the budget submitted, on the history of the convention,

etc.' The minimum period for requesting pre-financing and/or a guarantee is twelve months prior to the convention. The website claims that the Fund is a *'unique instrument in the international world of conventions'*.

Further details (including examples of finance provided): www.holland.com/meetings

Cyprus Tourism Organisation's 'Hospitality Programme for the Organisation of Conferences/Meetings in Cyprus'

The general aim of the programme is to promote Cyprus as an 'ideal conference destination', and for conference delegates and accompanying persons to experience the history, culture and gastronomy of Cyprus. The programme is administered by Cyprus Tourism Organisation (CTO).

Application criteria:

- A CTO application form must be submitted, with an accompanying letter, at least two months in advance of the conference/meeting. After the completion of the event, the required documentation should be submitted for payment of the agreed amount of hospitality funding (failure to supply appropriate invoices nullifies the agreement).
- Participation at the conference/meeting should include at least 15 persons from overseas.
- The CTO logo should be promoted on all printed and electronic media of the conference used outside Cyprus.
- Where it is feasible, two-minute campaign material on Cyprus should be projected in the framework of the conference.
- There should be special credits for the CTO hospitality (i.e. dinner/excursion).
- If they wish, a CTO representative should be able to participate free of charge.
- During the conference, there should be an option for CTO research to be undertaken among delegates to collect data in support of conference tourism.

Organisations eligible to apply for assistance under the programme are:

- non-profit organisations (excluding government, semi-government organisations as well as government services);
- academic/educational institutions.

Eligible expenses for the provision of hospitality include:

- gala dinner or welcome reception up to €15 per foreign participant; or
- excursion: complete coverage of the coach and licensed guide expenses and up to €15 per foreign participant for a meal that may be offered during the excursion; and
- provision of hospitality against receipt of air ticket/accommodation expenses for a keynote speaker, up to €800.

The CTO has also a 'Support Scheme for Conference Biddings for Cyprus', which offers local and overseas associations up to 80 per cent refund on their total bid presentation expenses, according to a Cyprus destination feature in *Association Meetings International* magazine (November 2010). Further information: www.visitcyprus.biz

Vienna Convention Bureau

Vienna Convention Bureau (VCB) manages a scheme of 'Financial Assistance for Conventions of Associations in Vienna'. The scheme is an incentive to attract international meetings to Vienna during the low season. VCB does not assume any event cancellation liability. The financial assistance is only available to association conventions.

To qualify for assistance, the association convention must meet the following criteria:

- *Internationality* – More than 50 per cent of attendees have to originate from countries other than Austria.
- *Timeframe* – The conference must take place in Vienna in the period November–March or July–August.
- *Accommodation* – Must be in Viennese hotels.

To apply for assistance, the convention organiser must submit an official request at least six months prior to the conference. The completed application must include:

- the exact title and date of the conference;
- the name of the conference venue in Vienna;
- the number of expected delegates;
- details of accommodation to be used in Vienna (category of hotels and duration of stay);
- a preliminary budget for the conference.

A Committee that meets three times a year decides upon each application. Confirmation of financial assistance is given in writing following the meeting and the confirmed amount is paid after the respective event. Payment is made to the conference organiser's account as soon as the following details have been received by VCB:

- for events of up to 500 participants, a list of participants. For events with more than 500 participants, country statistics for the participants;
- copies of invoices in respect of congress-related expenses (e.g. room rental, printing, translation/interpretation costs, etc.);
- bank account details for the remittance.

Pre-financing: it is possible for the organiser to receive 50 per cent of the amount allocated one year prior to the event. To take advantage of the pre-financing offer, a separate application has to be made to VCB. Further details: www.vienna.convention.at

The 'Glasgow Model'

The city of Glasgow has recognised the challenges facing organisers of association and not-for-profit sector conferences posed by potential falls in delegate numbers leading to loss-making events and the accrual of venue cancellation charges. To minimise such challenges and threats, it launched (September 2010) 'The Glasgow Model', designed as a unique business model between the association conference organisers, Glasgow City Marketing Bureau (GCMB) and the Scottish Exhibition and Conference Centre (SECC), based on the principles of creating equity, minimising risk and generating profit. Figure 4.3 shows the logo for the 'Glasgow Model'.

Logo for the 'Glasgow Model'

The construct of the Glasgow Model is, in the words of *Meetings & Incentive Travel* magazine (September 2010):

> straight out of the buyout chapter of a mergers and acquisitions manual: the front
> end price is cut but then rises on a sliding scale as delegate numbers grow beyond
> target. And there is an underlying belief that Glasgow's marketing expertise can drive
> up delegate numbers for all.

FIGURE 4.3 The Glasgow Model

Scott Taylor, Glasgow City Marketing Bureau Chief Executive, says (in a personal communication):

> *The environment in which associations operate is becoming more challenging and Glasgow uses its economic development drivers, operated by GCMB, to help organisers meet this challenge.*
>
> *With the Glasgow Model, the city shares the risk, has significant commitment to helping realise the strategy, and for the organiser to meet their objectives and KPIs (key performance indicators). The result is that, more often, success is a shared venture and guarantees of this scale are unprecedented in other cities.*
>
> *The Glasgow Model is a powerful way to create customer loyalty and de-risk an event. It has resulted in increasing our market share, and is influential in securing multi-year contracts. This will be reinforced by the city's rise up the ICCA ratings in welcoming an even greater number of international delegates year on year.*
>
> *In 2011–12, more than one in five tourists to Glasgow was a convention delegate, a trend set to increase during 2012–13.*

He says that the partnership is built on:

- transparency and trust (previous years' attendances must be available and accurate);
- sharing risk;
- guaranteed income by subvention;
- guaranteed venue discount;
- delegate build and delivery;
- multi-channel marketing and communications.

The city is a dynamic business partner with conference and event organisers providing marketing expertise and personnel, devising and undertaking multi-channel campaigns to boost attendance to record levels, and creating cost-neutral sponsorship opportunities to generate additional revenue streams. GCMB provides subvention assistance to an organiser, whilst the SECC provides a flexible cost structure based on delegate attendance. This combination reduces the level of financial output by an organiser at the planning stages, improves cashflow and reduces risk.

Figure 4.4 shows the GCMB staff participating in a fun run to create an alternative revenue stream for sponsorship during the Diabetes UK conference held in March 2012. GCMB helped to design the look and feel of the fun run, and produced packs for the runners and T-shirts.

Ben Goedegebuure, Director of Sales, SECC, comments:

> *The initiative is a direct response to concerns raised by clients worried about delegate numbers in this economic climate. We wanted to offer a way to reduce the risk to*

FIGURE 4.4 GCMB Team participating in Diabetes UK Fun Run

our client whilst sending a confident message from the destination that we can deliver on delegates. As a destination we're set up to help organisers boost attendance using the resources and connections we have throughout the city. The Glasgow Model is an extension of a unique collaborative approach that has already put Glasgow on the map as a world class events destination (www.myvenues.co.uk/news).

Scott Taylor adds:

The Glasgow Model is a unique commitment to a jointly shared business strategy with the conference organiser. We explicitly understand the importance of reputation and brand, and have a clear responsibility to deliver success through creating equity and profit for the association. The Glasgow combination offers a highly-differentiated business model that is incomparable to other cities' schemes. Together we unlock an easy-to-buy solution with support when you need it and a 360-degree marketing package that quickly builds delegate attendance. We are delighted that it is the first in the market place and believe that it will set the pace of change in our industry (www.myvenues.co.uk/news).

Ben Goedegebuure and Scott Taylor concluded:

The Glasgow Model continues to deliver advantages for conference organisers and remains unique in the market place (www.myvenues.co.uk/news).

CASE STUDY 4.2 Seoul Convention Bureau's three-step social media campaign in destination marketing

For the Seoul Convention Bureau (SCB), social media is a new electronic frontier for destination marketing. The key lies in adhering to the right strategy and, in 2011, the SCB employed a simple, three-step approach that quickly yielded dividends.

Plans to use social media as a means of attracting buyers to Seoul's business events assets began in 2010, a time when the city was enjoying unprecedented global attention as World Design Capital, UNESCO Capital of Creative Design, and host of the Seoul G-20 Summit. The SCB opened its official Facebook and Twitter accounts in the third quarter of 2010 and, by November, was testing the waters with its first online campaign, the Seoul Winter Promotion.

Utilising both social media platforms, the campaign focused upon countries from which Seoul draws the majority of its business tourists. Free roundtrip airfare was provided for one winner and partner from Singapore.

The primary goal of reaching out to buyers on a global scale required a long-term strategy. With the Winter Promotion an effective learning curve for logistics, including

FIGURE 4.5 Seoul skyline

partnerships with Seoul MICE Alliance members willing to contribute prizes in return for promotion, the SCB then drew upon its experiences for its next three phases:

The Seoul sizzling sweepstakes: building up an online network

The three-step strategy aimed to cast the net wide initially before sifting through the yield for the desired catch. September's Seoul Sizzling Sweepstakes, a month-long promotion in which entrants could win gift vouchers on a daily basis to a selection of the city's major business and entertainment venues, focused upon attracting a fan following. Promotions were handled via Facebook and Twitter, with the actual entries submitted to the SCB's official website. By the month's end, the SCB had that all-important foundation required for all social media: a readership.

The facts

- 700 participants;
- 25 participating local MICE-related businesses;
- 4,400 new Facebook 'likes' during event (950 per cent growth).

Figure 4.6 summarises responses to the Seoul Sizzling Sweepstakes campaign.

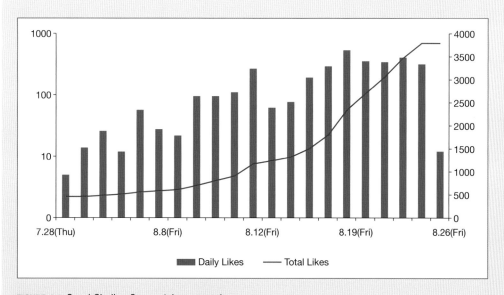

FIGURE 4.6 Seoul Sizzling Sweepstakes campaign

Spin-off benefits

- *General interest in the city's tourism, culture and cuisine increased*, as participation in the promotion led to an avalanche of publicity about Seoul via newsfeeds and Twitter RTs.

- *Top attractions in the city were given free advertising (at no extra cost to SCB),* and these businesses were put in touch with an ever-increasing audience of participants and followers – many of whom had never heard of their services and events before.
- *SCB's partners were happy with increased media exposure for a low cost.* Free advertising and the positive news articles that popped up throughout the web and travel magazines were a boon for participating businesses that had their name mentioned, all for merely offering an empty seat in a theatre or a meal voucher.

Steve's complete convention plan: marketing Seoul, your complete convention city

The November 2011 event helped to fine-tune the focus more specifically to Seoul as a business events capital. The promotion took the form of a weekly cartoon strip, following the adventures of Steve, a business tourist on a four-day itinerary stopover visit to Seoul for a conference. Capitalising on the campaign's episodic nature, the strip invited participants to help the character construct his itinerary, from the business hotel he would stay in to which of the city's tour programmes he would use in his free time. The winner was then given the chance to follow in his footsteps, starting with a free roundtrip airfare valid throughout 2012.

The promotion was well received, described as *'arguably one of the most creative social media campaigns ever run in the meetings and events industry'* by *Meetings: review*.

The facts

- Promotion drew 254 participants, many of whom commented several times about Seoul's meetings venues and attractions (which spills onto the participants' respective newsfeeds);
- 2,109 new Facebook 'likes' during event (153 per cent increase).

Spin-off benefits

- All spin-off benefits listed for the Seoul Sizzling Sweepstakes also applied to Steve's Complete Convention Plan – general interest in Seoul tourism increased, participating businesses received free advertising, and SCB's partners were happy with the increased media exposure across a variety of print and online media.
- There was a lot more interest and media attention for this second promotion, due to momentum from the first stage promotion and also for its creativity. Also, more so than the last promotion, followers on Twitter and 'likes' on Facebook were increasingly coming from international meetings industry professionals.

Increased exposure and further engaging the meetings community

With a growing Facebook following of over 6,000 and more than 1,000 Twitter followers, the Seoul Convention Bureau looks to capitalise on its successes of 2011. With a newfound network and an added emphasis on publicising the merits of Seoul's meetings industry, the SCB looks forward to navigating the uncharted waters of social media and continuing its third step of connecting with more meetings professionals online in 2012.

One of the challenges for the SCB will be to develop smaller, targeted promotions that work directly in the realm of the meetings industry. Plans are underway to bring short-term promotions to international industry tradeshows or large conferences in Seoul.

The main initiative (and an even larger challenge) is the current development of a viral promotion, run through multiple media such as social networking sites and online videos. If it has the desired effect, the SCB promotion will reach an enormous worldwide audience, while sticking to the core goals of promoting business tourism in Seoul and strengthening its brand identity – for a fraction of the cost of an international advertisement.

Value of the campaign for convention planners

Social media is just one of many tools in the marketing toolbox – one that is unfamiliar to many. SCB's experience has demonstrated that social media is very effective for destination publicity and branding, so SCB uses it to reach out to inform an ever-growing audience about the merits of business tourism in Seoul. It also allows SCB to keep a tight control on its brand identity by monitoring real-time feedback from their followers. SCB creates informative, yet fun initiatives on Facebook to help expand its network, but also to help catch the casual attention of busy meetings industry professionals.

The SCB realises that there is undiscovered potential for the use of new media, but has not yet used social media to communicate directly with industry professionals to conduct business. Finding a convention planner on Facebook or Twitter, getting them to like/follow you, and then messaging them are meant to get their attention and open a dialogue, not be a strategy for securing large bids and lucrative incentive trips. SCB staff are professionals, who continue to communicate with clients via phone and email, and follow up with polished documents, publicity materials and support.

This case study was compiled by Alexander Paik, PR Co-ordinator, Seoul Tourism Organisation (www.miceseoul.com).

CASE STUDY 4.3 Congress of the World Federation of Societies of Intensive and Critical Care Medicine (WFSICCM)

This case study describes the quadrennial world congress of the WFSICCM, a global federation which is a membership organisation comprised of national societies of intensive and critical care medicine. The federation was founded in 1974, has its headquarters in the UK and is governed by an elected council of 16 members who are each elected for an eight-year period in office. The WFSICCM is a membership organisation with 67 Society members and with further new membership applications pending. The combined individual membership of all societies exceeds 70,000 professionals. The overarching objective of the WFSICCM is to promote the highest standards of intensive and critical care medicine for all mankind, without discrimination. The world congress is regarded as a key element in the pursuit of this objective and this is reflected in a decision in 2011 to host future world congresses with a biennial frequency.

Key features of the world congress:

- It attracts 3,200–4,900 participants.
- They come from over 80 countries.
- The associated exhibition draws up to 75 exhibitors (industry, publishers and associations).
- The congress lasts for five days (with business meetings held during those five days).
- It includes some 295 hours of conference sessions which include scientific sessions, educational courses and free papers. A typical invited speaker faculty would be 450.

The locations of past and future world congresses

1st	1974	London
2nd	1977	Paris
3rd	1981	Washington DC
4th	1985	Jerusalem
5th	1989	Kyoto
6th	1993	Madrid
7th	1997	Ottawa
8th	2001	Sydney
9th	2005	Buenos Aires
10th	2009	Florence
11th	2013	Durban
12th	2015	Seoul (reflecting a change to a biennial frequency)
13th	2017	Rio de Janeiro

The selection process

- Six years ahead of time the WFSICCM Council announces the bid procedure for the next World Congress location. In 2011, Council voted unanimously that the frequency of world congresses would be biennial with effect from 2013 but the notification period will remain at six years. The bids to host the 2019 World Congress will be presented in August 2013.
- All WFSICCM member Societies who have paid their annual membership fees are entitled to submit a bid to host the World Congress.
- The WFSICCM is often approached by Professional Conference Organisers or Convention Bureaux for details of the bid procedures. All these enquiries are directed to the local society.
- Initially, each society is asked to provide a provisional notification of an intention to bid – this would normally be in January of the selection year. On receipt of this notification each society is provided with a resource pack to enable them to prepare their submission. This includes the selection criteria which Council has determined will influence the preferred choice of venue.
- In June of the selection year, societies are asked to confirm a definite intention to bid and this information is then used to plan the bid presentation timetable.
- In October of the selection year, societies are asked to provide a brief, two-page synopsis of their bid which is distributed to all Council members.
- In November of the selection year, all societies are invited to formally present their bid to a full meeting of the WFSICCM Council. The presentation order is decided by a random ballot.
- The presentations are strictly time-limited to ten minutes for presentation, ten minutes for questions and ten minutes to cover any feedback and the 'changeover time' between presentations.
- Following all presentations, Council members hold an open discussion about the relative merits of each presentation.
- Following this discussion the World Congress venue is selected by a secret ballot conducted among all Council members. In the first ballot, Council members rank their preferences to determine the leading two bids. A second ballot is then held comprising only these two bids and a winner is decided.
- The outcome of the ballot is announced at the end of the meeting with all bid delegations invited to attend this feedback session.

World Congress selection criteria

These include three main components: the geographical location, the host society and the proposed financial arrangements.

Geographical location

- What are the attractions of the host city from a professional, commercial (industry) and tourism perspective?
- What is the level of international flight access to the proposed venue?
- An assessment of the congress facilities and infrastructure including:
  - the Convention Centre
  - the price range of Congress hotels and hospitality
  - security and safety of delegates
  - culture and political climate.
- In what ways would selecting this Society contribute to the regional (and international) growth and development of critical care medicine?

The host society

- What are the relevant experiences of the Society in hosting an international congress with up to 5,000 delegates?
- What is the international reputation of the Society?
- Is one Society involved in the bid or are there others?
- Is the bid supported by local or regional critical care organisations?
- What is the Society's assessment of the level of confidence in ensuring a successful Congress?
- If selected, what plans does the host Society propose to engage with Council members and to provide timely updates (update every six months)?
- How will the World Congress be advertised and merchandised?
- In what ways would selecting this Society contribute to the regional and international development of critical care medicine?
- Are there any conflicts in the proposed dates or time of year such as other international meetings, vacations or religious festivals that may deter delegates from attending?

Financial arrangements

- What are the details of the proposed financial arrangements?
- What provisional budgets, if any, have been set?
- Do the proposed scales of Registration Fees make some provision to attract delegates from developing countries?
- What is the forecasted income for the World Federation?
- Does the financial proposal include any provision to fund meetings of Council in the time between selection and the World Congress?

Other desirable facilities or arrangements

- Free Wi-Fi access at the congress venue with all facilities within walking distance;
- opportunities to meet local government and healthcare representatives;
- plenty of places for delegates/attendees to meet and network;
- pre-congress educational workshops and post-congress tours;
- opportunities to host liaison or collaboration meetings with other professional organisations.

Compiled by Phil Taylor, Executive Director, WFSICCM. Further information on the WFSICCM can be accessed via its website: www.world-critical-care.org

SUMMARY

- The Internet is now a fundamental, indispensable tool in marketing for destinations, venues, event agencies and sector suppliers. Making appropriate investments in an organisation's website is absolutely essential, paying full attention to the site's design and structure, its navigability, content and copy, search engine optimisation, social media applications, and a range of other factors.
- In a few short years, social media has established itself as an accessible and cost effective way to communicate directly with target audiences. It has many uses in the meetings and conventions sector but, to make the most of these, organisations should develop a social media strategy and constantly measure how effective the strategy has been and refine it in the light of feedback received.
- Meeting planners and convention organisers are extremely busy people with a myriad of demands on their time. To persuade them to leave their workstations for 2–3 days in order to take part in a familiarisation visit or destination showcase event requires ever-greater creativity on the part of destination and venue marketing organisations. Such events have to be planned in ways which will ensure that suppliers can also demonstrate appropriate ROI for the time and money that they are investing in the event.
- There is a growing recognition globally of the importance of conference ambassador and local host programmes as a vehicle for identifying, bidding for and winning association congresses, both national and international. Different models of ambassador programme have emerged, including efforts to extend into the corporate conference market.
- The process of tendering and bidding for major events is absolutely crucial and it is vital that bids are designed and presented really professionally. It may well be that, to increase their chances of success, when destinations are bidding for a major event their bid will need to be supported by subvention assistance.

REVIEW AND DISCUSSION QUESTIONS

1 Analyse the ways in which conference venues can use social media as a marketing tool, highlighting the opportunities and challenges created by these types of applications.

2 Critically assess the role that subvention plays in bidding for conventions, and comment on whether 'buying in business' is a sustainable model for the future of the industry globally.

3 Undertake an in-depth analysis of a destination's conference ambassador programme, identifying weaknesses and also opportunities for future growth and development of the programme. Make suggestions as to how this could be achieved most effectively.

REFERENCES

BVEP (2011) *UK Subvention and Bid Support Practices for International Conferences and Events,* Business Visits and Events Partnership, available at www.businessvisitsandevents partnership.com

Davidson, R. and Rogers, T. (2006) *Marketing Destinations and Venues for Conferences, Conventions and Business Events*, Butterworth-Heinemann

Gurbuz, B. (2011) 'Social Media: "Joining the Conversation"', INCON e-newsletter (summer)

Hooker, J. (2010) 'Sharing the Pain and the Gain', *Meetings and Incentive Travel* magazine (September), available at www.meetpie.com

IACC (2012) *A Guide to Social Media 2012*, International Association of Conference Centres

ICCA (2010) *Congress Ambassador Programmes*, International Congress and Convention Association

Reiser, T. (2010) 'Experiences of Conference Ambassador Programmes Run by Destinations', in 'Conference Ambassador Programmes Online Survey', Fire Circle Ltd and Tony Rogers Conference and Event Services

CHAPTER **5**

Planning and staging successful conferences: an organiser's perspective

CHAPTER OBJECTIVES

www.routledge.com/cw/rogers

This chapter looks at:

- a general introduction to conference organising
- pre-conference planning and research
- budgeting and financial management
- sourcing and selecting a venue
- negotiating with venues
- programme planning
- event marketing
- conference management and production
- event evaluation and measuring return on investment (ROI)

It includes case studies on:

- outsourcing to a PCO or event management agency (mini case study)
- using Twitter at 'The Future Is You' conference (mini case study)
- Kenes Group – a global PCO company

and a Blue Paper on the applications of social media in convention planning.

LEARNING OUTCOMES

On completion of this chapter, you should be able to:

- discuss the strengths (and limitations) of conferences as a communications tool;
- describe the processes involved in organising a successful conference or convention;
- understand the role of a professional conference organiser (PCO);
- describe the principles and practice of calculating the return on investment (ROI) for events;
- appreciate the opportunities provided by the new social media and how/when these should best be used.

Introduction

The conference industry is based upon events of different kinds (including conventions and congresses, meetings, seminars, product launches, management retreats) and of different sizes and durations, requiring sophisticated planning and administration to ensure their success. Events are organised by people with varying degrees of knowledge and experience, some finding themselves responsible for organising conferences without much, if any, formal training. This chapter provides a framework for those who take up the challenge, and summarises the main processes involved in planning and staging an event.

A general introduction to conference organising

The organisation of a conference or meeting requires a similar strategic approach to that needed for planning and managing most other kinds of event. Clear objectives should be set from the beginning, a budget has to be established, a venue must be sourced and delegates' accommodation and travel arrangements made, a programme has to be prepared and the conference managed for its duration. Increasingly, health and safety and risk management, venue contracts and service guarantees, and changes in the national (and sometimes international) legislative framework are among a number of other aspects needing serious consideration, but there is not space to cover these adequately here. Then, after the conference is over, final administrative details have to be completed and some evaluation of the conference should take place. While there are different factors

to take into account when organising a conference for 500 delegates rather than one for 50, the essential components are the same.

Similar steps are required for the organisation of other events, such as sporting events, concerts, celebrations and rallies, whether these are of national or international significance like the football World Cup Finals or the Olympic Games, or of more localised importance, such as an antiques fair or agricultural show.

Organising conferences is a high-pressure activity, not recommended for those of a nervous disposition. Yet, well handled, it can be tremendously exhilarating and rewarding. It goes without saying that excellent organisational skills are a must, as are attention to detail and a willingness to work long and often irregular hours, especially in the immediate build-up period and during the event itself.

Conferences need to be planned with the precision of a military operation. Indeed, it is not surprising that a number of those now working successfully as conference organisers have come from a military background. Cotterell (1994) suggests that:

> *A conference for 200 people for two or three days is likely to take up to 250 hours or around six normal working weeks, even without counting the two or three 18-hour days which will be needed just prior to the event.*

But, in addition to hard work and attention to detail, conferences need a creativity and flair to be brought to them which will make them memorable occasions. They should live long in the memories of delegates, not only because of the benefits accruing from what has been shared and learned during the formal programme, but also for the opportunities they provide for informal networking and doing business, as well as socialising.

In some cases, companies and organisations will already have systems in place when the event is, for example, an annual event which runs along similar lines year after year. In other cases, it may be an entirely new event for which no previous organisational history or tradition exists. Both scenarios have their advantages and disadvantages:

- The regularly-held conference may operate smoothly with just some fine tuning and updating to established systems and procedures. It might, however, be failing to achieve its real potential as a conference, having become staid and predictable, and it may be that a completely fresh approach would be beneficial. The challenge for a new organiser will be to revolutionise the organisation of the conference without alienating too many of the staff or members (if it is a membership organisation) associated with the previous régime.
- Where there is no previous event history, an organiser has the benefit of beginning with a clean sheet of paper. There are no set ways of doing things, no established contacts, no *'venues that we always use'*. There is a freedom to bring something of his or her own identity to the event, to build up his or her own network of information

and suppliers, and to ensure that the event management systems are put in place to his or her own design. But such freedom brings with it a responsibility which can appear daunting if the organiser has been thrust into the role of running a conference with minimal training and experience.

This chapter attempts, therefore, to sketch out a framework for the successful organising of conferences. A number of books have been written already on this subject and the chapter will make reference to some of these in summarising the principles and steps needed to ensure that a conference is run effectively and maximises its return on investment (ROI) and return on objectives (ROO).

Pre-conference planning and research

The initial phase, of planning and research, is the one which lays the foundations for success. It is a crucial part of any event, and mistakes or oversights made at this stage can be difficult to remedy later on. It needs, therefore, to be approached thoroughly and systematically.

According to Carey (2000), it is also important to establish, at the outset,

> the degree of autonomy that you, as the planner, are being given. Crucially, what degree of control do you have over the budget? A word of advice: Think strategically and claim as much authority as you think you can get away with. A conference organiser who has to check back to a superior (or, worse still, a committee) on the times of tea or the biscuit selection is doomed to preside over chaos and remain forever a bean counter.

The initial planning phase is the time when the broad objectives for the conference must be set. These will vary from event to event. For example, the main objective for a meeting with a company's sales force may be to present new products, introduce a new incentive scheme, update them on sales performance and motivate them to reach higher targets, or inform them about a re-structuring of sales territories. The annual conference of American rose-growing societies (non-existent, as far as is known!) may have as its main aim to exchange information on new varieties of roses or to demonstrate the effectiveness of the latest pesticides, as well as maximising attendance and generating a profit. Fisher (2000) quotes the example of objectives set for a real FMCG (Fast Moving Consumer Goods) conference:

- to debate future strategy;
- to encourage delegates to get to know each other on a first-name basis;
- to agree the general direction of the group;
- to have an enjoyable, memorable experience.

Objectives should be clear and measurable: for example, an objective for a sales conference which is simply *'To launch new product X'* is hardly measurable, whereas *'To communicate the positioning, target audience, features, benefits and price structure of the new product X to all customer-facing staff'* would be. However, it is also important not to have too many objectives, as this can lead to confusion on the part of delegates and speakers. Measuring return on investment (ROI) and return on objectives (ROO) is increasingly an integral feature of any organiser's event management strategy, and is explored more fully in later in this chapter.

These broad objectives need to be supplemented with detailed answers to questions about the *'who, what, when, where, why and how'* (Maitland 1996) of the conference.

Who?

Pre-event planning needs to consider who the delegates will be, how many should be invited, and how many are expected to attend (essential for budgeting purposes). Is it appropriate for delegates' partners to be invited? Are there likely to be any special guests, including media representatives? Will there be any overseas delegates and, if so, is there a need to provide interpretation and translation facilities?

'Who?' also refers to the speakers who may be involved, either for presentations to plenary sessions or as leaders for workshops or 'breakout' sessions. Are there outside speakers to be invited, and will they require a fee as well as travel expenses?

'Who?' should also include the organising team, which may be just one person or a dedicated group of people, some of whom could include intermediary agencies as described in Chapter 2. When there is a team involved, not all of them will necessarily participate from the initial planning stage right through to post-event evaluation, but their degree of involvement is something which will need to be thought through early on. The more complex the event and the numbers involved in organising it, the more the need for some form of critical path analysis, mapping out the sequence of events in a logical order and within a realistic time-frame.

This is also the time to consider whether the conference should be organised in-house (using an organisation's own staff resources and expertise) or outsourced to a professional conference (or congress) organiser (PCO) or event management agency. A PCO can undertake all aspects of the management of an event (see Chapter 2 for a list of typical PCO services and also Case Study 5.1 below) or simply be contracted to manage certain elements. If the decision is taken to outsource to a PCO, it is normal to prepare a 'Request For Proposal' (RFP – sometimes termed 'Invitation to Tender') document which should include as much information as can be provided to enable those PCOs contacted to draw up a detailed and costed proposal for running the event. The RFP will cover the types of information shown later in this chapter under 'Sourcing and Selecting a Venue' but should also describe the target audience and how to reach them, the likely final attendance numbers, how speakers are identified (i.e. whether by invitation

CASE STUDY 5.1 Outsourcing to a PCO or event management agency

This mini case study is based largely on information from the Newcastle Gateshead Convention Bureau website (www.newcastlegateshead.com/meet).

To supplement the services provided to you by the host destination's convention bureau and your own administrative team, you may wish to consider the appointment of a professional conference organiser (PCO) or event management agency to manage all, or part, of your event.

A PCO is a company which specialises in event management and acts as a consultant to your conference organising committee. The PCO enacts the committee's decisions whilst using their experience and knowledge gained over many years in the business. Control of the event remains with the committee whilst the PCO acts as 'project manager' to ensure the administration runs effectively, leaving you more time to concentrate on the programme's content.

Do you need a PCO?

If there are elements of conference management for which you cannot provide the knowledge, resources (financial or human), time or technical facilities, a PCO can handle these for you.

When do you need a PCO?

A PCO can be brought in at different stages during the planning process but it is recommended that you consider your needs at the outset. The experience and expertise of a PCO can ensure you avoid the many pitfalls and unnecessary expenditure often encountered during the early stages of planning a conference.

How much does a PCO cost?

PCOs rarely publish set fees as they tailor their services exactly to suit your requirements (and your budget!).

Investing in PCO services, for all or part of your event's management, can not only ensure the smooth running of your conference but may also save (or even make) you money in the long run. Effective marketing can boost your delegate attendance and securing the right sponsorship can make or break the event, so an initial investment to bring in the professionals may pay dividends!

or through the submission of papers) and the number of speakers and/or abstracts (i.e. summaries of specialist research or current work projects with which they are involved), the number of foreign languages for print materials and sessions, the level and nature of sponsorship required, whether there is to be an exhibition running alongside the conference, the spending power of the participants, past history of the event, and an indication of how many PCO companies have been invited to tender. Some of the above headings relate particularly to national and international association and scientific conventions, rather than to corporate sector conferences. Chapter 4 contains an example of an actual RFP circulated to event management agencies for the management of an international corporate conference in the IT sector.

The International Association of Professional Congress Organisers (IAPCO) also has useful guidelines for appointing a PCO on its website (www.iapco.org). They include:

- how to choose the right PCO;
- how to choose the right core PCO.

Case Study 5.3 looks at the operation of Kenes Group, a global PCO company.

Strategic meetings management programmes (SMMPs) and meeting architecture

'Strategic meetings management programmes' (SMMPs) and 'meeting architecture' are relatively new terms in the conference industry lexicon, but they describe initiatives which are now having a major impact on the planning of meetings, conventions and other business events. They are both examined in more detail in Chapter 10.

What?

What kind of conference is being organised? Is it a corporate or association or government/public sector event? Is it a management retreat, training course, incentive event? A conference to update delegates on new developments in a scientific or medical field? A launch to dealers and trade media, or some other kind of event? Will delegates be listening and passive, or is there a high degree of participation, perhaps involving team building or outdoor activities?

What kind of message is the conference designed to convey? The organiser may have little or no control over this, as it may be something determined by senior managers or an organisation's 'conference committee', but it is imperative that he or she understands this clearly.

When?

Timing is another major consideration. All too often inadequate time is allowed to plan and prepare for a conference. The conference organiser may simply be given the conference dates and asked to ensure that it happens, and, indeed, may have made little input to the decision, even though his or her perspective is vital. The corporate sector, in particular, is notorious for allowing insufficient 'lead time'. Perhaps this is a reflection on the work that still needs to be done to raise the status of conference and event organisers to one which is on a par with an organisation's senior management team. In the final analysis, it is a company's reputation, not simply that of the conference organiser, which is in jeopardy if an event is poorly run.

Some flexibility on dates can also be helpful in securing the best possible rates from the chosen venue. The venue may be able to offer more favourable rates if the dates selected assist in its maximisation of yield (see Chapter 6).

Timing also needs to take into consideration the likely diary commitments of delegates. Are there any other events happening at the same time, or around that time, which might have an impact on delegate numbers? Is the conference occurring in a busy work period, or during holidays, or in winter months and, if so, what impact might any of these factors have?

Where?

Location needs to be determined at an early stage, whether this is expressed in rather broad terms such as a state/county or region of the country, or quite specifically such as New York, Nottingham, or 'within a 20-mile radius of Paris'. When deciding the ideal location, easy access to a motorway may be desirable (unless the event requires a venue off the beaten track). If many delegates are to use the train, location near a mainline station will be necessary, unless comprehensive local transport arrangements can be provided.

When events have an international dimension, with delegates arriving by plane, it is usually important to select a venue within reasonable travelling time of an international airport (often stipulated as 'no more than one or two hours' travel' from the gateway airport). Many hours sitting in a long-haul jet followed by several hours in transit around the country where the conference is to be held is not a recipe for a successful start to what will doubtless be a prestige event.

Does the location need to be a particular kind of venue to accommodate the event? Is there scope to explore an unusual venue, possibly to link in with the theme of the conference?

The choice of location may be taken out of the organiser's hands. He or she may be told to hold the event in a particular destination, or the conference may rotate around specific destinations/venues in a regular sequence. The organiser's role may simply be to draw up a shortlist of potential venues from which other people will make the final selection.

Why?

Maitland (1996) suggests that:

> The 'Why?' is almost certainly the most crucial question that needs to be asked at this stage. Don't ignore or underestimate it. You must be able to answer it well if you are going to proceed with your plans. Is 'because we always do it at this time of year' a good enough reason? It could be a huge waste of time and money if it is held for this reason alone. Are you staging it because it is the quickest and easiest way of putting across your important message to many people in a friendly and personal manner? That's a better motive. Consider carefully if a conference is really necessary. Are there less time-consuming and costly ways to achieve the same goals – perhaps a sales report, a promotional brochure or a press release?

And, of course, he might have added organising the event virtually! (See Chapter 10 for more information on virtual and hybrid events.)

How?

The format and duration of a conference are also very important factors, which will have an effect on some of the preceding considerations. Events requiring lots of syndicate rooms, as well as a main auditorium, plus exhibition space and catering areas will have a much more restricted range of options than events needing just one room with theatre-style seating for 75 people. Duration will also impact on venue availability, rates charged, accommodation requirements, and other factors. It may be appropriate to use videoconferencing technology or satellite conferencing, or to examine the benefits of webcasting (i.e. enabling delegates to attend 'virtually' via their computer screens as conference sessions are broadcast via the Internet) to increase attendance levels. Increasingly it will explore whether the event combines live, face-to-face sessions with virtual technology to create a hybrid event, a trend explored more fully in Chapter 10.

'How?' should also take into account the way in which an event fits into a company's overall marketing or training programme, and the general ethos of the company and its corporate social responsibility (CSR) objectives (a topic addressed in Chapter 7). Where a membership organisation is involved, such as a professional association or a trade union, how does a conference contribute to its communication links with members, and facilitate links between the members themselves? Are there ways in which these could be improved?

Fisher (2000) provides many useful tips on other practical aspects of managing an event, which there is not space to cover in this book. He describes the invitation process, the reception of delegates, travel and logistical arrangements, making the best use of refreshment and lunch breaks, handling overnight accommodation, the correct treatment of VIPs, the effective management of conference catering (traditionally the most common cause of problems and of delegate dissatisfaction), and organising a conference overseas.

A conference organiser must also undertake a risk assessment for his or her event and develop contingency plans for dealing with crises that might occur. Swarbrooke and Horner (2001) give examples of some of the commonest problems:

- keynote speakers who are unable to attend because of illness or travel problems;
- participants being seriously delayed or unable to attend at all due to transport difficulties or bad weather;
- overbooked hotels;
- fire alarms and bomb threats;
- failures of audio-visual equipment.

They contend, correctly, that:

> all these risks are foreseeable and the organiser should have in place contingency plans to implement if they arise – what we might term the 'what if' approach. This may involve having an alternative schedule in reserve, or a suitable additional set of audio-visual equipment available. It is important that everyone on the team knows about these contingency plans.

Risk assessment will also lead to taking out appropriate insurance cover for the event, and there are today a number of specialist event insurance providers operating at a global level.

The Fáilte Ireland website (www.meetinireland.com) contains a very useful planning steps checklist, available for free download. The checklist details the planning steps required in the countdown to a major conference, beginning two years in advance of the event and going right through to post-conference administration.

Budgeting and financial management

Assembling a budget is fundamental to the planning of any event. Anticipated costs impose parameters or a framework when putting the budget together and these, combined with an organiser's previous experience and detailed quotes from potential suppliers, provide the building blocks on which the budget is constructed. Whether the conference is being organised for a corporate organisation or for one in the not-for-profit sector, financial management is equally important. There are, however, some key differences:

- Within the corporate sector, the budget is set by the company. Budgets may be allocated per event or as an annual total budget which needs to be used effectively to finance a number of events. The budget is required to cover delegate expenses as well as the other costs associated with planning, promoting and staging the event.
- Within the not-for-profit sector (and with entrepreneurial conferences – see Chapter 2), conferences have to be income-generating with delegate fees being charged to defray costs. The events are designed to cover their own costs and (usually) make a profit which, in some cases, is used as a start-up fund to pay for the initial promotion and planning of the next event.
- Within the government and public sectors, either of the above approaches may apply.

Even so, the same principles hold good for all types of organisation: budgets must be drawn up to show projected income and expenditure, systems need to be in place to manage income and expenditure flows and, at the conclusion of the event, a balance sheet should be prepared to show actual income against expenditure. This balance sheet then forms the basis for planning the next event, particularly if it is one in a sequence of conferences taking place on a regular basis.

Income streams will vary according to the nature of the organisation and the event. With corporate events, the income source will be the company itself, but there may also be scope for attracting sponsorship for certain elements. With associations and other organisations in the not-for-profit sector, income will come primarily from delegate fees, although there may also be substantial opportunities to offset the costs of the conference through sponsorship and by running an associated exhibition. Trade union, political party and medical conferences and conventions, for example, often have concurrent exhibitions which attract exhibitors wishing to promote their products to the delegates. McCabe *et al.* (2000) also list income streams such as:

- grants – from government and/or other bodies;
- merchandising – money from the sale of items appertaining to the event, such as educational materials, clothing (T-shirts, hats) and videos/DVDs;
- advertising – money from the sale of advertising space, for example in the conference brochure, on clothing, and so on.

The NewcastleGateshead Convention Bureau website (www.newcastlegateshead.com/meet) has some useful guidelines on attracting sponsorship for a convention.

Many destinations are prepared to host a civic reception or banquet for delegates, as a form of welcome and expression of gratitude that the event is being held in their town or city. Some convention and visitor bureaux (CVBs) offer interest-free loans, particularly for events with a lead time of several years: the event organiser may incur expenses, especially promotional costs, well before any income is received from delegate fees. Loans are designed to assist with cash flow but will have to be re-paid once the event is over (and, if the conference has made a profit, the CVB may require a share of the profits) (see also the description of the Glasgow Model in Chapter 4).

Expenditure projections have to cover a whole host of items, but the main ones are usually:

- venue hire;
- catering costs;
- accommodation costs: delegates, partners, speakers/invited guests, organisers;
- speakers' expenses: travel costs, fees, subsistence, possibly presentation materials;
- delegate materials: written materials, CDs, badges, possibly gifts;
- social and partner programme costs: entertainment, transport, other venue hire, food and beverage;
- conference production costs: audio-visual equipment and technical staff to stage-manage the event plus, when appropriate, set construction;
- promotional costs: leaflets and publicity material, press releases, possibly advertising and/or direct mail, e-marketing;
- on-site staff (organiser) costs plus, in some cases, freelance event staff;
- miscellaneous costs: event insurance, security, couriers, interpreters, taxes (both local/national taxes and tax on profits).

Maitland (1996) provides a cashflow forecast template (see Table 5.1) for capturing event incomes and expenditures. This is a recognised way of keeping an overview of what is happening with the finances for an event, and helps to flag up any potential problem areas at an early stage.

Association and entrepreneurial conference organisers need to calculate the 'break-even' point for their events i.e. the point at which sufficient delegates have booked places to ensure that the conference does not run at a loss but, at the very least, covers its costs. McCabe *et al.* (2000) state that:

> break-even analysis is a tool that assists in the setting of prices. The basic concept is that at some level of sales (revenue), there will be sufficient income to cover the expenses of the convention or meeting . . . In calculating the break-even point, both fixed and variable costs are taken into consideration. The variable costs are relative to the volume of conference participants.

Figure 5.1 illustrates the break-even chart for a medical association conference for 400 delegates. Fixed costs include promotion and publicity, printing, brochures and delegate bags. Variable costs include food and beverage. The registration fee is £550.

It is now also possible to download workbooks and spreadsheets for tracking expenditure across a number of meetings/events.

Table 5.1 Cashflow forecast form

	Month			Month			Month			Month		
	Estimated	Actual	Variance	Estimated	Actual	Variance	Estimated	Actual	Variance	Estimated	Actual	Variance
A. INCOME												
Sponsors												
Delegates/Partners												
Other												
Total Income (A)												
B. EXPENDITURE												
Venue												
Accommodation/ housing												
Speakers/partners												
Delegates/partners												
Publicity												
Outside assistance (e.g. PCO/DMC)												
Rehearsals & production costs												
The programme												
Social programme activities												
Other, incl. taxes and contingency												
Total Expenditure (B)												
Net Cashflow (A–B)												
Opening Balance												
Closing Balance												

Source: Maitland (1996) (with some author's additions)

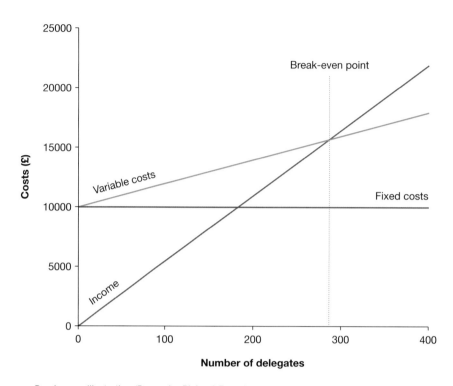

FIGURE 5.1 Break-even illustration (Drawn by Richard Evans)

The Convention Industry Council's *International Manual* (CIC 2005) examines budgeting from the perspective of organising events internationally. It suggests that:

> budgeting for international events is essentially the same process as budgeting for national and local events, with the added complications caused by currency and tax issues.

It explains how movements in currency exchange rates (which may float against one another, be fixed at a certain level, or even float within fixed limits) can have a major impact on the bottom line results of events, but the risks can be minimised with appropriate planning. Tax issues revolve more around implications for delegates and the organising company and whether it will be necessary to pay income or company tax because an event has been organised abroad. In some cases, the delegate is perceived to have received a taxable benefit from the company, and the company is potentially liable to pay any tax associated with providing a benefit to an employee. Local taxes in the form of sales taxes (paid on hotel stays or the purchase of goods from shops) or VAT (Value Added Tax) may also be payable by delegates. Organisers need to take advice from financial professionals and appropriate government agencies on tax, currency and similar financial issues.

Fisher (2000) suggests an allocation of budget for a typical corporate conference, drawing a distinction between fixed costs and variable costs, reproduced in Table 5.2.

Table 5.2 Budget allocations for a typical corporate conference

Fixed Costs	Likely Percentage
1. Production, staging and outside speakers	
2. Invitation process, marketing, design	
3. Conference rooms	
4. Agency fees, initial recce	
5. Signage	
6. Security, car parking set-up	35%
7. Cabaret, entertainment	
8. Registration costs	
9. Conference office costs, telephones, faxes	
10. Wet weather back-up, if applicable	
(Item 1 could be as much as 25% of total costs)	
Variable Costs (Per Delegate)	
1. Meals, breaks	
2. Drinks at meals, breaks	
3. Accommodation (housing)	
4. Travel	
5. Delegate print	
6. Table/room gifts	50%
7. Porterage, car parking per delegate	
8. Partner programme	
9. Late bar drinks	
10. Insurances, VAT (Value Added Tax)	
Contingency	
1. 10% to cover all contingencies for direct costs	15%
2. Allowance for currency movements (if abroad)	
Total Budget	100%

Sourcing and selecting a venue

There are many sources of information and advice to assist with choosing the venue most suited to a particular event. These include directories and brochures, websites and DVDs, trade exhibitions, trade media, and specialist agencies.

Directories and brochures

There are a number of annual directories available which provide a very useful reference source, some of which are international in their coverage, others national, and updated annually. Examples of international directories updated annually include:

- *Worldwide Convention Centres Directory*, published by CAT Publications – www.meetpie.com;
- *Guide to Accommodation, Wedding Venues and Meeting Venues*, as well as a series of Recommended Hotel Guides covering privately owned and independently run hotels throughout the world – published by Condé Nast Johansens.

Most, if not all, international trade associations (see Chapter 9) produce member directories (increasingly in electronic format via their websites) detailing their memberships and the services available through the trade association, which may include a venue finding and enquiry referral service. From a client (i.e. meeting planner) perspective, membership of a trade association by a venue or convention bureau can give a greater assurance of accredited standards and quality service.

At a national level, directories or brochures are produced by trade associations, by national convention bureaux and tourist boards, by hotel chains, and by venue consortia of the kind listed in Chapter 3. In the UK, UBM Plc (organiser of the 'International Confex' exhibition) publishes an annual guide to venues in the British Isles ('Venuefinder.com Blue and Green'), complementing its online venue finding service www.venuefinder.com.

All venues produce some form of promotional brochure and conference organisers may find it helpful to keep up-to-date copies of such information for those venues they use on a regular basis. They should also consider obtaining a set of *destination guides*, produced by most conference destinations (CVBs) and generally updated annually or biennially. These tend to be produced in A4 or quarto format, and describe (almost) all of the venues in a destination as well as summarising attractions, communications, support services and other features – in recent years the trend has been for much of this information to be stored on destination websites for ease of updating and to reduce the costs of printing, but hard copy guides can still be valuable companions.

Websites and DVDs

Computer software packages, listing conference venues, have been in existence since the early 1990s, although it is fair to say that the early versions struggled to achieve widespread acceptance among conference organisers. Nowadays, websites and DVDs have replaced the more traditional software format. Three of the leading Internet-based venue finding and enquiry systems are: www.venuedirectory.com, www.cvent.com and www.starcite.com. Sites such as these allow browsers to enter their own venue search criteria online, and details of venues that match are supplied to them within a matter of seconds. Browsers can then look at detailed information on the venues, including images, and may also be able to undertake a 'virtual' tour of the venue. There is also the facility to send a specific enquiry ('RFP') to venues shortlisted.

Many of the directories and brochures referred to in the previous section above can also be accessed electronically through their respective websites.

For those conference organisers who prefer to source their own venues, rather than use an intermediary organisation, websites and venue brochures/directories are a useful way of whittling down the options to a manageable shortlist. They do not, however, obviate the need to visit venues before making a final choice. Computer or printed images and text can help, but they do not replace the need to see a venue at first hand and meet the staff.

As Cotterell (1994) says, inspection visits:

> are important because there is much that cannot be ascertained from a brochure. The experienced organiser will travel to a venue the way most delegates will, to experience at first hand any problems with finding it or reaching it. Judgements will be made on the overall first impressions, the attitude of the staff, the quality, colours, style and condition of furnishings, the ease of getting from one area to another, and so on. Many experienced organisers make a check-list of points they need to cover. It is sometimes easier to attend one of the group inspection visits organised by hotels, tourist boards, convention bureaux, trade associations and some trade magazines. These give an opportunity, often over a weekend, to inspect a variety of venues within a location in the company of other organisers, an aspect that can be a most valuable opportunity to add to one's own personal network.

Trade exhibitions

There are a number of trade shows and exhibitions specifically designed for conference organisers and meeting planners, where the exhibitors include conference venues and destinations, conference service suppliers, intermediary agencies, transport companies and trade magazines. The benefit for conference organisers is that an exhibition enables them to make contact with potential suppliers, all under one roof – people it would be very expensive and time-consuming to contact individually away from the show. Exhibitions are a good way of updating information files, making personal contacts, finding out about new developments and facilities. Many exhibitions also have a seminar programme running alongside, covering topics of relevance to conference organisers in their everyday work.

Examples of major industry exhibitions include:

- *EIBTM (European Incentive and Business Travel and Meetings Exhibition)* – An international exhibition held in Barcelona, Spain in November and organised by Reed Travel Exhibitions. Several thousand buyers are hosted to the show each year by the organisers, who provide complimentary flights and overnight hotel accommodation. Further details: www.eibtm.com
- *IMEX* – Another highly international exhibition (see Chapter 1) held at Messe Frankfurt, Germany in April or May each year, and also including a major programme for hosted buyers. IMEX incorporates a German trade show, Meetings Made In Germany. Further information: www.imex-frankfurt.com
- *International Confex* – The largest of the British shows which is held at ExCeL, London (usually late February/early March). Exhibitors are British and overseas companies and organisations. Organised by UBM Plc. Further information: www.international-confex.com
- *AIME (Asia Incentives and Meetings Exhibition)* – Held at the Melbourne Exhibition and Convention Centre, Australia in February (first staged in 1993). Organised by Reed Travel Exhibitions. Further details: www.aime.com.au
- *IT&CMA (Incentive Travel and Conventions, Meetings Asia)* – This show has been running since 1993, and has been held annually in Thailand since 2002. It is organised by TTG Asia Media Pte Ltd. Further details: www.eventseye.com/fairs

Trade media

Conference industry trade magazines (both printed and electronic formats or ezines) and their associated websites are a valuable source of up-to-date news and features on conference venues and destinations, both national and international. As well as articles reviewing the facilities and attractions of specific areas, some magazines also include price comparisons between venues and case studies of events which illustrate how other organisers have staged events in particular locations.

Readers of trade magazines need to bear in mind that all of the magazines depend for their survival on attracting advertising support from conference venues and destinations, a fact which can sometimes influence editorial content. Despite this caveat, trade magazines are an important source of information and provide a service which does not exist elsewhere. They also contain many other articles, for example on trends and statistics and new legislation, which provide essential background for professional buyers.

Agencies

Various agencies provide specialist venue finding services. These include venue finding agencies, professional conference organisers (PCOs) and event management agencies, conference production companies, and destination management companies (DMCs) (see Chapter 2). Agency services are usually free to buyers (unless the agencies are also involved in the planning and organisation of a conference), with commission being charged to the venues where business is placed.

Whichever source(s) of information organisers choose to use (one of the most popular sources, not listed above, is that of peer group recommendations i.e. recommendations of venues by colleagues or by other conference organisers), they will need to have at their fingertips the answers to questions about their event which will be posed by venue staff or intermediary agencies. They will require information on:

- the nature of the conference/event and its key objectives;
- duration of the event (including any build-up and break-down time for stage sets, exhibition stands, etc.);
- proposed dates (and any possible flexibility with these to secure the best deal);
- number of delegates/partners/exhibitors/speakers;
- preferred location(s);
- type of venue sought and space/meeting room requirements, with room layouts;
- technical and audio-visual equipment needed and whether a specialist conference production company is to be used;
- catering requirements, with any special arrangements (e.g. private dining, receptions, entertainment);
- accommodation (numbers, types of bedroom);
- social programme activities/requirements (where appropriate);
- budget;
- deadline for receipt of information and details of the decision-making process.

Venue inspection checklist

Once a shortlist of potentially suitable venues has been produced, the next step is to inspect these venues by visiting in person. When undertaking an inspection visit, it is useful to go armed with a checklist of questions, such as:

- Is there the correct combination of rooms available for plenary sessions, syndicate groups, catering, possibly an accompanying exhibition?
- Is there good access for disabled delegates? Is the venue equipped in other ways to meet the many different disabilities that delegates (and speakers) may have?

- What style of seating will be needed? U-shape, boardroom, theatre-style, classroom, hollow square and herringbone are just some of the options (see Figure 5.2). For the purposes of calculations, a room which seats 100 delegates theatre-style will seat 50 classroom-style, 25 hollow square/boardroom/U-shape, and about 75 for dinner/lunch at round tables/top table with sprigs.
- Do the meeting rooms have natural light? If so, can the rooms be blacked out satisfactorily?
- How noisy is the heating and air conditioning system?
- If the event is residential, how many bedrooms will be available at the venue, and how many of these are single/double/twin bedrooms? Is it important for all delegates to sleep under the same roof, or can they be accommodated in different hotels and transported to the conference venue?
- Does the venue have leisure facilities and, if so, are they available to delegates free of charge?
- What are the options for social activities in the vicinity, if there is time in the conference programme for these?
- Does the venue have a dedicated conference co-ordinator (or team) who can assist with the detailed planning and arrangements?
- Are there other venue staff with whom you will be working and, if so, when will you be able to meet them? At what stage will the sales manager – usually the conference organiser's initial point of contact – pass on the booking details to colleagues, who then become the main points of reference?
- Are there in-house technical staff to operate audio-visual equipment? If so, is there an additional charge for using their services? If there are no such staff on site, what arrangements does the venue have with independent audio-visual companies, and what do they charge? What audio-visual equipment is needed during the event? (Normally this can be decided quite close to the event, unless the requirements are specialised or the event is a large one requiring substantial equipment and sophisticated production.) Is there Wi-Fi in the venue, and is it freely available?
- Can the venue offer any transport assistance for delegates travelling by public transport (e.g. collecting them by minibus from the airport or railway station)? How much car parking space does the venue have?
- Is there a high turnover of staff in the venue, which might create problems in the build-up? Does the venue team give the impression of being experienced, professional, easy-to-work-with?

Carey (1997) provides a series of checklists for conference organisers. An example of one of these is given in Figure 5.3.

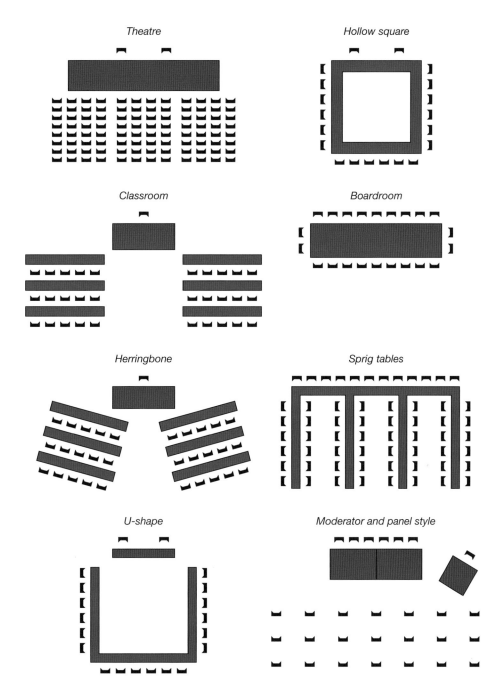

FIGURE 5.2 Seating options

To attend a site inspection without a checklist is a recipe for extra work, as vital questions will remain unasked and important features remain uninspected. Every conference brings its own demands but if you investigate the following you will be halfway there.

A. Location
- Independent access[1]
- Freight access[1]
- Easy to find? (well signed?)
- Proximity to:[2]
  - Main entrance and car park
  - Meal areas and kitchens
  - Fresh air
  - Lifts
  - Toilets and cloakrooms
  - Telephones
  - Break-out rooms
- Disabled access

B. Fixtures
- Decor
- Wall and floor materials[3]
- Pillars/obstructions
- Room shape and partitions[4]
- Location of doors
- Where doors lead to[5]
- Fire exits[6]
- Natural light/views

- Chandeliers and mirrors[7]
- Stage area and access to it
- Registration area
- Light switches or regulators
- Power and telephone points[8]
- Temperature controls (location)[9]
- Blackout curtains
- Acoustics
- Ceiling height[10]

C. Non-fixtures
- Chairs (comfort factor)
- Tables (size and coverings)
- Table furniture[11]
- Signage

D. General
- Cleanliness
- Overall comfort
- Capacity
- Ambience
- Pre-function space
- Smell

Notes:
1. Direct on to concourse, foyer or street.
2. Explore for yourself.
3. Should be sound absorbent, not bright and not 'busy'.
4. Are partitions really soundproof?
5. Beware doors that open on to kitchens or garbage areas.
6. Are they blocked or locked?
7. Chandeliers can impede projection. Mirrors toss light from projectors and lecterns indiscriminately around a room.
8. You may need lots for PCs, modems and fax machines.
9. Are they in the room?
10. High enough for maximum screen height.
11. What is provided? e.g. Water, cordials, note pads, mints.

Did you hear about the organizer who checked the dimensions of the access doors with the venue (over the phone) and computed that the car would fit through them? Sadly, he was unaware until the day of the launch that the room he had booked wasn't on the ground floor!

FIGURE 5.3 Meeting room checklist

Negotiating with venues

Once a shortlist of suitable venues has been produced and inspection visits made, the process of negotiating a final rate or package with the preferred venue takes place. Conference organisers should be aware of a venue's need to maximise yield from its bookings (as described in Chapter 6) but, nonetheless, there is almost always scope to negotiate on a venue's published delegate rates.

Carey (1997) suggests that:

As a professional conference organiser, you are in a powerful position to negotiate a good deal with your chosen venue and it can be tempting to bully the management into ridiculously low room, food and beverage rates. This may make you feel good and impress your Finance Director but it will almost certainly jeopardize the vital relationship between you and the venue. As a rule, it is better to pay a reasonable rate for facilities and accommodation and then negotiate added value and service.

In short, good negotiation is about creating a win-win situation for both the event organiser and the venue, but also about building relationships and partnerships, and doing business with people who want to do business with you.

Some flexibility on the part of the organiser can assist in the negotiation process, particularly if this can help to make a booking even more attractive in the eyes of the venue. The following points should also be borne in mind:

- Only negotiate with venue staff who have the authority to make decisions.
- Underline and sell the stature and value of your event to the venue.
- It is a good sign if the venue asks lots of questions about your event. Give them as much information as possible *before* discussing rates.
- Be prepared by doing your homework on the venue's 'rack' (i.e. published) rates and having a copy of the venue's brochure on file before discussing a deal. Establish what the venue's tariffs are for other types of business.
- Give the venue manager an indication of your budget (unless it is higher than their published rates!).
- If you can offer some flexibility on dates/timings, you are likely to get a better deal, bearing in mind that venues are seeking back-to-back bookings. If the event is to be held midweek, rates charged are likely to be higher than at weekends. Significant reductions can be achieved by holding an event at least partially over a weekend when occupancy levels, especially for hotels, are generally lower.
- The scope for negotiation will also depend on the time of year (autumn and spring are the peak seasons for conferences, and so the busiest for the venues), the number of delegates, nature of the organisation (lower rates may be available for not-for-profit organisations).
- Published rates do not cover the same package from venue to venue. It is, therefore, important to examine what the rates do actually include. The provision of audio-visual equipment is one of the areas where wide variations can exist.
- While most venues (and certainly almost all hotels) promote a delegate package (expressed either as a non-residential or eight-hour or day delegate rate OR as a residential or 24-hour delegate rate), it is also possible to ask for room hire and catering charges separately, and sometimes these may be cheaper than an integrated package.

Cotterell (1994) puts forward a number of strategies to be used by conference buyers in the negotiation process, including:

- be prepared – for example, know the prices charged by the venue to other clients (if possible), and know the prices charged by similar venues in the area;
- be nice, but gain respect;
- don't lie;
- be flexible;
- never reveal deadlines;
- name drop;
- hint at other business to be placed;
- be patient;
- disclaim responsibility (for the final decision);
- don't underestimate the sellers.

Programme planning

It is of prime importance that the conference programme matches the overall objectives set at the initial planning stage. The content, style and pace of the programme will, of course, vary from event to event. There is now a strong business orientation to most conferences, plus a clear requirement for even large conferences to be more participatory, inviting delegate contributions to plenary presentations and, particularly, through a greater use of syndicate sessions and appropriate technology. There is also a requirement for programmes to cater for different delegate needs: this may be less of a concern for corporate conferences where delegates' levels of experience and expertise can be checked and controlled, but a challenge for association conferences where delegates are self-selecting to a much greater extent and will have disparate levels of experience.

The choice of speakers, and leaders of syndicate or workshop sessions, is crucial to the success of the formal conference programme. In some cases, decisions about speakers may be imposed upon the organiser by senior managers or a conference committee. Where this is the case, the organiser's role is to ensure that speakers are properly briefed about the aims for the conference as well as for their own presentation, and that all of the technical and environmental factors (room layout, audio-visual facilities, introductory speeches) are carefully planned to create a successful 'performance'.

Richard John (2011) makes the point that, in today's conference, 'content is king' and he stresses the importance of choosing speakers who can identify with the needs of their audience:

So many conferences have been packed full of speakers talking about how they went up Mount Everest using a pogo stick, which is fine, but has no real value to your organisation. Glib, perma-tanned speakers are being replaced by those who really

do have a genuine and original story to tell, and who can explain how to apply their lessons to your organisation. Without that, you're just enjoying some theatre, and it's probably more expensive than the best West End show.

When the organiser has to take on the task of sourcing speakers, imagination and recommendation should be uppermost in his or her mind, probably in equal proportions. It is often stimulating for delegates to listen to a speaker with new ideas or controversial views, and a rousing opening session which generates discussion and debate may be just the spark needed to ensure a lively and productive conference. But few organisers will be willing to put their own reputations on the line by inviting relatively unknown speakers to the platform, unless they come recommended by others. Colleagues and peers are clearly an important source of such speaker recommendations. Other sources can include trade associations, editors of trade magazines, university or college departments, speaker bureaux and professional conference organisers.

Some conferences are strictly business events with little or no free time. Others, particularly in the association sector, combine a business programme with a social programme. The social itinerary is another area where an organiser has an opportunity to display his or her creativity and really make the conference memorable. The social programme should allow delegates to mix informally and network (for many this is often the most worthwhile part of the event), but also to experience something of the destination in which the conference is being staged. It may be possible for social activities to extend, in a lighthearted way, the theme of the conference. Invaluable assistance in the design of social programmes is available from the local convention bureau or conference office, as well as from PCOs and, especially, DMCs. Examples of social events organised by the author for trade association conferences in the UK have included:

- a tour of the Whisky Heritage Centre in Edinburgh followed by dinner, concluding with a late-evening guided tour of the narrow streets around Edinburgh Castle by a 'ghost' (Adam Lyal Deceased) – a truly haunting experience!;
- a banquet in the splendour of Cardiff Castle featuring Welsh dancers and a male voice choir;
- a Caribbean evening in Leicester, with delegates in Caribbean costume being entertained by steel bands and cabaret;
- a torchlit drinks reception in the Roman baths in Bath, followed by a banquet in the Pump Room;
- a formal whisky tasting, under instruction, at Glamis Castle near Dundee followed by a tour of the Castle and a sumptuous banquet;
- a boat trip to the island of Sark (from a conference in Guernsey) with rides by horse-drawn carriage and bicycle (there are no cars on Sark), followed by dinner.

Each of these gave the event a unique character and made it an enjoyable and memorable experience.

Event marketing

Marketing is an essential part of the event management process. There is little point in devoting a great deal of time and resources to the organisation of a conference, if few people bother to attend. The marketing should begin at the earliest possible stage, even if this only entails publicising brief details of the event so that potential delegates have reserved the date in their diary.

Event marketing is not just about maximising delegate numbers. It also creates a positive attitude towards the event for everyone concerned (speakers, delegates, venue and suppliers, trade media, etc.) and helps to raise its profile, both within its own industry sector but also within the conference sector.

Clearly the greater the budget for marketing, the more that can be done, but much can still be achieved without a huge promotional 'pot'. The following are some ideas that can be used or adapted to meet the needs of any organisation:

- Ensure that the printed brochure/leaflet used to promote the event, containing the conference programme, is of the highest standard affordable. Increasingly the programme is also produced in electronic format as a PDF which can be disseminated by email to potential delegates, and/or be posted onto appropriate websites. The programme sets the tone for the event and, if well done, goes a long way to creating interest in, and positive expectations from, the conference. It should contain:

  - an introduction (possibly in the form of an invitation/welcome from the organisation's chief executive or chair);
  - the conference programme (in as much detail as is confirmed at this stage – a final programme can be circulated nearer the event to registered delegates);
  - short biographies of speakers and contributors;
  - upbeat information on the venue (and destination) being used, ideally with some photographs;
  - details of any event sponsors;
  - a booking form (either as part of the leaflet or as a separate insert);
  - if the conference has been held previously, favourable quotations from delegates should be included in the promotional material and programme brochure. Peer group quotes are one of the most effective ways of generating interest.

- A PR strategy should be prepared for the event (although not normally applicable to corporate conferences). This will include the issue of press releases to help create awareness of the conference and raise its profile as an event 'not-to-be-missed'. As well as giving key facts and figures about the conference, the releases should contain details of new or controversial issues and topics to be discussed at the conference, quotes from the organisers and keynote speaker(s) (where appropriate), and set out briefly what the conference is intended to achieve.

- Direct marketing, including e-marketing, is one of the main marketing tools to be used, especially with association and entrepreneurial conferences, but is dependent on access to a good quality database of potential invitees.
- Maximise use of the Internet by developing a site for the event and/or incorporating full event details in other websites. The website may offer online registration facilities, including payment over the web, but the site must be secure and all data encrypted.
- Advertising may also be appropriate when promoting an entrepreneurial type of event, and sometimes when marketing to the association sector where delegates can choose whether or not to attend. Advertising should normally be used to complement other press and PR activity, rather than being used in isolation.

The following additional tips are based on an article written by Robin Lokerman, Chief Executive Officer of MCI Group's Institutional Division, published in *Conference & Meetings World* magazine (Lokerman 2011).

Planning and delivering a conference involves many thousands of people hours, but even the most impeccably organised event can fail to achieve the anticipated numbers of fee-paying delegates. Inevitably this reflects a weakness in event promotion. So what are the key elements in successful conference marketing? A well prepared marketing plan should consider the following promotional elements:

Market analysis

To reach your target audience it is vital to first identify it. If you don't have this information, capture it by sending out a free email survey.

Brainstorm

Avoid the 'inside looking out syndrome' and capture valuable data by brainstorming with past and potential attendees to develop the value proposition of the conference.

Event branding

Promote the conference as a 'must attend' event by identifying a catchy theme or positioning statement for it e.g. *'All the latest advances in XYZ under one roof'*.

Conference logo/livery

Engage a competent designer to create a conference style sheet. Don't rely on the association's logo – customise a conference identity. Avoid non-standard fonts and colours – they will be lost in most web browsers.

Promotional items

Merchandise is back in vogue as a creative way of promoting a conference. Delegates attending the 2011 Site International Conference in Las Vegas received redeemable gambling chips. A promotional DVD can be inexpensively created by 'topping and tailing' local convention bureau footage with a welcome message from the conference chairperson. Footage from a previous event is also effective.

Website

A low cost web presence, preferably one with an easily updateable Content Management System (CMS), is necessary. Spend funds on marketing the site rather than flash animation. Enable analytics to gauge where delegates are coming from and use this data to help target relevant markets. Use tools such as Search Engine Optimisation (SEO) and Adwards to improve the site rankings.

Email promotion

Email communication is cheap but it is also the least effective promotional method. Ninety-five per cent of all email is spam and filters are increasingly aggressive. Always use the same email address to send conference-related email; ideally from the conference's own domain.

Promotion at other events

Engage with delegates by setting up a display booth at a kindred association conference.

Social media

In its simplest form, social media is about using Facebook, YouTube and Twitter to blog, and flog people, ideas and products. Gen Y and Z may use it, but it is not widely used by mainstream Gen X or Baby Boomers, often the main source of delegate revenue. Reflect on your target audience before investing in social media tactics. (See below for a more in-depth exposition of the use of social media in event marketing and management.)

Direct mail

Secure fewer than 20 per cent new delegates at your event and you are regressing. Consider buying mail/email lists and designing a special campaign to generate interest.

CASE STUDY 5.2 Using Twitter at 'The Future Is You' Conference

'The Future Is You' is a conference for final year events management students held as part of the annual *International Confex* tradeshow at London's ExCeL venue – the conference is organised by the author in conjunction with PCO Rose Padmore of Opening Doors & Venues. For the 2012 event, the organisers were very keen to create a feeling of 'here and now' delegate engagement, particularly as the audience were primarily of the digital native category (i.e. born and brought up during the age of digital technology and thus familiar with computers and the Internet from an early age).

The Twitter hashtag #studentyouconfex was introduced, by email, to all registered delegates a couple of days prior to the event to encourage 'real time' conversation and provide a platform for gauging immediate reaction. Using hashtags before relevant key-words in tweets enables the creation of a mini 'real time' community because, when clicking on a hashtagged word in any message, all the other tweets also using it are revealed.

Initial comments and conversations pre-conference indicated a general feeling of looking forward to the event, as well as moans about the early start on the actual morning! During the conference a few positive speaker reviews were posted – as well as some comments about the quality of refreshments. However, the lack of Wi-Fi in the conference room meant that only phones with 3G would actually operate.

Post-event comments were also very interesting and, although it was a short-lived community, it served its purpose and the intention is that, for 2013, if Wi-Fi is available, a live Twitter feed will be displayed on a plasma screen to encourage others to join in.

Telemarketing

It's effective but can be costly and the process of building and cleaning appropriate lists can be time-consuming. Ask the volunteer committee to contact 10–20 associates and ask them in turn to contact another 10–20. A message coming from a trusted referrer is highly effective.

Media relations

If budget allows, profile speakers to the media during the conference and leverage any press coverage after the conference.

Time path

The overall conference time path should include:

- promotional opportunities/deadlines (e.g. cross-promotion at similar conferences; through journals);
- printed material deadlines (e.g. first announcement; call for papers; registration brochure; handbook; abstracts volume);
- scientific programme and speaker deadlines (e.g. deadline for abstract submission; review procedures; deadline for full papers; audio-visual requirements);
- registration requirements/deadlines (e.g. early bird deadline);
- sponsorship/trade deadlines (e.g. deadlines for confirming sponsors).

Finally, the old adage that you have to spend money to make money rings true. Research shows it's rare for more than 2 per cent of conference budget to be spent on marketing the event.

Conference management and production

The general management of a conference requires, in Carey's (1997) words, *'common sense, forethought, meticulous planning and attention to detail, team work and sometimes crisis management'*. Much of the administration can be enhanced by the use of event management software packages, which are designed to handle delegate registrations and correspondence, itinerary planning, accommodation arrangements, abstract management, speaker liaison, exhibition management, invoicing, report production, delegate evaluations and other aspects – the jargon term is 'meetings procurement solutions'. Increasingly such products are also available as web-based tools which allow online registrations and other real-time applications. Examples of such meetings procurement solutions include:

- Events Pro produced by Certain (see www.certainevents.com);
- Meetings technology solutions from Cvent (see www.cvent.com);
- Strategic meetings management technology produced by Starcite + Active Network (see www.starcite.com);
- Eventbookings.NET produced by UK company Eventbookings.com (see www.event bookings.com).

There is a very useful free e-newsletter detailing the latest developments in technology and web applications for meetings, hospitality and travel industry professionals, circulated free of charge every two months and compiled by Corbin Ball. It is entitled 'Corbin's

Techtalk Newsletter' – anyone wishing to be added to the circulation list should email him at: corbin@corbinball.com.

It is useful to provide delegates, either in advance or at the registration desk, with a printed itinerary detailing the timing and location of individual sessions, particularly important when there are a number of sessions running concurrently or 'in parallel'. When this is the case, delegates will normally have been asked to pre-select the sessions of most interest to them and it is worth producing a reminder list of these sessions for them, perhaps with a list of the other delegates who have chosen the same sessions. Delegate badges can now have a microchip inserted to track whether delegates are attending the correct conference sessions or which stands they have visited in a major exhibition, while other networking devices allow delegates to identify and make contact with individuals who are of particular interest to them.

It should be remembered that a conference is an event which needs to be stage-managed and which requires a very professional approach to its production and presentation on the day. Through familiarity with television programmes and other broadcast media, delegates now expect the same high standards of presentation in their working environments. Multimedia shows are not just about glitz – they really do get the message across. Poorly produced slides or overheads, problems with projectors or microphones, ill-prepared chairmen, intrusive air conditioning, uncomfortable seating are just some of the all too frequently voiced criticisms of conferences and all are less and less acceptable. What is more, all can and should be avoided with proper planning.

While the message is, of course, more important than the medium used to convey it, the message may get lost or misinterpreted if not presented in a way which holds delegates' attention. For this reason, the appropriate use of audio-visual technology should be discussed with speakers, who will usually have their own ideas about how best to make their presentations. If something more than just an overhead projector and flipchart, or data projector and computer, are to be used, an organiser should look at employing a specialist conference production company. The services of such companies are not cheap, but their costs can be built into the budget and will minimise the risk of embarrassing crises, as well as reassuring speakers that their presentations will not be plagued by technical hitches.

Wherever possible, speakers should participate in rehearsals, both to familiarise themselves with the room and technical equipment to be used, and also to run through the sequence of introductions and cues to be used with the session chairman.

Technology is now on the market which allows an entire conference to be recorded on video, audio and in text format, translated into any language and placed on a DVD to be played back on a computer by the delegate (or, of course, sold to those who were unable to attend the conference, both to extend the conference audience and to generate additional income streams for the organisers). Some products contain a complete 'virtual' environment, allowing delegates to walk between lecture theatres and meeting rooms as if present at the conference.

Other technology tips include:

- Check whether any speakers' PowerPoint presentations have video embedded in them – and whether the speakers need access to the web for online demonstrations.
- Are social media to be used for directing questions to speakers? If so, ensure there is a delay on questions appearing and be very prepared for blunt questions!
- Check on the venue's bandwidth as many delegates will wish to check their emails during the event – ensure there is sufficient bandwidth for them to do so.
- Is the venue's Wi-Fi free of charge? Bear in mind that 'free' is no guarantee of quality or size of bandwidth.
- Encrypt the Wi-Fi network using an alphanumerical password and the best encryption possible.

Chapter 10 will outline some of the other developments and applications of technology, including the growing use of hybrid events.

Event evaluation and measuring return on investment (ROI)

Once the conference is over, an evaluation of the event needs to take place as soon as possible. Ideally, delegates should complete assessments for each session as soon as it ends or shortly afterwards, either through a printed questionnaire or an online evaluation form. Delegates attending the 22nd World Congress of Dermatology in Seoul in 2011 used an optical mark recognition questionnaire system to generate feedback. Delegate itineraries can include evaluation questionnaires (a sample is shown at Figure 5.4) for each session, as well as an overall evaluation sheet for completion at the end of the conference. Feedback from delegates is essential in assessing the success of the conference. It is also very important as a means of gathering ideas for future events. It may be appropriate for delegate questionnaires to be completed anonymously to encourage honest comments, and some form of incentive can also increase the number of responses.

In some cases, of course, a fully objective appraisal of the conference will not be possible until months later, as the outcomes of the event are translated into improved sales, enhanced performances, a more effective sharing of information, or whatever objectives were set in the first place.

The organiser will also want to evaluate how, from his or her perspective, the conference was managed and to what extent it met the set objectives. Ideas for improving those aspects which did not work well should emerge, and the more successful elements can be developed further in the future.

An appraisal should also take place with the venue. In the author's experience, this is an area where many venues lose marks. Discussions between the venue and the client

CONVENTION SESSION 1 - EVALUATION SHEET

Session Title:

Session Date:

Presenter:

The following is a general questionnaire, some statements may not be applicable to this session. If so, please omit.

Please indicate the extent to which you agree or disagree with the following statements regarding this session. (4 = strongly agree, 1 = strongly disagree; circle one number only.)

	Strongly Agree			Strongly Disagree
The speaker demonstrated knowledge of the subject	4	3	2	1
The speaker was effective in communicating the subject matter	4	3	2	1
The subject matter was of relevance and interest	4	3	2	1
The visual aids/handouts formed a useful part of the presentation	4	3	2	1
The question and answer session was of benefit	4	3	2	1
I learnt new skills/gained new insight and understanding	4	3	2	1

- **My overall impression of the session was:**

  _____

  _____

  _____

  _____

- **Additional Comments:**

  _____

  _____

  _____

  _____

FIGURE 5.4 Evaluation questionnaire (Source: British Association of Conference Destinations)

after the event seem to be the exception, whereas they should be the norm. Even when an event appears to have run smoothly, there will always be scope for further improvement. Venues should take the initiative in following up with clients to assess all aspects of their performance.

It is worthwhile preparing a post-conference/convention report: a detailed summary of every aspect of the event, from total attendance to room usage to food and beverage functions and more. It will take time to prepare such an in-depth document, but the rewards are worth the effort. It is both an invaluable reference tool for planning next year's conference (it is much easier reading through a detailed four-page or five-page summary document than having to work through bulky files), and a powerful negotiating tool since it contains accurate figures from the conference, including details of all revenue spent at the conference venue.

Return on investment (ROI)/return on objectives (ROO)

It is increasingly essential for conferences and business events to demonstrate that they are providing appropriate returns on the investments that companies and organisations are making in them. Such events are required to show that they have led to greater productivity, higher sales, enhanced performance by the individuals who have attended them, better team morale, more effective team collaborations, and so forth. The Event ROI Institute defines return on investment (ROI) as the net meeting benefits achieved when set against the total costs of a meeting.

This means that it is no longer sufficient simply to carry out evaluations after an event in the form of reaction and satisfaction surveys among delegates. Companies now demand to know how effective their meetings and events have been. As budgets come under closer scrutiny, more companies are asking questions such as: *'Why are we holding this meeting?' 'Could we achieve our objectives more effectively?'* – the kinds of questions it was suggested earlier in this chapter that event organisers should always be asking.

The challenge for conference organisers and meeting planners is to find a consistent way of measuring the effectiveness of their events, one that will convince the procurement department and chief financial officer of the return on their investment.

The Event ROI Institute (www.eventroi.org) actively promotes the ROI Methodology as a robust and logical approach to ROI measurement. This emphasises the importance of setting objectives for a return on investment before the meeting takes place so that, post event, an assessment can be made of the extent to which the objectives were met. The ROI Methodology sets objectives and measures results at six levels, from Level 0 to Level 5. The information below is taken from a paper entitled 'The ROI Methodology' written by Dr Elling Hamso (2009) of the Event ROI Institute, and reproduced with permission:

- *ROI Objectives (Level 5): Setting the desired ROI or profit from the event, its contribution to shareholder value in the business world, or its contribution to the*

mission of a non-profit organisation. From this level, objectives are cascaded downwards to Level 0 which is called the Target Audience. Results are measured in the opposite direction, from Level 0 to Level 5, as shown in the ROI pyramid [Figure 5.5].

- *Impact Objectives (Level 4): The Impact, or Business Impact, is the ultimate value contribution of the event to its stakeholders. The Impact is used in the profit and ROI calculations. For a customer event, the Impact is usually sales. For an internal event, it is typically organisational effectiveness.*

- *Behaviour Objectives (Level 3): What do the guests or participants at meetings and events need to do, during and after the event, in order to create value for the stakeholders? The answers may well be different for different categories of participants. Some actions may be significant (e.g. buy the product) whereas others only make a small contribution to value, maybe increasing the probability of a purchase (e.g. ask for more information, share knowledge with colleagues, investigate alternative solutions, etc.). The behavioural change may involve ceasing to do something, doing something differently, or taking some new actions as a result of attending the event.*

- *Learning Objectives (Level 2): What cognitive change (i.e. learning) is required for the participants to change their behaviour? All behaviour change is pre-empted by cognitive change. The cognitive change might be subconscious, but something always has to change in the mind before behaviour changes.*

- *Satisfaction and Learning Environment Objectives (Level 1): How can we design a learning environment which will make cognitive change most effective? Learning is influenced by the state of mind of the learner as well as ambient factors (e.g. room temperature and air quality), instructional design, speaker quality, etc.*

- *Target Audience Objectives (Level 0): Finally, how do we ensure that the right people are attending? Do they have opportunities to apply what they learn to the benefit of their stakeholders? Are they learning something new, which will change their behaviour?*

Once the objectives have been set, the meeting planner can calculate a return on investment by comparing the monetary benefits to the cost of the meeting. An example of the calculation made would be as follows, for a meeting costing £80,000 and with the benefits of the meeting being valued at £240,000:

$$\text{Benefits/Cost Ratio} = \frac{\text{Meeting Benefits}}{\text{Meeting Costs}} \quad \text{i.e.} \quad \frac{£240,000}{£80,000} = 3$$

$$\text{ROI} = \frac{\text{Net Meeting Benefits}}{\text{Meeting Costs}} \quad \text{i.e.} \quad \frac{£160,000}{£80,000} = 200\%$$

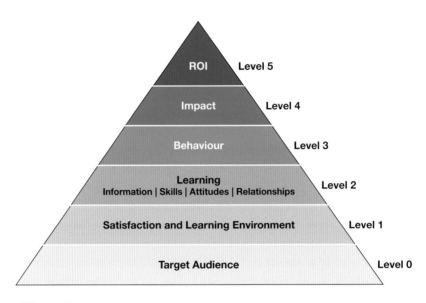

FIGURE 5.5 ROI pyramid

2011 research by Meeting Professionals International (MPI) has shown that few companies have a formal strategy in place for measuring the value of their meetings and events. The research, which was part of the MPI study into the Business Value of Meetings (BVOM), found that there were a lot of perceived challenges into what it takes to measure efficiently and effectively the business value of meetings and events. It also found that:

- companies that are measuring are relying on traditional satisfaction surveys and are not beginning with design concepts and clear objectives;
- many corporate cultures embrace measures of value other than traditional ROI. They want to know if a meeting has accomplished its stated objectives, because this implies a business value, even if that value is not reduced to a monetary quantity;
- there are significant differences in definitions between North America, Asia and Europe;
- most planners perceive good measurement as too complicated or expensive. Many organisations successfully measuring the BVOM focus on only a few key elements, making the actual costs of measurement less than most perceive;
- measures vary by meeting type: educational, sales, networking, etc.

MPI's BVOM study revealed several benefits resulting from proper measurement, reporting and planning (summarised in an article 'Perception vs Reality' in *Conference & Meetings World* magazine: Colston 2012):

- **Clarity of Purpose** – *by understanding the measurable outcomes, organisers and planners can make their meetings more cost efficient and more clearly align their activities and environments with clear objectives.*
- **Quantification of Meeting Success** – *meeting professionals and the organisations they serve learn how much needs to be done to accomplish their goals by creating, deploying and reporting on measures of meeting success. This allows them to establish budgets, make strategic decisions about meeting logistics, design goals and establish realistic expectations.*
- **Identification of Strengths and Weaknesses** – *by understanding a meeting's strengths and weaknesses, professionals can better concentrate resources where they are needed most and lever asset areas.*
- **Creation of Better Measures** – *gaining insights into meeting performance relative to objectives requires trial and error to get meaningful information for the lowest cost. Implementing an intentional and planned strategy for understanding the business value of events leads meeting professionals to develop better measures over time, making the process more valuable.*
- **Comprehensive Measures** – *each individual measure can be assessed for value. New measures can be introduced to help understand and use that information. This process results in more comprehensive views of the business value of meetings and leads to a better understanding of the contribution of meetings to an organisation, and in many cases leads to good approximations of ROI.*
- **Easier Evaluations** – *successful strategies for understanding the business value of meetings lead to a process for improving meetings. This is central to assessing value. As meetings become better, they become more clearly aligned with objectives, therefore more effective. The reduction of time, money and personnel, combined with clearly stated objectives, makes the actual costs and benefits of meetings easier to evaluate. Events with unclear purposes are difficult to assess, because proper budgets and outcomes are speculative.*

For a measurement strategy to be effective, it needs to be implemented as part of a process in which stakeholders are engaged, objectives defined, measures are appropriate and results are used to make improvements to meetings and the process itself.

An interview with Dr Elling Hamso of the Event ROI Institute by *Meetings:review* (June 2011) quoted Dr Hamso as saying:

> *There is more serious talk about ROI now, not only for meetings and events, but right across the marketing mix, including social media. There is a well proven industry standard methodology for measuring the effectiveness of meetings and events – it is simply a matter of putting it to practical use, and that takes time. Data collection technology is developing fast, online surveys migrate to mobile devices, audience response systems are becoming cheap and effective. The great thing is that*

everything digital is measurable, like the event's digital footprint as a measure of social media engagement. We are moving up the Chain of Impact, but there are still some hills to climb before we have a good grasp of bottom-line value.

Dr Hamso further comments:

The economic downturn was a forceful reminder that, if you can't prove the value you bring to the table, then your budgets are cut. And I agree with those who cut the budgets. If you are not reasonably confident that a meeting or event will add to the bottom line, don't take the risk, and don't spend the money. This is the only sensible and responsible management action. If results are not properly measured, it invariably means that proper detailed and measurable objectives are not set, and without proper objectives, most of the budget will be wasted anyway as you don't really know why you're spending it.

2012 research among meeting planners entitled 'The Power of 10', commissioned by IMEX-Frankfurt and carried out by Fast Future Research, revealed that 91 per cent of the planners who responded strongly agreed or agreed that '*To reduce its vulnerability to economic cycles, the business events industry must demonstrate a tangible return on investment for event owners, delegates, sponsors, exhibitors and other key stakeholders*'.

For further details on the European Event ROI Institute, including opportunities to participate in free ROI webinars, visit: www.eventroi.org. The ROI White Paper may be downloaded free of charge from this website. Additional information may be found at: www.scribd.com/eventroialumni. Information on MPI's Business Value of Meetings research can be accessed at: www.mpiweb.org/bvom

CASE STUDY 5.3 The Kenes Group

Introduction and background

Kenes Group is a specialised company providing international congress management services as well as professional management support and execution for medical scientific societies. In its aim to be the 'first among equals', Kenes Group has developed targeted supporting expertise such as full marketing communication, branding media and communication services, specialised educational services offering online accredited learning based on congress content, as well as expertise and skills to optimise meeting connectivity and exchange.

Kenes was formed in 1965 by Mr Gideon Rivlin, who, from day one, interpreted the role of a professional congress organiser as being the enabler and caretaker of a perfect congress without financial concerns for his clients, enabling them to enjoy

a content-rich and worry-free meeting or congress. Mr Gideon Rivlin is still serving the company as Chairman of the Board while his son, Dan Rivlin, is the current Managing Director of the Kenes Group.

The Kenes Group is registered and headquartered in Geneva, Switzerland with group management and operational offices in Geneva, Tel Aviv and Amsterdam. Some 500 proud professionals in a multi-talented and multi-cultural team work within the Kenes Group at Group headquarters and in regional offices in Asia and Latin America, in national offices in Germany, United Kingdom, Spain, Turkey, India, Brazil and in an association management team in Geneva and the USA. Although allowing for local differences in culture and style, all Kenes offices are supported by Kenes systems and backed up by managerial and operational departments enabling the delivery of a guaranteed level of service worldwide.

Figure 5.6 is an organigram showing the provision of services across the Kenes Group.

Mission, vision and values

The Kenes Company mission, vision and its values are totally connected with its dedication to servicing medical, life sciences and healthcare communities of practitioners and scientists:

- *Mission:* Kenes strives to improve lives by leading and facilitating the global exchange and management of medical knowledge.
- *Vision:* Kenes endeavours to enhance its legacy as a leading and innovative provider of unhindered access to scientific knowledge and education throughout the world.
- *Company values:* accountability, corporate social responsibility, excellent service, pioneering spirit, teamwork and transparency.

Some facts

Since 1965, 2,857 conferences have been organised by Kenes in 104 countries; 46 years of experience; 115,000 conference attendees per year; 108 long-term core PCO clients have asked Kenes to organise their conferences time after time and some 30 medical and scientific organisations with some 40,000 individual/societal members are supported by Kenes Association Management professionals. www.kenes.com gives an actual overview of all congresses organised and congresses planned.

Knowledge worth sharing

'Knowledge Worth Sharing', chosen by Kenes Group as the unifying motto, is a manifestation of the values and brand promise of the company. Kenes Group clients have a wealth of important medical and scientific knowledge that needs to be shared. And the role of Kenes is to facilitate the distribution of that knowledge through

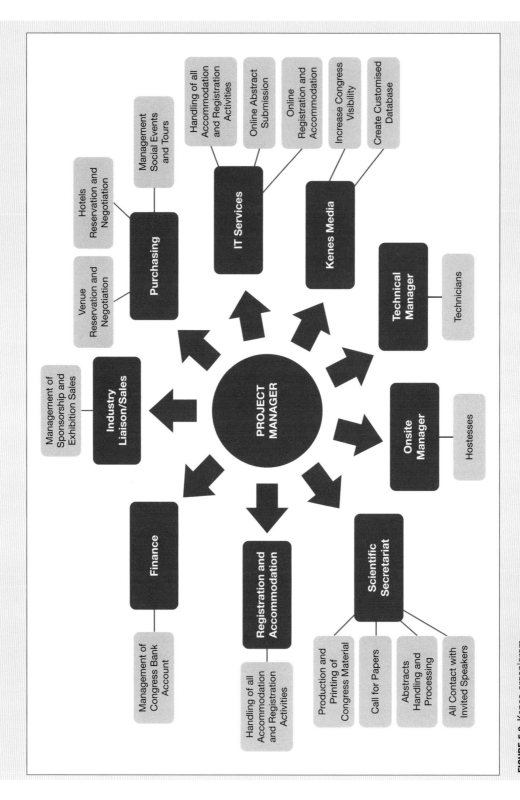

FIGURE 5.6 Kenes organigram

congresses, association management and the development of knowledge portals, in the most efficient and innovative way – for the organisation and for the individual end user. Thus the services Kenes provides include all that is necessary to deliver a high level, professional and functional range of services:

- full conference and association management;
- industry relations and creation of exhibitions supporting congresses;
- full media planning and execution;
- delegate registration, booking and providing of hotel accommodation;
- preparing and executing of all technical requirements from simple to complicated audio-visuals;
- signage and room settings;
- from webcasting to knowledge portal development;
- from hostesses to ingenious meeting communication support;
- from programme planning, and accreditation, to accounting and financing;
- planning to organisation of social events.

An up-to-date and modern interpretation of how the founding father of Kenes saw his role. To enable and be the caretaker of a perfect congress without financial concerns for its clients, enabling them to enjoy a content-rich and worry-free meeting or congress focused on optimal networking and learning opportunities for delegates and members. Giving them the support and development for robust and relevant scientific organisations, taking the needs of all stakeholders as a matter of course.

Market trends

Kenes Group is keenly aware of market changes and trends and adapts itself accordingly, by upgrading its existing services and systems worldwide, by developing and fostering as operational skills not only practical operations but the skills and knowhow of adult learning and interactivity in live environments, by utilising the latest communication skills and techniques such as social media, hybrid meetings and well thought through meeting architecture, by being as green a company as possible and by further expanding its operations into countries and regions that matter.

This case study was written by Quirine Laman Trip, Kenes Group Director Business Development (www.kenes.com)

Social media blue paper

The following information is based on a Blue Paper entitled 'Social Media Handbook for Conventions' published in 2011 by Lykle de Vries and Ronald Mulder of De Ondernemers BV, which is now available (in Dutch) in book form (De Vries and Mulder 2011).

General introduction

Social media influence the way in which we communicate, cooperate and share information. This offers major opportunities for conventions. And conventions in 2011 will get a grip on social media, and vice versa.

The world is becoming increasingly smaller and, therefore, way bigger

Even just a few years ago it may have been a problem if the expert on your discipline lived in Bangkok, but this is far less important these days. Sharing knowledge is easier than ever, and more information is available than ever before. The expert in Bangkok can be in constant touch with other experts around the world. People who are interested can often view/read the information, and even contact the expert directly for questions. It used to be extremely valuable, and required, that a speaker share his or her knowledge during a convention. These days this is far less necessary, as knowledge is shared anywhere and anytime.

The largest audience is outside the auditorium

During a convention, delegates are inspired, knowledge is shared or decisions are made. In many cases, the number of interested parties or possible contributors is larger outside the auditorium than inside. By using social media you can open up that 'outside auditorium'. You share what happens and, where desired or necessary, you allow the people outside the auditorium to interact. This yields new dynamics, new opportunities and new aspects to which you have to pay attention.

The discussion is ongoing and so, therefore, is knowledge sharing

As a result, the value of the physical meeting of people during an event or convention also changes. Experts, pro-ams and interested parties continuously exchange knowledge, as a result of which the boundaries between these groups are blurring. For this reason, conventions are no longer a stand-alone moment of sharing knowledge, but one element of the ongoing discussion.

The paradigm of the sending expert and receiving visitor is shifting

The convention of the future is not an event for sending only. Visitors are increasingly more independent and share their opinions by way of several channels. They no longer want to be restricted to asking their questions after the convention, they also want to contribute their own experiences and expertise during the lecture. Visitors increasingly attend with a view to participating rather than consuming. Use this to your advantage! This is valuable input when preparing your convention. Why come up with elements yourselves that you think will satisfy the needs of the convention visitors while you can ask them? Being an organiser is no longer about being the gatekeeper who decides what will and will not be discussed during a convention.

Shift from gatekeeper to custodian

Rather than deciding what is said exactly, and by whom, an organiser is increasingly more responsible for managing all conversations, both offline and online, before, during and after the convention. If you do this well, your convention will remain relevant for your discipline and your target audience. If you do not manage to successfully play the role of custodian, you will find that fewer speakers and delegates will be interested in your convention.

Marketing versus word of mouth

The marketing and promotion of a convention or event is subject to the same changes. Traditional advertising and promotions are increasingly less effective, while targeted promotion is more and more easy. A well-read weblog on a certain topic is a better place to inform visitors about an upcoming convention than a flyer that is inserted in a trade journal, and usually cheaper.

Prior to the convention

When you do the spadework for the next edition of your event or convention, do take some additional time to research how you can use your social media to advantage. Check out opportunities to create a buzz prior to the event, in order that people become aware that an interesting event is upcoming that they will wish to attend. Also consider how you can usefully use your social media during the event. Finally, prepare what you wish to happen in the social media after the event.

Step 1: Determine the relevant online channels

Investigate which online channels are relevant for the attendees of your event. Do they spend time on Hyves? Do they meet on specific online forums? Are there relevant groups on LinkedIn where they discuss professional matters? And, while you are at it, try to find out who they listen to. If you have prepared your event well, you will, of course, know who the first league leaders are within the discipline but, possibly, there are other bloggers, Twitter users and forum tigers with a good reputation. Draw up a list with:

- influential forums/blogs;
- influential individuals;
- influential Twitter users;
- influential or relevant Facebook/LinkedIn groups.

There are three platforms that are the most obvious to use, at the time of writing this Blue Paper:

- *Twitter* – Do your attendees a favour and make Twitter lists of all important Twitter users in the discipline.
- *LinkedIn* – Create LinkedIn groups and make these 'communities of practice'. Pool all knowledge on the smartest questions to formulate the discipline. Pool the knowledge to find the best/newest/most refreshing speakers in the domain.
- Use *Facebook* – See LinkedIn.

Step 2: What is it about?

The event probably only has one or a few topics. This is usually a very general topic, such as the annual meeting of poodle breeders, and sometimes a very specific topic, for instance Arduino Meet-ups. To ensure that you get a lively discussion, you must define the topics as clearly as possible. This is why you draw up a list with the following information:

- Determine the main topics of the event/convention.
- Who has anything relevant to say about this? Choose from the list of influentials you drew up under step 1.
- Which questions can you put to your attendees/delegates? For an event on a very specific topic, you can probably do this quite quickly. If the event is more general in nature, it will take you quite some time to ensure that you identify the correct current topics.
- To whom shall I put these questions? Again, use the list you drew up under step 1.
- Determine who are the speakers and authorities at the event/convention.
- Who of these can enter into the discussion? If you are lucky, all the people involved will be enthusiastic about the event that they are preparing for together. You can share this enthusiasm with the rest of the world by allowing these people to share their enthusiasm with their own public.

- Encourage your speakers to write about the convention on their blogs and/or send tweets. Ask them to keep their LinkedIn connections abreast of the progress. Supply them with text that they can include in their newsletters or can respond to on their blog.
- Who wants to connect with whom? An essential aspect of being together in the same physical location is that people can really connect, and can get to know others. Is your convention a meeting place for old friends? They have different requirements than if the aim of your convention is to connect people who have never met before.
- Make it easy for delegates to find one another online afterwards:

  - if you use name tags, make sure the Twitter names are shown in a large enough and easy-to-read font;
  - show the delegates list online, with email addresses, LinkedIn information and Twitter accounts;
  - have your participants register for your event on LinkedIn or Facebook, in order that this is done automatically.

- And finally: where do you want the conversations to take place? You will probably consider your convention's website the most likely platform. However, is this able to support the conversations after the event? Who will be the website administrator? Are there online places where the discussion is currently taking place? These may be better places to guarantee continuity as others already organise this.

Step 3: Draw up the plan

Draw up a plan with the above ingredients:

- Which channels do you want to use to discuss which questions with your attendees prior to the event?
- Decide on a hashtag in order that everyone will find all online content.
- Are you going to stimulate your attendees with statements?
- Will you encourage your attendees to contribute?
- Will you facilitate exclusive, virtual meetings with the speakers?

Be as specific as you can when drawing up the plan. Your plan must provide the answers to the following questions:

- When will we do this?
- In which order will we do this?
- Which persons within our organisation will monitor which aspects?
- How do we monitor progress and results? (Possibilities are Google Analytics and TribeMonitor. Also see the list of tools below!

Step 4: Inform the world prior to the event

Prior to the convention you must inform the world that you will actively use social media. Blog, make your hashtag known. Ensure that the people outside the auditorium are excited and able to and eager to participate.

Step 5: Organise the facilities

Make sure there are ample Internet facilities during the convention. Free and open Wi-Fi would be wonderful, especially if there is no good 3G connection. Social media without the Internet is a tad difficult. Have a number of laptops/iMacs available that delegates can use; iMacs can be rented via MacRent.

During the convention

With a well-defined social media plan you will have a flying start to your convention. However, you will have to make it happen! You will have to spend the time and energy to guarantee a highly effective combination of offline and online activities.

Step 1: Make it visible

Make the online content visible during the convention. Ensure that your convention delegates see what happens online. Put up screens on which tweets, Facebook mentions, photos, videos and other online content is shown as soon as these come online. Help people make their content visible and findable online by telling them which hashtag you use.

Make sure that someone is available at each lecture and workshop session to share the main items with the world via Twitter. Ask people to take photos and put these online with the correct tags. Have people walk around who can post short quotes of speakers and delegates online. Share the energy and the contents with the world. It goes without saying that you also post this on the convention's website, possibly with live video-streams.

Step 2: Integrate the online content in the offline sessions

Make sure that someone is available in each auditorium and at each workshop or lecture to monitor the online activities and comments. This person can give feedback on what happens online at suitable times and, for instance, convey questions from outside the room, in consultation with the speaker or session leader.

Step 3: Make the sessions truly interactive

When you execute all these online matters properly, but still have your speakers speak in the traditional fashion to the audience from a stage, you will disappoint the attendees

who wish to actively participate. Organise your convention differently, in order that inter-action is much more encouraged:

- Limit speakers to short Pecha Kucha-like presentations, after which you give the floor to attendees who wish to comment or ask questions.
- Make your convention a BarCamp. Leave some timeslots open on purpose, and stimulate your attendees to have their say, and to subsequently enter into a discussion with other participants.
- Unconference your conference. Let the attendees decide on the convention programme.
- Provide an Open Space. Allow room for dynamics, but keep a tight rein on the contents. Form follows function works very explicitly in this setting. If the speaker on the stage is the only person with a microphone, one-way communication will result. Make groups smaller, appoint well-trained moderators and discussion leaders, and monitor true interaction.

After the convention

The event is over. The venue has been tidied, the relevant people were thanked and you survived the after party or final drinks party. Now is the time to take stock of what relevant matters have been shared. Now is the time to see what people thought about the event, and to draw up the broad outlines for the next edition.

Step 1: Publish your content and gather attendee-generated content

Make sure that you post the shared content online soon, such as videos of the lectures, scripts of the speakers' presentations. Have trainees write reports, or post reflections by experts. Also gather the photos, videos, tweets and other visitor-generated content. Do try to tag this content and give it the right keywords, to ensure that it can be easily found at a later stage. Mark useful content from others as 'favourite'. Ideally, all this content should be accessible in one online place. Were questions put to the speakers from people outside the auditorium? Ask the speaker to respond to these questions after the event. A blog post would be great, but an open, shared Google Doc may be more appropriate.

Listen to what your attendees have to say. Communicate clearly which content was attendee-generated. Do not begrudge them the exposure and the limelight, but expand on it.

Step 2: Invite the world to respond

With some luck, points of view were formulated and shared during your convention, statements people like to respond to. In the olden days you asked journalists to write about these, but now you may possibly ask the influentials whom you found during the preparation stage to write a report and post it online. Dare to take the plunge and ask for feedback. Use Speakonomy.com, for instance, to invite the attendees to assess the speakers.

Step 3: Use the power of the 'players'

Who stood out during the event? Are these people willing to continue to moderate/govern the conversations, supported by you? Ask them! They may be only too happy to do this, as it will make them visible as experts or oracles. If you have smartly organised the registrations for your convention, you will, moreover, have a database chock-a-block with the personal and contact data of all speakers and participants. If, moreover, you have duly asked them whether you may use those data to share information, you can send a newsletter soon after the event to pass on lots of knowledge and to inform people about the possibilities to stay in touch. Contributions by participants and experts could be the basis for a newsletter that can provide all interested parties with relevant information, in the run-up to the next convention.

Step 4: Take stock, learn and improve

Review the original plan, and the results achieved. Investigate what could have worked better, decide what did not work at all. Every group of people has their own preference. You may find that the attendees of your convention are much more active on LinkedIn than other social media. Make sure you adjust your plans for the next event accordingly.

Hacks and other findings that may offer results

- What do you do if no one uses social media? Employ ten students with iPhones to report on what is happening.
- Arrange Wi-Fi or check that there is a 3G connection at the venue.
- Use offline means and people to announce your social media jokes. Hang up posters. Have speakers mention it fifteen times. Have cute young people walk around in T-shirts. Hand out stickers.

Tools

To use before, during and after the convention:

- *Storify.com* – Allows you to easily gather and save tweets after the event.
- *Twitterfountain.com* – Project a Twitter fountain on a huge screen, showing both tweets and photos on a particular topic.

- *MindMeister.com* – During lectures and workshops you have people make a real-time mindmap of the lecture/workshop and show this on a large screen. Afterwards you hand out these mindmaps as convention documentation.
- *Google Docs* – Google Docs are online documents that can easily be shared with several writers and viewers. This not only saves forwarding PDF files, but also enables documents to be written simultaneously, by people from around the world.
- *U-stream* – For streaming live video. Not everyone can attend your convention. Stream live video to enable people to watch and listen to the lectures during the convention. The streamed video can also be viewed afterwards, and is an excellent video archive of your convention.
- *Speakonomy.com* – Let your attendees assess the speakers. This helps you to decide which speakers fit in best with your attendees, rather than the other way around.
- *Mindz.com* – Brings your attendees together in its online community, Plaza.
- *www.twoppy.com* – Twoppy puts you on your attendees' smartphones, from which they communicate with the rest of the world about your convention.
- *www.triqle.eu/content/triqles-whats* – What's on provides your participants with a realtime, online schedule on their smartphones.
- *YouTube.com* – To share the convention videos with the world.
- *Vimeo.com* – To share the convention videos with the world.
- *Slideshare.net* – To share all presentations online. You can even add the audio recordings of the lectures.
- No money for an expensive convention website? Reserve a domain name and create a free website with wordpress.com, tumblr.com or posterous.com.
- *Twitter accounts* – For the convention organisers. Have them tweet on the preparations, the topics, the speakers.
- *Soundcloud.com* – To share audio recordings, e.g. the recordings of lectures, but better still, short interviews with speakers and visitors. These are easy to make with the Soundcloud iPhone app and easy to find online.
- *Google Analytics* – Analyses the visits to your website. Where do your visitors come from? Via which other sites are they referred? What search term did they use to get to your site?
- *Tweetreach* – To determine the social scope of your content.

To view details of a new book on social media applications for the convention industry written by Lykle de Vries and Ronald Mulder, visit: http://deondernemers.nl/bluepaper/handboek-social-media-voor-congressen-en-events/

SUMMARY

- The planning of a conference involves steps which are similar to those involved in the staging of many other events. It demands a logical approach and great attention to detail on the part of an organiser, but also affords scope for creativity and imagination.

- At the outset, clear objectives for the conference should be set and as much information collected as possible about the participants, programme, timing, location and format. Financial aspects are another important part of the planning process: budgets need to be drawn up and, where appropriate, cashflow forecasts prepared.

- The selection of a suitable venue is crucial to the success of any event, and time and resources should be allocated to ensuring that the right choice is made. Various forms of assistance in venue finding are available, including directories, brochures, computer software and websites, exhibitions, magazines and specialist agencies. Once a shortlist of the most suitable venues has been completed, inspection visits are made and negotiations take place between organisers and venues to determine an agreed package.

- Planning the detail of the conference programme should always take account of the objectives set for the event from the start. The choice of speakers is a critical factor in delegate perceptions of the event. Social programmes present an ideal opportunity for organisers to bring something distinctive and memorable to an event.

- Marketing the conference needs to begin at the earliest possible moment, ideally at the previous year's event if it is one in a regular sequence. Various promotional tools are available, designed to increase the profile of the conference as well as to maximize delegate numbers, and to distribute the message of the conference globally and over an extended period of time.

- No conference ends with the closing session. Organisers should spend time evaluating the event through feedback from delegates and other interested parties. Ideas for improving future events will emerge from this evaluation process.

- It is increasingly important for events to demonstrate that they are providing appropriate returns on the investments being made in them by companies and organisations. Full evaluations using consistent and robust methodologies should now be an essential part of all events.

- Social media influence the ways in which we communicate, cooperate and share information, offering major opportunities for convention organisers and attendees, but requiring a professional and informed approach if these opportunities are to be maximised.

REVIEW AND DISCUSSION QUESTIONS

1   Analyse the key factors that influence a conference budget. Critically discuss how a monitoring framework should be used in managing event budgets, and analyse the relationship between income and expenditure in relation to meeting financial objectives.

2   Experience shows that most complaints from delegates are about food and beverages (F&B) served during the conference. Analyse, with examples, the different roles that F&B plays at conferences and discuss how conference organisers can plan F&B to make this aspect of their events as successful as possible.

3   You have twelve months to plan a new medical association conference for 300 delegates (plus partners). There is no previous event history. Produce a schedule which details the actions and decisions required on a month-by-month basis in the planning and staging of the conference. The schedule should include a budget and cashflow forecasts. The conference committee has given you an initial promotional budget of £3,000 and asked you to make a profit of £5,000 which can be used as a start-up fund for the following year's conference. Demonstrate how this will be achieved.

4   Critically analyse how ethical issues may arise from the following aspects of organising an event: choice of venues and accommodation, ideas expressed in the Request for Proposal, gifts from suppliers and attendance on fam. trips.

REFERENCES

Carey, Tony (1997) *Crisis or Conference!*, The Industrial Society

—— (2000) 'Planning the Planning', *Meeting Planner* magazine, 4 (16) (Winter)

CIC (2005) *The Convention Industry Council International Manual*, The Convention Industry Council

Colston, Paul (2012) 'Perception vs Reality', *Conference & Meetings World* magazine (Issue 67)

Cotterell, Peter (1994) *Conferences: An Organiser's Guide*, Hodder & Stoughton

De Vries, L. and Mulder, R. (2011) *Social Media Handbook for Conventions*, available at http://deondernemers.nl/bluepaper/handboek-social-media-voor-congressen-en-events/

Fisher, John G. (2000) *How to Run a Successful Conference*, 3rd edn, Kogan Page

Hamso, Elling (2009) *The ROI Methodology*, Event ROI Institute

John, R. (2011) 'Content is King', *Conference News* magazine (October)

Lokerman, R. (2011) 'Sixteen Steps to Market', *Conference & Meetings World* magazine (June)

McCabe, V., Poole, B. and Leiper, N. (2000) *The Business and Management of Conventions*, John Wiley & Sons

Maitland, Iain (1996) *How to Organise a Conference*, Gower Publishing Limited

Swarbrooke, John and Horner, Susan (2001) *Business Travel and Tourism*, Butterworth-Heinemann

FURTHER READING

Allen, Judy (2002) *The Business of Event Planning*, John Wiley & Sons

Appleby, P. (2005) *Organising A Conference*, How To Books Ltd

Bladen, C., Kennell, J., Abson, A. and Wilde, N., *Events Management: An Introduction*, Routledge

Bowdin, G. A. J., McDonnell, I., Allen, J. and O'Toole, W. (2010) *Events Management*, Butterworth-Heinemann

Carey, Tony (1999) *Professional Meeting Management: A European Handbook*, MPI Foundation

Cook, P. and John, R. (2011) *Risk It!*, Standard Copyright Licence

Craven, R. E. and Johnson, L. (2006) *The Complete Idiot's Guide to Meeting and Event Planning*, Alpha

Friedman S. (2003) *Meeting and Event Planning for Dummies*, John Wiley & Sons

Goldblatt, J. J. (1997) *Special Events: Best Practices in Modern Event Management*, 2nd edn, Van Nostrand Reinhold

Hoyle, L. (2002) *Event Marketing: How to Successfully Promote Events, Festivals, Conventions, and Expositions*, John Wiley & Sons

Phillips, J., Breining, M. and Pulliam Phillips, P. (2008) *Return on Investment in Meetings and Events*, Butterworth-Heinemann

Seekings, D. and Farrer, J. (1999) *How to Organise Successful Conferences and Meetings*, Kogan Page

Torrence, Sara R. (1996) *How to Run Scientific and Technical Meetings*, Van Nostrand Reinhold International

IAPCO publications (available at www.iapco.org):

- *First Steps for a Medical Meeting*
- *First Steps in the Preparation of an International Meeting*
- *Guidelines for Co-operation between the International Association, the National Organising Committee and the PCO*
- *Guidelines for the International Scientific Programme Committee*
- *Guidelines on Poster Presentations*
- *Housing Guidelines*
- *How to Choose the Right PCO*
- *Sponsorship Prospectus*

INCON publication (available at http://www.incon-pco.com):

- *International Meetings: Ten Steps to Success*

CHAPTER 6

Conference management: a venue perspective

CHAPTER OBJECTIVES

This chapter looks at:

- professional inspection visits and showrounds
- yield management and 'REVPAR'
- negotiating with clients

It includes case studies on:

- China National Convention Center, Beijing
- Highgate House, Northamptonshire, England
- The Celtic Manor Resort, Newport, Wales

www.routledge.com/cw/rogers

LEARNING OUTCOMES

On completion of this chapter, you should be able to:

- understand how conference venues seek to maximise and retain business;
- explain the meaning of esoteric terms such as 'yield management' and 'REVPAR';
- describe best practice in conducting showrounds of venues and in negotiating with conference clients;
- appreciate the various approaches to venue management adopted by different types of conference venues.

Introduction

Organising a successful conference is dependent upon many interlinking factors, not least of which is effective communications and teamwork between the conference organiser and the conference venue. Chapter 5 has looked at the management of an event from the standpoint of the organiser, whether this is the 'end user' or 'buyer' (corporation, association, public body, etc.) who has ownership of the event, or a PCO or intermediary organisation acting on behalf of the end user. This chapter explores conference management from the perspective of the venue or 'supplier', and describes the team approach within a venue, and between venue and client, to deliver successful events.

Professional inspection visits and showrounds

For conference and meeting venues, a key part of the sales and marketing process is the opportunity to show a potential client the benefits and attractions of their venue through a personal showround or inspection. In the author's experience, this is often an activity in which venues fail to do justice to themselves because the showround is conducted by inexperienced, untrained and ill-informed staff who fail to sell the benefits of their venue effectively and so fail to convince the customer that his or her event will be successful if held there. The guidelines below set out how such visits should be handled by the venue to maximise the chances of winning the business.

The showround provides an opportunity to:

- build a rapport with the client which demonstrates an understanding of his or her needs;

- develop the client's confidence in the venue team;
- address detail, recognise and use confidence signals, remembering that clients cannot sample the actual service before an event.

Careful preparation and planning are vital. When the appointment for the showround is being made, the following should be covered:

- Decide on the appropriate level of hospitality to be offered and whether this should involve an overnight stay.
- Check that the right staff and the correct facilities will be available on the proposed visit date.
- Ensure the client's correct contact details are held, including mobile/cell phone number for emergency contact, and numbers of people visiting.
- Clarify the client's travel arrangements (e.g. arrival time, time available to spend at the venue, method of transport being used).

A written acknowledgement of the appointment and arrangements should be sent, with reassurances of meeting any specific interests or concerns (e.g. availability of the chef), and enclosing full venue location details.

Before the visit takes place, internal communications within the venue should determine the appropriate venue personnel (numbers, job role, specialist knowledge) to meet the client. Full details of the client should be circulated, including the reason for the visit. Agreement will be needed on the appropriate layout for the conference rooms (subject to other commitments). And, finally, the person overseeing the showround should check that he or she has the authority and knowledge to cover any potential areas of negotiation, has got the necessary venue and destination product knowledge to hand, and has prepared a photo file of the venue (especially if the conference rooms are not available or are set up for a different kind of event).

On the day of the visit, the 'welcome' from the venue Reception staff must show that the client is expected. Appropriate introductions should be made, refreshments offered, and the agenda for the visit re-confirmed. The venue representative(s) will need to:

- discuss the enquiry in a logical way (chronologically);
- clarify the client's needs, objectives and priorities for the event;
- show an interest in the client's organisation, products/services and future development;
- use open questions, listen carefully to replies, check understanding where necessary;
- give the client a site plan of the venue, showing its general layout and indicating the route of the showround;
- show those parts of the venue relevant to the client;
- highlight the venue's benefits based on the client's needs (rather than just listing the 'features' of the venue);

- introduce and involve appropriate personnel;
- if appropriate, show the grounds and/or leisure facilities, and kitchens;
- and, throughout the visit, invite questions, check understanding, make notes, indicate locations on the floor plan as they relate to different aspects of the client's event, and look/listen for buying signals.

At the conclusion of the visit, it is important to find a quiet corner with the client to summarise the event, check and overcome any concerns, clarify the next step(s), and agree a time for the next contact. The 'close' should include a reaffirmation of interest in staging the client's event. After the visit, there should be a written follow-up with the client, and the venue's sales follow-up system should be updated. In due course, feedback on the visit to the venue staff should be given.

Yield management and 'REVPAR'

The 1990s saw the adoption of the theory and practice of yield management by conference venues, hotels especially. The application of yield management is seen most importantly towards the end of the marketing process, at the time when a customer (conference organiser) is negotiating a booking with his or her chosen or shortlisted venue.

Yield management aims to *'maximise revenue by adjusting prices to suit market demand'* (Huyton and Peters 1997). It *'emphasizes high rates on high demand days and high occupancy when demand is low. The focus of yield management is to maximise revenue every day, not for seasons or periods. It places the needs of the customer secondary to those of the hotel.'*

Huyton and Peters suggest that:

> For many years prospective hotel guests have become used to bargaining for their room rates or at least expecting that a room, at the rate they normally pay, will be available. Hotels have been seen by their customers as simply providers of rooms and beds. The idea that they are organised establishments, whose sole purpose is to make money for the owners, appears not to be a part of hotel guests' thinking. For as many years as this attitude has been expressed by customers, the hotel industry has permitted it by acceding to guests' needs, wants and whims. The idea seems to have been that we should be grateful for who we can get to come and stay. Yield management has turned this aspect of hotel operation on its head. What the system now tells the customer is that there are certain rooms set aside at certain price categories and, once they are full, you will have to pay more.

Yield management principles apply not just to the sale of bedrooms. Hartley and Rand (1997) explain that:

> For a venue having conference, function and/or exhibition space, yield management systems, designed to increase the overall profitability of the venue, must include consideration of many factors beyond room inventory and room pricing. While the yield-related information needed to handle a bedroom booking can be assessed relatively quickly, conference function and exhibition space can be sold and used in many different ways and for many different purposes – combinations of which will produce significantly varying profit potential. Ultimately, yield will be determined by how you sell the total facilities available.

Hartley and Rand outline a 'Conference Capacity Strategy' which a venue's sales team should develop in order to maximise yield from conference business. The Strategy looks at business mix, market strength and competitive edge, profitability, lead times and refused business. They expound the factors and techniques involved in allocating capacity to particular enquiries, and give practical tips on how to secure the business. They contend that:

> Price, and the way the pricing issue is managed by the venue, are components of the 'package' that the venue constructs at this stage of the enquiry. The overall relevance and quality of the package will be determining factors in winning or losing the business.

They strongly discourage the frequently used terminology of 'eight-hour', '24-hour' or 'day delegate rates', preferring to use 'residential' and 'non-residential rates' as more appropriate terminology. They put forward what they describe as a:

> Radical but still potentially flexible approach: the 'up to' tariff where the maximum rate is quoted as the published rate but it is still apparent that a reduced tariff may be available, dependent on the overall attractiveness of the booking to the venue.

Figure 6.1 (taken from Hartley and Rand 1997) illustrates the measurement of conference capacity yield in a venue over a period of one week, showing the potential and actual realised figures.

Revenue per available room (REVPAR) is often used as the definitive measure of a hotel's performance, replacing or complementing the measurement of occupancy and average rate. And yet, too often, too few people in a hotel fully understand the significance of this measurement. Similarly, too many people think that REVPAR and yield are the same measurement. Many hotels which claim to practise yield management are simply measuring REVPAR on a daily basis and staff are incapable of explaining to a guest why different rates are charged on different days for the same room.

	Target (potential) (week)	Actual realized (week)
Accommodation Number of bedrooms (allocated to conference sector) Accommodation rate	400 rooms £70	325 rooms £65
Conference space (capacity of 850* sq. mtrs) *inc. private dining facilities		
Revenue per sq. m	£93	£75

Conference sector bedroom yield

$$\frac{\text{Rooms sold}}{\text{Rooms available for sale}} \times \frac{\text{Average rate of rooms sold}}{\text{Average rate potential}} = \frac{325}{400} \times \frac{65}{70} = \frac{21125}{28\,000} = 75\%$$

Conference space – revenue earned

$$\frac{\text{Revenue per sq. m realized} \times 850}{\text{Potential revenue per sq. m} \times 850} = \frac{£75 \times 850}{£93 \times 850} = \frac{63\,750}{79\,050} = 81\%$$

Conference sector capacity yield

$$\frac{\text{Accommodation revenue realized} + \text{Conference space revenue realized}}{\text{Accommodation revenue potential} + \text{Conference space revenue potential}} \times 100$$

$$\frac{21125 + 63\,750}{28000 + 79050} \times 100 = \frac{84875}{107050} \times 100 = 79\%$$

FIGURE 6.1 Conference capacity yield in a venue over a period of one week

Yield management and revenue management (as opposed to REVPAR) are one and the same thing. Essentially they are an approach to increasing profit by responding to what we know about the past, what we know about the present and what we think will happen in the future. In other words, we are trying to sell the right room at the right time, at the right price to the right person. You could say that this is nothing new, but on the other hand many hotels are focused on occupancy or average rate and make most decisions on a very short-term basis. Yield management is a systematic approach to simultaneously optimising both average rate and occupancy, the ultimate aim being 100 per cent yield i.e. 100 per cent occupancy at rack rate (the published rate).

Yield is derived from the basic economic theory of supply and demand. In times of high demand, high prices can be charged. Conversely, when demand is low, prices will be lowered. Also, when supply is limited, prices rise and when there is an over-supply, prices drop. We are trying to match supply and demand by establishing a customer's willingness to pay a certain price.

Yield management only really operates in hotels and airlines by virtue of the following:

- Capacity is relatively fixed.
- Demand is derived from distinct market segments.

- Inventory (bedroom and meeting room stock) is perishable (see below).
- The product is often sold well in advance of consumption.
- Demand fluctuates significantly.

Whilst airlines started using yield management in the 1970s, hotels have only really been using it in a disciplined way since the mid-1990s. The common factor in both industries is that if a seat or bedroom is empty on one flight/night, it cannot be sold twice the next day to make up lost revenues (it is thus a 'perishable' product). This is unlike most other industries whereby sales shortfalls today can be made up at some time in the future. Also, other industries can increase and decrease manufacturing output to match fluctuations in demand, but a hotel cannot increase or decrease its number of bedrooms or meeting rooms to match demand.

Yield is measured as a percentage, being the actual room revenue as a percentage of total room revenue (see Figure 6.1). The closer it is to 100, the better the yield is, but a typical hotel will achieve around 60 per cent yield. A yield measurement enables comparisons between hotels of different standards and in different countries.

REVPAR is a monetary amount and is calculated by dividing the total room revenue by the total number of rooms. The psychological disadvantage of both these measurements is that they will be lower than the traditional measurements of occupancy and average rate. But, they are a truer reflection of a business's performance.

Yield management is about forecasting, discounting, managing inventories, over-booking, evaluating group (including conference) enquiries, redirecting demand and logical, rational pricing. Essentially the key to successful yield management is the ability to differentiate customers who are prepared to pay high prices from those who are prepared to change their travel plans to secure low prices, or make a commitment well in advance to secure the low price.

Negotiating with clients

The principles and practice of yield management provide the backcloth against which sales activity takes place, one key element of which is negotiating with the venue's conference clients. Some aspects of negotiating have already been touched on (see section on 'Professional inspection visits and showrounds' above). However, there are a number of other factors which a venue will need to consider as part of this negotiation process, all of which link with the objectives of maximising occupancy and yield, and help in determining whether a venue wants a particular piece of business and, if so, at what rate. Such factors include:

- decisions on the correct business mix for the venue (identifying the most appropriate conference market segments (see Chapter 2) as well as other types of business if, for example, the venue is a hotel also seeking individual business travellers, leisure tourists, coach groups, etc.);

- dates – accepting business that allows the venue to maximise bookings on 365 days a year, including factors such as whether the event is weekday or weekend or a combination of the two;
- timings of a meeting or conference – if, for example, the event does not start until the afternoon or evening, is there an opportunity to sell the meeting room(s) to another client for the first part of this day?;
- duration and seasonality;
- numbers of delegates, bedroom occupancy, and overall value of the piece of business;
- numbers of meeting rooms required, and the implications this might have for other potential business that might have to be refused;
- future opportunities for business from this client.

Before commencing negotiations, it is also important for the venue sales manager to prepare fully through an understanding of the market in order to:

- know the main sources of business for the venue;
- understand market segmentation and the different types of conference clients with different types of events, objectives, budgets. What is the market position of the client?;
- keep abreast of the current state of the conference market (strengths and weaknesses, trends) and of the general economy (local/national and increasingly international);
- be aware of the venue's principal competitors;
- be fully informed of major events in the locality (sporting, cultural, business) which will have an impact on demand for bedrooms and possibly function rooms.

A venue needs to decide, prior to negotiation, what the ideal outcome would be, but also what a realistic outcome would be and, finally, what its fallback position should be.

Once negotiations start, it is important to establish at an early stage what are the important criteria (i.e. critical factors in determining how successful an event has been) for the client; what alternatives are available (both other venues being considered but also alternative dates and formats for the event to allow maximum flexibility); whether the buyer/organiser has any concessions to offer and, if so, what he or she might be expecting in return; and what concessions the venue can bring to the negotiating table which will cost little but be perceived as adding value by the client.

Venue case studies

This section of the chapter elaborates on points made in previous sections: it looks at the ways in which three different types of venue are structured and operated to enable them to compete effectively in winning and retaining conference business through the delivery of successful events. It examines a purpose-built convention centre, a residential training and conference centre, and a resort hotel.

CASE STUDY 6.1 China National Convention Center, Beijing, China

Olympic legacy best practice

Opened in November 2009, the China National Convention Center (CNCC) is the largest and most recent purpose-built convention centre in China providing international standard convention and exhibition facilities and customer-oriented service. It is located in the heart of the Olympic Green adjacent to the National Stadium (Bird's Nest), the National Aquatics Center (Water Cube) and the National Indoor

FIGURE 6.2 China National Convention Centre

Stadium. During the 2008 Beijing Olympic Games, CNCC served as the main press centre and the international broadcasting location as well as providing the venue for fencing and pistol shooting competitions. After two years' successful operation as a convention centre, CNCC has secured its position in the list of China's leading venues and is widely regarded as a best practice example of an Olympic Games legacy.

The CNCC complex

The CNCC complex overall has a total of 530,000 m² (5,704,872 ft²) gross floor area containing the Center, two hotels, two commercial towers providing office space plus support services in a small mall – food court, health club, convenience store – and over 1,000 car parking spaces located below the Center. The four-star CNCC Grand Hotel with 420 rooms and the five-star Intercontinental Hotel with 337 rooms are connected to the Center by walkways. The city's subway line arrives at CNCC directly and the North 4th Ring Road links the area to the arterial road system of the city and to Beijing Capital International Airport.

CNCC has been designed to provide spacious and comfortable operating areas, with high standard facilities for conventions, exhibitions, special events, banqueting and corporate meetings. It has over 23,600 m² (254,028 ft²) of flexible meeting space. The largest, the Plenary Hall, can seat 6,000 delegates in theatre style. Six exhibition halls plus general exhibition areas total 40,000 m² (430,556 ft²) of exhibition space. Well-equipped kitchens and experienced staff can provide catering services for over 10,000 people simultaneously.

The CNCC area is equivalent to two city blocks located on the Olympic Green Boulevard, the extension of the main north–south axis of the city which also passes through the Forbidden City and Tian An Men Square. The design of the roof follows the concept of curvilinear architecture based on ancient Chinese architectural traditions. The mid-section over the exhibition halls is set lower and emphasizes a link between the two upward curving ends – this design symbolises a bridge of communication between peoples of the world.

Business mix

By the end of 2011, CNCC had hosted 1,267 meetings and 145 exhibitions in total since its opening, attracting more than one million conference attendees and another 1.14 million exhibition visitors. Figure 6.3 shows the breakdown of CNCC business in terms of the number of the events. Meetings are the dominant category of business at CNCC, accounting for 84 per cent of all events. It is worth mentioning that the percentage of banquets shown only refers to the dedicated banquet event. In reality, many meetings and exhibitions require banqueting services. The income generated from banqueting services actually accounts for around 25 per cent of total revenue. The ability to provide large scale catering services is also a key selling point of CNCC.

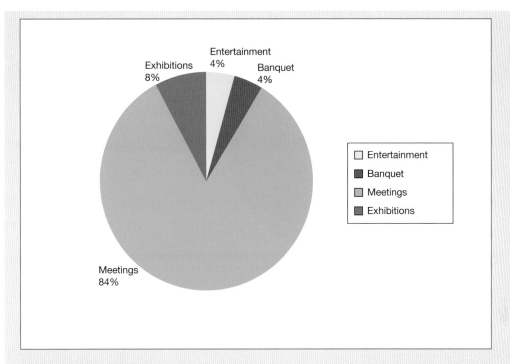

FIGURE 6.3 CNCC business mix

In terms of meetings, the corporate meetings sector holds the largest business share at 56 per cent, followed by association meetings (32 per cent) and government meetings (12 per cent) – see Figure 6.4. The revenue also reflects the dominance of corporate meetings which amounts to 52 per cent of total revenue generated. Unlike many western countries, the segment of government meetings is significant in China, especially in Beijing as the capital city where central government offices and all ministries are located. For CNCC, most of the large scale and the more lively corporate meetings are from technology (IT), media and telecommunications industries. In terms of association meetings, science and medical congresses are the two main areas. China has established that the medical, scientific and technology-related meetings are the highest priority to attract to the country and the pattern of CNCC events follows this prioritisation.

Enquiry handling procedures

Meeting planners and PCOs can reach CNCC sales staff for enquiries by all means including a telephone hotline, email, fax, sms/text and in person. Normally, the handling of enquiries follows a pre-defined process so as to ensure that each request has been well understood and actioned. When a booking enquiry arrives, sales staff not only provide feedback to the customer but also request detailed information about the event and the organiser before advising on availability in order to ensure clashes

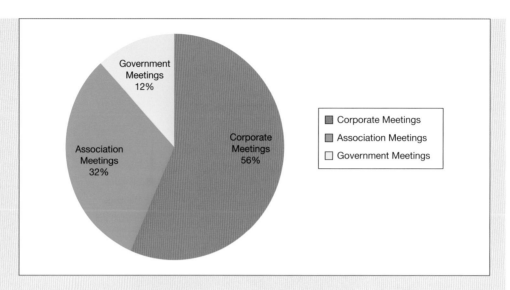

FIGURE 6.4 CNCC business share by sector

with other events are avoided in a very busy venue. Based on the information collected, sales staff assess whether the event will bring any potential risk to the Center in terms of the activity undertaken and audience profile and whether the proposed date and time conflict with existing bookings in terms of the client industry or attendee profile. If all answers are NO, the next step is inputting the booking into the EBMS system, reviewing any seasonal discount that can be applied and generating a formal proposal. Negotiation is a way of life with sales in China and is sure to follow. Figure 6.5 provides a flowchart showing the enquiry handling process.

After the contract is signed, the file is forwarded to the CNCC event planning department who generate the event order and create the internal work orders distributing them to related departments such as food and beverage (F&B), IT, security, operations, etc. Event planning staff always go back to the customer to make sure that their needs will be well fulfilled and they remain as the main contact through to the event delivery stage and they keep up-to-date on all adjustments and changes to these requirements during the build-up towards the event. After the event, a

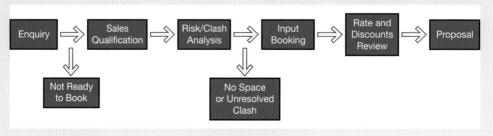

FIGURE 6.5 CNCC enquiry handling flowchart

customer evaluation form is passed to the client as a follow-up. As a new venue in China this feedback is essential and serves as a good reference to understand customers' experiences with CNCC and their future intention to come back with other events. It also provides ideas for improvement to CNCC services.

Mr Liu Haiying, CEO of CNCC, said:

> Service quality is the most important component to affect a customer's experience with us. We want both organiser and attendees to leave CNCC happy – in this way they will come back.

Emphasising the importance of service quality, CNCC launched the 'Service Quality Year 2012' initiative. This initiative includes:

- training to give staff a better understanding of clients;
- client satisfaction research conducted by an appointed external research company;
- establishing the regular use of a CRM module within the EBMS system to record all client contact history;
- working closer with other properties under the same ownership of the Beijing North Star Group to provide clients with a more convenient and competitive product package.

Staff cross training

Besides common skill training programmes, CNCC provides all staff with the opportunity to work in other departments and receive hands-on training for 2–3 months each time. Mr Liu believes that:

> Learning the skills for certain positions is important, but understanding how other departments work is equally vital to successful interaction throughout the company.

Cross training provides staff with a good opportunity to have a full picture of the total work flow. This helps them to work better and more closely with each other in the future and enhances the overall service quality. 'It is also a process of building up quality human resources which can only be a win–win situation for staff, clients and the company,' commented Mr Liu.

Since opening, CNCC has played a critical role in attracting meetings and exhibitions to Beijing and brought enhanced economic impact to the overall industry. Unlike many other convention centres in Europe and North America, CNCC's development was an investment by a private owner, who also manages the facility, as opposed to being local government-owned and run. The pressure on ROI is obvious, which is in fact an impetus for CNCC to quickly develop new services and stay competitive. In 2012 CNCC had bookings as far ahead as 2020.

Looking to the future CNCC management appreciates the fast pace of development of the convention industry in China and is committed to staying 'ahead of the game'. As the teams in the venue gain in experience, reviews are continually undertaken to fine-tune the business services and to support the increasing awareness of opportunities in China for international meeting planners. CNCC is proud to be seen not only as a leading professional venue in Asia but also as an information source for running meetings in China.

This case study was compiled by Jennifer Salsbury, CNCC Senior Director Sales and Marketing, and Sarah Wang, Communications Manager (www.cncchina.com).

CASE STUDY 6.2 Highgate House, Northamptonshire, England

In 1964 Highgate House, a seventeenth-century country house in Northamptonshire, was bought by the Chudleys as a family home and guest house. Recognising a gap in the market and Highgate House's capability in catering for large groups, it soon began to develop as a specialist venue for groups of business people wishing to meet.

Today Highgate House continues to be run by the Chudley family, who have since developed the 'Sundial Group' brand. Sundial Group specialises in conferences, meetings and training events with three separate areas of the company focusing on different elements of corporate hospitality. Sundial Teamscapes offers expertise in people and team development, Sundial Options and Solutions is a venue finding and event management agency, whilst Sundial Venues, perhaps the most well known branch of Sundial within the meetings industry, is made up of three dedicated conference centres in country house venues across the UK.

Highgate House has received such awards as 'Number One UK Venue' (BDRC Continental's 'VenueVerdict' survey 2010) and 'England's Best Business Tourism Establishment' (EnjoyEngland Awards for Excellence 2011). It focuses on creating the right environment for conference and business guests through investing in specialist meeting facilities and expert equipment. Distinguishing features of these high standard meeting rooms are natural daylight, specialist heavy duty, non-glare tables with ergonomic eight-hour conference chairs, screens with computer connectivity for projections, flip charts with markers and a stationery 'toolkit' including name place cards, as well as a direct-dial telephone with a speed-dial button to the dedicated conference services team who are trained in the set-up and operation of all IT equipment.

Meetings business

Highgate House operates primarily as a specialist conference venue. Annual revenue from meetings is of the order of £3 million with the single largest client (a central

FIGURE 6.6 Highgate House

government department) accounting for about 12 per cent of business. Other key clients come from the following industry sectors, but in all more than 20 sectors are well represented:

- food industry;
- professional bodies and associations;
- retail;
- charity sector;
- construction;
- financial services.

Tim Chudley, Managing Director of Sundial Group, explains:

> *Over the years we have seen a gradual change in the character and type of meetings we host. For many years smaller meetings were mostly described as management training and featured a group of middle ranking or senior executives attending a structured educational event for continuing professional development. Specialist lecturers required a formal learning environment and classroom type setting. Increasingly the character of meetings has evolved into less structured, strategic planning and discussion, detailed communication events or peer to peer learning and teambuilding. Clients also like to use our facilities for recruitment or assessment centres which often have very high staff to delegate ratio. Larger*

events have changed less and continue to be product launches, company conferences or motivation and reward which may feature outdoor fun activities and a gala dinner.

Enquiry handling procedures

Highgate House's sales team follows a detailed Sundial enquiry handling procedure to ensure that all enquiries are handled professionally and efficiently. The guidelines are as follows:

- An enquiry form must be completed on the database through asking open questions to invite maximum detail and be led by the customer to ascertain exactly what they would like for their event.
- Where there is an issue of limited availability due to a provisional booking, a specific time (within 24 hours) is given to call the client back for clarification of venue availability. Where there is a fixed event date for which the venue is already booked, the client is handed to the Sundial Options & Solutions team who will offer expertise in finding an appropriate alternative venue.
- Where there is venue availability, a provisional booking is proposed to the client and a contract will be sent to them immediately.
- A guided site-inspection and a dinner/lunch invitation is offered for every enquiry. If travelling by train, Highgate House offers to meet the client at the station (sometimes by the General Manager) or sends a private hire taxi to ensure a sense of maximum hospitality is achieved.
- Following the site inspection, the client is contacted again (within 24 hours) to establish their opinions and further discuss their decision-making process. If the client is not going to book Highgate House, a specific reason is asked for and noted on the initial enquiry form – this is important for future learning opportunities for the entire team.
- If the booking is to confirm, a contract is sent right away and Highgate House aims to receive the completed contract back from the client within five days.
- Highgate House employs a 'mystery shopping' service which regularly examines its systems and processes and provides valuable call handling and follow-up feedback for the team.

Event servicing and management, plus post-event activity/follow-up

Highgate House understands communication as a paramount element of proving and maintaining a reputation for providing an excellent service. Once the customer's key representative is identified (known by Highgate House as the 'event host'), they are allocated one of Highgate House's dedicated event planners; from this point on this member of the Highgate House team will be the host's event manager. Having one

point of contact at the venue, which is someone with experience in planning and orchestrating conferences, makes for smooth communication between the client event host and all the various departments at the venue (whether this is the conference services team, the chefs or the groundsmen). The event manager works with the host in planning every detail of their event, including accompanying the host during their initial site inspection, communicating with regards to the finer details and planning in the run up to the event, meeting them on site on the day of their event and being on hand throughout the event. The post-event follow-up and feedback is also communicated via the dedicated event manager.

The event host is also supported during their event by the dedicated and experienced conference services team who ensure that everything with the conference runs smoothly, from technology to furniture set-up and the provision of appropriate equipment. New clients are always greeted by the General Manager, who aims to greet every host wherever possible.

Client retention

Each week Highgate House collates the results from the BDRC Continental feedback systems to keep track of the venue's performance in every area, from enquiry handling to the cleanliness of the venue, the quality of food served, appearance of the facilities and the quality of the service experience among other categories. Tim Chudley explains:

> This data is openly shared with all team members and contributes Key Performance Indicators (KPIs) towards our 'Balanced Scorecard' system for the measurement of individual, departmental and organisational performance. Our Balanced Scorecard also includes measures for staff satisfaction, financial results and environmental performance.

Highgate House has consistently achieved industry leading levels of client retention and 'net promoter score' (individuals who report 9 or 10 out of 10 to the question, 'How likely are you to recommend?').

Staff training and development

At Highgate House the training and developing of employees is considered vital and continual, for the benefit of every employee personally and the business. Employees are trained to provide an outstanding hospitality environment, with the needs of the conference guest in mind. BDRC Continental results show continual improvement in the 'softer' aspects of service, such as 'understanding objectives' and high scores for flexibility and responsiveness and friendliness and helpfulness.

Sundial has created its own internal training programmes including 'Through the customers' eyes', which is aimed at developing key customer service skills and has won a National Training Award. 'Through the customers' eyes' encourages the staff to view the service that they deliver from the customers' viewpoint, thereby increasing empathy and improving service. Sundial has also won awards in developing employees and in Investors in People. A staff organisational chart is shown at Figure 6.7.

Tim Chudley comments:

> To achieve the 'can do' attitude that many clients value we have established a comparatively flat, self-managed management structure. Our heads of department are very hands on and lead by example. The most senior managers and directors are happy to carry our guests' bags and open doors for others. All our team members are encouraged to take responsibility and use their initiative. Highgate House is nonetheless organised in a traditional departmental way so that we have clear lines of responsibility and localised skills where needed.

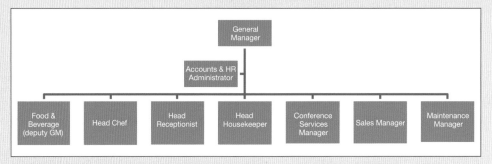

FIGURE 6.7 Highgate House staff organisation chart

The case study was written by Lotty Chudley, Group Communications and PR Manager, Sundial Group (www.sundialgroup.com).

CASE STUDY 6.3 The Celtic Manor Resort, Newport, Wales

Introduction

The Celtic Manor Resort has long been recognised as a jewel in the crown of Britain's business destinations, having been voted the UK's Top Conference Hotel for five years running since 2007.

After staging one of the world's largest and most iconic sporting events, the Ryder Cup in 2010, the resort was also named the UK's Best Hotel at the Meetings and Incentive Travel Awards in 2011 and 2012.

Only two hours from London, world-class facilities include a 400-bedroom resort, award-winning convention centre and exhibition hall, 31 meeting rooms, six restaurants, two luxurious spas and health clubs, and three championship golf courses.

FIGURE 6.8 Celtic Manor Resort

Catering for everything from large conferences to meetings, exhibitions, corporate golf days, incentive trips, banquets, product launches, concerts and other events, the Resort's dedicated event management team is committed to delivering the highest level of service, providing professional and technical support.

In addition to a luxury five star 330-room Resort Hotel, state-of-the-art convention centre and exhibition hall, the Resort also features a historic nineteenth-century Manor House with 70 bedrooms and a 200-year-old country inn restaurant with six bedrooms, The Newbridge on Usk. Two large golf clubhouses – The Lodge and The Twenty Ten Clubhouse – offer further conference and banqueting suites and function rooms for private dining.

Conference and meeting facilities

The conference and meeting facilities at the Celtic Manor Resort include:

- a purpose-built convention centre;
- a 1,200 m^2 exhibition hall;
- state-of-the-art facilities;
- a dedicated entrance and reception;
- the Caernarfon Suite for up to 1,500 delegates;
- banqueting for up to 800;
- 31 additional syndicate and meeting rooms;
- organiser's office and business centre;
- a rooftop garden and barbecue terrace;
- the 330-room Resort Hotel;
- the 70-room nineteenth-century Manor House hotel.

Conference and meetings business

Just over a million people passed through the Celtic Manor Resort in 2011, about a quarter of whom were delegates at conferences and events. Conference revenues (included related bedroom income) were in excess of £12 million in 2011, up 11 per cent on 2010.

Clients are drawn from a range of sectors, including:

- banking, finance and insurance;
- retail;
- pharmaceuticals;
- societies;
- associations;
- education.

Enquiry handling procedures

The resort employs a corporate relations field sales team of six people who generate business from both new and existing clients. Enquiries are handled by a dedicated events team. The in-house events team convert the enquiries generated by the corporate relations team, event agencies or other channels into business.

On receipt of an enquiry, the events team is able to check availability and produce proposals for the client. It follows up these leads and, working in tandem with the corporate relations team, turns these proposals into contracts.

Event servicing and management

Events booked with upward of 100 delegates or £50,000 in value, or smaller events for key account holders or other VIPs, are assigned to one of a team of six event managers. This team is responsible for co-ordinating all the client's requirements, working with the client and its event organiser(s) to deliver the logistics of the event:

- The assigned event manager will handle all the details from contract, through planning the delivery with the client to hosting the event to a detailed brief.
- The event managers work to a detailed checklist to ensure as much of the minutiae of any event is known and prepared in advance.
- The event manager relays the requirements of the event to the Resort's conference and banqueting team and other internal teams where appropriate, and oversees their delivery of services.
- The event manager will work long and unsocial hours with big events to make sure they are on hand to implement any late changes and additional requests from the client.
- Post-event, the event manager will sit down with the client to complete an event debrief form.

- Event managers also work with the corporate relations team to bring repeat enquiries back into the system. Bookings lost at the enquiry stage, past bookings and previous leads all stay on the system and are monitored.

Business Development Director, Jill Manley, commented:

> *No stone is left unturned in the reports produced for a monthly Corporate Relations meeting. We have very thorough procedures in place to ensure all past clients are contacted for possible repeat business and any potential new leads are followed up rigorously.*

Customer relationship management (CRM)

The corporate relations team keeps in regular touch with established clients and potential new clients and uses the Resort's leisure facilities to entertain clients and showcase the offering for events.

Interested clients will be given a 'Wow' showaround of all the Resort's events facilities and numerous site visits are held every week to fully inform existing and potential clients of all the facilities. Additional hospitality is provided to valued clients and targeted potential new clients during special events like the ISPS Handa Wales Open (a charitable organisation, principally promoting blind and disabled golf) and Elemis Polo at the Manor. Hospitality is sold at both these large sporting events and offers an ideal opportunity to entertain key clients and hopefully win new business.

In addition, the Resort usually runs two dedicated familiarisation trips every year when clients will be hosted for one or two nights and be treated to a full itinerary showcasing facilities and activities.

The Resort also runs an annual programme to incentivise large events. Any conference organiser booking an event worth more than £100,000 in 2012 won a £750 voucher to spend at celebrated jeweller Tiffany & Co. In 2011 it was a similar reward to spend on designer shoes.

Jill Manley said:

> *We recognise that event organisers are among our most important contacts. We appreciate the hard work they put in and are delighted to be able to offer them a gift as a thank you for bringing big bookings our way.*

Staff training and development

The Celtic Manor Resort is committed to the ongoing training of all employees from induction for new recruits to regular courses for senior management.

Every department works to a training plan for all employees and there is an umbrella Celtic College training programme which covers all training and encourages employees to earn external qualifications, like NVQs (national vocational qualifications), where appropriate. The resort is also an Investor in People.

This case study was written by Paul Williams, PR Manager, The Celtic Manor Resort (www.celtic-manor.com).

SUMMARY

- Venues must adopt a customer focus in their sales and marketing strategies and in their service delivery, while aiming to maximise return on investment through their approach to, inter alia, yield management and client negotiations.
- Different management and organisational approaches are adopted by distinct types of venue, with detailed examples included of three highly successful venues.

REVIEW AND DISCUSSION QUESTIONS

1 'Investments in a venue's physical product (meeting rooms, audio-visual technology, furniture and decor, bedrooms, etc.) can compensate for any failings in service delivery by the venue's operational team.' Discuss and debate and illustrate with specific examples.

2 Critically review the personal selling and the sales promotion activities that conference venues may use in order to generate sales and build relationships with their clients.

3 Analyse a range of conference venue operational management models and structures and assess which are the most successful, and why.

REFERENCES

Hartley, Jerry and Rand, Peter (1997) 'Conference Sector Capacity Management', in Yeoman, I. and Ingold, A. (eds) *Yield Management Strategies for the Service Industries*, Cassell

Huyton, J. and Peters, S. (1997) 'Application of Yield Management to the Hotel Industry', in Yeoman, I. and Ingold, A. (eds) *Yield Management Strategies for the Service Industries*, Cassell

FURTHER READING

Davidson, R. and Rogers, T. (2006) *Marketing Destinations and Venues for Conferences, Conventions and Business Events*, Butterworth-Heinemann

McCabe, V., Poole, B., Weeks, P. and Leiper, N. (2000) *The Business and Management of Conventions*, Wiley

Shone, Anton (1998) *The Business of Conferences*, Butterworth-Heinemann

The economic, social and environmental impacts of conferences and conventions

This chapter looks at:

- factors affecting conference sector demand
- the economic impact of the conventions industry
- social impacts and legacies
- environmental impacts and sustainability issues

It includes case studies on:

- the Conventa exhibition's sustainability features
- Vancouver Convention Centre, Vancouver, Canada

www.routledge.com/cw/rogers

LEARNING OUTCOMES

On completion of this chapter, you should be able to:

- appreciate the value of the conference industry in economic terms;
- explain the factors affecting the demand for conference activity;
- understand the concept of multipliers;
- assess the variety and importance of the social impacts of conventions on participants and on host communities;
- appreciate the myriad of ways in which any negative environmental impacts of conferences and business events may be mitigated and describe the positive approaches to sustainable event management now being developed around the world.

Introduction

Conferences are a vital economic benefactor for both local and national economies. Investment in conference facilities and infrastructure can bring substantial returns through the expenditure of organisers and delegates (and accompanying persons), with both direct and indirect benefits for the destinations in which conferences are held. However, there are also social benefits for event attendees and for the communities which host these events, and occasionally negative social impacts. Environmental and sustainability issues have come to the fore since the start of the new millennium, and the minimising of harmful effects on the environment is now a core objective for most organisers of conferences, conventions and other business events.

Factors affecting conference sector demand

The health of national and international economies

In line with most other industries, demand for conferences is driven to a large extent by the buoyancy of both national economies and the global economy. There is strong evidence to show that, during periods of economic recession, business activity levels decline and conferences may be cancelled or, more typically, run on much lower budgets. At such times companies trade down, reducing delegate numbers, cutting out the residential aspect of conferences, spending less on catering and using lower quality venues (for example 3-star hotels rather than 4-star).

Similarly, fluctuations in the value of a country's currency can have both positive and negative effects on its conference industry: a weakening of the currency may assist it to win more international events as costs for incoming delegates and organisers will be lower and the country may be perceived as good value for money. However, it will be more difficult, and certainly more expensive, for delegates to travel abroad from that country to attend conferences and meetings because of the relative weakness of their national currency. The opposite situation applies when a currency is strong compared with other currencies.

However, one of the positive characteristics of the conference industry is its resilience, even in times of economic downturn. While there may be a trading down, many events still go ahead: public companies are required to hold an Annual General Meeting for their shareholders, senior managers need to engage in management retreats to explore ways of reviving their business, new products are launched, staff have to be trained and motivated, sales forces need to be brought together for briefings, and many other types of 'conference' take place, albeit with reduced budgets.

The impact of crises, conflicts and emergency situations

'September 11th' (or '9/11') is a phrase now firmly embedded in the international lexicon, describing an appalling act of terrorism in New York which had an immediate, catastrophic impact on travel in North America. It led to the cancellation or postponement of conferences and meetings scheduled to take place in the weeks and months following. Conference delegates and business travellers refused to attend events held more than a short distance from their homes.

Other crises (epidemics such as SARS, volcanic ash clouds, wars, agricultural disasters such as the foot-and-mouth outbreak that affected the UK in 2001, for example) also have a negative impact on the demand for conferences in the countries and regions where they occur. Sometimes the impact is short-lived, sometimes it may be more prolonged.

Paradoxically, crises and disasters can also stimulate demand for meetings, training courses and international conferences; '9/11', for example, heightened awareness of the need for security and crisis management strategies as an integral part of overall conference management, generating seminars and training courses to address this educational and information need. Sendai, in Japan, which suffered dreadfully following the 2011 earthquake and tsunami, was by 2012 busy attracting a whole host of international meetings: on civic disaster preparedness and communication; on specialist engineering and water management; on earthquake science; on financial and reconstruction issues. In a similar way, wars and threats of wars lead to international meetings and conferences in an attempt to find a peaceful solution to the causes of conflict.

Technological Influences

Another factor affecting demand for conference facilities is the availability and enhanced performance of satellite, video and teleconferencing technology and social media applications, and the use of webcasts for broadcasting conferences over the Internet. The CAT (2011) *British Meetings and Events Industry Survey 2011–12*, conducted among corporate and association buyers, found that around 60 per cent were using social media, between 10–20 per cent were using virtual meetings, around 5 per cent QR (Quick Response) codes, 5–10 per cent apps for delegate information, and 1 per cent of corporate buyers were using holograms as part of their presentation technologies.

Webcasting allows individuals to attend a conference or meeting as 'virtual' delegates by sitting at their computer screens and listening to speaker presentations through an electronic link, either in real time or post-event – the current expectation is that this technology will widen conference attendance by making an event affordable and accessible to a much greater, global audience, rather than reduce the numbers of delegates wishing to attend an event in person.

More venues have invested in the installation of video and teleconferencing facilities in an effort to win new niche markets. Venues are also being required to provide wireless (Wi-Fi) technology, although issues of bandwidth, quality and pricing remain. See also Chapters 4, 5 and 10.

Social factors and working patterns

Social factors must have some effect on people's interest in conferencing, although little research has been undertaken to quantify these. Predictions that, for example, many more people would be working from or at home by the end of the last millennium have not proved to be entirely correct. However, if the 'office-in-the-home' should become a more common feature of everyday life in the future, its end result might well be an increased demand for conferences as people respond to their gregarious instincts by coming together in regular, face-to-face meetings.

Changes in a country's industrial and commercial structures can also have an impact on the demand for conference facilities. In the UK, for example, reductions in trade union membership since 1980 have led to trade unions merging which, in turn, has meant fewer trade union conferences (particularly affecting seaside conference destinations) but with higher attendances than previously. Some resort destinations, the traditional hosts of many trade union conferences, have found that their conference venues may no longer be big enough to accommodate their former clients.

Finally, it should be noted that fluctuations in conference demand are more noticeable in the corporate sector than in the association sector, often because of factors such as lead times. Corporate events, with relatively short lead times, can respond quickly to changing economic situations. Association conventions, with much longer lead times and frequently much larger delegate numbers, find it less easy to adapt but can also

take a longer term view and avoid what may sometimes prove to be a panic reaction to a particular situation (while still retaining the ability to react to emergencies such as that encountered after '9/11').

The economic impact of the conventions industry

Measurements of economic impact

Assessments of the value of the conference industry to most countries are at best only estimates, based on information drawn from national and local surveys. Calculations of the value, or economic impact, of conferences measure the net change in the local (or national) economy resulting from the hosting of conferences and business events i.e. what difference such events have made to levels of expenditure, income and employment. These calculations must also take account of a number of factors, outlined by Cooper *et al.* (1993), which apply to the tourism industry as a whole:

> Tourists spend their money on a wide variety of goods and services. They purchase accommodation, food and beverage, communications, entertainment services, goods from retail outlets and tour/travel services, to name just a few. This money may be seen as an injection of demand into the host economy: that is, demand which would otherwise not be present. However, the value of tourist expenditure represents only a partial picture of the economic impact. The full assessment of economic impact must take into account other aspects, including:
>
> * indirect and induced effects;
> * leakages of expenditure out of the local economy;
> * displacement and opportunity costs.

Cooper *et al.* refer to the 'cascading' effect of tourist expenditure, with the benefits of tourist spending being felt in hotels, restaurants, taxi firms, and shops and then permeating through the rest of the economy. From this total direct impact, however, must be subtracted the cost of:

> imports necessary to supply those front-line goods and services . . . for example, hotels purchase the services of builders, accountants, banks, food and beverage suppliers, and many others.

These suppliers, in turn, purchase goods and services from other suppliers, generating further rounds of economic activity, known as the indirect effect:

> The indirect effect will not involve all of the monies spent by tourists during the direct effect, since some of that money will leak out of circulation through imports, savings

and taxation. Finally, during the direct and indirect rounds of expenditure, income will accrue to local residents in the form of wages, salaries, distributed profit, rent and interest. This addition to the local income will, in part, be re-spent in the local economy on goods and services, and this will generate yet further rounds of economic activity. It is only when all three levels of impact (direct plus indirect plus induced) are estimated that the full positive economic impact of tourism expenditure is fully assessed.

Cooper *et al.* also make reference to certain 'negative economic impacts' of tourist expenditure. These include opportunity costs and displacement effects. Opportunity costs refer to the use of resources such as labour and capital for the benefit of one industry rather than another. Decisions to invest limited capital resources in tourism infrastructure, for example, will have negative impacts on other industries which failed to attract that investment:

Where tourism development substitutes one form of expenditure and economic activity for another, this is known as the displacement effect. Displacement can take place when tourism development is undertaken at the expense of another industry, and is generally referred to as the opportunity cost of the development. However, it is more commonly referred to when a new tourism project is seen to take away custom from an existing facility. For instance, if a destination finds that its all-inclusive hotels are running at high occupancy levels and returning a reasonable yield on investment, the construction of an additional all-inclusive hotel may simply reduce the occupancy levels of the existing establishments, and the destination may find that its overall tourism activity has not increased by as much as the new business from the development. This is displacement.

Figure 7.1 illustrates the measurement of net economic impact arising from tourist expenditure in an area through the application of the tourism multiplier concept (Heeley 1980).

The use of multipliers

Measurement of the economic impact of tourist spending is effected by using multiplier analysis. Various types of multiplier exist, and it is important to use the correct multipliers for specific functions, such as those measuring the additional revenue or employment for an area arising from tourist expenditure. However, the formulas used to calculate the net impact of conferences and similar events are complex and resource-intensive to administer. For these reasons many industry professionals, required to give account of the value of conference and business tourism to their city or area, tend to use the 'gross' figures rather than the 'net' impact figures i.e. the total gross expenditure calculated by multiplying:

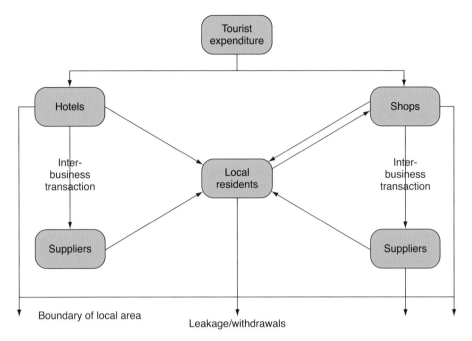

FIGURE 7.1 Measurement of net economic impact from tourist expenditure through the application of the tourism multiplier concept. Source: Dr John Heeley, University of East Anglia

- number of delegates/attendees;
- delegate spending (which varies by delegates' country of origin and by type of event);
- number of days' duration of the event;
- any additional days (i.e. for delegates staying on after the event or arriving early before the event starts);
- additional members of the group (e.g. spouses/partners);
- organisers' (and others') spending.

The totals arrived at only measure the direct expenditure to a destination and do not, therefore, take into account the negative effects (opportunity costs, displacement and leakages) referred to above.

Some examples of the economic impact of conference and convention activity on destinations and venues follow.

Examples of the economic impact of convention activity

Canada

Economic impact analysis is not new for the global meetings and conventions industry. Previous editions of this book have given detailed examples of work undertaken in various countries to measure and evaluate the economic significance of the sector. However, research undertaken in Canada in 2006 and published as *The Economic Contribution of Meetings Activity in Canada* (MPIFC 2008) was the first to use a measurement methodology developed by the United Nations World Tourism Organization (UNWTO) for the meetings industry (see Chapter 1 for more details), and it is likely that this will become the standard approach to be adopted by other countries in the future. Subsequent to the Canadian study, similar studies have been completed in the USA, Mexico and Denmark, and, at the time of writing (spring 2012), the author understands that other studies using the same methodology are being planned for France, Switzerland and the UK. It is a very positive sign of the increasing maturation of the conference and convention industry.

The Canadian study was commissioned by Meeting Professionals International Foundation Canada (MPIFC) and conducted by Maritz Research and the Conference Board of Canada. It neatly summarises the challenges and opportunities for measuring the economic impact of meetings:

> For anyone involved in measuring the impact of the tourism sector, the challenges facing the meetings sector are not new. For years, tourism researchers knew that the sector had a huge impact on the economy – locally, nationally, and globally. Identifying that impact was not easy – the difficulties of defining and measuring all visitors and collecting data on both their expenditures, and the revenues received by the myriad businesses that serve them, required the development and implementation of a new customized accounting framework.
>
> In 2001, after more than a decade of research and negotiation, the tourism sector developed and finalised the design of a 'Tourism Satellite Account' (TSA) that precisely defined the tourism-related activity that goes on within the economy as a whole. With the meetings economy facing the same types of measurement challenges, meetings organisations realised that their best hopes for defining their sector's economic contribution lie in a similar approach.

The MPI Foundation Canada study (MPIFC 2008) found that:

- in 2006, 1,517 venues hosted 671,000 meetings across Canada, of which 476,900 meetings, more than 75 per cent of the total activity, took place in hotels and resorts (see also Table 7.1);

- the size of individual meetings ranged from 10 – the minimum attendance in MPIFC's definition of a meeting – to tens of thousands;
- the 70.2 million people who attended meetings in Canada in 2006 included 65.5 million delegates, 452,000 exhibitors, and 3.3 million professional speakers or other paid attendees;
- across all meeting types, a total of 32.5 million participants attended activities in hotels and resorts, followed by 31.4 million in purpose-built venues and 4.9 million in special event venues;
- 40.4 million participants (57.5 per cent) were local, having travelled less than 40 kilometres to reach their meetings. 16.6 million (23.6 per cent) were based in the host province, 10.9 million (15.5 per cent) travelled within Canada, and 2.4 million (3.4 per cent) travelled internationally;
- meetings in Canada generated $32.2 billion in direct spending in 2006 ($23.3 billion by meeting participants and $8.9 billion by non-participant sponsors and stakeholders). Average spending was higher for delegates who travelled farther to attend a meeting, and for delegates attending trade shows (see also Table 7.2 for a breakdown of expenditures associated with the organisation of meetings);
- international trade show delegates, followed very closely by international visitors attending conferences, conventions or congresses, accounted for the highest per-person expenditures;
- meetings activity in 2006 generated the equivalent of 235,500 full-year jobs. Only 31,900 (13.5 per cent) of those jobs – 16,000 at meeting venues, and 15,900 among meeting organisers – were concentrated in meetings industries, showing that meetings are an incredibly effective employment creator for other parts of the economy;
- in addition to the 235,500 full-year jobs in meetings, tourism and other related industries, meetings activity supported, through indirect effects, an additional 195,800 jobs, and through induced effects 152,200 more positions, for a grand total of 583,500 full-year equivalent jobs;
- the totals point to a sector that creates employment at a rate of one full-year equivalent job for every $55,155 in direct spending on meetings activity;
- although the direct industry output of meetings activity in Canada was $32.2 billion, every dollar spent on meetings activity in 2006 resulted in another $1.21 in spin-off activity in some other part of the economy. Indirect and induced effects accounted for $20.2 billion and $18.7 billion respectively, for total industry output of $71.1 billion;
- considering the direct, indirect and induced effects on taxes, meetings activity returned total revenues of $7.3 billion to the federal government, $6.2 billion to the provinces, and nearly $1.1 billion to municipalities, for a total of $14.6 billion. It produced a total of $3.8 billion in income taxes, $2.1 bilion in social security contributions, $1.9 billion in federal Goods and Services Tax (GST), nearly $1.7 billion in provincial sales taxes, nearly $3 billion in other federal and provincial taxes and service fees, and $1.1 billion in corporate taxes.

7 Economic, social and environmental impacts

Table 7.1 Venues in Canada hosting events	Meetings		By Venue			
	Total Number of Meetings	Share of Total (%)	Purpose-built	Hotels/ Resorts	Special Event	Other
Conferences/Conventions/ Congresses	126,000	18.80	3,800	105,400	14,800	2,200
Consumer Shows/Consumer Exhibitions	7,000	1.0	900	4,400	1,000	300
Trade Shows/Business Exhibitions	11,000	1.60	1,000	8,100	1,400	500
Incentive Meetings	12,000	1.80	400	9,100	1,100	1,100
Other Business Meetings	391,000	58.30	12,800	300,700	62,700	15,300
Other Meetings	124,000	18.50	5,100	49,200	66,600	3,000
Total	671,000	100.00	24,000	476,900	147,400	22,400

Source: *The Economic Contribution of Meetings Activity in Canada* (MPIFC 2008)

Publication of the Canadian study marked a sea-change in our understanding of the economic benefits of meetings and convention activity, not just in Canada but also around the world, and it is to be hoped that the adoption of similar research methodologies in other countries will add further to the momentum generated by the MPIFC project, increasing the recognition and profile of meetings and conventions as major wealth generators for local and national economies.

Studies using the same methodology as the Canadian study have subsequently been completed in the USA, Mexico and Denmark. A few key facts from the three studies again reinforce the enormous, and often undervalued, contribution that meetings and business events can make to national economies.

USA

- Nearly 1.8 million meetings took place in the USA in 2009, attended by an estimated 205 million participants.
- Total direct spending associated with US meetings activity in 2009 is estimated at $263 billion.
- Total output of US meetings activity (i.e. direct, indirect and induced effects) in 2009 is estimated at $907 billion.
- Meetings activity supported 6.3 million jobs and generated $271 billion in total labour income.

Table 7.2 Event expenditure in Canada	
Goods and Services	**Expenditure ($)**
Venue hire	753,063,000
Food and beverage	2,935,629,000
Equipment/production/technical costs	959,301,000
Administration	629,436,000
Advertising and promotion of meeting	341,889,000
All Internet and online/web-based services or promotions	120,498,000
Keynote speaker and other sponsored attendees	391,043,000
Insurance	12,949,000
Other facility costs	112,953,000
Meeting management company/destination management company (DMC)	173,417,000
Printing	357,697,000
Temporary agency staff	87,437,000
Company staff (food and beverage, travel, accommodation)	246,123,000
Audio-visual and staging	644,259,000
Décor	430,145,000
Entertainment	178,676,000
Gifts and awards	166,256,000
Shipping	23,961,000
Sponsor expenses	48,415,000
Delegate materials (delegate bags, give-aways, etc.)	84,811,000
Transportation (organisation purposes only – non-delegate)	274,619,000
Accommodation (organisation purposes only – non-delegate)	368,546,000
Meeting organisation fee income/management fees from clients	1,942,845,000
Other	820,098,000
Total Spending	12,104,066,000

Source: *The Economic Contribution of Meetings Activity in Canada* (MPIFC 2008)

Mexico

- In 2010, 197,400 meetings were held, attended by 23 million participants. Of these meetings, 131,000 were corporate events, 28,000 conferences and conventions, 6,300 incentive trips, 4,400 consumer shows, and the remainder consisted of other types of events.
- Meetings in Mexico generated 24.3 million room nights.
- Expenditure on meetings totalled $18.1 billion.
- The contribution of meetings to gross domestic product was valued at $12 billion, with a further $13 billion in indirect effects.
- Meetings generate 441,300 direct jobs and 342,400 indirect jobs, and $4.7 billion in employment income.

Denmark

- In 2010 the Danish meetings industry created a direct annual turnover of DKK20.8 billion (approx. £2.24 billion), of which DKK11.4 billion (£1.23 billion) was the cost of meetings and DKK9.4 billion (£1.01 billion) was spending by delegates, including accommodation, transport and shopping.
- The total number of meetings held in Denmark in 2010 was 187,900, involving 6.9 million delegates.
- About 17 per cent of meetings activity came from international delegates, with 928,000 'commercial foreign delegates' visiting Denmark in 2010 for meetings, contributing DKK3.5 billion (£377 million) to the local economy and spending DKK3,070 (£330) per delegate per day.
- Some 37,900 jobs are generated due to the direct and derived effects of the industry, 1.4 per cent of total employment in Denmark.

Durban

Economic impact studies are, of course, not only undertaken at a national level. They are frequently carried out by cities and other local/regional destinations to assess the importance of conference and business events activity for a discrete location. For example, a study published in late 2011 by the International Convention Centre Durban (ICCD), South Africa, assessed the impact of the Centre's work on the KwaZulu-Natal region. It found that, in the five-year period from 2006, the ICCD generated R11.4 billion (€1 billion) for the region. The ICCD was also responsible for:

- creating 3,376 direct and 4,462 indirect jobs during the 2010–11 financial year, generating 1,432,866 delegate and visitor days in Durban;
- being a net generator of R467 million (€43.2 million) in foreign exchange, up from R363 million (€33.6 million) in the previous financial year;
- contributing R246 million (€22.8 million) in tax revenues, up from R234 million (€21.6 million) in the previous year.

The ICCD Chief Executive, Julie-May Ellingson, commented:

> The ICCD was originally developed as a catalyst for economic development for the city at a cost of R800 million (74 million euro). It has more than delivered its return on investment for the city and province. (Source: Meetings:review, 7 November 2011)

Impacts for suppliers

The benefits of conference and convention activity are felt by a wide range of supplier organisations in a destination. Two political conferences held in the UK can provide an

interesting insight into the scale of such benefits enjoyed, for example, by specialist caterers. The 11,000 delegates and 2,000 global media attending the UK Labour Party's 2011 convention held at the ACC Liverpool consumed:

- 4,800 canapés;
- 3,500 bottles of wine;
- 1,900 jugs of iced water;
- 10,500 sandwiches;
- 16,000 cups of tea and coffee.

The event was estimated to have generated £15 million in economic benefit for the city. Not to be outdone, the Conservative Party Conference held at Manchester Central in 2011:

- required 425 catering staff to service delegates' needs;
- consumed 15,000 litres of milk in teas, coffees and general cooking – 13,200 teas and coffees were served during the four-day conference;
- required 20,000 pieces of bread to be buttered in one day.

The impact on delegate waistlines was not measured at either event!

Social impacts and legacies

The social impacts, in some cases more aptly termed legacies, of convention activity are experienced both by the individuals who attend conventions and similar business events, and by the destination communities which host or stage the events.

Individual delegate impacts

Business Events Sydney (BESydney 2011) published a report entitled *Beyond Tourism Benefits: Measuring the Social Legacies of Business Events* which, as the title suggests, examines the wider social legacy benefits to derive from international congresses, aside from the kinds of economic impact benefits described earlier in this chapter. The report was based on an online survey of approximately 13,200 attendees – comprising delegates, sponsors, exhibitors and members of the organising committee – to five international congresses held in Sydney over the previous two years.

The study builds on an earlier study, *A Scoping Study of Business Events: Beyond Tourism Benefits* (BESydney 2010), which had established that the benefits derived from business events extend well beyond the tourism contribution. The range of legacies identified in the 2010 study is presented in Table 7.3.

Table 7.3 Legacies of business events

Knowledge expansion
- Growing local knowledge
- Knowledge improving education
- Knowledge improving professional practice

Networking, relationships and collaboration
- Access to networking opportunities for local practitioners and researchers
- Networking fosters creation of long-term relationships
- Networking as a catalyst for knowledge expansion and research development
- Networking as a catalyst for research collaborations
- Research collaborations lead to development of new products and technologies

Educational outcomes
- Opportunities for local postgraduate research students
- Increased attractiveness of education sector

Fundraising and future research capacity
- Fundraising opportunities
- Greater access to government and/or private sector funding sources

Raising awareness and profiling
- Generating awareness of sector-specific issues
- Raising awareness of broader societal issues
- Profiling local organisations, associations, and/or centres
- A catalyst for government support

Showcasing and destination reputation
- Showcasing local talent
- Enhancing Sydney's reputation as a leader

Source: *A Scoping Study of Business Events: Beyond Tourism Benefits* (BESydney 2010)

The 2011 study, therefore, represents the second stage of the project, commissioned on behalf of and carried out with the assistance of BESydney. It confirms that:

> *Congresses have facilitated the dissemination of new knowledge, ideas, techniques, materials, and technologies by providing Sydney/New South Wales-based educators, practitioners and researchers with access to a network of international colleagues. This networking affords local delegates with new business and research collaborations, which can generate innovation, ideas and research agendas for many years to come . . . Business events provide a supporting platform from which the growth of intercultural friendships can occur.*
>
> *Business events are shared social contexts that take people away from their established routines. Through this social context the sharing of knowledge and ideas occurs and common meanings are developed through their interactions. It is not surprising that this research has found a direct connection between the staging of*

business events and an extensive range of benefits and outcomes beyond the tourism spend. These benefits and outcomes can be considered as leaving legacies in five different areas:

- *intrinsic;*
- *practice;*
- *social;*
- *economic;*
- *attitudinal.*

The legacies of these benefits and outcomes are not mutually exclusive: one benefit and outcome may have multiple legacies.

Intrinsic legacies *are the opportunities afforded by congresses to delegates to develop their knowledge, skills and practices to fulfil part of their potential to work within the chosen industry sector. The ability to express and share in a collaborative environment their knowledge, skills and practices to the extent that they have already been developed is an additional benefit*

Practice legacies *result from the skills and knowledge that delegates gain – such as learning new insights, surgical techniques, sharing new ideas and identifying solutions to solving problems – being directly integrated into their professional practices and organisations*

Social legacies *represent the camaraderie that develops around the congress, the appeal of engaging with other like-minded people, the relationships that are enhanced and developed and the broader benefits that accrue to the communities in which the congress is held. Business events develop a social space that is important as it facilitates and reinforces social interaction and, in turn, influences the effectiveness of collaborative learning*

Economic legacies *are realised for three reasons. First, social networks affect the flow and the quality of information. Moving in different circles from one's own group connects people to a wider world. Therefore, any new acquaintances can be better sources when we need to go beyond what our own group knows. Second, trust is built as people come to know and understand others. As information is often subtle, nuanced and difficult to verify, people will rely on people they know. Congresses are intense periods during which the social interaction is fostered, resulting in benefits and outcomes that have both intangible and tangible economic effects such as dissemination of new knowledge, building knowledge and capabilities, improved workforce practices, better education, new investments, enhanced funding and better industry sector policies*

Attitudinal legacies *arise from the reactions of delegates through their experiences at the congress, and from governments, the private sector and other individuals who become aware of important issues that are communicated through the international and local media.*

Both reports may be downloaded free of charge from the Business Events Sydney website (www.businesseventssydney.com.au).

Several other cities which, like Sydney, are members of the Future Convention Cities Initiative (FCCI) were reported in May 2012 to be planning similar research studies. Such cities include Toronto and Durban, with London, Seoul and San Francisco also expected to follow suit.

Social impacts and legacies for host communities

The early years of the twenty-first century have witnessed a growing trend for conferences, conventions and incentive events to leave a lasting legacy of community improvements in the destinations which host these events, perhaps driven by a wider demand across society for companies and businesses to behave ethically and demonstrate a social awareness and responsibility in their links with the countries and societies in which they operate. Davidson (2009) notes:

> *Many people within the new generation of participants in business tourism events are uncomfortable with the type of conspicuous consumption that often characterises such events. This is particularly the case when lavishly-funded meetings and incentive trips take place against a background of disadvantaged communities or in developing countries. Consequently, one of the main differences between twentieth century and twenty-first century business tourism events is the current widespread desire, particularly among younger, Generation Y, participants, to somehow make a difference and give something back to the communities where their corporate meetings and incentive trips take place. This is becoming known as the social legacy of business tourism, and it is one of the key trends driving the design of such events today.*

Davidson suggests that:

> *Social legacy relates to the People aspect of the triple bottom line of corporate social responsibility or CSR (People, Planet and Profit) and, as such, goes far beyond the simple greening of business tourism events. While the planet-centred greening of events involves practices such as recycling materials, hosting paperless meetings, choosing meetings destinations served by public transport and building green clauses into contracts with suppliers, social legacy also takes into account how a meeting or incentive trip impacts upon the people and economy of the local community.*

There are now many interesting and innovative examples of how convention and meeting organisers and attendees have interacted with local communities to provide some form of social legacy. They range from donations to local charities (of money, clothes, food,

toys, for example) to engaging in construction and renovation projects to providing speakers to local schools and colleges. On a familiarisation visit to Thailand in 2011, a group of 120 meetings and exhibition industry buyers took part in a corporate social responsibility activity, helping to construct a multi-purpose building for children of the Wat Khok community. Delegates to Meeting Professionals International's 2010 annual congress held in Vancouver were given opportunities to take part in a range of social legacy activities, including puppy socialisation for the Pacific Assistance Dog Society, a charity which helps those with visual and hearing impairments.

However, it would be misleading to suggest that there are no dangers or challenges with social legacy activities embedded into convention and incentive programmes. There is always a risk that they are undertaken to generate good PR coverage for the company or association, rather than to create any lasting benefit for the host community. Davidson recommends that:

> *Social legacy activities are most effective and convincing when they take place within the wider context of the company's existing CSR policy. This lends coherence and continuity to such activities, focusing, where they exist, on the company's established contacts and the causes that it already supports.*

There are, of course, other potential negative social impacts from conventions. One example is the disruption to the local community that can be caused when a major convention comes to town, especially where there is a need for high levels of security. This can mean that the area surrounding the convention centre is cordoned off during the convention and often for some days in advance, making it a no-go area for local residents and reducing trade for shops and other businesses in the vicinity. Similarly, restaurants may be full with delegates eating out, traffic may be congested and public transport overloaded. While most local communities now recognise that such inconveniences are a price worth paying because of the wider economic benefits, there is often still a minority of residents who voice criticisms.

Environmental impacts and sustainability issues

Few news broadcasts today are completed without some reference to environmental issues such as global warming, carbon emissions, and the very sustainability of our planet. These same issues have also become mainstream concerns and challenges within the conference and conventions industry. Barbara Maple, at the time President of the International Association of Congress Centres (AIPC), President of the Vancouver Convention and Exhibition Centre, President of the Joint Meetings Industry Council and Chairman of the World Council for Venue Management, listed four reasons for this in an article entitled 'Green Meetings: Does Anyone Really Care?' (Maple 2007):

Our communities will increasingly expect it of us. We and our activities are highly visible wherever we operate, and attract a lot of attention from the local community: this means people expect that we will take a leadership role in implementing more programmes where the good of the community is at stake. At the same time, we are often government-owned and operated, which means we are under pressure to set an example in this regard.

The second reason is that our clients will increasingly want it because their own members will want it. Environmental concern has gone from being a 'cause' to simply an expectation; people today just assume that environmental concerns are being addressed because they have become a fact of life in most parts of the world. For this reason, the people who make up the membership of the organisations whose events we host will be applying more pressure on organisers to address the role environmental and sustainability considerations can play in their events. This, in turn, will make sustainability issues and the record of a centre in this regard more of a decision factor for meeting planners.

The third reason sustainability will become a bigger factor is that it will contribute to cost-effective operations, particularly in key areas like energy. One of the big points of the sustainability concept is that industries must manage long term costs if they are to be successful in an ongoing way, and the costs of energy and waste management are among the largest and least predictable we face as facility managers. Like so many other aspects of environmental management, it is often only when there are significant cost implications that action gets taken.

Finally, this whole area will increasingly be a matter of law, as communities and governments in many parts of the world strengthen their regulations around how businesses manage their environmental and social impacts. Just as issues like smoking have moved from the encouragement stage to outright prohibition, so we can expect that what are today seen as being good practices will likely become legal requirements as community expectations evolve.

She concluded that:

The results of all this will affect many different areas of facility management: everything from building operations and environmental control measures to how new facilities are designed and constructed, and even how we market and sell our facilities. We will, for example, likely have to get more involved with our clients to make sure that they comply with community sustainability expectations when they hold their events in our cities. This is now simply a 'good thing to do', but will increasingly be a requirement for being allowed to operate at all.

An MPI Foundation Canada White Paper entitled *The Economic Impact of Meetings and Events* (MPIFC 2008) described the opportunity to 'green' meetings and events and

improve the eco-efficiency of the facilities that host them as an *'important trend with significant economic potential for the meetings industry'*. It went on to say:

> *Increasingly, meeting professionals are recognizing that green practices like recycling and re-use can translate into lower onsite costs. On the facilities side of the industry, a handful of trendsetters have achieved dollar savings by reducing the energy and water they consume and the waste they generate – and have gained a distinct marketing advantage by positioning themselves as green venues.*

When the Canadian government was hosting the Eleventh Conference of the Parties to the Framework Convention on Climate Change, also known as the Kyoto Protocol, in Montreal in 2005, it committed to organising an environmentally friendly, carbon-neutral conference. The plans included:

- reducing greenhouse gas emissions, in partnership with the provincial electrical utility, Hydro-Québec;
- distributing 4,750 free transit passes to attendees and conference volunteers;
- using hybrid, ethanol, and biodiesel vehicles for conference shuttles;
- minimising the need for shuttles, by locating 19 of 50 conference hotels within walking distance of the convention centre;
- introducing a catering plan that included fair trade coffee service, composting of food waste, and a strong commitment to recycling;
- turning off all non-essential electrical equipment at night, and specifying EnergyStar standards for rented equipment;
- using canvas delegate bags and functional gifts to minimize waste;
- reducing the volume and environmental impact of the printing process through double-sided production on EcoLogo™ paper, on-demand printing, wireless Internet access for attendees, and the use of vegetable-based inks.

It is interesting to note how the practices and objectives outlined above have, over subsequent years, become truly mainstream for many conference and convention organisers. At the same time, there have been a number of significant developments at an international level designed to integrate sustainability criteria and activities into a wide range of business events, including the publication of formal Standards to provide guidance on sustainable event management. For example:

British Standard 8901: Sustainability Management System for Events

BS8901 was launched as a draft standard in November 2007. After a consultation process with the events industry, a revised draft standard was released in 2009 with the title

'BS8901: 2009 Sustainability Management System for Events – Specification with Guidance for Use'. The purpose of BS8901 is to help the events industry to conduct business operations in a more sustainable manner. The standard is applicable to the full range of events and needs to be applied to the full life-cycle of an event (i.e. from conception to final review) as well as extended throughout the supply chain. It is based on the Plan-Do-Check-Act process that is already used in event project management and requires measuring and monitoring of performance and the identification of Key Performance Indicators (KPIs) within a context of continuous improvement.

The standard is also described as 'proportional' – in other words, an organisation's or individual's role and position in the supply chain, its size, capacity to adopt the system and ability to implement it will determine which requirements of the standard apply.

BS8901 applies to event clients, event organisers/management, venues, and related supply chains. Like ISO9001 (Quality Management System), ISO18001 (Health and Safety Management System) and ISO27001 (Information Security Management System), BS8901 is a standard enabling certification to be provided. Certification is for the management system used by an organisation to manage its event-orientated activities, products and services and *can* be for one event only. The event, therefore, is considered to be the 'output' of the system.

Copenhagen Sustainable Meetings Protocol

The Copenhagen Sustainable Meetings Protocol (CSMP) offers a flexible, umbrella framework that can be used to organise large, complex meetings in a more sustainable way. The protocol is not a standard that provides accreditation or certification – rather it is intended to help planners manage their meetings sustainably. The CSMP aims to complement other existing guides present in the market, and it is not only targeted at corporate, government and association event organisers, but also consultants and managers in venues and large hotels. It is designed to be used in combination with the 'COP15 Event Sustainability Report'.

The CSM is divided into chapters on: sustainable event management; introduction to the Protocol framework; leadership and commitment; strategic approach to stakeholder engagement; operational integration; governance; and sustainability and the future of the meetings industry.

Development of ISO 20121: International Standard for Sustainable Event Management

This new international standard for sustainable event management was developed by over 30 countries and was launched in June 2012. The aim is to provide an international standard following the worldwide adoption of the British Standard for Sustainable

Event Management (BS8901). ISO 20121 is an event sustainability management system standard which addresses the implementation of sustainability within the events industry. It is not a list of actions which each event must take, because every event is different – instead it is a framework to ensure that sustainability is considered at every point. The framework is likely to include:

- identifying issues: users of the standard will identify where their behaviour negatively impacts socially, economically or environmentally;
- stakeholder engagement: users of the standard will share their issues with stakeholders to ensure all issues are identified;
- objective setting: users will set objectives and targets for how to address their specific issues.

The standard can be used by individuals or companies who plan events and also by the events supply chain, including venues. Thailand Convention & Exhibition Bureau announced in May 2012 that it would be looking to introduce the system to its MICE industry players in 2012, with a formal launch in July 2012, the first Asian country to do so.

APEX and ASTM green meetings and events standards

The very first green meetings and events standards were launched by the Convention Industry Council's Accepted Practices Exchange (APEX) and The American Society for Testing and Materials International (ASTM) in February 2012. The APEX/ASTM standards are broken down into nine individual sector standards, covering all facets of event planning and management:

- audio-visual;
- communication and marketing materials;
- destinations;
- exhibits/exhibitions;
- food and beverage;
- meeting venue;
- on-site office;
- transportation;
- accommodation(s).

The standards are available for purchase individually (the costs range between US$40 and US$46) or as a full package for US$149. For more details visit: www.astm.org/BOOKSTORE/COMPS/GREENMTGS.htm

Event Organisers Sector Supplement (EOSS)

This document, developed over a two-year period by a team of volunteers drawn from event agencies, government, labour and civil society organisations and published in January 2012 by the Global Reporting Initiative, is intended to help event organisers report their sustainability performance and provide quantitative and qualitative information on sustainability issues. In addition to more widely applicable issues such as greenhouse gas emissions and waste, the guidance assists event organisers to report on more specific issues including attendee travel, the legacy of the event, and initiatives taken at the event to promote sustainability and transparency.

The supplement has three sections covering profile, management approach and performance indicators:

- *Profile*: how to disclose the event's or organisation's strategy, profile and governance structures.
- *Management approach*: how an event organiser addresses a given set of sustainability topics in order to provide context for understanding performance in a specific area.
- *Performance indicators*: specific indicators that elicit comparable information on the economic, environmental and social performance of the organisation and/or event.

The Supplement offers different levels of reporting (from Level C up to Level A) and provides structure, indicators and advice.

To download the guidelines (which are free of charge), visit: https://www.global reporting.org/reporting/sector-guidance/event-organizers/Pages/default.aspx

It is apparent that many cities and destinations have recognised the importance of staging sustainable meetings and events, but probably none more so than cities and countries in Scandinavia. In March 2012, the five Scandinavian countries of Finland, Iceland, Denmark, Norway and Sweden established what was claimed to be the first sustainable meetings region in the world. They each signed an Accord, the first of its kind in the world, outlining 10 specific actions to which the signatories would commit. A major aim of the initiative is to reduce the Scandinavian meetings industry's CO_2 footprint by 20 per cent by the year 2020. The Accord also includes the use of environmentally friendly transport, giving back to the local community, advocating to clients the use of responsible, sustainable and certified suppliers, sharing knowledge and learning from others. Project leader, Guy Bigwood of MCI Sustainability Services, commented (www.meetpie.com – 16 March 2012):

> This project is unique in its scale and collaborative nature. For the last two years we have engaged the Scandinavian ICCA members to define a shared vision for the future of meetings and events. We feel this innovative model of leadership collaboration

will result in destinations that are positioned to capture new business from the rapidly expanding sustainable marketplace.

One of the partners in the Scandinavian Accord, Denmark, has also created its own Danish Sustainable Events Initiative (DSEI). DSEI was developed through the collaborative efforts of private and public stakeholders in the Danish meetings industry, designed to showcase and improve Danish actions to profit from sustainability in action.

The meetings industry has supported the American city of Denver's sustainability programme. For example, in 2011 the 250,000th tree was planted in front of the Colorado Convention Center, as part of Colorado's Mile High Million initiative and with the help of organisers and suppliers from the corporate events industry. The tree marked a milestone towards the target of adding a further 750,000 trees to Denver's urban environment by 2025. The aim of the initiative is to provide '*a cleaner, more beautiful environment for locals and visitors, and motivate individuals to become life-long stewards of the city's natural environment*'. Denver's many green initiatives include:

- the LEED-certified* Colorado Convention Center, which has one of the largest solar arrays on its roof and a full-time staff member dedicated to assisting events planners with their sustainable initiatives (*LEED stands for Leadership in Energy and Environmental Design and is a rating system by the Green Building Council);
- a well-developed farm-to-table programme supported by local independent restaurants, under the 'Eat Greener Denver' banner;
- the Rocky Mountain greener venues partnership through which 10 establishments share best sustainable practices;
- visit Denver's online resources to help meeting planners provide green options to their clients and convention attendees – from carbon calculators to green vendors.

Vienna Convention Bureau, Austria, has become a licensee of the Austrian EcoLogo and is now authorised not only to assist conferences in matters relating to environmental impact, but also to certify them as 'Green Meetings'. The EcoLogo was awarded to the Convention Bureau by Austria's Minister for the Environment, and it means that the Bureau is licensed to certify as Green Meetings those conferences whose organisers take climate protection, regional value-added and social compatibility into account. The Green Meetings EcoLogo was created in 2009 by the Austrian Ministry of Life and the Consumers' Association of Austria. In order to obtain certification, an organiser needs a licensee, such as the Vienna Convention Bureau, who can not only handle the formal certification process but is also bound by strict environmental protection regulations.

Case Study 7.1 illustrates the practical steps taken by an industry trade exhibition, 'Conventa', to minimise any negative impacts on the environment and to maximise its sustainability credentials.

CASE STUDY 7.1 The Conventa Exhibition's sustainability features

Conventa, the South East Europe trade show described more fully in Chapter 2, lays great emphasis on its sustainability credentials.

From conception to planning and implementation, Conventa makes sustainable decisions to decrease the generation of waste, choose products with a high recycled content and reuse or donate materials. Conventa uses local knowledge, partners with local suppliers and engages members of civil society to support the local economy and promote local traditions and heritage. By facilitating personal contacts between a hosted buyer community and the wide choice of meetings supplier businesses, Conventa provides the platform for business negotiations. Conventa, therefore, creates business opportunities leading to further growth of the regional meeting industry markets. In line with its three key sustainability issues of engaging stakeholders, keeping it local and implementing a 4R policy for its waste management practices (i.e. rethink, reduce, recycle, reuse), Conventa aims to achieve its strategic goal of serving the interests of people, planet and profit.

In 2012 Conventa focused on assessing its environmental, economic and social impacts and on implementing sustainable practices. Seeing the complex nature of sustainability and the number of partners and suppliers involved, Conventa focused on measuring and reporting on a selected number of metrics. By assessing the sustainability performance of the trade show, Conventa can gain a greater under-standing of its sustainable management, identify areas for improvement and allow for future comparisons. Each trade show partner was asked to commit to one sustainable measure in his or her respected area, track respective indicators and report. Details of the sustainable measures and measurements are shown in Table 7.4.

Conventa sustainable management, led by Go.Mice agency, is based on the principles of international sustainable event standards, including BS8901, a draft version of ISO20121 and APEX Green Meeting standards, Global Reporting Initiative Event Supplement.

Other useful sources of information on green and sustainable issues with reference to the conference and conventions industry include:

- www.greenmeetings.info
- www.thecarbonconsultancy.co.uk
- www.eventia.org.uk
- www.bluegreenmeetings.org

There is an excellent website providing tools, resources and case studies for measuring the economic, environmental and social impacts of events, originally developed by Sport UK. The website address is: www.eventimpacts.com and it contains resources at basic, intermediate and advanced levels.

Table 7.4 Conventa's sustainability metrics

VENUE

Sustainable commitment	With a modern system of waste separation which includes 11 different types of waste, GR – Ljubljana Exhibition and Convention Centre commits to collect all waste separately according to the appropriate fractions.
Sustainable performance indicator	GR commits to measure and report on the total weight of waste by type and disposal method.
Sustainable commitment	In line with implementing a number of energy efficient measures, Cankarjev dom commits to reduce energy consumption by encouraging Conventa participants to use stairs instead of taking the elevator.
Sustainable performance indicator	Cankarjev dom undertakes to report on energy savings by participants taking stairs.

TRANSPORT

Sustainable commitment	For a smooth running of the event, Kompas DMC provides a shuttle service with a low emission fleet for participants travelling between the venues, accommodation providers and point of arrival and departure.
Sustainable performance indicator	To establish a benchmark of transport emissions within the Conventa programme, Kompas DMC commits to measure the distance travelled and fuel consumption.

ACCOMMODATION

Sustainable commitment	Grand Hotel Union commits to use paper products which have a high recycled content for signage and welcome notes within the Conventa programme.
Sustainable performance indicator	Grand Hotel Union undertakes to report on paper use within the Conventa programme.
Sustainable commitment	Best Western Premier Hotel Slon adopts the policy of rethinking, reducing and reusing 100% organic centrepieces for the Academy Conventa Module.
Sustainable performance indicator	Best Western Premier Hotel Slon is to report on economic and environmental savings.

CATERING

Sustainable commitment	Jezersek Catering plans menus with up to 95% of milk and dairy products, up to 70% of meat and 50% of vegetables sourced locally. Information on the origin of food and beverages is made available to Conventa participants.
Sustainable performance indicator	Jezersek is to measure the amount of local products used in menus for Conventa.

EXHIBIT

Sustainable commitment	Signage at exhibit stands is made from recycled cardboard. Signage is designed with reuse in mind; therefore stand numbers are printed separately from company names.
Sustainable performance indicator	Go.Mice undertakes to report on the volume of produced, recycled or to be reused signage at exhibit stands.
Sustainable commitment	Printed materials are designed and written in a generic way instead of specific way (not including the event date or CGP specific of the year), to allow them to be reused for future editions of the trade show.
Sustainable performance indicator	Go.Mice is to report on the number of printed materials to be reused for future trade shows and the number of materials to be donated to the cultural-ecological fellowship Smet Umet that, combining art, ecology, design, creates new products from waste.

COMMUNICATION

Sustainable commitment	To minimise paper use, all relevant information, presentations and catalogues are provided via electronic media: Conventa webpage, mobile application, sms text communication and multidata devices.
Sustainable performance indicator	Go.Mice is to measure the volume of printed materials for the Conventa catalogue, Conventa Daily and Conventa floor-plan as well as the number of downloads of these materials.
Sustainable commitment	In addition to providing standard participant communication, Go.Mice prepared sustainable guidelines for exhibitors and for hosted buyers to help them understand how to integrate sustainable actions into their exhibit and travel arrangements.
Sustainable performance indicator	In the Conventa evaluation form, participants are asked to give their opinion concerning the sustainable initiatives within the show programme. The outcome of the survey and the feedback obtained are evaluated and used for the quality assurance of the following trade shows.

EVENT PRODUCTION

Sustainable commitment	Ljubljana Tourism/Convention Bureau, the host of the Ljubljana Pre-Conventa day, incorporated sustainable considerations while designing the fam trip programme, in particular as regards food and beverage. This includes their commitment to plan in-season, local and fresh menus for a light lunch at the Ljubljana Castle, dinner at the Pri Vitezu restaurant and a luncheon at the 'Skyscraper'.
Sustainable performance indicator	Ljubljana Tourism/Convention Bureau is to provide relevant data for measurements of the food products' sustainability used in the scope of the Ljubljana Pre-Conventa day.

Case Study 7.2 examines how a major convention centre, Vancouver, has been designed and is managed to create positive economic, social and environmental benefits for Vancouver and British Columbia.

CASE STUDY 7.2 Vancouver Convention Centre, Canada

Introduction, background, investment

Located on Vancouver's waterfront with a dramatic mountain backdrop, the Vancouver Convention Centre (VCC) offers one of the most beautiful settings in the world as well as convenient access to all the major visitor amenities in the downtown (city centre) core.

The Vancouver Convention Centre opened in July 1987 after originally serving as the Canada Pavilion at the World's Fair in 1986. After 20 years of successful operation,

FIGURE 7.2 Vancouver, showing Vancouver Convention Centre

the Centre had outgrown its facility and an expansion was necessary to meet the growing demands of the meetings and events industry in Vancouver.

Opened in April 2009, the West building expansion has tripled the facility's capacity for a combined total of 466,500 ft^2 (43,340 m^2) flexible meeting and function space. Notable features of the West building include the largest waterfront ballroom in Canada at 53,000 ft^2 (4,920 m^2); floor to ceiling windows offering breathtaking mountain and harbour views throughout; and a convenient 295 ft (90 m) harbour concourse connector that joins the West building to the existing East facility.

The West building expansion also provided an opportunity to include new public spaces on the waterfront that did not previously exist, including over 130,000 ft^2 (12,080 m^2) of new waterfront walkway and bike-lane surrounding the facility. The Centre also features over 120,000 ft^2 (11,150 m^2) of public plaza space, perfect for clients to use to enhance their events, and for informal gatherings and community events like Canada Day celebrations and cultural activities. The West building also features a unique, thematic art programme by local and international artists.

The overall goals for the expansion were to:

- meet the demand in the global market for Vancouver to host larger conventions;
- increase the number and size of events taking place in Vancouver;
- triple the number of attendees compared to prior average attendance.

With the increased capacity VCC has been able to meet those objectives – to accommodate much larger conventions and events, and compete at a global level. The total cost of expansion (including the cost to refurbish the existing East building) was CA$836 million.

The first-ever repeat winner of the International Association of Congress Centres' (AIPC) APEX award for 'World's Best Convention Centre' (2002, 2008), the Vancouver Convention Centre has distinguished itself as a highly attractive, uniquely located, environmentally sustainable and service-excellence oriented facility. The facility has earned numerous industry awards, including the International Association of Venue Managers' 2011 Venue Excellence Award, AIPC's 2011 Innovation Award recognising the Centre's Service Excellence Program, as well as AIPC's Quality Standards Certification in the gold level in 2011. The Centre is also the world's first and only convention centre to have earned LEED (Leadership in Energy and Environmental Design) Platinum certification.

VCC mission and objectives

Since opening in 1987, VCC's mandate has been to generate economic and community benefits for British Columbia through the management and marketing of the province's premier convention and exhibition facility.

Apart from the objective to generate economic activity for the province, VCC has the following organisational purpose:

> To elevate Vancouver as the global leader and convention destination of choice, by creating inspiring and sustainable experiences for: its clients, its team, and its community.

VCC's organisational purpose is much more than an inspirational statement. It has become the foundation from which VCC formed an innovative, organisational-wide programme to elevate its service standards, brand promise and delivery.

Comprised of distinctive service practices and standards reflecting VCC's organisational Purpose, Values and Guest Service Promise, the Service Excellence Program touches every area of operation, every department, every partner supplier and every employee. Ultimately, VCC's goal is to provide an unparalleled experience – where every guest receives the highest level of service at each and every touch point, and recognises that VCC is committed to 100 per cent customer satisfaction.

VCC's business mix

The Vancouver Convention Centre has a diverse business mix, including the following key markets:

- Canadian and US associations;
- Canadian and US corporations;
- international associations and societies;
- Canadian trade and consumer show organisers.

With an expanded convention centre, Vancouver is competing with larger facilities in North America and around the world and attracting larger conferences than could previously be accommodated. An unprecedented level of events has been hosted at the facility since the opening of the West building.

The fiscal year to 31 March 2012 proved to be Vancouver's most successful convention year ever with 567 events in total, including 58 conventions. This included the largest convention in Vancouver's history, SIGGRAPH 2011, the 38th annual conference of the Special Interest Group on Computer Graphics and Interactive Techniques that brought over 16,000 delegates to the city. Due to the success of the 2011 meeting, SIGGRAPH announced their plans to return to Vancouver for their 2014 convention.

Bookings continue to be strong for the future, with major conventions booked through to 2022.

As British Columbia's premier meeting and convention facility, the Vancouver Convention Centre generates millions of dollars in economic activity for the province each year.

VCC's sustainability credentials and features

Since its inception in 1987 and prior to global interest in sustainability, the Vancouver Convention Centre has taken steps to manage and minimise its impact on the environment. The facility's sustainability programmes are focused around ongoing building operations; pursuing upgrades to enable the facility to qualify for key environmental/conservation certifications; staff engagement; client engagement; and community engagement. While these initiatives have formed a very strong environmental foundation over the last two decades, VCC continues to identify and capitalise on new opportunities that will enhance its sustainability programme.

The Centre's West building expansion offered the perfect opportunity to design and build a facility that is 'green' in innovative ways, while setting new standards in the industry. The West building was awarded LEED (Leadership in Energy and Environmental Design) Platinum certification by the Canada Green Building Council in February 2010, and is the only convention centre in the world to have earned the highest LEED rating.

FIGURE 7.3 Vancouver Convention Centre living roof image

Examples of VCC's sustainable practices and features include:

- a six-acre living roof, the largest living roof in Canada and the largest non-industrial living roof in North America. The roof is landscaped with more than 400,000 indigenous plants and grasses, providing a natural habitat for birds, bees and other insects. The roof is designed to act as an insulator, reducing heat gains in the summer and heat losses in the winter;
- four beehives installed on the living roof. The bees pollinate the roof's plants and surrounding vegetation, while providing honey for use in the Centre's scratch kitchen;
- a sophisticated drainage and water recovery system, which has successfully reduced potable water use;
- an extensive facility-wide recycling programme that recycles an average of 180,000 kg of materials annually;
- adoption of a green housekeeping programme, which includes the use of only Green Seal Certified and EcoLogo Certified cleaning products;
- a restored marine habitat built into the foundation of the building, as 40 per cent of the West building is built over the harbour. The marine habitat mitigates the Centre's environmental footprint while promoting the development of marine life. Water quality in the area has improved dramatically, with the growth of a diverse variety of marine species;
- a seawater heating and cooling system that takes advantage of the adjacent seawater to produce cooling for the building during warmer months and heating in cooler months;
- operation of a 'scratch' kitchen, utilising primarily fresh, local and seasonal ingredients. VCC's commitment to promoting and using locally grown products means less energy consumption for transporting products to its door;
- natural light maximised throughout the building;
- local British Columbia wood products used throughout the building;
- supporting clients to create sustainable meetings, and zero-waste and zero-carbon events in collaboration with their suppliers.

VCC's community role

Apart from generating significant economic benefits for Vancouver and the province from the conventions and events attracted to the city, VCC supports a variety of community initiatives. For instance, the facility has been a long-time supporter of the Social Purchasing Portal, which is part of a non-profit organisation known as Building Opportunities with Business (BOB). BOB works to strengthen Vancouver's inner-city community by working with local businesses to improve employment opportunities and increase investment in the inner-city.

VCC supports BOB through use of the Social Purchasing Portal (SPP), which identifies the businesses who are partners with BOB in providing employment, growth and development opportunities in the inner-city neighbourhood. VCC's procurement practices encourage buying from the list of SPP suppliers whenever possible, putting social corporate responsibility into practice and creating a social value for the community. This lets VCC align with the community in a meaningful way without compromising its business goals and reflects its values of 'Respect, Responsibility and Excellence'. VCC has also changed its organics recycling vendor to an SPP vendor offering an improved scope of services.

The recognised charity for the Convention Centre is the Greater Vancouver Food Bank Society. The partnership includes provision of space for fundraising activities, participation in year-round activities to generate food donations as well as funds, and facilitating donations from interested clients and events. VCC also participates in CANstruction(r) Vancouver, a canned food sculpture design competition, where all food items are donated to the local Food Bank.

VCC also has a partnership with United We Can. VCC's returnable containers (e.g. cans and bottles) are collected and donated to this charity. United We Can is a local organisation that advocates for marginalised people and the environment. They provide people with support, training, and 'green collar jobs'. These jobs help lift people out of poverty and help create community opportunities.

In addition to the facility's formal involvement with BOB, the local Food Bank and United We Can, the Centre recognises the valuable work of numerous charitable organisations by offering special flexibility in booking and operating policies to facilitate their events in the building.

Engaging the community on a regular basis is a priority to VCC in order to raise awareness of its business, the value and significance of conventions hosted in Vancouver, and its commitment to environmental sustainability. One of VCC's initiatives is its popular Public Tour Program. Over 11,100 members of the community have been toured through the facility since April 2009 when the West building expansion opened.

Apart from its general public tours, VCC also hosts tours for groups with special interests in the facility from hospitality students to professionals in architecture, landscape architecture, engineering and urban planning. In 2011 alone, VCC hosted over 1,100 students on 56 different tours.

VCC also participates in the City of Vancouver's Green Building Audio Tours, allowing the public and guests to learn about the Centre's sustainability features and practices using their personal mobile devices.

Recognising the important role of social media and the technological sophistication of its clients and community, VCC stays closely connected with them via Facebook, Twitter, LinkedIn, YouTube, Flickr and FourSquare. These social media platforms allow

VCC to share news and updates, answer questions from its stakeholders, raise the profile of its clients' events and make recommendations to delegates.

Members of the Executive and leadership teams are also active in the community and industry, regularly delivering presentations and participating in panel discussions for industry groups, hospitality partners, etc.

Customer feedback on VCC

VCC has had excellent responses from its clients and their delegates. The most notable measurement of its success is based on the strong results of VCC's online Client Feedback Survey, developed and launched with client input representing each of the facility's major markets. In addition to measuring a client's satisfaction with services and suppliers, the survey also measures loyalty, overall perceived value of the VCC, pride with using the facility and trust in the facility.

Through less formal channels, VCC regularly receives comments from its guests about how much they enjoy the facility, the harbour views, the natural light, the flexibility of space, and how they appreciate and recognise the VCC team for being solution-oriented and committed to excellent service. It's also wonderful to hear comments from VCC clients about the easy and walkable proximity of hotels, restaurants, and other features of being on the waterfront in downtown Vancouver.

This case study was compiled by Jinny Wu, Communications Manager, Vancouver Convention Centre (www.vancouverconventioncentre.com).

SUMMARY

- Calculations of the economic impact of conference business must take into account a number of negative economic impacts, such as opportunity costs and displacement costs, as well as the cascade of positive benefits, in order to arrive at an accurate assessment of net beneficial effects.
- Measurement of the economic impact of tourist spending is achieved by the use of multipliers. Multipliers can be used to measure income generated and employment supported, among other things.
- National surveys and local studies confirm that conferences, conventions and business events provide substantial economic benefits for those countries which have embraced the sector vigorously and invested in the necessary infrastructure to attract and retain such business. They sustain jobs which are all-year-round and bring income through delegate expenditure which benefits many sections of local communities.

- Research has provided a better understanding of the social benefits accruing to delegates who participate in conventions and congresses. The events offer a shared social context and provide lasting benefits in terms of knowledge and skills development, creating networks for international collaboration and learning, stimulating investment and better industry sector policies, and more besides.
- Communities which act as hosts to conventions and congresses and incentive groups may receive practical benefits as the events interact with the communities and seek to leave a lasting social legacy and contribute to community development and enhancement.
- Conferences and conventions have unavoidable negative environmental impacts but there is now much evidence of good practice globally to reduce or minimise such impacts and ensure that events are managed to high sustainability criteria, guided by formal International Standards.

REVIEW AND DISCUSSION QUESTIONS

1   With reference to the relevant literature, give a critical analysis of the impacts of conferences and events on the natural environment. Describe the measures being taken by the industry to control and mitigate these impacts.

2   Review the principal issues and challenges regarding the supply of reliable research and data for the conference industry. How could such research and data be improved?

3   Critically assess the social impacts and legacies of conference activity, for individuals and communities. Suggest ways in which the positive benefits could be further enhanced.

REFERENCES

BESydney (2010) *A Scoping Study of Business Events: Beyond Tourism Benefits*, Business Events Sydney

—— (2011) *Beyond Tourism Benefits: Measuring the Social Legacies of Business Events*, Business Events Sydney

CAT (2011) *British Meetings and Events Industry Survey 2011–12*, CAT Publications, available at www.meetpie.com

Cooper, C., Fletcher, J., Gilbert, D. and Wanhill, S. (1993) *Tourism Principles and Practice*, Addison Wesley Longman Ltd

Davidson, R. (2009) 'Business Tourism: Providing a Social Legacy', *Tourism Insights*, VisitBritain (September), available at www.insights.org.uk/ (accessed 12 August 2012)

Heeley, J. (1980) *Tourism and Local Government: With Special Reference to the County of Norfolk*, Vol. 1, University of East Anglia, p. 72

Maple, B. (2007) 'Green Meetings: Does Anyone Really Care?', *Conference & Meetings World* magazine (January)

MPIFC (2008) *The Economic Contribution of Meetings Activity in Canada*, MPI Foundation Canada, with Maritz Research and the Conference Board of Canada

8

Developing the industry's workforce: creating a profession

CHAPTER OBJECTIVES

This chapter looks at:

- developing appropriate skills
- creating a profession
- education and learning, training and CPD opportunities
- careers in the conference industry
- salary levels

It includes case studies in the form of career profiles of personalities within the international conference industry. They are:

- a destination and community organisation marketer and consultant – Linda H. DiMario
- an event exhibition director – Duncan Reid
- an event agency chief executive – Leigh Jagger
- a convention bureau director – Christian Mutschlechner
- a journalist and editor of conference industry magazines – Paul Colston

www.routledge.com/cw/rogers

LEARNING OUTCOMES

On completion of this chapter, you should be able to:

* identify the skills and personal qualities needed for a successful career in the conference industry;
* understand the opportunities available for continuing professional development;
* describe the various initiatives designed to create a profession of event management;
* define the types of career opportunities available within the industry;
* appreciate how leading figures in the industry have reached their current positions, and what they see as the rewards and satisfactions of their jobs.

Introduction

The conference industry depends for its success and future profitability on attracting people with the highest-quality interpersonal and organisational skills. Such skills are equally important to both the buying and supply sides of the industry. Education and learning programmes, coupled with training and continuing professional development (CPD) courses specific to the conference sector, have emerged and are increasing in number and quality. Professional competency standards have been developed and qualifications and certification now exist. Stimulating and rewarding careers can be enjoyed, although clear entry routes and progression paths do not yet exist in most countries.

Developing appropriate skills

The conference industry is, by definition, about people. The word 'confer' implies a discussion or meeting involving two or more people. It follows, therefore, that those wishing to make their career in the industry need to be 'people' people. They need to have very good interpersonal skills and enjoy mixing with a very wide range of people. Diplomacy, flexibility, tact, patience, friendliness, approachability, a sense of humour, a team player, are just some of the personal qualities needed for success.

A variety of other skills and characteristics is also required depending upon the actual position occupied. For example, a paper published in the UK, entitled 'Addressing the skills and labour needs of the events industry' (Kent *et al.* 2010), described the skill sets

required by event organisers working for intermediary agencies in the following terms, based around the three occupational levels of account director, account manager and account/event executive. It said that the main skill needs associated with these roles, as with those for in-house organisers, are wide-ranging.

Account directors need skills in:

- people management and leadership;
- strategy and budget management;
- solid understanding of suppliers.

Account managers need:

- people management;
- project management;
- ability to liaise and build relationships with clients;
- supplier management.

Account/event executives need:

- excellent verbal and written communication;
- excellent organisation and administrative skills;
- customer service;
- degree in event management desirable.

In today's competitive marketplace, the average account manager needs a greater breadth of skills than ever before. A broad mix of finance, marketing, communications and creative skills, combined with a first-class customer service ethic and unsurpassed organisational skills are all but essential. Technical capabilities are also much sought after. Today's technological advances bring with them many exciting opportunities, but with the opportunities come challenges. Event organisers need a workforce prepared to embrace new technology in order to provide the market with the sophisticated and professional service it is increasingly demanding.

The following job vacancy descriptions are based on actual advertisements and are quoted to highlight the types of skills needed for different posts.

- *Conference Manager*: We are looking for a conference manager with a minimum of three years' experience to work for a specialist medical events company. Strong organisational and administrative skills are essential along with a flexible approach to work and the ability to work on your own initiative. You will be expected to manage all logistical aspects of your allocated conferences and manage their budgets accordingly. You will be liaising with suppliers, venues and clients and so excellent communication skills are key. This role is suitable for someone with an outgoing personality, strong work ethic and who is looking for a new challenge.

- *Conference and Publicity Co-ordinator*: Are you a graduate with experience of organising major high-profile conferences and publicity events? Do you have proven knowledge of media and public relations? Have you at least two years' experience of project management and budgetary control? If you fit this description, you could be responsible for the planning, marketing and co-ordination of events, an Annual Conference and Exhibition and public relations for . . . (a professional medical association). You will lead a small dynamic team and, in addition to the stated skills, will be able to prioritise and juggle tasks and will have excellent oral, written, presentation, negotiation and decision-making skills. The post is likely to attract candidates who are computer literate, are ambitious, have established media contacts and enjoy UK travel.

- *Event Co-ordinator (with a conference centre)*: Acting as principal contact between the Centre and the client, developing, organising and managing events to ensure client requirements are carried out to the highest standard with the main objective of securing repeat and increased business. It is essential that the successful applicant has proven experience of organising events where the focus is on high quality customer care/service, possesses excellent communication skills together with the ability to produce detailed and accurate documentation. Applicants must be team players who are organised, thorough, able to work in a pressurised environment and possess a high level of motivation. This is a role for a dedicated and highly committed individual.

- *Conference organisers*: An international company, based in London, seeks two people to join its training and seminars office. We produce high level seminars for ministers and senior officials of foreign governments. Skills required: an analytical mind, ability to work under pressure, attention to detail, experience of seminars or courses, interest in world affairs, knowledge of languages (especially Spanish, Russian, French), excellent written skills and ability to deal with senior people.

- *Head of convention bureau*: Convention bureau seeks conference/meetings/exhibitions/incentive industry professional to drive the marketing and selling of this international city as a business destination, working closely with – and providing benefit for – the range of hotels, venues and professional service suppliers in this market. Candidates will need three to five years' experience in at least one of these specialist sectors and will, ideally, have a wide network of UK and overseas contacts. A blend of marketing and sales skills will impress, but the prime requirement is the personal confidence to build positive and productive relationships with both prospective clients and the destination's suppliers.

A number of skills and personal characteristics recur in this small selection of advertisements. Some also re-appear later in the chapter, identified by leading conference

industry figures as important requirements when they outline their own career profiles. The industry is broad enough to accommodate people with various working backgrounds and educational qualifications, but the common thread is the ability to build productive relationships with a wide variety of people (colleagues, clients and customers, suppliers, the media, and others) and to enjoy doing so.

Research has consistently shown that, where conference organisers and meeting planners have problems with venues, it is not, for the most part, with the facilities and equipment but with staff service, specifically a lack of professionalism and friendliness. As the physical attributes of conference venues become more standardised and of a generally acceptable level, it is likely to be the quality of the staff which will differentiate one from another. This point was expressed very lucidly in a report published in the UK by the Department of National Heritage (DNH) – now Department for Culture, Media and Sport (DNH 1996). Entitled *Tourism: Competing with the Best – People Working in Tourism and Hospitality*, the report said that:

> *The quality of personal service is perhaps more important to tourism and hospitality than to any other industry. Consumers who buy one of this industry's products will often have made a significant financial investment, but also an emotional investment and an investment of time. Of course the physical product – the facilities of the holiday village, the distinctiveness of the tourist attraction, the appointments of the hotel, the quality of the restaurant's food – is very important to them. But during the period customers are in the establishment, they will have many interactions with people: some indirect, with the management and chefs and cleaners; and many direct, with the front-line staff. The quality of those interactions is an integral part of the experience and has the potential to delight or disappoint the consumer. We do not believe that this potential is there to the same extent in any other employing sector.*

The DNH report rightly claims that:

> *Excellent service at a competitive price can only be provided by competent, well-managed and well-motivated people. This means recruiting the right people in the first place, equipping them with the skills they need, managing staff well to create motivation, job satisfaction, and high productivity.*

The conference industry is a wonderful, dynamic, seductive industry but one which still fails to command the recognition it deserves. For it to achieve its full potential and be appreciated as a major benefactor to national economies, both sides of the industry must embrace and maintain the same high standards of integrity and professionalism. The status of the conference organiser must be raised to that of a real profession, of equal standing with solicitors, accountants, scientists or engineers.

There is a need to invest in education and training programmes for buyers, to develop career structures so that experience and expertise are retained within the meetings industry, to ensure that the rapidly growing number of college and university courses on conference/events management and business tourism are in tune with the industry's needs, and to provide recognised qualifications in line with other professions.

Buyers and suppliers are inter-dependent, neither can succeed without the other. Effective collaboration and partnerships should be born of respect for the skills and knowledge of each other, built on mutual trust and confidence.

To translate such needs and aspirations into reality will depend to a great extent upon developments to education and learning, training and continuing professional development (CPD) programmes.

Creating a profession

Before looking at the international provision of education and professional development programmes, it is worth noting that one of the underlying objectives for the conference and business events industry's development is its progression from being an 'industry' to becoming a 'profession'. Bowdin *et al.* (2011) describe the characteristics of a profession as:

- *a body of knowledge – this is the library of the profession. It is made up of information from other professions such as logistics, contract management and marketing. Journals and textbooks describe the body of knowledge and continually refine it;*
- *a methodology – this is made up of a series of processes or tasks, which can be described and taught. The risk management process is an example;*
- *heuristics – these are 'rules of thumb', stories and descriptions of experience that can be learned only 'on the job'.*

They suggest that:

Event management is gradually collating and describing these three areas. In the past, 'rule of thumb' was the main method of organising events. The recognition and description of the processes used to create the event – that is, the methodology – is the 'eureka' moment when events management progressed from being a skill to becoming a profession.

The events management body of knowledge (EMBOK) is being defined and developed. The purpose of EMBOK is to create a framework of the knowledge and processes used in event management that may be customised to meet the needs of various cultures, governments, education programmes and organisations (www.embok.org). A practical

example of the type of knowledge 'domains' covered by EMBOK is given below in the description of the Events Management International Competency Standards (EMICS).

Competency standards in events management

Alongside the creation of EMBOK is the development of competency standards for events management. In the United Kingdom, for example, competency standards were developed for the National Vocational Qualifications, while similar standards have also been developed in Australia, Canada and South Africa. Bowdin *et al.* (2011) suggest that:

> A competency standard for events management gives the industry a benchmark to measure excellence in management. Previously this benchmark was the success of the event; however, stakeholders cannot wait until the event is over to find out whether the event management was competent – by then it is too late.

Events Management International Competency Standards (EMICS) have been developed by the Canadian Tourism Human Resource Council (CTHRC) in cooperation with industry participants from 20 countries (Emerit 2011). The standards contain a comprehensive summary of the functions, tasks and competencies required to work in event management. They describe in detail the skills, knowledge and attitudes that employers and clients are looking for when obtaining professional services to plan, implement and evaluate different types of events, nationally and internationally.

The international standards cover a number of 'domains', including:

- strategic planning;
- project management;
- risk management;
- financial management;
- human resources;
- stakeholder management;
- meeting or event design;
- site management;
- marketing;
- professionalism.

Full details of the standards can be downloaded at www.emerit.ca under the 'Free Downloads – Occupational Standards' link (see also the reference under the CMP programme below).

Meeting Professionals International (MPI) has also been developing a comprehensive set of competency standards, known as the Meetings and Business Events Competency Standards (MBECS), launched in summer 2011. A product of several international boards, governmental bodies, task forces and MPI itself, MBECS are designed to provide a detailed catalogue of the skills needed to be a meetings professional.

The Standards cover twelve areas:

- Strategic planning:
  - manage strategic plan for meeting or event
  - develop sustainability plan for meeting or event
  - measure value of meeting or business event.
- Project management:
  - plan meeting or event project
  - manage meeting or event project
  - risk management.
- Financial management:
  - develop financial resources
  - manage budget
  - manage monetary transactions
  - administration.
- Human resources:
  - manage human resources plan
  - acquire staff and volunteers.

The 12 major categories cover 33 individual skills which are, in turn, informed by sub-skills. The full standards can be downloaded from the MPI website (www.mpiweb.org/mbecs).

International events qualifications framework

The Canadian Tourism Human Resource Council (CTHRC), in addition to its leading involvement with EMICS, and with the help of a global advisory group of experts, facilitated the beginning of an International Events Qualifications Framework (IEQF) during 2011–12. At the time of writing (April 2012), the concept for the IEQF had been completed. The aim is that the IEQF will provide an outline of applicable levels of learning and types of event qualifications which is to be recognised nationally within an increasing number of countries and internationally in the industry. It will not be a regulated frame-work, but will provide an industry-recognised benchmarking resource for the events industry. The IEQF project recommends a process that enables referencing of different qualifications or types of event qualifications (e.g. certificates, diplomas, degrees and industry certifications) awarded by different learning and training providers (e.g. academia, industry professional bodies) against benchmark levels related to role responsibilities within the professional workplace. These role/responsibility levels – support, co-ordinate, manage and direct – are the common ground for all event qualifications.

The various initiatives described in this section clearly show that important steps are being taken by the conference and events 'industry' as it moves towards the creation of a true profession.

Education and learning, training and CPD opportunities

This section looks at the existing provision of education and learning programmes, training courses, and opportunities for continuing professional development (CPD) which are available internationally, and are co-ordinated and administered by industry associations and professional bodies. There is also, of course, substantial provision offered at a national level via trade and professional bodies, in the form of short courses and training workshops, although it is often the case that such provision is uncertificated and does not lead to recognised professional qualifications.

In parallel with the courses offered by industry bodies and professional associations, there are rapidly growing numbers of educational programmes provided by universities, in some cases offered as distance learning programmes, at undergraduate and postgraduate levels. There is not sufficient space in this book to give more than an example of such provision – readers are encouraged to examine university prospectuses in their own country but also to benchmark such national provision against courses and programmes offered by universities outside their own country, especially where distance learning facilities are available.

There are also private sector training providers. This can include the trade media, as well as specialist event management training companies.

Courses and qualifications offered by industry bodies internationally

International Association of Professional Congress Organisers (IAPCO)

The International Association of Professional Congress Organisers (IAPCO) runs courses at several levels through its Training Academy. The best known is the annual IAPCO Seminar on Professional Congress Organisation, popularly known as the Wolfsberg Seminar, first staged in 1975. This is a five-day seminar held in Switzerland in late January and it provides a comprehensive training programme for those at all levels involved in conference organisation, international conference destination promotion or ancillary services. In-depth topics covered include: today's association/corporate/ government meetings, congress promotion, creating the project plan, bids, finance and budgeting, information technology, sponsorship and exhibitions, contracts/insurance/ risk management, presentation skills, programmes, promoting a congress, delegate management and much more including tutorials on a variety of topics as requested by the participants. IAPCO also runs the Meetings Masterclass, a course for those with a minimum of six years' experience in the business. Held also at Wolfsberg, Switzerland, in January each year, topics at the Masterclass revolve round: service organisations, risk management, technology, contract management, sponsorship, human resource and meeting client expectations. Attendance at the Masterclass is strictly limited in number and is a highly interactive course. IAPCO also runs regional and national seminars, in co-operation with governments, tourist authorities or destination hosts, which typically cover 2½ days of concentrated sessions similar to those presented at the Wolfsberg Seminar.

Full details on all IAPCO courses are available from: International Association of Professional Congress Organisers. Email: info@iapco.org (www.iapco.org).

Certification in Meetings Management (CMM)

The mission of the Certification in Meetings Management (CMM) programme, which is administered by Meeting Professionals International (MPI), is to select, educate, and certify management-level meeting and event professionals. The focus of the certification is to provide continuing educational enhancements to the strategic decision-making ability of these leaders to manage and deliver exceptional meetings and events that drive organisational success.

The CMM educational programme is an intensive learning opportunity designed for experienced and highly accomplished members of the global meetings industry community seeking personal career advancement and professional recognition.

The five-day programme (undertaken residentially) enhances the strategic decision-making ability of these leaders, enabling delivery of exceptional meetings and events that drive organisational success. The CMM certification and resulting designation is among the most prestigious in the meetings and events industry. The programme is continually updated and revitalised with curriculum enhancements for today's evolving business culture.

To qualify for the CMM certification, candidates will be:

* management-level meeting and event professionals with a minimum of ten years' experience in the industry;
* business leaders who have existing expertise in all aspects of meeting management including logistics, budgets, people, legal/contracts, and marketing and communications.

Further details on the CMM are available from: Meeting Professionals International, 3030 LBJ Freeway, Suite 1700, Dallas, Texas 75234, USA. Tel: +1 972 702 3000. Email: information@mpiweb.org (www.mpiweb.org/education/cmm).

Certified Meeting Professional (CMP)

The Certified Meeting Professional (CMP) programme recognises individuals who have achieved the industry's highest standard of professionalism. The CMP was established in 1985 and is administered by the Convention Industry Council. Since its inception over 14,000 individuals in 36 countries and territories have earned the CMP designation. The CMP credential increases the proficiency of meeting professionals by:

* identifying a body of knowledge;
* establishing a level of knowledge and performance necessary for certification;
* stimulating the advancement of the art and science of meeting management;
* increasing the value of practitioners to their employers;
* recognising and raising industry standards, practices and ethics;
* maximising the value received from the products and services provided by Certified Meeting Professionals.

Through the CMP programme, individuals who are employed in meeting management pursue continuing education, increase their industry involvement, and gain industry-wide recognition. The CMM qualification does not affect the status of the CMP designation. In fact, the CMM is structured to complement, rather than compete with, the CMP designation: the former is more strategic in approach, the latter more tactical.

To qualify for the CMP examination, a candidate must demonstrate a minimum number of years in the industry as well as having acquired a minimum number of continuing education hours. From July 2012, the CMP paper-based exam changed to a computer-based model. The electronic advance coincided with the regular update of the CMP exam and the introduction of CMP International Standards (see below), enhancing the global relevance of the certification. The exam is administered four times a year during a ten-day testing window at more than 450 testing centres around the world. There are online courses as well as local study groups which can assist in preparing for the exam.

Certification demonstrates that the certified meeting professional has evolved through self-study and industry-promoted education which, when combined with the individual's experience and practical knowledge, has led to their ability to obtain certification. CMP certification holders:

* are recognised by peers for their professionalism and expertise;
* are able to contribute to the development of industry best practices;
* act as role models to junior meeting professionals;
* participate in ensuring industry standards.

CMP international standards

The CMP International Standards (CMP-IS) are the body of knowledge for the Certified Meeting Professional programme and examination. The CMP-IS defines and categorises the skills, competencies and abilities an individual needs to be successful in the profession. The CMP-IS, completed in 2011, represents the most significant enhancement to the CMP body of knowledge since the start of the CMP programme in 1985. The CMP-IS is the result of a multi-year project that involved many stakeholders including subject matter experts, educators and CMP designation holders. In developing the CMP-IS, the Convention Industry Council partnered with the Canadian Tourism Human Resource Council (CTHRC), which completed a job analysis in 2009 for their new standard, *Event Management – International Competency Standard*. The project also utilised Meeting Professionals International's (MPI) Meetings and Business Events Competency Standard (MBECS), which are aligned with CTHRC's competency standards.

The full Standards can be downloaded from the Convention Industry Council website and/or from www.emerit.ca

Further details on the CMP and CMP-IS are available from: Convention Industry Council, 700 N Fairfax, Suite 510, Alexandria, VA 22314, USA. Tel:+1 571 527 3116 (www.conventionindustry.org).

Certified Destination Management Executive (CDME) and Professional in Destination Management (PDM)

The Certified Destination Management Executive (CDME) and Professional in Destination Management (PDM) programmes have been developed by Destination Marketing Association International (DMAI) to provide a dedicated professional education curriculum and testing for individuals employed in the destination management and marketing industry.

The CDME programme is an advanced educational programme for experienced and career-minded DMO executives looking for senior-level professional development courses. Its focus is on vision, leadership, productivity and the implementation of business strategies. Demonstrating the value of a destination team and improving personal performance through effective organisational and industry leadership are the expected outcomes. Those completing the programme successfully receive their professional certification and are entitled to use the CDME credential.

The course requires completion of three 'core' courses:

- Strategic Issues in Destination Management;
- Destination Marketing Planning;
- Destination Leadership.

Each of these courses is two and a half days in length and scheduled throughout the year. Participants must also take a minimum of two 'elective' courses, chosen from nearly 30 topics ranging from targeted destination themes to specific job disciplines within a DMO.

The courses are also open to staff of non-DMAI member organisations, although at a higher cost. The costs (as at January 2012) are US$1,350 per core course for DMAI member bureau staff, and US$1,825 for non-member bureau staff. The elective courses are US$795 each for DMAI member bureau staff and US$1,095 for non-member bureau staff.

The PDM programme leads to completion of a Certificate and is designed for DMO professionals seeking the knowledge and skills that will help to ensure successful careers in destination management. The PDM Certificate requires completion of 40 credits within a five-year period. Credits are tracked only for individuals with an individual DMAI membership. In addition to an initial 'Fundamentals of Destination Management' course (1.5 credits), there are four required courses each resulting in one credit:

- Communications in Destination Management;
- Destination Marketing;
- Destination Product Development;
- Information Technology for Destination Management.

These programmes can be taken upon registration and attendance at DMAI's Annual Convention. DMAI is in the process of revising these programmes for access online with individual pricing by course. The balance of the 40 credits is earned through a variety of educational offerings at DMAI's annual meetings.

Further details on the CDME and PDM programmes are available from: Manager of Education, Destination Marketing Association International, 2025 M Street NW, Suite 500, Washington DC 20036, USA. Tel: +1 202 296 7888. Email: info@destinationmarketing. org (www.destinationmarketing.org).

European Cities Marketing (ECM)

European Cities Marketing (ECM) has been running an annual Summer School since 1987, held in a different country each year (normally end of August/early September). The 2011 and 2012 Summer Schools took place in Krakow (Poland) and Dubrovnik (Croatia) respectively.

The primary goal of the ECM Summer School is to provide a solid basic education for those just starting out in the meetings industry. Uniquely, it brings students face-to-face with leading industry practitioners through a seminar that reflects the latest trends, new technologies and practices. It seeks to maintain the highest standard of course content, retaining and recruiting the very best speakers, and giving up-to-date examples showcasing the latest trends in the industry.

The concept of the course is based on a number of lectures in combination with practical training and interactive group work. Details of the programme can be found at the ECM website (see below). Members of faculty are renowned experts who are very willing to share their knowledge with the students. Participants have a unique opportunity to receive first-hand information and are encouraged to develop contacts with the speakers in a relaxed atmosphere. The 2012 Summer School focused on:

- how to create a marketing plan to promote a city or region;
- the decision-making processes of corporate and association clients as they relate to meeting and congress planning;
- how to find clients: databases and research;
- how to establish a client database;
- the role of intermediaries (PCOs and DMCs);
- to bid or not to bid;
- green meetings, the principle of sustainability for cities and conference centres.

The charm and family atmosphere of the ECM Summer School offer the chance to establish life-long contacts and friendships.

In addition to the Summer School, ECM organises three seminars per year with the aim of developing knowledge and expertise in the fields of city tourism, conventions, and city marketing. The June 2012 seminar focused on the BRIC (Brazil, Russia, India and China) markets, for example.

Further details from: European Cities Marketing, 29d Rue de Talant, 21000 Dijon, France. Tel: +33 380 56 02 04. Email: headoffice@europeancitiesmarketing.com (www.europeancitiesmarketing.com).

Professional Convention Management Association (PCMA)

The Professional Convention Management Association (PCMA) provides educational programmes for meeting professionals, hotels, convention and visitor bureaux, and others in the meetings industry. PCMA views lifelong learning as the key to an inspiring job and continued career advancement. PCMA is recognised as a leader in the meetings industry for providing high quality senior education, innovative resources, and networking opportunities designed to help build relationships critical to success. Educational opportunities are delivered through seminars, self-study courses, reference materials and distance learning programmes. They include: the annual PCMA Convening Leaders which takes place each January and is one of the industry's premier educational events; the PCMA Education Conference; the Certified Meeting Professional (CMP) Online Prep Course (the '*only online course specifically endorsed by the Convention Industry Council*'); and the CASE (Certified Association Sales Executive) Program (designed to help meetings industry suppliers better understand the needs of their association customers).

Professional Meeting Management®, fifth edition (PMM5), is the essential desktop reference for meeting professionals. This book includes all the topics to help plan smarter, faster, and more efficiently than ever before! For both meeting planners and suppliers, a quick reference for the seasoned professional and a thorough training tool for new staff. The Instructor Resource Center provides classroom learning resources including test items, activities, discussion questions, checklists, case studies and more. Further details from the PCMA website or direct from Kendall/Hunt Publishers.

Further information: PCMA, 35 E Wacker Dr, Suite 500, Chicago, IL 60601, USA. Tel: +1 312 423 7262 (www.pcma.org/education/).

Certified in Exhibition Management (CEM)

The Certified in Exhibition Management (CEM) designation was created in 1975 to provide a professional qualification for individuals in the exhibitions and events industry. The designation was formed to raise professional standards and is recognised throughout the industry as the premier mark of professional achievement. To begin the CEM learning programme, new candidates must have three years of full-time experience in the exhibitions and events industry. To earn the designation, participants must complete a nine-part programme within three years. Advanced level courses are also available for CEMs to continue their professional education and obtain recertification.

The CEM programme is administered by the International Association of Exhibitions and Events (IAEE). It offers both face-to-face and online learning opportunities for those studying for CEM accreditation.

Further details from: International Association of Exhibitions and Events, 12700 Park Central Drive, Suite 308, Dallas, Texas 75251, USA. Tel: +1 972 458 8002. Email: info@iaee.com (www.iaee.com).

Certified Event Management Professional (CEMP)

At the time of writing (April 2012), details of a new Certified Event Management Professional (CEMP) certification programme were becoming available. This new certification would be one of the outputs from industry discussions about international qualification frameworks and the development of certification based on the EMICS (Events Management International Competency Standard) (see above for details). The framework would lead to a Certified Event Management Professional (with co-ordinator and manager levels below this), drawing in formal qualifications plus industry certifications such as CMP and CMM (see above). The initiative is being spearheaded by the Canadian Tourism Human Resource Council (CTHRC), which conducted pilot administration of the scheme during 2011. Certificants demonstrate that they meet the standard through a rigorous competency assessment model, involving an assessment of applied knowledge through a written exam; an evidence-based measure of performance, through a case study/portfolio submission and peer jury; and demonstration of a minimum level of experience; with renewal requirements every two years.

Table 8.1 LMU programmes		
Programme Title	**Attendance Mode**	**Qualification Achieved**
Conference & Exhibitions Management	Full-time or Part-time	BA
Conference & Exhibitions Management	Full-time or Part-time	BA (Hons)
Events Management	Distance Learning and Part-time	MSc
Events Management	Distance Learning and Part-time	Postgraduate Certificate
Events Management	Distance Learning and Part-time	Postgraduate Diploma
Events Management	Full-time, Sandwich, Part-time	BA (Hons)
International Events Management	Full-time or Part-time	MSc
International Events Management	Full-time or Part-time	Postgraduate Certificate
International Events Management	Full-time or Part-time	Postgraduate Diploma

University programmes and qualifications

Since the beginning of the new millennium, there has been an explosion of courses in event management offered by universities and colleges, and in certain instances schools are also developing curricula for event courses. In the UK alone, there are believed to be over 60 further and higher education institutions offering full-time, part-time and distance learning programmes. An example of one such institution, Leeds Metropolitan University, is given in Table 8.1 to illustrate the range and depth of such provision – the table only shows courses related to 'business events'. In total, some 20 programmes in event management were on offer at the university's UK Centre for Events Management in April 2012, at various levels and with differing foci – other event-related disciplines included event fundraising and sponsorship, international festivals management, managing cultural and major events, responsible events, sports event management (http://courses.leedsmet.ac.uk).

Careers in the conference industry

Unlike many other sectors, the business visits and events industry does not yet have clear entry routes or easily identified career progression paths. It is one of the facets which illustrate its relative immaturity as an industry. This lack of structure may be somewhat frustrating and confusing for those, both within and outside the industry, who have set their sights on reaching a particular career goal but are uncertain about how best to get there. At the same time, however, this lack of precedent and structure can encourage a greater fluidity and freedom of movement between jobs. There is often no

set requirement to progress in a particular way, or to have obtained specific qualifications before being able to move on.

Many of those now working in the industry have come to it as a second or third career. This is not surprising in view of the need to be at ease in dealing with a wide range of people, or in coping with a last-minute crisis in the build-up to a high-profile conference – situations which require a reasonable maturity and some experience of life.

Relatively few of the occupations in conferences and business events offer regular '9–5' working hours. On the contrary, many involve long hours in the build-up to an event, weekend working, travel delays, pressure and stress caused by working to tight deadlines, pre-event anxiety, having to deal with difficult people and disrupted social life, as the worst aspects of the job.

On the plus side, industry employees often cite the benefits such as: enjoying the variety of work, the absence of routine, the diversity of tasks, the wide range of places and locations visited along with the interaction with people – participants, clients and suppliers. The chance to be creative and face the differing work challenges are also seen as real positives.

When applying for jobs, previous experience in hotel and catering, sales and marketing, business administration, secretarial work, financial management, local government administration, training, travel and transport, or leisure and tourism can be advantageous, depending upon the position being considered. But many other backgrounds and disciplines can also give very relevant skills and knowledge, provided that these are combined with a natural affinity for working with people.

For those looking to find employment straight from university or college, vacancies do arise in event agencies (e.g. administrative posts, assisting in venue finding, as junior account executives) and in event venues (as assistant conference and banqueting co-ordinators, or in venue sales and marketing). It can be possible for new graduates to obtain posts in destination marketing organisations, although more often one or two years' previous experience in sales and marketing is desirable.

Relatively few conference/event organisers, especially within the corporate sector, are full-time. They are first and foremost secretaries/PAs, marketing assistants/managers, training managers, or public relations executives, who find themselves asked to organise events on behalf of their department or company. Their role in conference/event organising may, of course, develop if they prove to have the right talents and enthusiasm and if this meets the company's own development needs.

Other openings arise, from time to time, in the business visits and events industry trade associations and, for those with an interest in publishing, in the industry's trade magazines and electronic media (either in advertising sales or, for those with some journalistic background, as part of the editorial team).

Before beginning a career within conferencing/events, it is probably helpful to know whether one's interest is primarily in the buying (i.e. working as a conference/event organiser for a company, association, public body) or supply side (i.e. working for a conference/event venue, for an audio-visual company, or other supplier of services) of the industry. It is, of course, quite possible at a later stage to switch from one side to the other, and an understanding of how both buyers and suppliers operate is obviously important and beneficial. It is a moot point whether intermediary agencies are best described as buyers or suppliers. Their activities certainly revolve around venue finding and event management, but they do this by providing a service to their clients, the actual buyers.

It should be stressed that most companies and organisations operating within the business events industry are small, employing limited numbers of people. They cannot offer multiple career opportunities and endless possibilities for progression. But their smallness does often ensure that there is a great variety of work with considerable responsibility and lots of scope to display initiative. It does also mean that it is possible, quite quickly, to get to know many of the players in the industry, building friendships and networks of colleagues nationally and, indeed, across the world.

Many job advertisements do not cite 'conference' or 'event organisation' in the job title, nor as a primary function, but mention it as part of the overall duties in the role to be performed. These advertisements can be related to marketing, public relations, project management, communications and publishing, as well as those relating to charities and welfare organisations.

The industry is broad enough to accommodate people with various working backgrounds and educational qualifications, but the common thread is the ability to build productive relationships with a wide variety of people (colleagues, clients and customers, suppliers, the media, and others) and to enjoy doing so.

Salary levels

Perusal of vacancies in trade magazines or on websites is one good way to obtain information on salary or compensation levels for different types of positions within the industry. Another useful indicator are surveys undertaken by industry magazines, recruitment agencies and trade associations.

In the UK, trade magazine *Event*, in association with specialist events sector recruitment consultancy esprecruitment and market research consultancy Zing Insights, carries out an annual 'Event Industry Salary Survey'. The 2011 survey questionnaire (*Event* 2011) was distributed to over 15,000 event industry professionals. A sample of the findings from the 2011 survey (published spring 2012) is reproduced in Table 8.2. The table is instructive in its coverage of job titles prevalent in the sector. It also provides valuable insights into: the actual number of hours worked per week; average holiday or vacation entitlements; employer recruitment activity; frequency of salary reviews; promotion prospects; job motivation factors; job satisfaction levels; useful sources of job vacancy information; and a range of other issues. The full survey can be viewed free of charge at: www.esprecruitment.co.uk

Table 8.2 Salary levels

Job Title/Sector	Average Salary (£) 2010	Minimum Salary (£) 2011	Maximum Salary (£) 2011	Average Salary (£) 2011
1. Event Director				
Exhibition Director	55,200	45,000	80,000	55,000
Event Management Agency Account Director	58,000	40,000	75,000	55,000
Hotel Director of Sales	68,500	42,000	95,000	68,000
Hotel Director of Events	44,000	36,000	53,000	42,000
Production Company: Head of Production	59,000	45,000	80,000	65,000
Venue Sales & Marketing Director	50,000	45,000	100,000	52,500
Venue Operations Director	56,000	45,000	95,000	60,000
Event Services: Project Director	61,500	35,200	78,000	60,500
Commercial Conferences: Conference Director	50,500	40,100	70,100	50,100
Charity/Public Sector Head of Events/Conferences	45,000	38,000	65,200	48,000
Corporate In-house Head of Events/Conferences	68,000	65,000	120,000	70,100
Conference & Incentive Agency: Account/Operations Director	46,000	38,000	75,000	48,000
2. Event Manager				
Exhibition Marketing Manager	35,000	26,000	45,000	33,000
Exhibition Operations Manager	32,000	26,000	45,000	32,500
Event Management Agency Account Manager	30,500	24,000	32,000	30,000
Hotel Sales Manager	27,000	25,200	34,100	28,000
Hotel Conference & Banqueting Manager	24,000	19,000	31,200	25,000
Production Company: Production Manager	38,000	25,000	48,000	32,000
Venue Ops./Event Manager	22,000	18,000	26,000	24,000
Event Services Project Manager	32,000	22,000	50,100	34,000
Commercial Conferences: Conference Manager	31,750	27,000	35,000	32,000
Charity/Public Sector Event/Conference Manager	30,000	26,000	35,500	30,200
Corporate In-house Event Manager	36,500	30,000	48,500	38,000
Conference & Incentive Agency Event/Account Manager	30,000	25,000	38,000	30,000
3. Event Executive/Co-ordinator				
Exhibition Sales Executive	22,000	18,500	27,500	22,150
Exhibition Ops. Executive	21,000	18,500	25,000	22,000
Event Management Agency Event/Account Executive	24,000	19,000	26,000	23,100
Hotel Sales Executive	22,500	18,750	26,000	23,000
Hotel Conference & Banqueting Co-ordinator	18,000	16,000	21,500	18,500
Production Company: Production Co-ordinator	22,000	17,000	27,000	21,000
Venue Sales Executive	23,250	18,000	25,000	22,500
Event Services Business Development Executive	24,000	20,500	28,000	23,800
Commercial Conferences: Conference Co-ordinator	25,000	23,000	27,500	25,000
Charity/Public Sector Event/Conference Co-ordinator	24,500	19,500	28,000	25,000
Corporate In-house Event Co-ordinator	30,000	25,000	40,000	32,000
Conference & Incentive Agency Account Executive	23,000	20,000	25,000	23,000

Source: *Event* Magazine in association with esprecruitment and Zing Insights (reproduced with permission)

Career profiles of leading industry figures

The last section of this chapter contains a series of career profiles written by personalities within the international conference industry. They each describe their current jobs and those aspects of their work which they find rewarding and fulfilling. Some also outline the parts of their work which they find less enjoyable. And previous career experiences, including education and training, are touched on, together with the provision of useful advice and tips for those considering venturing along a similar career path. It is hoped that these profiles will be instructive and maybe inspirational, encouraging some of the readers of this book to want to follow in their footsteps and forge their own careers in the infinitely varied and endlessly stimulating conference industry. Their specific experience, in the order in which they appear, is as:

* destination and community organisation marketer and consultant: Linda H. DiMario;
* event director: Duncan Reid;
* event agency chief executive: Leigh Jagger;
* convention bureau director: Christian Mutschlechner;
* journalist and editor of conference industry magazines: Paul Colston.

Linda H. DiMario, DiMario and Associates

FIGURE 8.1
Linda H. DiMario

DiMario and Associates is a destination and community marketing organisation working with towns, cities, counties, DMOs and EDOs to compete more effectively. My experience is as former President and CEO of Arlington, TX, CVB and Long Beach, CA, CVB; VP Sales and Marketing Tucson, AZ, CVB and Oakland, CA, CVB; ten years hotel sales and marketing with Hilton, Queen Mary Hotel and Disneyland Hotel; professional meeting planner, owner Northwest Conventions, Inc.; political campaign manager.

Destination marketing is the toughest job in the world, soldiers, police officers and firefighters aside! We don't own, operate or manage the assets we sell and promote. We don't control price point or point of purchase. We don't control distribution. We don't control sales and marketing. We don't control customer experience delivery. Millions of people define us. Thousands of people speak for us.

I know just a handful of people who took a straight line to destination marketing. And usually that was because their father or mother was involved. After all, when was the last time you heard someone say, '*I want to be a destination marketer when I grow up?*' The old joke in the industry about '*not even my mother understands what I do*'

holds just as true today as it did when I entered the business over 30 years ago. The idea that we 'sell' a city or community is quite beyond comprehension. And it is certainly one of the reasons that our segment of the tourism industry is still overshadowed by other better known segments like air, hotel, convention centre or attraction. So, rather than dwell on the facts, let's focus on what everyone else is missing!

Almost all of us who find our way into destination marketing do so by way of a detour or two. We find out about a DMO when we are a hotel or attraction sales manager. We discover the job opportunities when we work with a DMO or serve on their Board. We learn about a DMO's mission if we lead a Chamber of Commerce or serve on a city council or as city staff responsible for funding a DMO. In other words, we 'bump into' the work and career opportunity quite by accident and usually through association.

In my case, politics and all its twists and turns led me to destination marketing – and it was not a direct route. Managing political campaigns brought me into contact with contributors and fundraising events at hotels. These contacts helped me transition my organisational skills into meeting and event planning, which – as we know – took me back into hotels and intersecting with DMOs. But when my hotel was sold, my options were to transfer to Denver or take advantage of an opportunity with a DMO. No contest! I was intrigued by the opportunity to sell a destination. Excited to offer my clients an arsenal of hotel options, attractions and experiences as opposed to a single hotel. I thought it would be an opportunity to put my full skill set to work – political, sales, marketing and management. I was right. And I never looked back.

Destination marketing (and many say, management) is a rich and rewarding opportunity for the right person. If you like the nuance of influencing people as opposed to the overt exercise of power, you will be well suited to lead a DMO. If you like rallying people with disparate agendas to serve a common purpose, as opposed to operating unilaterally, you will be well suited to lead a DMO. If you see the value in divergent perspectives and enjoy the process of identifying points of intersection, you will be well suited to lead a DMO. If you like both the visionary aspect and the task-oriented aspects of management, you will be well suited to lead a DMO. If you like strategising, harnessing and directing resources to deliver a specific result, you will be well suited to lead a DMO. If you like building relationships, developing partnerships and forging collaborations to advance a plan of action, as opposed to the 'my way or the highway' approach, you will be well suited to lead a DMO. If you are an active listener and an engaging speaker, you will be well suited to lead a DMO. If you are energised by finding solutions and exploring options, you will be well suited to lead a DMO. If you don't mind who gets the credit as long as the job gets done, you will be well suited to lead a DMO. If you have a passion for making a difference, you will be well suited to lead a DMO. If you like the notion of working at something that is bigger than self, you will thrive in DMO work.

These characteristics are more than a wish list. These characteristics describe the predispositions necessary to lead a destination marketing organisation in the twenty-first century. The days when knowing how to sell and market were considered the most important skill set are over. Now, a DMO leader must be a skilled politician, strategist, consensus builder, mediator, networker and fundraiser. And sometimes, even a therapist! DMO work is challenging on many levels. It is not for the faint of heart or thin-skinned. It is for the confident and capable. It is for those who are curious and passionate about their vision. And it is for those who believe that making people happy is a very important mission.

It's all about relationships

I learned the value and benefits of making a good first impression and cultivating quality relationships early on. At a national convention of association leadership and meeting planners, we were treated to a cruise of the San Francisco Bay. Attending as National Sales Manager for the Disneyland Hotel, it was an opportunity to connect with potential clients. I had the good fortune of meeting and spending time with a national association CEO from Georgia. He and his wife were enjoying their first trip to San Francisco and I became their tour guide. Between showing them the sights and sharing stories and anecdotes of the area while we cruised, we discussed his national meetings. He explained that they always selected convention hotels in close proximity to manufacturing plants that produced member products – and he knew that there wasn't such a manufacturing plant anywhere around the Disneyland Hotel. I remember feeling disappointed at the time but I really enjoyed these genuinely nice people. So, I figured that I would just work harder the next day!

The next day, the CEO made a visit to our exhibit booth to re-connect and thank me for my time and express his wife's appreciation for the 'tour'. I still held out no hope that it would develop into any convention business but the fact that he appreciated the time I had spent with them made it all worthwhile.

Flash forward three weeks: I am sitting in my office and the CEO called. He said, *'You see that manufacturing plant next to the Disneyland Hotel?'* Foolishly, I answered, *'No.'* To which he responded, *'Look again. I am bringing a convention to the Disneyland Hotel next year.'*

Making an authentic connection with customers will always reap benefits and results – if not in direct business, then in recommendations and referrals.

It is all about relationships.

Many years ago, I was lamenting the lack of social conscience in my tourism work to a former college friend who was engaged in very important legal work on behalf of great social causes of the day. His response changed my perception of our work forever. He told me to remember that while he was forced to work with the bottom-side of life, I was lucky enough to work the top-side of life. He told me to

never underestimate the value to men, women and children of good times, laughter, memories and positive travel experiences. He told me that life was tough for most and the work I did contributed to making people happy. He told me to be proud.

And from that day to this day, I see this work through a different prism. It is a journey to make people happy. And throughout this journey I discovered much about myself and others – some good, some not so good – but always valuable. Life is a series of learning experiences and DMO work affords many lessons. It's not enough to be right. There is likely someone else who thinks they are more right. It's not enough to have compelling facts. There are always other facts that can be used to distract from your position. It's not enough to produce good or even great results. There are always other needs and expectations that may supersede the value of your results. There will always be those who do not know what you do or care what you do. And there will always be those who believe that your work provides no benefit regardless of how the benefits are framed. But when the work is done well and with conviction, it is satisfying and rewarding to stand back and look at it through the eyes of those whose lives you touched in small and large ways.

George Bernard Shaw's quote from his play *Mrs Warren's Profession* has always been a favourite of mine because it captures the singular determination required to meet and manage today's challenges:

> *People are always blaming their circumstances for what they are. I don't believe in circumstances. The people who get on in this world are the people who get up and look for the circumstances they want, and if they can't find them, make them.*

Whether it is a destination, a hotel, an attraction or other tourism industry segment, there will always be circumstances seemingly beyond our control – competition, weather, political environments, catastrophic events and misaligned agendas just to name a few. It is our responsibility to manage, mitigate or change those circumstances in ways that empower people to positively impact a destination or experience. It is our responsibility to make people happy – and in so doing, make a difference.

Duncan Reid, Event Director, Clarion Events

FIGURE 8.2
Duncan Reid

The journey

There are hundreds of event courses up and down the UK turning out thousands of event graduates each year but, 15 years ago when I started work, there were no event courses at all. The industry was still in its infancy and the change that has happened over my career to date has been dramatic. For any aspiring organisers in the late 1990s you just fell into it, there was no formalised university training, no real theories and certainly no textbooks. I first met Tony Rogers when I was running 'International Confex', the large annual UK exhibition for event organisers, so when he asked if I wanted to contribute to the third edition of his book I could only say 'Yes'. You see, whilst the industry has come a long way, it has a lot further to go as it looks to professionalise and this is a process we can all help and be a part of.

I suppose my individual journey started at college when I was doing my A-Levels. We used to put on parties for the other students and, when I went to university, I carried this on, running nights at the Student Union, and in clubs and bars in West London, where I was 'studying'. Like many people I had no idea what I wanted to do when I left university and I'd chosen my course – Media Studies and Psychology – based on the small amount of time they wanted me to attend lectures. From what I can remember, the one thing I did have at university was a lot of fun and ideally I wanted to find a job that was going to let me carry on doing this.

The media section in Monday's *Guardian* newspaper always had pages and pages of media sales jobs. I needed money and someone suggested, as I was quite good at talking rubbish, that I might be suited to sales. I applied for a role working at a publishing company in Woolwich. I didn't know what publishing or media sales was, I didn't even know where Woolwich was, but I went along for a group interview with 15 other people. It was like an episode of *The Apprentice* and, as the day went on, we completed tasks and slowly people were sent home if they failed. Finally there were only two of us left and we both got offered jobs.

Anyway, the following week I started work, selling classified advertising for a trade magazine similar to those on the end of the TV programme *Have I Got News For You*. It wasn't glamorous but, within a few months, I'd been promoted a few times so the money was OK. My big break came when the publishing company I worked for decided to buy an events company. Shortly after, the events part of the business had a vacancy appear on their leading computer game event – I applied internally and was successful.

For a guy in his twenties, working on a computer game event was the dream job. I got to fly around the world selling exhibition space on a market-leading show, seeing some great countries and at the same time playing lots of computer games. It was before the accountants really came to the computer game sector and we had some great parties and events. Sony PlayStation would take over big warehouses in East London and turn them into fantastic parties. They'd book artists like Jamiroquai, Faithless and Pulp to headline and you'd get to play the latest console games months before release.

After one edition of the computer game show my role developed so it wasn't just about client sales. I got involved in all the elements of the event from marketing to logistics. It was during this stage of my career that I really learnt how to make events effective. I learnt about marketing campaigns from attracting a visitor to understanding how to make them stay. I also learnt about the operational side. Everything from putting better features into the show to ensuring we had engaging content in the seminars. All this helped refine and deliver a better product that we could then sell more effectively for the following edition.

In 2005 I left the gaming sector behind as I got the opportunity to head up the market-leading 'International Confex', the big exhibition for event organisers and its sister website, www.venuefinder.com. We built a great team and over five editions grew attendance from around 9,000 to nearly 15,000 at its peak. We rolled out a series of initiatives from promoting the voice of one unified trade body, to the support of continuing professional development (CPD), to charity initiatives and industry-wide CSR schemes. We also lobbied the UK government hard to take note of our industry, which it finally did.

Now my career has moved on again and I work for Clarion Events, one of the leading exhibition and conference organisers, on its flagship event, DSEI. The exhibition takes over the whole of ExCeL (London) and is attended by royalty, visitors from 121 countries and over 50 Members of Parliament. For the first edition I worked on, we grew attendance from 25,000 to nearly 29,000 using many of the skills I picked up on Confex and the computer game show as well as the enthusiasm of a new team. I've found that it's not till the second or third edition of an event that you really refine the proposition, so we will see what this will hold. Everything, you see, takes time.

This is a great industry to work in and whilst I may have fallen into it because I had a natural flair for organising, I'm glad I did. Most of it has been good fun but in any career you make your own luck by working hard. Certainly there have been bad times. One day, for example, Sony sent a press release out saying they were never doing the computer game show again but it is how you recover from setbacks like this that really defines you. The next games event we did was probably my best one as it made us up our game dramatically.

To be successful in this sector you need a good team with a range of skills because no one can run an event on their own. There are probably some core skills that it helps if you all have like being organised with a strong attention to detail. You need to be a creative, adaptive and resourceful problem-solver and, ultimately, calm under pressure because, no matter how much you plan, something will always go wrong. It's about what you do next and how you respond that counts.

The future

The industry is ever changing and over the next 15 years I expect it to continue to professionalise. Academia will be more ingrained in the work place with many students from event courses running their own businesses. We will see a rise in the use of continuing professional development (CPD) amongst employees due to the broad range of learning on offer. This, in turn, will create a virtuous circle of improvements for the sector as industry sees the benefits academia brings and invests more back in it. This relationship is currently in its infancy.

Hopefully we will have further government recognition of the sector. Events are fantastic contributors to a country and to that country's economy. They can change lives and rebuild and regenerate whole communities. They can be productive and deliver memorable experiences whilst making money for clients and the Exchequer.

In my career I've found it beneficial to attend the many trade events that cover the sector. The best way to meet people, network and learn about this industry is at the event industry events. It's also good to practise what we preach! And if you can't do that, read the many industry magazines and websites and keep learning.

As I mentioned at the beginning of this piece, I fell into event organising but, if I were going to give someone starting out three simple tips, they would be these:

- Work hard and demonstrate a 'can do' attitude in everything you do. Employers want hard-working staff that will pick up a project and run with it. They want to know that you will do your utmost to make the event a success.
- It can be hard to get your first break and, with thousands of other well qualified graduates to compete with, your CV (or résumé) needs to stand out. Build your CV by volunteering for any event that will take you. If you have practical experience to add to that theory, you're going to be better positioned than someone who hasn't. You might just get offered a job by one of the people you volunteer for as well.
- And, finally, don't forget to have fun! This is truly a great industry with some great people and great products. If you're good and work hard you'll get to travel the world and have some great experiences.

For all of us the journey's only just begun . . .

Leigh Jagger, CEO, Banks Sadler

FIGURE 8.3
Leigh Jagger

Banks Sadler, one of Europe's leading event management agencies employing over 160 staff across five different offices – London, York, Paris, Dusseldorf and New York – provides event management services for over 35 contracted global clients across a number of different industry sectors running over 400 events worldwide per year and managing over 16,000 bookings.

I suspect that, like many of my generation, ending up in the field of event management was a happy accident! Having studied languages and business studies at Oxford Polytechnic, I was very fortunate to find myself doing a work placement at Mercedes Benz in Stuttgart in the sport sponsorship department. You'd have thought that this would have triggered my interest in a career in events, but even then I can't say that I realised that this would be the life for me!

Fortunately, fate stepped in again and, after graduation, I took an administration position at the College of Petroleum and Energy Studies. The College organised oil and gas training courses in the UK but wanted to start offering courses overseas. Very quickly, I found myself co-ordinating a series of training courses in Southeast Asia; that was when I really became hooked.

The College was a relatively small company, so I was involved in every aspect of the courses – from initial conception and discussion with the course leaders, negotiating speaker fees, finding venues, marketing the courses, through to registering the delegates and then spending weeks onsite overseas. A baptism of fire but ultimately a great indicator as to what life in the events industry is like.

I spent the next four years alternating between putting courses together and travelling to Asia to manage them for 4–6 weeks at a time. You learn quickly when you are running events on your own overseas; whatever happens, you just need to find a solution. Working in a different time zone (we didn't have such luxuries as email or mobile phones), I would often have to wait 12 hours before I got any feedback from my office. Whether it was my company credit card being stolen just as I needed to pay for the gala dinner, finding myself stranded in the red light district of Bangkok in the early hours of the morning, or having to find somewhere open on a Sunday to reprint all the course manuals in 24 hours because the originals were stuck in customs (whilst not speaking a word of Thai) – all these experiences gave me the confidence to know that, when it came to pulling an event together, I could remain calm and carry on!

After four very enjoyable years, I was yearning for the excitement of a London life and so moved to join the commercial conference world at IIR. My roles there were slightly different: responsibilities were mostly focused around researching and putting together topical conference agendas and persuading leading industry experts to come along and speak at the event. We marketed the event out via various channels and delegates paid to come along. Although similar in some ways to my previous events experience, with commercial conferences I was much more responsible for content, speakers, getting sponsorship and, of course, the bottom line.

After two years running events at IIR, I was hungry for a new challenge and so joined EuroForum, a competitor who specialised in financial, legal and telecommunications events, to set up a new team. I was lucky enough, two years later, to be offered the role of Managing Director managing a team of 50 people. No longer running events myself, but having to delegate instead, was a huge learning curve in itself. In my experience, event managers tend to have a slight tendency to be 'control freaks' and so moving into a senior management position and having to learn the art of successful delegation was a definite challenge!

Following an enjoyable ten years in the commercial conference world, I decided I needed to spread my wings further and explore other parts of the events industry. After a short period of time working with ExCeL London during their build phase, advising on how the venue could better work with the conference world, I was approached about an exciting opportunity to join an event management agency – Banks Sadler.

When I joined Banks Sadler, we were a team of 40 people based in London; now there are over 160 of us working from five different offices across the world with more soon to follow. I've been at Banks Sadler for 12 years but it is as exciting today as the day I started. We work alongside some of the world's leading companies and making sure our events are fresh, exciting and that they constantly meet and exceed our clients' expectations gives me a great buzz!

Banks Sadler celebrated 30 years in business in 2012; it is amazing to see how our industry has changed over that time and how our industry has become so much more professional. At one point in time, just being a well organised and fairly 'unflappable' person was a good enough foundation to embark on a career in the events world – now the skill set we look for goes far beyond that. Creative, commercial, good with budgets, trained in risk assessment, preferably with numerous languages . . . the list goes on.

I was lucky and fell into a growing industry but currently it's a much more competitive place to be. Of course, there are now many courses available to ensure that prospective new event managers grasp the basics before embarking on their careers but, in addition to anything you can learn, for me personally, I can attribute three clear differentiators to those who go on to be really successful in the events industry:

Firstly, the people who make their mark in the industry are those that can communicate well with people at all levels. Having the confidence and ability to

communicate equally well with your key client stakeholder as you do liaising and negotiating with your supplier base, or even your own internal team, can make the difference between being a real star performer and being just a decent event manager.

The second characteristic that makes someone shine for me is the ability to be solutions-focused. In my experience no one responds well to being told '*No, we can't do that.*' Not everything is possible but, being seen to offer alternative solutions and think outside the box, will ensure that you are always asked to be part of the team addressing the problem!

Last, but not least, for me is the ability to remain calm in the face of adversity. The events industry can often throw a few curve balls at you when you are not expecting them. Whatever it is, you would always prefer to be in the hands of a cool, calm professional with a contingency plan than a drama queen. Flapping gets you nowhere and panic and negativity are contagious!

So as you set off on your career in event management, be warned you will no doubt come in for a lot of stick from your friends and family who will view all of your events as glorified holidays! Despite all my protestations over the years, I can see that the events world does sound a bit more fun than the usual 9–5 job. I have been fortunate enough to visit some amazing countries, stay in some beautiful hotels and eat in some fabulous restaurants – but don't be fooled. For every glamorous story, I can equally recite a string of moments I would rather forget! Whether it is sitting in a windowless office stuffing badges until 3 am, being yelled at by the MD of a global company after he got lost en route to the gala dinner, having large event groups in both New York and Madrid when the terrorists' attacks took place, or having people stranded all over the world by volcanic ash . . . I could go on! But it is these moments, even more so than when things are going smoothly, when an event manager really shows their true value. In fact, the reality is that, if things are going well, your clients should barely notice you are there!

In an interview recently someone asked me what part of my job I love most. As I tried to answer I realised just how lucky I am; actually, I pretty much love all of it. The events industry can be demanding, stressful and exhausting but I have always found it to be great fun, challenging and incredibly rewarding. The industry attracts passionate, motivated and inspirational people and that's why I love it just as much now as I did when I joined over 20 years ago.

The industry has moved on at such a great pace over the last few years and, with technology now playing such an integral part in terms of content, communications and delivery, I can't even begin to imagine what the industry will look like in 30 years' time. Fortunately that won't be my problem – I will probably be busy organising the summer fete in my retirement home by then.

Christian Mutschlechner, Director, Vienna Convention Bureau

FIGURE 8.4
Christian Mutschlechner

If there is one stable element in my career and the business I am in, the meetings industry, it is change.

When I started my business life, which has been basically spent only in the meetings industry, I worked for a local PCO (professional congress organiser) in Vienna. In the late 1970s the profession of a PCO was rather unknown and, due to the structure of the business, we dealt exclusively with our local representatives from European or international associations. It was a time where our key communication tools were telephone lines and telex machines (does anyone remember how to work with telex machines, spending hours on the machine to send confirmations worldwide?). But it was also an excellent school in which to learn, to understand and to get prepared for all the changes I experienced later on.

Adapting to the change and to new tools was, and is, one of the key issues: using electronic typewriters with a memory function; using the first Text machines from Xerox to work on scientific abstracts; entering the era of fax machines; starting to adapt daily work to the era of personal computers; watching the market became inundated with CD-ROMs; the appearance of email as a new communication tool; the creation of webpages; the move into the social web phenomenon. All these elements always begged the key question – is it a temporary hype or will it be a sustainable development? Fax machines are already disappearing; we never lived the CD-ROM time in my office, we switched directly to the webpage; and whether the social web etc. will last, we do not know yet. The question was always: do we need to adapt to this change in our daily work?

At the beginning of the 1990s I became Director of the Vienna Convention Bureau, which had been operational since 1969 as part of the Vienna Tourist Board and, until then, also part of the sales promotion department. When I took over the Vienna Convention Bureau it became a separate department and my challenge was to re-engineer the Bureau. Having been a supplier in the city and experienced cooperation with the Vienna Convention Bureau, it was clear to me that we needed a drastic change or a drastic move from being a passive 'institution' to being a proactive, highly professional Bureau – on the one hand, representing and being a spokesperson for the whole meeting industry in Vienna and, on the other, needing to convince potential clients that, despite being a not-for-profit organisation, you can still operate to high professional standards like a private sector, commercial company. With the team I built up, we managed that over the years and today the Vienna Convention Bureau is, for many, the benchmark bureau.

One of my first targets when I took over the Bureau was to create the first ever city-wide meetings industry statistics for Vienna. This was a major step forward in generating recognition of the meetings industry in our city and, by providing robust data, we also managed to create interest among our local politicians. Subsequent cooperation with the University of Economy to develop economic impact data was a further major breakthrough and is still a benchmark for many other destinations.

Change in the market has happened since I took over the Bureau and is still happening. One of the philosophies we have, and I have, is that as a leading bureau you need to be among the key followers of change or even drive the change. Sometimes your investments of time and money fail because the project or vision is not yet sustainable, or sometimes it is just too early for the market – but if we do not take the risk we might be confronted with facts which we cannot influence any more.

For me one of the key successes, also reflecting change, was the foundation of the ACForum – an association of Europe-based European and international associations organising meetings with more than 2,000 delegates and where a major part of the organisational tasks is within the head office of the association (rather than being outsourced to a PCO or others). Discovering in personal meetings with some association representatives that they never meet each other gave us the idea of founding the ACForum. At the time of its foundation I went through hard times with many industry colleagues who did not understand or see the vision behind this project. Ten years later, the ACForum is still not a very large association (there are around 30 member associations, representing approx. 300,000 delegates per year), but it is becoming more and more significant in our industry. We were the initiator but we are not a member!

Change also accompanied my time as ICCA president. Having been on the Board of Directors from 1997 to 2002, it had already become clear to me that, as a global association, we also needed to increase the global representation on the Board of Directors. This was an important change within ICCA governance – at that time the vast majority of members were Europeans – but we managed to convince our members that being global means also living and guiding our association globally. We also managed to reduce the number of membership categories from seven to five so that our association structure more accurately reflected how our clients see and perceive things. This change was only possible with an excellent Board of Directors, ready to support this vision and this move.

Change is also on the agenda in the years ahead: for many years, decades even, meetings were seen from the supply side as mainly a logistical task or challenge, but scientific associations running congresses are today managed by a new generation of people who are more questioning and more ready to adapt the meetings they organise to a changing audience. A key focus for the future will be how the individual delegate can:

- make the experience of attending a meeting an unforgettable one;
- increase the scientific input and output for delegates;
- create an environment in the venue and in the meeting that supports and enhances the quality experience of our delegates.

The meetings industry (suppliers and clients) will be opened up to different fields of science and experimentation will take place around what kinds of knowledge and know-how can be introduced, such as the impact of different lighting on delegates, on science transmission, on the attendance, etc.

One of the key changes through which I lived in the past and still live through today is that our industry established its own definition, the acronym MICE, which is rarely understood by outsiders. The term is slowly disappearing and, after a lot of work by many industry associations, we managed to agree on the term 'meetings industry' and we also managed to establish a globally recognised economic measurement tool for our industry. I was part of this development and I am proud that this dramatic change has already resulted in three national studies (in Canada, USA and Mexico) into the value of the meetings industry in those countries, and also providing comparisons with other national industries. We have made a start and there is still a long way to go, but the first case studies prove that it is possible to achieve a change of perception of our industry among the general public and politicians.

You can only drive and live change if there is also a certain stability – and that is the team at the Vienna Convention Bureau, a team which has been around without change for nine years. This team stability allows me to look forward, to try things and sometimes also to be successful and to be recognised as a leading Convention Bureau, but also as a person who drives and initiates change. Without my team this would not have been possible.

There is one sentence which I have tried to follow over the years and which is on my desk: '*I find the real thing in this world is not so much where we stand, but the direction in which we are going.*'

Paul Colston, Managing Editor, *Conference News* and *Conference & Meetings World*

FIGURE 8.5
Paul Colston

I remember my first day in the job as editor of *Conference News* magazine was straight in at the deep end with all the sights and sounds of a very busy 'International Confex' show, March 2005, at London's Earls Court. I was struck immediately by the buzz and extrovert nature of the meetings industry and the people in it. It had been a sector, I confess, I had not thought too deeply about in my previous career. As I walked along the aisles that first day I was impressed with the engaging exhibitors and mostly well-designed stands. The feeling of community was palpable.

Most of those who gave me a warm welcome to the meetings industry seemed to have arrived in it more by accident than training, as in my own case. Most seemed to stay.

I graduated with an honours degree in Russian from Manchester University before going into journalism as an editor at the international press agency Novosti. It was a time when Mikhail Gorbachev was shaking up the old USSR and there were plenty of stories to excite a young journalist keen to be part of the big issues of the day. The 'meetings' I reported on then tended to be on the dry side: concerned with topics such as arms control and geopolitics. My ability to speak Russian did lead to some marvellous opportunities early in my career to meet and interview global celebrities, including chess champions Garry Kasparov and Anatoly Karpov at the world chess championship showdown in London; as well as ice hockey and gymnastics stars and footballers.

My experience at Novosti also enabled me to 'warm up' an icebreaker at an early MPI conference session on 'crisis management'. As our North American shoulder-padded power dressers from CVBs Stateside urged us to list the worst disaster we'd been involved in professionally, the good ladies of LA, Denver and New York duly listed experiences including bus transfers going awry, hotel salad bars leading to food poisoning and other such meeting planning mishaps. When my turn came I mentioned that I'd had to field telephone calls to the USSR Embassy's press department in London when Chernobyl's nuclear reactor No. 4 blew up in April 1986. More than a few stomach problems there, I'm afraid.

The new markets of the East were very much to the forefront as opportunities for the international meetings industry when I was invited to Mash Media Group to launch the first truly global English language magazine for the industry, *Conference & Meetings World*. I was fortunate to step also into a working atmosphere steeped in the UK's broadest publishing portfolio of events industry magazines, including *Exhibition News*, *Exhibition World*, *Exhibiting* and *Conference News*. The exciting Mash Media project had always been a meritocracy where you see the results of your labours.

Keeping an outsider's perspective can be a benefit and inoculation against getting too steeped in jargon, acronyms and industry cabals. The trade press should challenge as well as champion and provide platforms for the inspirers and innovators and the coming generation of thought leaders.

The role of editor has allowed me to travel widely and, for a person interested in foreign languages and cultures, it has been a real treat catching a ride on the conference carousel.

Stamina and energy

While our events industry is full of entrepreneurs and creative ideas and types, the speed of interaction and pace of work can be demanding. You need good stamina allied to a healthy hinterland in your personal life.

The international perspectives I have been privileged to gather have helped me better understand the strengths and weaknesses of our UK industry. Are we really the best in the world as we are often told by the likes of our national tourism leaders? Or could we be learning more from the successful models of the German Messes and Asia's innovative and quality-driven approach to delivering meetings and events, such as the model in Singapore and Hong Kong?

Where we do excel clearly in the UK is at education for the sector and the exponential growth of events management courses in Britain has proved popular with international students, even if higher fees have deterred somewhat the natives from taking up places in the same numbers. Our *Conference News* columnist and University of Greenwich senior lecturer Rob Davidson is one shining example of Britain's best on the international meetings stage, inspiring students and bringing back examples of world best practice.

This is greatly encouraging for a country that has lost ground in some of its former key industries, such as manufacturing. Birmingham, for example, is now better known for its delivery of big conferences and events than for producing cars.

The UK and its meetings industry's best prospects, I feel, lie with the new knowledge economy. Just look at the content of internationally successful trade shows such as IMEX and the Reed stable of IBTMs and the education that goes into making them the model to copy. These hosted buyer models are being exported Stateside successfully at AIBTM and IMEX America.

In the events publishing world we have managed to change the axis of work from print to servicing digital media and it has been exciting leading our teams into co-creating new platforms for discussion. Mash Media was first in the UK industry to introduce digital page turning versions of its magazines.

Being part of a vibrant, entrepreneurial and confident sector is stimulating and rewarding. The meetings industry uses the most modern information tools and apps, and combined with the enduring power of 'face-to-face' contact, means it is a sector where you can do business right in the vanguard of innovation and technology.

The meetings industry is also very collaborative and I have enjoyed joining forces with our industry's professional associations and famous acronyms such as the MIA, ICCA, UFI, the HBAA and a whole host of others that embrace a wealth of talent and gifted doers and givers.

Sometimes, of course, '*if your face is crooked, you need to look in the mirror*' and we seized an opportunity at Mash Media to redesign all our magazines in April 2011. In bringing in a revolutionary design, I believe we raised the bar for our industry's trade press in terms of design and content.

The challenges can often be daunting and you can't afford to stand still. I am proud to admit taking several leaves out of the books of some of our finest industry entrepreneurs. A couple of examples: Emma Cartmell, who bravely took on the Leeds Hospitality Show (now the Conference and Hospitality Show) in the depths of the recession; re-engineered it and built it incrementally into the biggest industry trade show in our sector in the North. *Conference News* was proud to back her as a media partner when others did not deem it necessary to pay much attention to a small show.

Likewise, the team at Venuemasters who have built a very solid marketing organisation and show in the academic venue sector. *Conference News* again was proud to stand shoulder to shoulder on the trade show floor with these people of great integrity as they grew their events.

When I do retire from this industry I will be spoilt for choice as I rewind the memory banks for amusing incidents. Up among the great moments was the time in Abu Dhabi when the team at Reed took exhibitors and press out into the desert for a social evening, following the launch of their GIBTM trade show. There was a Bedouin feast, with live music, rhythmical dancing by the camel drivers and demonstrations of falconry and Arab art and craft. Reed's group show director Paul Kennedy persuaded me to have a Bedouin tattoo. Emboldened by a couple of beers, I settled into the big cushion in the tattooist's tent, rolled up my sleeve and, upon being asked through an interpreter what kind of drawing I would like on my arm, I replied: '*Can she do a church, as in the Everton Football Club crest*' (the only team with a chapel inside its stadium)? Assured our Bedouin artist could, I turned around to watch the dancing for 20 minutes as the tattooist got to work. Proud of her 'religious building' as the word 'church' had translated into Arabic, our Bedouin artist pointed out a lovely design of a classical mosque on my arm. Panic set in as I envisaged a hard time at security in Heathrow should I be picked out for a full body search, and also at the thought of explaining to my wife why I had a mosque tattooed on my arm! The henna used also lasted a good three weeks and not the three days as promised by the Reed team . . . I like to think

I'm big enough to take a joke and published the image in our magazines. Sometimes you get to make the news yourself!

On a more serious side, our sector's attention to accreditation and standards is highly laudable. My advice to anyone coming into this industry is to immerse yourself in it; spend time with some of the most interesting people you can find (and not just the ones that talk the loudest or who have the biggest reputations). You may wish to pick up a few techniques for eating on the move, balancing food, drinks, sometimes a camera and a digital recorder, too, and learning to handle multiple venue show rounds with good grace.

My advice would be to approach the industry and your tasks in the right way and you will get your reward and a multitude of lasting friendships.

SUMMARY

- Excellent interpersonal skills are essential to anyone looking to make a career in the conference industry. A range of other qualities will also be needed, including organisational ability, IT skills, strategic and financial planning, a facility for working well under pressure, being a team player, creative skills and communication skills.
- As the quality of the physical conference product (venues, equipment, infrastructure) reaches a generally acceptable standard, it will be the quality of service delivered by the industry's employees which will distinguish one venue or destination or supplier from another.
- There are a number of important initiatives, at various stages of development, which are helping to professionalise the industry. They include the establishment of an events management body of knowledge, international competency standards, and an international qualifications framework.
- The conference industry and the education sector were initially slow to develop appropriate education and training opportunities for the industry's workforce and for potential new entrants. This situation is now changing as educational institutions and professional associations develop full-time, part-time, distance learning and short course programmes, with certification.
- The industry is broad enough to welcome into its ranks people from diverse employment backgrounds and disciplines. The lack of clear career structures and progression routes can be confusing and frustrating, but also stimulates greater fluidity and freedom of movement between jobs.
- The conference industry offers a rich diversity of employment opportunities. Few people will become millionaires, but the rewards in terms of job satisfaction, fun, creativity, and building friendships around the world are rich indeed.

REVIEW AND DISCUSSION QUESTIONS

1   Assess the differences between an 'industry' and a 'profession'. Review the steps being taken by the conference and events sector to professionalise and to turn event management into the next genuine profession. What are the main barriers to potential success, and how might these be overcome?

2   The hotel sector has a reputation for high staff turnover in certain countries, with insufficiently trained staff and limited career opportunities. To what extent is this an accurate description of the hotel sector in your country? What measures should be taken to change perceptions of the sector and ensure that it really does attract, and retain, the highest calibre of personnel?

3   Analyse the structure of post-entry training, CPD and qualifications provision for conference sector employees in your country. To what extent should such provision be available at a national level or, as an international industry, should we be looking at a range of international standards, courses and qualifications?

REFERENCES

Bowdin, G., Allen, J., O'Toole, W., Harris, R. and McDonnell, I. (2011) *Events Management*, 3rd edn, Butterworth-Heinemann

DNH (1996) *Tourism: Competing with the Best – People Working in Tourism and Hospitality*, UK Department of National Heritage (now Department for Culture, Media and Sport)

Emerit (2011) *International Competency Standards: Setting International Benchmarks*, Canadian Tourism Human Resource Council, available at www.emerit.ca

Event (2011) 'Event Industry Salary Survey 2011'*, Event* magazine in association with esprecruitment and Zing Insights, available at www.zinginsights.com/salarysurveyreport.pdf (accessed 13 August 2012)

Kent, M.-C., Moss, C., Jordan, N. and Rogers, T. (2010) 'Addressing the skills and labour needs of the events industry', position paper for discussion at the Events Skills seminar, Confex, 22 February, available at www.businesstourismpartnership.com (accessed 13 August 2012)

CHAPTER 9

Leading industry organisations

CHAPTER OBJECTIVES

This chapter looks at:

- the activities of key international organisations and associations
- the roles of selected national trade and professional associations
- online communities of industry professionals

and includes an assessment of the conference industry's fragmentation.

www.routledge.com/cw/rogers

LEARNING OUTCOMES

On completion of this chapter, you should be able to:

- understand the roles of the major trade and professional organisations in the conference and conventions industry;
- discuss the areas of complementarity and duplication between the different bodies.

Introduction

The conference industry has been described, or more accurately criticised, as being 'fragmented', because of its multiplicity of representative bodies and organisational structures. Even those working full-time within the industry are frequently confused by the bewildering array of abbreviations and acronyms in use. At an international level, a number of professional and trade associations and industry forums, almost all established since 1950, frequently compete with one another for members but also engage in important collaborations on specific projects and initiatives, seeking to raise standards, increase recognition for the economic importance of conferences and business events, and develop a clear vision for the evolution of the industry through the twenty-first century. This chapter attempts to identify the key players and explain their current roles.

The role of international organisations and associations

AIPC: The International Association of Convention Centres

AIPC represents a global network of 170 leading centres in 54 countries with the active involvement of more than 800 management-level professionals worldwide. It is committed to encouraging and recognising excellence in convention centre management, based on the diverse experience and expertise of its international representation, and maintains a variety of educational, research, networking and standards programmes to achieve this. AIPC also celebrates and promotes the essential role of the international meetings industry in supporting economic, academic and professional development and enhancing global relations amongst highly diverse business and cultural interests.

AIPC programme activities include:

- conducting industry research and analysis;
- preparing technical publications;

- carrying out training, educational and professional development activities including the comprehensive AIPC Academy programme;
- maintaining global marketing and communications for the industry;
- facilitating member networking and information exchange forums;
- maintaining performance standards including the AIPC Quality Standards programme;
- recognising management excellence through awards programmes such as the AIPC Apex Award for 'World's Best Congress Centre' and the 'AIPC Innovation Award'.

AIPC also ensures that the convention centre perspective is prominently represented in the advancement of the industry by addressing key opportunities and challenges facing members and actively engaging with government, business and media audiences on issues of importance to the future success of the industry.

Contact details: Marianne de Raay, Secretary General, AIPC, 55 rue de l'Amazone, B-1060 Brussels, Belgium. Tel: +32 496 235 327. Email: Marianne.de.raay@aipc.org (www.aipc.org).

American Society of Association Executives (ASAE)

Although not directly a conference industry trade association, ASAE (American Society of Association Executives) is, nonetheless, a very important body for the international convention industry because of the scale of convention activity undertaken by its members.

ASAE is an individual-membership organisation of more than 21,000 association executives and industry partners representing 10,000 organisations. ASAE members manage leading trade associations, individual-membership societies, and voluntary organisations across the United States and in nearly 50 countries around the world.

With support of the ASAE Foundation, a separate, related non-profit entity, ASAE is the premier source of learning, knowledge and future-oriented research for the association and non-profit profession. ASAE provides ideas and resources – ranging from a monthly magazine and books to educational programming and other products and services – as well as advocacy to enhance the power and performance of the association and non-profit community.

ASAE believes that associations have the power to transform society for the better. ASAE's passion is to help association professionals achieve previously unimaginable levels of performance. The organisation does this by nurturing a community of smart, creative, and interesting people: its members.

Contact details: ASAE and The Center for Association Leadership, 1575 I Street NW, Washington DC 20005, USA. Tel: +1 202 371 0940. Email: ASAEservices@asaecenter. org (www.asaecenter.org).

Association Internationale des Villes Francophones de Congrès (AIVFC)

Formed in 1975, the Association internationale des villes francophones de congrès (AIVFC: International Association of French-speaking Congress Cities) now has over 50 members spread across the main French-speaking countries of Europe, America and Africa. Its principal objectives can be summarised as *'exchange, act, promote, innovate, communicate and anticipate'*:

* exchanging experiences by organising regular seminars and continuous training;
* acting by being present in international trade exhibitions, and by sharing information on congresses that might potentially interest other members;
* promoting the French language by encouraging clients to use simultaneous translation for their congresses, and by creating and distributing a glossary of French congress terms;
* innovating as a constant and continuous state for members;
* communicating through PR activity and the AIVFC website;
* anticipating and observing the evolution of occupations and professions in the field of congresses and related events.

Contact details: Association internationale des villes francophones de congrès, Palais des Congrès-Expositions, Dijon-Bourgogne – Centre Clémenceau, 3 boulevard de Champagne, BP 67827, 21078 Dijon Cedex, France. Tel: +33 (0) 3 80 77 39 00. Email: contact@dijon-congrexpo.com (www.aivfc-congres.com).

Confederation of Latin American Congress Organising Entities and Related Activities (COCAL)

Established in 1985, COCAL is a civil, not-for-profit body of Latin American professional conference organisers specialising in congresses and events. The Confederation's vision is to establish the Latin American meetings industry at the highest level internationally, combining cutting-edge technology with the region's natural strengths and beauty. COCAL's specific objectives are to:

* enhance the training of the sector's managers and professionals;
* agree a set of ethical and commercial principles and standards;
* contribute to the promotion of the countries of Latin America and building collaborative relationships between them;
* represent the region at an international level.

Contact details: Confederation of Latin American Congress Organising Entities and Related Activities. Email: secretaria@cocal.org (www.cocal.org).

Convention Industry Council (CIC)

The Convention Industry Council's (CIC) 32 member organisations represent more than 103,500 individuals as well as 19,500 firms and properties involved in the meetings, conventions and exhibitions industry. Formed in 1949, the mission of CIC is to provide a forum for member organisations seeking to exchange information on global trends and topics, promulgate excellence in best practices and guidelines, collaborate on industry issues and advocate the meetings, conventions, exhibitions and events industry.

CIC is well known for its Certified Meeting Professional (CMP) programme (see Chapter 8) and the CMP International Standards. CIC is also responsible for the Hall of Leaders Program (which seeks to recognise industry leadership) and the Accepted Practices Exchange (APEX) (see also Chapter 1). Through the APEX initiative and in partnership with the American Society for Testing and Materials International (ASTM), professionals in the meetings industry have access to the very first green meetings and event standards in the areas of audio-visual, communication and marketing materials, destinations, exhibits/exhibitions, food and beverage, meeting venue, on-site office, transportation, and accommodation, which are available for purchase through ASTM (www.astm.org).

Contact details: Convention Industry Council, 700 N Fairfax, Suite 510, Alexandria, VA 22314, USA. Tel: +1 571 527 3116. Email: cichq@conventionindustry.org (www.conventionindustry.org).

Destination Marketing Association International (DMAI)

The Destination Marketing Association International (DMAI) is the world's largest and most reliable resource for official destination marketing organisations (DMOs), from city-level convention and visitors bureaux to national tourism boards. Formerly the International Association of Convention and Visitor Bureaus until August 2005, the association has worked to enhance the professionalism, effectiveness and image of more than 3,000 professionals from 600 destination marketing organisations in 25 countries since 1914.

The association protects and advances the success of destination marketing, offers cutting-edge educational and professional development programmes for destination marketing professionals, and provides a voluntary accreditation programme for DMOs called the Destination Marketing Accreditation Program (DMAP). DMAI maintains a premier convention and meetings database, empowerMINT, that contains data on over 34,000 association and corporate meetings from more than 17,000 organisations (mainly headquartered in North America). DMAI also sponsors two annual *Destinations Showcase* tradeshow events in Washington DC and Chicago, highlighting exhibiting destinations to thousands of qualified meeting professionals.

The Destination and Travel Foundation was established in 1993 to enhance and complement the association and the destination management profession through research, education, visioning and developing resources and partnerships for those efforts.

Further information is available from: Destination Marketing Association International, 2025 M Street NW, Suite 500, Washington DC 20036, USA. Tel: +1 202 296 7888. Fax: +1 202 296 7889. Email: info@destinationmarketing.org (www.destinationmarketing.org).

European Association of Event Centres (EVVC)

The European Association of Event Centres (EVVC), founded in 1955, is a leading umbrella organisation for event and convention centres, arenas, and other multi-purpose halls in Europe. It represents about 700 locations in Germany, Austria, Switzerland and other European countries. The EVVC acts as a platform for the active exchange of experiences and information between its members and offers various services, seminars and consultation services.

The main activities of EVVC include communication and exchange with the industry and with other associations, support for technical developments, market research, and lobbying. For its members EVVC provides agreements with partners from different industry sectors (hotels, technology, software, etc.), support in marketing activities, the organisation of workshops and seminars, and information exchange and consultancy on tax and legal issues.

Further information is available from: European Association of Event Centres, Ludwigstrasse 3, D-61348 Bad Homburg, Germany. Tel: +49 61 72 27 96 900. Fax: +49 61 72 27 96 909. Email: info@evvc.org (www.evvc.org).

European Cities Marketing (ECM)

European Cities Marketing provides a platform on a pan-European basis for cities to perform better in their convention and tourism activities through the exchange of knowledge and best practice within a city marketing framework. European Cities Marketing was created following the merger of the former European Cities Tourism (ECT) and the European Federation of Conference Towns (EFCT) in 2007. It is now promoting and linking the interests of more than 120 members from more than 100 major cities in 32 countries. The network is composed of two forums: Conventions and Tourism.

The Conventions Forum aims to teach destinations and convention bureaux to act as a professional 'one-stop-shop' for professional meeting planners. The 'Meet Europe' event and 'Mercado' workshop organised by ECM offer face-to-face meetings between buyers and suppliers. The Conventions Forum also arranges the ECM Summer School for all people starting work in the meetings industry (see Chapter 7 for more details), while its Politicians' Forum (organised in cooperation with IMEX) aims to educate and inform local politicians about the economic importance of the meetings industry, as well as providing the opportunity to debate current issues.

ECM's Tourism Forum provides a range of services for those of its members focused on the leisure tourism sector.

The annual programme of activity includes three meetings per year with all ECM members including ECM's general assembly and conference, other meetings, workshops, seminars and research studies. ECM intranet – a virtual network giving access to online discussions, a library, news and projects – is also one of the member benefits.

Further information is available from: European Cities Marketing, 29D rue de Talant, F-21000 Dijon, France. Tel: +33 380 56 02 04. Fax: +33 380 56 02 05. Email: headoffice @europeancitiesmarketing.com (www.europeancitiesmarketing.com).

European Federation of the Associations of Professional Congress Organisers (EFAPCO)

EFAPCO was formed in 2004 to complement the activities of the national associations of PCOs operating across Europe and to ensure a united and strong voice within the European Union. The EFAPCO network now embraces 13 national associations representing well over 1,450 companies and organisations active in the meetings industry.

The Federation's specific objectives are to:

- increase the recognition of professional congress organisers within the European Union;
- promote the interests of European PCOs, their clients and their suppliers;
- raise and maintain the highest professional standards across the meetings industry with the provision of education and training opportunities;
- grow the business of PCOs across Europe;
- monitor, propose and advise on European Union legislation which has an impact on the meetings industry;
- assess the challenges and problems faced by PCOs and to promote relevant solutions;
- provide opportunities for networking and the exchange of ideas and experiences;
- further and encourage the commercial relationships between members and their clients;
- provide relevant information to international public authorities;
- play an active role within other European and global organisations working in the meetings and events industry.

As at summer 2012 EFAPCO had 13 full members representing: Belgium, Czech Republic, France, Germany, Greece, Hungary, Ireland, Italy, Poland, Portugal, Slovakia, Spain and the United Kingdom.

Contact details: EFAPCO Executive Office, Av 5 de Outubro, 53, 2. 1050–048, Lisbon, Portugal. Tel: +351 213 155 135 (www.efapco.eu).

Global Business Travel Association (GBTA)

The Global Business Travel Association (GBTA) is one of the world's premier business travel and meetings organisations. For more than 40 years, the association has dedicated itself to the professional development of its members and the advancement of the business travel and meetings management community. It is a critical source for information and resources on the business travel industry.

Collectively, GBTA's 5,000-plus corporate members manage over US$340 billion of global business travel and meetings expenditures annually. GBTA supports its network of 17,000 individual business and government travel and meetings managers, as well as travel service providers, through education and research, networking and events, and advocacy:

- *Education and Research* – GBTA's wide array of education forums and seminars are aimed at helping business travel management professionals to advance their careers and become better-informed leaders. The GBTA Foundation is the education and research arm of the association and provides the only master's-level accredited course and professional designation for the corporate travel professional. Education initiatives and research findings are designed to equip travellers with the knowledge they need.
- *Networking and Events* – GBTA provides valuable programmes, tailored and targeted to support the business travel professional's success in the corporate world. GBTA offers a comprehensive calendar of events and networking opportunities. Through GBTA's relationships with affiliated US local chapters and business travel organisations around the world, members can stay connected both locally and globally.
- *Advocacy* – GBTA's government relations programme brings the collective voice of business travel to Washington. It monitors legislative policies affecting the business travel industry and the work of other industry associations and companies to provide research to demonstrate the value of business travel to the federal government and promote the role of the travel manager.

GBTA membership provides networking and marketing opportunities at all levels bringing together business travel buyer and supplier professionals from around the globe:

- *Peer Networking* – Members benefit from access to the industry's leading network of corporate and government travel decision–makers and purchasers through committees, events and local chapters.
- *Discounts* – Benefits include discounts on advertising/sponsorship opportunities, event and exhibitor fees, and professional certifications.
- *Tools and Resources* – Members can access requests for proposals (RFPs), research/ surveys, white papers, newsletters and online career centres.

Contact details: Global Business Travel Association, 123 North Pitt Street, Alexandria, Virginia 22314, USA. Tel: +1 703 684 0836. Fax:+1 703 684 0263. Email: info@gbta.org (www.gbta.org).

International Association of Conference Centres (IACC)

The International Association of Conference Centres (IACC) is a not-for-profit organisation whose vision is to be '*A community of passionate people and organizations delivering innovative and exceptional meeting experiences*'. The '*Thought Leader on the Meeting Experience*', IACC represents its members by defining and promoting the IACC Meeting Concept and providing learning opportunities.

IACC's core strategic priorities are to create and promote the IACC brand; develop and ensure adherence to quality standards; create, identify and communicate meeting trends and statistics; provide learning experiences to members; and foster strategic alliances with industry organisations.

In 2012 IACC had more than 300 member conference centres in three chapters: Australia Asia-Pacific; Americas; and Europe.

Benefits of membership include:

- marketing and branding of IACC and its members throughout the meetings industry;
- representation through the IACC website and other online portals;
- access to industry trends and statistics;
- professional education programme;
- a global programme of conferences and events;
- Copper Skillet chef competition.

In addition to its conference centre members, IACC also offers 'Individual and Associate Membership' for organisations providing products and services to enhance the meetings experience.

Contact details: International Association of Conference Centres, 243 North Lindbergh Boulevard, Saint Louis, Missouri 63141, USA. Tel: +1 314 993 8575. Fax: +1 314 993 8919. Email: info@iacconline.org (www.iacconline.org).

International Association of Exhibitions and Events (IAEE)

The International Association of Exhibitions and Events (IAEE) began life in 1928 as the National Association for Exposition Managers (and subsequently traded as the International Association for Exhibition Management, until November 2006). Today IAEE is the largest international association for individuals who conduct and support exhibitions around the world.

The mission of IAEE is to promote the unique value of exhibitions and other events that bring buyers and suppliers together, such as roadshows, conferences with an exhibition component, and proprietary corporate exhibitions. IAEE is a principal resource for those who plan, produce and service the industry.

It oversees the 'Certified in Exhibition Management' (CEM) programme and awards the designation of CEM to those who complete the programme successfully. The CEM was created to raise professional standards and provide a vehicle for certification in the exhibition industry.

Further information from: International Association of Exhibitions and Events, 12700 Park Central Drive, Suite 308, Dallas, Texas 75251, USA. Tel: +1 972 458 8002. Email: info@iaee.com (www.iaee.com). IAEE also maintains offices in Europe, Asia-Pacific and China.

International Association of Professional Congress Organisers (IAPCO)

Helping the world to meet

The International Association of Professional Congress Organisers (IAPCO) is the international association for professional congress organisers (PCOs), serving the needs of PCOs and international meeting planners all over the world. It is exclusively for organisers of international meetings and special events and has 120 members in 42 countries around the world (as at February 2012) including intergovernmental organisations (European Parliament; IMF/World Bank; Asian and European Development Banks).

IAPCO aims are:

- to further the recognition of the profession of the congress organiser;
- to further and maintain a high professional standard in the organisation and administration of congresses, conferences, and other international and national meetings or special events;
- to undertake and promote the study of theoretical and practical aspects of international congresses;
- to undertake research work concerning all problems confronting professional organisers of international meetings to seek and promote relevant solutions;
- to establish and maintain effective relations with other organisations concerned in any way with international meetings;
- to develop a programme of educational courses through its Training Academy;
- to offer a forum for PCOs;
- to encourage meetings' convenors to seek the assistance of reputable PCOs;
- to provide members with opportunities to exchange ideas and experiences.

Quality assurance

Since the founding members met in 1968 to establish this international association, IAPCO has set standards for an industry which has grown dramatically in terms of service and economic impact. The IAPCO logo is a global quality branding for professional meeting planners and managers specialising in international events whose membership is universally recognised as a sign of excellence by clients and other suppliers within the conference industry. Prospective members are required to provide evidence of their experience, competence, client references and quality procedures for consideration by the IAPCO Council before membership applications are considered. There is an on-going compulsory quality maintenance programme to ensure that existing members retain the exacting standards required for IAPCO membership, which includes verification of two annual congresses by the Quality Committee, an annual Self-Assessment programme and attendance at IAPCO's Annual Seminar on Quality Management.

Sustainability

IAPCO recognises the increasing importance of environmental sustainability to its members and to the wider conventions and incentives industry, as both a business and an ethical issue. IAPCO feels it is important to take steps now to incorporate environmental sustainability into its core vision and implements a Code of Sustainable Practice.

IAPCO training academy

IAPCO has an unparalleled record in conference education. IAPCO's educational programmes contribute to the Certified Meeting Professional Programme (CMP) and the Meeting Management Programme (CMM).

The IAPCO Annual Seminar on Professional Congress Organisation, popularly known as the 'Wolfsberg Seminar' due to its location, was first staged in 1975. Since then over 2,100 participants from more than 70 countries have completed the week-long Seminar, entitling them to an IAPCO Seminar Certificate (see Chapter 8 for further details). This is one of the world's most comprehensive training programmes for executives involved in conference organisation, international conference-destination promotion or ancillary activities.

The Meetings Masterclass was established in 2011 and is fast becoming an essential educational ingredient for training 'senior executives with more than 6 years' decision-making experience in the meetings industry'. Introduced by popular demand from former 'Wolfsberg' participants, the Masterclass is held at IAPCO's educational home in Wolfsberg. In addition, IAPCO National and Regional Seminars are staged at the invitation of local hosts.

IAPCO internationally

IAPCO is a founder member of the Joint Meetings Industry Council (JMIC), a worldwide council of international associations whose representatives meet on a regular basis to report on new initiatives and explore ways in which they can co-operate in conference education, publications and research.

IAPCO is actively involved in initiatives with other meeting industry partners and organisations such as the International Pharmaceutical Congress Advisory Association (IPCCA) and the Healthcare Convention and Exhibitors Association (HCEA), founding the Healthcare Congress Alliance to develop a better understanding of specific needs and interests as well as common guidelines between the different industry players involved in conference organisation.

A member of CIC, the Convention Industry Council, IAPCO plays an active part in the international arena, and openly supports the 'Face Time. It Matters' campaign launched in 2010 to promote the benefits of meeting face-to-face.

IAPCO publications

In addition to the international quarterly newsletter, *The PCO*, IAPCO publishes a range of useful conference guidelines for PCOs, planners and suppliers, such as:

* Request for Proposal (RfPs) for the Appointment of a PCO for International Meetings;
* Request for Proposal (RfPs) for the Appointment of a PCO for National Meetings;
* How to Choose the Right PCO;
* How to Choose the Right Core PCO;
* Bidding for a Congress;
* First Steps for the Chairman in the Preparation of an International Meeting;
* Guidelines for Co-operation between the International Association, the National Organising Committee (NOC)/Local Organising Committee (LOC) and the PCO;
* Guidelines for the International Scientific Programme Committee;
* Poster Presentations for an International or National Congress.

Guides and publications from the Healthcare Congress Alliance

* First Steps in the Preparation of an International Medical Meeting for the Chairman;
* Sponsorship Prospectus;
* Security and Safety at Healthcare Congresses;
* Accountability Issues in Healthcare Congress Management.

Meetings industry terminology

* The congress industry's leading dictionary of over 900 words in 12 languages;
* Supplement – incorporating Chinese, simplified and traditional;
* Supplement – incorporating Russian.

In addition, members of IAPCO receive the benefits of additional guideline documentation, such as:

- guidelines for managing the scientific programme – extended;
- national fact sheets for working outside the country of own offices;
- continuing medical education surveys;
- PCO check-list;
- code of European Federation of Pharmaceutical Industries and Associations;
- code of International Federation of Pharmaceutical Manufacturers and Associations;
- site inspection handbook;
- sustainable practice check-list.

IAPCO is active on Twitter, tweeting only relevant news and information for the benefit of all in the meetings industry; as well as managing various professional congress organiser sites on LinkedIn and contributes to IAPCO news on Facebook.

Annual survey

An annual survey of IAPCO members is undertaken to identify the position of IAPCO members in the meetings marketplace. The results of the survey show a steady increase in business and the major impact and contribution that IAPCO members make to the meetings industry. IAPCO members (2010 results) organise in excess of 6,100 meetings annually, representing some 2.24 million delegates and 0.54 million m^2 exhibition space, representing an economic impact in the region of €3.638 billion, increasing year on year.

Contact details: International Association of Professional Congress Organisers. Email: info@iapco.org (www.iapco.org).

International Congress and Convention Association (ICCA)

The International Congress and Convention Association (ICCA) was founded in 1963 and is the most global of all the international meetings industry trade associations. Its membership (numbering over 920 companies and organisations in almost 90 countries in 2012) is organised in eleven chapters representing regions of the world, and five industry sectors comprising meetings management, transport, destination marketing, venues, and meetings support.

ICCA's mission statement says: '*ICCA is the global community for the meetings industry, enabling its members to generate and maintain significant competitive advantage*'. ICCA's stated USPs are the global, cross-regional and cross-sectoral networking for senior executives, and its unique access to the international association meetings market, particularly its unique database on past and future international association meetings.

ICCA membership benefits and services include:

- Business opportunities:
  - online associations database, with data supplied by members and qualified by 13 full-time researchers
  - provision of hot leads on association events
  - client/supplier business workshops
  - business leads exchange at ICCA member events.

- Promotion:
  - ICCA pavilions for members to exhibit at international trade shows
  - listing/advertising in a widely distributed membership directory
  - listing/advertising in a wide range of educational publications aimed at international meeting planners
  - ICCA Intelligence – an online resource published four times a year and distributed to over 2,500 international association clients
  - PR kit: a comprehensive database of meetings media and guidance on achieving a positive PR profile.

- Education:
  - ICCA Congress, which is recognised as one of the industry's thought-leadership forums, and which moves around the world attracting approximately 1,000 industry leaders
  - ICCA research, sales and marketing programme for frontline executives and middle managers
  - ICCA Forum for young professionals/youth forum
  - association expert seminar
  - chapter meetings
  - wide variety of publications on penetrating the association meetings market.

- Networking:
  - ICCA Congress
  - client/member networking evenings at major trade shows such as IMEX and EIBTM
  - members update online
  - chapter meetings.

ICCA is a member of the Joint Meetings Industry Council and the Convention Industry Council, and is an Associate Member of the United Nations World Tourism Organization, and a Gold partner of the Green Meetings Industry Council.

Contact details: ICCA, Toren A, De Entrée 57, 1101 BH Amsterdam, The Netherlands. Tel: +31 20 398 1919. Fax: +31 20 699 0781. Email: icca@icca.nl (www.iccaworld.com).

ICCA also maintains regional offices in Malaysia, Uruguay and the USA, which run their own regional events and business opportunities for members.

International Pharmaceutical Congress Advisory Association (IPCAA)

Membership of the International Pharmaceutical Congress Advisory Association (IPCAA) is open to internationally active healthcare companies engaged in medical congresses. All member companies must maintain a permanent healthcare-oriented research programme. IPCAA represents in excess of 23 healthcare companies from around the world with its Code of Conduct and Guidelines seen as the basis for interactions between medical societies, congress organisers and the healthcare industry.

IPCAA's mission is to '*ensure the most beneficial outcome for all parties involved in medical congresses, through the development of common and consistent congress policies and through recognised partnerships with medical societies*'. IPCAA's main objectives are to:

- promote the highest possible standards at medical congresses;
- establish a common and consistent congress policy through recognised partnership with medical societies;
- ensure optimum benefit for all parties involved in medical congresses;
- exchange experience, data and documentation on medical congresses;
- organise meetings of members to exchange knowledge and information about medical congresses;
- organise training courses and seminars for those involved in medical congress management;
- maintain a code of conduct and guidelines on the organisation of, and participation in, medical congresses.

IPCAA is a member of the Healthcare Congress Alliance. This provides an excellent consolidated overview on the running of medical congresses worldwide.

Contact details: International Pharmaceutical Congress Advisory Association, PO Box 182, CH-4013 Basel, Switzerland. Tel: +41 61 821 3133. Email: secretariat @ipcaa.org (www.ipcaa.org).

International Special Events Society (ISES)

ISES was founded in 1987 to foster enlightened performance through education, while promoting ethical conduct. ISES works to focus professionals on the 'event as a whole' rather than its individual parts. The solid peer network that ISES provides helps special events professionals to produce outstanding results for clients while establishing positive working relationships with other event colleagues.

ISES's mission is to educate, advance and promote the special events industry and its network of professionals along with related industries. To that end, ISES strives to:

- uphold the integrity of the special events profession to the general public through its 'Principles of Professional Conduct and Ethics';
- acquire and disseminate useful business information;
- foster a spirit of cooperation among members and other special events professionals;
- cultivate high standards of business practices.

Membership of the International Special Events Society or ISES is comprised of over 7,200 professionals in almost 40 countries representing special event planners and producers (from festivals to trade shows), caterers, decorators, florists, destination management companies, rental companies, special effects experts, tent suppliers, audio-visual technicians, event and convention co-ordinators, balloon artists, educators, journalists, hotel sales managers, speciality entertainers, convention centre managers, and many more professional disciplines.

Contact details: ISES, 401 North Michigan Avenue, Chicago, Illinois 60611, USA. Tel: +1 312 321 6853. Email: info@ises.com (www.ises.com).

The Joint Meetings Industry Council (JMIC)

The Joint Meetings Industry Council was established in 1978 as a vehicle for creating a forum for the exchange of information and perspectives amongst international associations involved in various aspects of the meetings industry. It is now engaged in the process of building better communications and linkages amongst member organisations and advancing industry profile along with a greater appreciation of the value the industry brings to the global economy.

JMIC members include:

- AACVB (the Asian Association of Convention and Visitor Bureaus);
- AIPC (the International Association of Congress Centres);
- COCAL (the Latin American Confederation of PCO and Related Companies);
- DMAI (Destination Marketing Association International);
- ECM (European Cities Marketing);

- EFAPCO (the European Federation of Associations of Professional Congress Organisers);
- EVVC (the European Association of Event Centres);
- IAEE (International Association of Exhibitions and Events);
- IAPCO (the International Association of Professional Congress Organisers);
- ICCA (the International Congress and Convention Association);
- MPI (Meeting Professionals International);
- PCMA (the Professional Convention Association Management Association);
- Site (the Society of Incentive and Travel Executives);
- UFI (the Global Association of the Exhibition Industry).

It is also supported by the CIC (Convention Industry Council).

Contact details are those for whichever member body is currently acting as JMIC President. Since 2004 this has been the International Association of Convention Centres (AIPC) (www.themeetingsindustry.org/jmic_home.html).

Meeting Professionals International (MPI)

Meeting Professionals International (MPI) is a vibrant global community of business professionals who specialise in the meeting and event industry. As at February 2012, membership comprised of more than 21,000 members belonging to 71 chapters and clubs worldwide.

MPI is the sum total of its members' ideas, goals, knowledge and talents, committed to advancing business events as integral to business success. It is also committed to delivering constant professional development and business opportunities. Each MPI member brings what they have to the community. Each takes away what they need. After four decades of building an outstanding association, MPI remains committed to growing the meeting and event industry, proving the business value of meetings and evolving to deliver what its members need to survive and thrive by providing human connections to knowledge and ideas, relationships and marketplaces.

Further information is available from: Meeting Professionals International, 3030 LBJ Freeway, Suite 1700, Dallas, Texas 75234, USA. Tel: +1 972 702 3000. Fax: +1 972 702 3070. Email: information@mpiweb.org (www.mpiweb.org).

MPI European Office, 22 Route de Grundhof, L-6315 Beaufort, Grand Duchy of Luxembourg. Tel: +352 2687 6141. Fax: +352 2687 6343. Email: dscaillet@mpiweb.org.

Professional Convention Management Association (PCMA)

Founded in 1956, the mission of the Professional Convention Management Association (PCMA) is to deliver superior and innovative education and promote the value of professional convention management. Membership of PCMA was initially restricted to meeting managers in the medical and healthcare fields. Through the years, PCMA's initial focus shifted to providing both networking and educational opportunities for meeting professionals at all levels, plus suppliers, faculty and students. PCMA now represents nearly 6,000 members from 17 chapters in the USA, Canada and Mexico.

In 1985 PCMA created the PCMA Education Foundation, designed to support educational programmes to improve professionalism in the meetings industry and to provide university-level meeting management curriculum through fundraising and grant-giving.

Since 1956, PCMA's signature educational event has been its annual Meeting, *Convening Leaders*. Over the years, attendance has grown from six in 1956 to over 3,750 in 2012. The meeting takes place in January and features numerous educational sessions and networking opportunities. Education sessions are designed to deliver new strategies and innovative solutions to attendees.

The Foundation has published the fifth edition of *Professional Meeting Management*, widely recognised in North America as the 'bible' of the industry. PCMA has also published *Convene* magazine since 1986. One of the leading industry magazines, *Convene* is published monthly and distributed to more than 35,000 subscribers.

Contact details: Professional Convention Management Association, 35 East Wacker Drive, Suite 500, Chicago, Illinois 60601, USA. Tel: +1 312 423 7262. Email: communications@pcma.org (www.pcma.org).

Society of Incentive and Travel Executives (Site)

The Society of Incentive and Travel Executives, which trades as 'Site', has grown since its inception more than 35 years ago to more than 2,000 members in 90 countries with 30 local and regional chapters. It is the only global authority connecting motivational experiences with business results. The community of Site professionals brings best-in-class solutions, insights and global connections to maximise the business impact of motivational experiences regardless of industry, region or culture. Site serves as the source of expertise, knowledge and personal connections that will catapult and sustain professional growth, and help build the value of extraordinary, motivational experiences worldwide.

Site offers members and industry colleagues many opportunities to connect through events and online forums. A full list of the membership benefits is accessible on the Site website.

Contact details: Site, 401 North Michigan Avenue, Suite 2200, Chicago, Illinois 60611, USA. Tel: +1 312 6673 5930. Email: site@siteglobal.com (www.siteglobal.com). Follow Site on Twitter under SiteGlobal.

Union of International Associations (UIA)

The Union of International Associations (UIA) was formed in 1907 as the Central Office of International Associations, becoming the UIA in 1910. It was created in an endeavour

to co-ordinate international organisation initiatives, with emphasis on documentation, including a very extensive library and museum function. Gradually the focus has shifted to promoting internationality, as well as to a role in representing the collective views of international bodies where possible, especially on technical issues.

The UIA is an independent, non-governmental, not-for-profit body that undertakes and promotes study and research into international organisations. Of particular importance to the conference industry is the UIA's production of statistics on international congresses and conventions, statistics which have been collected annually since 1949. The meetings taken into consideration are those organised or sponsored by international organisations appearing in the UIA publications *Yearbook of International Organizations* and *International Congress Calendar*. The UIA publishes its 'International Meeting Statistics' on an annual basis (some of its 2010 conference statistics are reproduced in Chapter 1). UIA publications are available in printed and online formats.

Contact details: Union of International Associations, Congress Department, Rue Washington 40, B-1050 Brussels, Belgium. Tel: +32 2 640 4109. Email: uia@uia.be (www.uia.org).

The roles of selected national trade associations

In addition to the international industry associations described above, there is a much larger number of trade bodies operating at a national level. This section provides brief profiles of a small selection of these as examples of the types of organisations to be found within individual countries.

Association of Australian Convention Bureaux Inc. (AACB)

The Association of Australian Convention Bureaux Inc. (AACB) consists of 17 city and regional bureaux dedicated to marketing their specific region as a premier business events destination. The mission of the Association is '*to represent the collective interests of Australian convention bureaux*'. While recognising the specific destination marketing role of individual bureaux, the AACB plays a role in promoting Australia internationally through major publicity campaigns launched in conjunction with national partners such as Business Events Australia (BEA, a division of Tourism Australia). As an incentive for individual bureaux to promote their city/area internationally, the AACB holds approved body status for eligible bureaux to receive a rebate on international marketing expenditure through the Export Market Development Grant scheme.

In addition to its promotional role, the AACB has several key focus areas:

- an annual convention bureaux performance report;
- ongoing research leading to business events (BE) market intelligence;

- bureaux staff education;
- a national domestic marketing and education campaign targeting BE buyers;
- providing a marketing policy development forum;
- liaison with Business Events Australia (BEA), the Committee for Economic Development of Australia (CEDA), Austrade and similar bodies in order to develop activities which promote Australia as a business events destination;
- lobbying and government liaison.

Some detail

- *Information and research* – The AACB'S 'Annual Australian Convention Bureaux Performance Report' generates relevant and timely statistical reports for effective advocacy, planning and performance review. Each year updated information from bureaux is provided to BEA for compilation of the sector's Events Calendar. This Calendar lists details for confirmed events and is aimed at assisting with delegate boosting to conventions, trade shows and exhibitions. The AACB was also involved with the joint National Business Events Survey (NBES) in partnership with the Cooperative Research Centre for Sustainable Tourism (CRC) and the business events industry. The survey measures the size, scope and value of the segment and AACB continues with updating elements of this survey for its marketing and industry partners such as BEA and the Business Events Council of Australia (BECA).
- *Education* – An annual staff conference is held for members to develop sound professional practices, educate members and provide networking opportunities. In addition, a Staff Scholarship and Staff Prize (for newcomers to bureaux) are offered annually to encourage excellence, in partnership with BEA and Qantas.
- *Lobbying and government liaison* – As a representative body, the AACB works through BECA to communicate a co-ordinated industry view and voice to the Governments of Australia and to the public, thus strengthening industry influence on policy formulation.

Contact details: Association of Australian Convention Bureaux Inc., Level 13, 80 William Street, Woolloomooloo 2011, New South Wales, Australia. Tel: +61 (0)2 9326 9133. Fax: +61 (0)2 9326 9676. Email: info@aacb.org.au (www.aacb.org.au).

Association of British Professional Conference Organisers (ABPCO)

ABPCO was founded in 1981 and incorporated as a company limited by guarantee in 1987. ABPCO is the UK organisation for Professional Conference and Event Organisers, their industry colleagues and those studying for or pursuing a career in the meetings industry. The formation of ABPCO was the result of leading Professional Conference

Organisers wishing to harness their collective experience to maintain and enhance the quality standards they set within the meetings industry.

ABPCO is one of very few UK conference and event industry associations to select Full and Associate Members based on peer assessment, meaning that clients and suppliers can expect ABPCO Members to deliver business and ethical standards in the management of national and international association and corporate conferences, seminars, meetings, exhibitions and other events.

ABPCO offers Corporate Membership to those organisations working in the conference and event service and supply sectors; Entry Level Membership to those studying for or pursuing a career in the industry; and Academy Membership to those academic institutions offering conference, event, tourism and hospitality-related courses. All Members are required to uphold an agreed Code of Practice.

In 2012 ABPCO had almost 150 members who organised an estimated 3,500 conferences and events a year.

ABPCO's mission

ABPCO's mission is to develop and enhance the professional status of conference and event organisers and increase the recognition given to its members and to ABPCO as the leading representative of the profession in the British Isles.

ABPCO's strategic aims

ABPCO's strategic aims are to:

- position ABPCO as the leading body representing the interests of professional conference organisers and increase its profile and recognition;
- constantly develop and enhance the benefits it provides to ABPCO members by creating opportunities for networking and by encouraging its members to achieve the highest possible standards of excellence;
- raise standards of professionalism across the meetings industry through the provision of education, training and personal development opportunities;
- increase the volume and value of business being won by ABPCO members through a range of marketing activities.

ABPCO membership benefits

The benefits of ABPCO membership include:

- *Recognition and accreditation* – To achieve full or associate ABPCO membership, professional conference and event organisers are required to demonstrate a high level of experience and proven competence. The status of ABPCO membership confers a clear commercial advantage when bidding for contracts or when applying for new positions within the industry.

- *Networking* – Through ABPCO member meetings, workshops and events, along with ABPCO's social media presence on LinkedIn, Facebook and Twitter, members can share ideas and experiences and create mutually beneficial relationships with a peer group of event organisers and industry colleagues.
- *Business leads* – Full ABPCO members can gain access to business leads and enquiries received through the ABPCO website RFP facility from individuals, companies or associations wishing to employ a professional conference or event organiser. In addition, all members' details are shown on the ABPCO website.
- *Training and education* – Professional development opportunities are available through the regular ABPCO events programme, with a focus on educational content and keynote sessions and workshops run by high level speakers and industry professionals.
- *Others* – Other benefits include access to a free VAT advice line; special event insurance cover rates and advice; and representation to Government via ABPCO's membership of the Business Visits and Events Partnership (www.businessvisitsand eventspartnership.com).

Contact details: Association of British Professional Conference Organisers, Barn Down, 2 Pool Row, Main Street, Willersey, Gloucestershire, WR12 7PJ, England. Tel: +44 (0)7947 369255. Email: heatherlishman@abpoc.org (www.abpco.org).

Brazilian Association of Event Organisers (ABEOC)

Founded in 1977, the Brazilian Association of Event Organisers (Associação Brasileira de Empresas de Eventos – ABEOC) is a public, not-for-profit and non-political entity whose objective is to bring together those service companies specialising in events and to co-ordinate, direct and protect their interests at a national level. Its members include companies which organise, promote and provide services within the events sector (www.abeoc.org.br).

Eventia

Eventia is recognised as the official trade body of the events and live marketing industry providing leadership and representation on important issues to Government, regulators and the corporate community. The association was created in January 2006, following a merger between two complementary associations: the Incentive Travel and Meetings Association (ITMA) and the Corporate Events Association (CEA). The British Association of Conference Destinations was subsumed into Eventia in January 2009.

Eventia promotes the highest standards of professionalism and best practice in the industry. All members of the association adhere to a Code of Practice which governs the spirit and method of all commercial activities and conduct of business.

Eventia's activities and objectives include:

- to raise the profile and importance of the events medium as a key component in the marketing communications mix;
- to be a conduit for the exchange of ideas and expertise in events through training, education and events;
- to be a centre of excellence of providing commentary, guidance and advice on all legal and other regulatory issues affecting members' businesses;
- to provide a forum for the exchange of non-competitive information;
- to be a central representative body to put the views of the events industry to government departments and agencies, Parliament, the European Commission, and other relevant organisations;
- to arrange networking events and introductions between event organiser and partner members;
- recognition of excellence through awards programmes;
- to support the future of the industry by providing links between course providers and industry ensuring the relevance of degrees, diplomas and training provided by third parties; and to facilitate student placement throughout the industry;
- to share and uphold standards and best practice.

Eventia's members are:

- *Event organiser members* – UK-based companies that organise events taking place in the UK or overseas.
- *Partner members* – Companies trading in the UK that provide services to event organisers.
- *British destination members* – Conference offices and convention bureaux in the UK.
- *National tourist offices* – Providing services to event organisers.
- *Overseas partner members* – Companies trading from addresses outside the UK that provide services to event organisers.
- *Affiliate members* – Organisations, associations and academic institutions whose activities are complementary to those of Eventia.
- *Freelance members* – Self-employed individuals providing freelance services to event organisers.

Contact details: Eventia, 5th Floor, Galbraith House, 141 Great Charles Street, Birmingham, B3 3LG, England. Tel: +44 (0)121 212 1400. Fax: +44 (0)121 212 3131. Email: info@eventia.org.uk. Twitter: @Eventia (www.eventia.org.uk).

Hellenic Association of Professional Congress Organizers (HAPCO)

The Hellenic Association of Professional Congress Organizers (HAPCO) was established in 1996 to represent congress tourism professionals and to promote the congress industry throughout Greece. Since its establishment, HAPCO has developed into one of the principal institutions in the Greek tourism sector and has been acknowledged as an official partner of the Greek State on issues relating to congress tourism.

The 110 members of HAPCO (as at March 2012) stand out for their dynamic involvement in the tourism industry. They include PCOs, conference centres, convention centres and resort hotels, hotels with conference facilities, audio-visual companies, as well as companies offering a range of services related to congress organisation and support. Thanks to their specialisation, know-how and considerable experience, they offer high-class services that bolster the competitiveness of Greek congress tourism.

HAPCO promotes the aims of the Greek congress industry and implements actions that contribute to both its prestige and its effectiveness. By setting high quality standards, supporting specialised training for professionals in the field and constantly improving existing infrastructure, it has laid the foundations for the steady growth and development of congress tourism in Greece.

As part of its efforts to develop and establish itself in the congress sector, HAPCO seeks to:

- promote the services of its members in the national and international meetings market;
- contribute to the diversity and competitiveness of the Greek meetings industry;
- promote its views and proposals to public and private national stakeholders, contributing to the systematic development of Greek congress tourism;
- provide specialised education and training to executives in the tourism sector on matters relating to congress tourism;
- promote quality specifications and raise standards of professionalism that enhance the prestige and image of the Greek meetings industry.

Contact details: Hellenic Association of Professional Congress Organizers, 2–4 Alkmeonidon Street, 16121 Athens, Greece. Tel: +30 210 72 56 541. Fax: +30 210 72 58 487. Email: hapco@hapco.gr (www.hapco.gr).

Meetings Industry Association (MIA)

The Meetings Industry Association (MIA) is one of the leading associations for the UK meetings industry, reflecting the needs of the buyer, improving the standards of the supplier. It was established in 1990 and has around 500 organisations in membership,

drawn from the supply side of the conference industry in the UK and Ireland, but also offers free membership, with associated benefits, to buyers.

The MIA aims to improve the quality of service and facilities offered by its members, encouraging the highest possible standards through its industry-recognised accreditation scheme AIM (Accredited in Meetings), which is a prerequisite of MIA membership. AIM has three levels: Entry, Silver and Gold. The MIA seeks to strengthen the position of its members' businesses in an increasingly competitive marketplace and raise the profile of the United Kingdom as an international meeting and conference destination. Specific member services and benefits include:

- AIM accreditation, the industry-recognised meetings standard;
- marketing opportunities via the MIA website, AIM website, newsletters, publications, exhibition representation, sponsorship and media relations;
- sales opportunities;
- inclusion within Solution, the automated online event proposal system for AIM venues used by buyers;
- networking at MIA national and regional events (an annual general meeting, the MIA List celebratory lunch, educational events, general managers and principals business lunches);
- specialised training courses through the MIA Learning and Development Academy;
- access to the MIA Pathfinder report, a snapshot of industry trends published every quarter;
- access to best practice guidelines and contract templates;
- consultancy and arbitration services.

Contact details: Meetings Industry Association, PO Box 515, Kelmarsh, Northampton NN6 9XW, England. Tel: +44 (0)845 230 5508. Fax: +44 (0)845 230 7708. Email: info@mia-uk.org (www.mia-uk.org).

Meetings and Events Australia (MEA)

Meetings and Events Australia (MEA), formerly known as the Meetings Industry Association of Australia (MIAA), is a national, independent not-for-profit organisation dedicated to fostering professionalism and excellence in all aspects of meetings management. It also promotes the value and effectiveness of meetings as an important high-yield sector of business travel and tourism. MEA offers professional development programmes and accreditation. It also disseminates information, provides a forum for its members to discuss current issues, and represents the industry to government.

In order to achieve these broad aims, it has set for itself a number of 'key result areas', which include:

- creating business opportunities and facilitating business-to-business relationships;
- encouraging better business practice;
- promoting professional development;
- providing information, forums and advice that lead to improved business performance;
- promoting the value of meetings and the business events industry;
- acting in an advocacy capacity in respect of pertinent industry issues;
- managing a sustainable association.

Members of MEA comprise meetings management companies, special event organisers, venues, staging/AV service providers, convention/visitors/tourist organisations and bureaux, and a range of meetings and events industry suppliers and services.

Contact details: Meetings and Events Australia, Level 1, Suites 5 and 6, 1 McLaren Street, North Sydney, New South Wales 2060, Australia. Tel: +61 2 9929 5400. Email: mea@mea.org.au (www.meetingsevents.com.au).

Southern African Association for the Conference Industry (SAACI)

The South African Association for the Conference Industry (SAACI) was formally established in 1987 and represents every type of business that is involved in Southern Africa's meetings, incentives, conferences, events and exhibition industry – venues, organisers and providers of any type of service, big or small. Over 25 years, SAACI membership and endorsement have become the ultimate recognition of professionalism in the conference industry. SAACI is always first with the latest industry information and trends, and effectively represents the industry on all relevant business tourism forums, but also to government.

SAACI has a national board and four regional branches:

- Northern Territories;
- Western Cape;
- Eastern Cape;
- KwaZulu-Natal.

Each of the branches is made up of specialist forums where members can participate, depending on the specific sector of the conference industry in which they work. The forums are:

- conferences and events (CandE);
- venues;
- services;
- destination marketing;
- exhibitions;

- transport;
- technical.

Membership benefits – members:

- may use the SAACI logo;
- are listed on the website database and in the annual yearbook;
- receive the official journal: *Southern Africa Conference, Exhibition and Events Guide;*
- receive *SAACImatters*, the monthly newsletter;
- can network with professionals across the industry;
- attend the annual congress and exhibition as well as regional events;
- have a gateway to knowledge, information and contacts.

Contact details: Southern African Association for the Conference Industry, National Office, PO Box 1279, Halfwayhouse, 1685, South Africa. Tel: +27 11 805 7272. Email: info@saaci.co.za (www.saaci.co.za).

Online communities of industry professionals

The digital age has also witnessed the development of a range of online communities, bringing together individuals with specific niche interests to communicate, share ideas and issues, collaborate on projects, learn together, and so forth. Such online services complement, rather than compete with, the more traditional membership organisations described above.

A number of these communities can be found through portals such as LinkedIn, while i-Meet.com (established in 2008) claims to have over 65,000 members in 173 countries worldwide (as at November 2011). i-Meet.com's website has sections for planners and suppliers as well as a media portal.

An assessment of the conference industry's fragmentation

It cannot be denied that the tourism and hospitality industry is fragmented. It is composed of thousands of mainly small operators and businesses, providing accommodation, restaurants, attractions, coach and taxi services, and so forth. The conference sector shares this same infrastructure, but also encompasses conference venues and other suppliers specific to the industry. With the exception of chain hotels and selected groups of dedicated conference centres, conference venues are, for the most part, run as discrete business units, independent of any centralised management or structure.

The sense of fragmentation is reinforced by the apparent proliferation of trade associations and similar bodies representing segments of the conference industry. In comparison with many other professions and industries, such as the oil/petroleum and aviation industries or the legal profession, the conference industry can be said to lack a single, cohesive voice.

At another level, however, the industry enjoys a very real sense of unity across the world. It is characterised by an openness and sharing, by friendships and networking between colleagues, which are immensely attractive and create almost a sense of family.

There is undoubtedly scope to bring some greater harmonisation to the industry, and there would also be benefits arising from a rationalisation of the industry's representative bodies, but it is to be hoped that these can be achieved without damaging the international friendship and collaboration which are such an important, and winsome, feature of the conference and conventions sector today.

SUMMARY

- There are many trade associations and professional bodies operating within the conference sector, at national, continental and international levels.
- Some have clearly defined roles and a niche membership which is not being served by other associations.
- Some, however, appear to duplicate the activities of other associations, suggesting that rationalisations and mergers may become necessary both to ensure their own survival and for the wider health of the industry.

REVIEW AND DISCUSSION QUESTIONS

1   Assess the extent to which the description of the conference sector as 'fragmented' is justified. Is there a greater degree of fragmentation within the conference and business events sector than in the leisure tourism sector?

2   Read through the descriptions of the various international and national trade bodies described in this chapter. Identify those characteristics that are common to a number of the bodies and comment on why these seem to be important. Then make a list of some of the key unique features that differentiate one from another. What features and services would you expect to be crucial to the future survival and prosperity of these associations?

3   'There should just be one conference industry association per country.' Discuss the pros and cons of such a development.

CHAPTER **10**

The future: trends, challenges and opportunities

CHAPTER OBJECTIVES

This chapter looks at:

- understanding and promoting the value of the conference, meetings and business events industry
- technology applications and trends
- virtual, face-to-face or hybrid?
- corporate social responsibility (CSR)
- the future of meetings and conventions

It includes mini case studies on:

- the 29th International Congress of Ophthalmology, Sydney
- an app for the 6th International Congress on Modern Trends and Perspectives in Total Hip and Knee Arthroplasties, Rome

www.routledge.com/cw/rogers

LEARNING OUTCOMES

On completion of this chapter, you should be able to:

- understand the key drivers of conferences and business events and the range of benefits they bring to participants as well as to host cities and communities;

- assess how the marketing of the sector is being undertaken to politicians and to the wider business community;

- appreciate the range and impacts of technology on the sector;

- identify key trends impacting the ways in which people confer, both face-to-face and virtually, and appreciate the benefits of hybrid events;

- explain the relevance of corporate social responsibility (CSR) to the conference and events sector;

- understand some of the mega trends which will influence the future shape and activity of the industry.

Introduction

Satellite technology now gives us instant communications across our planet. The Internet provides access to an ever-expanding encyclopaedia of information and knowledge. Both phenomena enable us to understand and evaluate more effectively the opportunities and threats facing us in many aspects of our daily lives. What insights can we glean into the trends, challenges, issues, opportunities and threats affecting the twenty-first-century conference and conventions industry, and how will they shape its future development?

Understanding and promoting the value of the conference, meetings and business events industry

Reference has already been made in Chapters 1 and 7 to the benefits of conferences and meetings and to their economic, social and environmental impacts. It is clear that the sector is a huge force for good in our world, but much work remains to be done to convey the scope and scale of its benefits to a wider audience.

There is still a lack of understanding and recognition of the value that conferences and meetings generate in terms of professional development, knowledge transfer, investment generation, technical progress and all the other areas that define why these events happen in the first place. In reality, meetings, conventions and exhibitions are, in the words of a paper published by the Joint Meetings Industry Council (JMIC 2008):

primary engines of both economic and professional development, key vehicles for not just sharing information – something that, in many cases, can be done just as effectively on the Internet – but building the kind of understanding, relationships and confidence that can only be achieved on a face-to-face basis.

The JMIC paper describes '*three critical areas of interface which the meetings industry has with the broader economy, whether that be at a global level or in the context of an individual community*'. The first of these is the economic role, explained in Chapter 7. The second is the business development role:

which reaches far beyond the immediate effects of event-related spending. For a start, meetings, conventions and exhibitions attract business audiences that wouldn't necessarily otherwise visit a particular destination, and who are more likely to be investors and decision-makers than other types of visitors. In this way, events serve to expose the host city and its investment opportunities to a whole new audience – a process that can rival even the most highly evolved economic and investment development programmes mounted by the business community. At the same time, they provide a vehicle for local business and professional groups to host colleagues and create a showcase for local products and services, all key elements in the economic development process.

But, the paper suggests:

above all, there are the benefits associated with the community enhancement role – because these are the ones that most directly impact the largest number of people in a community. For a start, meetings and conventions create access to a wide range of professional development opportunities for local residents by making these more accessible to those in the community. Major, or even regional, gatherings bring what is often world class knowledge and expertise within the grasp of local businesses and professionals, improving overall knowledge in ways that would not otherwise be possible. When such gains are made in areas such as the medical or research fields, the benefits to the rest of the community can be very profound in terms of how they improve the overall quality of life.

But even without this effect there are ways that the community benefits in a very tangible way from the meetings, conventions and exhibitions taking place there. For a start, it justifies and in large part finances the development of facilities that can then be used for the community's own events and celebrations. But, best of all, the arrival of non-resident delegates means a lot of new tax revenues from outside of the usual local tax base which can and will be applied to supporting ongoing community services.

The paper concludes, however, by describing an even more important role, one which goes to the heart of what meetings are all about, which is:

> *The importance they have in bringing together diverse interests and cultures to address common challenges. Meetings, conventions and exhibitions not only support professional, research, technology and academic development – the pivotal activities that underpin global progress – but they also help build networks and bridge cultural differences that threaten world order and advancement. The simple fact is, meetings are vehicles for finding solutions to global issues – and that is something we will have no shortage of in the years ahead!*

The challenge, therefore, is how to communicate all of these benefits through positive messages to a myriad of audiences: political (local, national and international), business, academic, community, and others. It is encouraging to note a number of initiatives taking place around the world. One such is the creation of 'National Meetings Weeks' being run on an annual basis in several countries. First begun in the UK at the beginning of the new millennium, these 'Weeks' have enjoyed some success in raising the profile and understanding of the sector. In the UK, 'National Meetings Week' has evolved into a six-month campaign entitled 'Britain for Events', and this campaign has been instrumental in the creation of an All-Party Parliamentary Group for Events, the first time that a group of national politicians has come together to lobby for and support the Events sector. The campaign was also successful in gaining endorsement from the British Prime Minister, David Cameron. The 'Britain for Events' campaign is overseen by the Business Visits and Events Partnership, an umbrella body that brings together over 20 representative bodies and trade associations from the sector (www.businessvisitsand eventspartnership.com).

The trade show, IMEX-Frankfurt, includes as part of the proceedings an annual Politicians Forum, designed to bring together both local and national politicians from a number of countries to debate key issues in support of the business events sector (www.imex-frankfurt.com).

In Australia, the Business Events Council (BECA) (www.businesseventscouncil.org.au) was created in 1994 to bring the business events industry and community together and to speak with one voice. Its purpose was, and is, to foster the development of the industry as a united entity and to raise the profile of business events to government and to the business community. Perhaps inevitably this is still a 'work in progress', acknowledged by the Executive Manager of BECA, Inge Garofani, who was quoted (Garofani 2012) as saying:

> *Business and association meetings and events are an undervalued contributor to the economy and community in Australia. They provide not only the tangible benefits of room nights and delegate spend but a far greater contribution to the nation. They*

have a ripple effect like a stone in a pond where the initial impact is small and defined but the real impact is in the ripples flowing outwards. These ripples are where we provide the greatest benefit to Australia. We bring international experts to Australia to share knowledge, educate our community and this leads to great legacies and benefits, both financial and non-financial.

A BECA paper (Jago and Deery 2010) emphasises the important role that business events can play in fostering innovation. Entitled *Delivering Innovation, Knowledge and Performance: The Role of Business Events*, the paper recommends:

- As fostering innovation is such an important national building endeavour and business events have a key role to play in this activity, strategies need to be identified that can best leverage the role of business events, particularly in key industry sectors targeted for growth by government.
- Given the view that the impacts of business events are largely synonymous with tourism, there need to be greater efforts made to raise awareness within key government portfolios and industry sectors as to the broader value and potential of business events.
- At a time when Australian universities are under substantial pressure to cut costs, a campaign should be launched to highlight the important role that business events play in helping researchers create and disseminate innovation. The benefits to individual universities hosting international research conferences should also be highlighted.
- More effort should be made to encourage associations and companies to assess the ROI of the business events they stage so that the outcomes from these events are captured and there is wider recognition of the benefits that can be derived.

A meeting convened by the Joint Meetings Industry Council (JMIC) in London in May 2011 agreed on five steps to broaden understanding of the benefits to accrue from meetings and conventions:

- to carry out inventory/comparative analysis of existing valuation models and develop a means for achieving greater consistency among these;
- to encourage the development of local applications for economic impact models in order to generate better data for use in individual communities;
- to create a protocol for assembling value-added 'output' values with emphasis on the use of case studies and examples to illustrate major areas of benefit;
- to identify key audiences along with their priority information requirements and develop a communications 'tool kit' to assist in this process;
- to encourage event owners to assume a more active role in measuring and communicating value.

Case Study 10.1 illustrates a tangible benefit to derive from an international association congress, namely the funding of an ophthalmology foundation for research and training.

CASE STUDY 10.1 29th International Congress of Ophthalmology 2002, Sydney

The 29th International Congress of Ophthalmology was held in Sydney, Australia in 2002. In the years immediately prior, the meeting had been sliding, losing delegates and sponsor support. It came to Sydney, ran exceptionally well, setting new standards. It also made a financial surplus of AU$1.8 million. One third of this surplus went to the world body and the balance of AU$1.2 million stayed in Australia and was used to set up the Eye Foundation. This fund is professionally managed and is used for research and to train ophthalmologists locally and regionally. Australia's hosting of the world congress made this possible.

Technology applications and trends

Technology in the conference and meetings industry is developing at an ever-faster pace, with new applications coming onto the market on a very regular basis. Understanding and keeping pace with these developments is a continual challenge, but is an essential part of the conference organiser's role. The need to maximise the opportunities afforded by these new technologies is vital to remain competitive. They may help to reduce costs, generate new income streams, improve the efficiency and effectiveness of meetings, enhance the delegate experience, extend the life and spread of a conference.

In an article entitled *Selecting the Right Meeting Planning Technology: A Step-by-Step Guide* (Ball 2005), Corbin Ball, a well-known speaker, writer and consultant focusing on the meetings, events and tradeshow industries (www.corbinball.com), lists the following areas where meetings technology tools can help:

- abstract and educational content management;
- association and membership tracking;
- attendee/delegate matchmaking and networking;
- auctions and fundraising;
- audience polling;
- badge making;
- banquet seating;
- contact management;
- customer relationship management;
- event websites and portal management;
- exhibition sales and floorplan management;

- incentive tracking;
- lead retrieval;
- marketing, communication and attendance building;
- meeting specification;
- meetings consolidation, procurement and request for proposal (RFP) management;
- onsite technology (registration, cyber cafes, product directories, Internet access);
- registration;
- room diagramming;
- scheduling;
- site/venue selection;
- speaker management;
- surveys;
- travel and ground transportation management;
- virtual meetings and shows.

Selecting the right virtual technology

Teleconferencing

Teleconferencing, or the act of meeting via the telephone, is one of the simplest and most cost-effective forms of meeting. It requires a telephone at each location and a long distance service provider. The pros and cons of teleconferencing include:

Pros

- Decisions can be made quickly, and problems can be handled immediately, without wasting time on extensive planning and travel. This allows participants to address client needs and changing markets faster.
- Teleconferencing is one of the simplest and most cost-effective forms of meeting. There is little or no capital investment, and the price is relatively low. The only additional cost is the fee to the service provider and any long distance charges that accrue.
- Contacts can participate from anywhere, as long as they are near a phone.

Cons

- Meeting without visual communication can sometimes be difficult. There is no way to read facial expressions or body language over the phone.
- Some people are easily distracted from phone conversations. A well-planned teleconference can minimise the risk of this, however.
- Some people find it hard talking in a vacuum and might refrain from participating, whereas face-to-face they might be more chatty.

However, the traditional teleconference is changing, with the advent of Skype and also the impact of new conference furniture. For example, interactive screens and virtual flip charts allow information from laptops, scanned images and video to be input onto flip charts (and/or participants can write by hand onto the flipcharts), with the images being transmitted simultaneously to a flip chart or computer in a remote location. Participants can share their laptop screen, actively add content and annotate just as if they were physically present in the room with the initiator of the original message.

Videoconferencing

Videoconferencing is a set of interactive telecommunication technologies which allows two or more locations to interact via two-way video and audio transmissions simultaneously. Videoconferencing first appeared in the 1980s, but did not attract wide usage because of high costs, unreliable and incompatible technologies, and poor quality images. However, over the past couple of decades, major improvements have been made to the technology and the costs have fallen substantially. Some venues have invested in videoconferencing suites designed to replicate the appearance and feel of face-to-face meetings.

High speed Internet connectivity has become more widely available at a reasonable cost and the cost of video capture and display technology has decreased. Consequently personal video teleconference systems based on a webcam, personal computer system, software compression and broadband Internet connectivity have become affordable for the general public. The hardware used for this technology has continued to improve in quality, and prices have dropped dramatically. The availability of free software (often as part of chat programmes) has made software-based videoconferencing accessible to many. For many years, futurists have envisaged a future where telephone conversations will take place as actual face-to-face encounters with video as well as audio. Desktop PC videoconferencing promised to make this a reality, although it remains to be seen whether there is widespread enthusiasm for video calling.

Videoconferencing provides students with the opportunity to learn by participating in a two-way communication platform. Furthermore, teachers and lecturers from all over the world can be brought to classes in remote or otherwise isolated places. Students from diverse communities and backgrounds can come together to learn about one another. Students are able to explore, communicate, analyse and share information and ideas about one another. Through videoconferencing students can visit another part of the world to speak to others, visit a zoo, a museum and so on, as 'virtual field trips'.

Videoconferencing can enable individuals in faraway places to have meetings at short notice. Time and money that used to be spent on travelling can be used to have short meetings. Technology such as VOIP (voice over Internet protocol – the Internet protocol is the internationally agreed standard for communicating data across and between networks; VOIP is also known as IP telephony or IPT) can be used in conjunction with desktop videoconferencing to enable face-to-face business meetings to take place

without leaving the desktop. The technology is also used for telecommuting, in which employees work from home.

The arrival of Internet protocol communications and the plummeting cost of big TV screens have ushered in a new generation of videoconferencing systems – a technology dubbed 'telepresence'. A telepresence suite looks much like a boardroom, except that the table has very large flat screens along one side. When the screens are switched on, the images show a similar boardroom, as if a mirror was mounted across the table. The others taking part are shown in full size, as realistically as possible. Instead of having a single microphone over each screen, microphones are placed around the room to pick up the direction in which a person is speaking. Participants in the virtual 'boardroom' then turn to look at them, as if they were all in the same room. Both boardrooms have the same whiteboard showing the same presentations, and documents can even be 'passed' across the table by inserting them into a scanner in one room and printing them out in the other.

Beaming

'Beam me up Scotty' – that simple phrase reminds us of Captain Kirk, whisked from alien worlds back to the Starship *Enterprise* via the magic of 'teleporting', in the cult TV series *Star Trek*. Beaming, of a kind, is no longer pure science fiction. It is the name of an international project funded by the European Commission to investigate how a person can visit a remote location via the Internet and feel fully immersed in the new environment. The visitor may be embodied as an avatar or a robot, interacting with real people. Motion capture technology, robots, 3D glasses and special haptic suits with body sensors can all be used to create a rich, realistic experience which reproduces that holy grail: 'presence'.

According to a BBC News Magazine article (Peter 2012), project leader Mel Slater, Professor of Virtual Environments at University College London, calls beaming augmented reality, rather than virtual reality. In beaming – unlike the virtual worlds of computer games and the Second Life website – the robot or avatar interacts with real people in a real place.

The article suggests that '*teleconferencing and videoconferencing would be transformed, once beaming is able to convey the non-verbal communication that people value, reducing the need for businessmen to jet around the world*'.

Podcasting

Corbin Ball (2006b) defines podcasting as a '*method of distributing audio or video programs over the Internet to be played on portable digital players or personal computers*'. He explains that it is possible to subscribe to podcasts in a manner similar to e-newsletters, or by searching through the podcast offerings of iTunes (www.itunes.com) and RSS (really simple syndication) sites; or by simply clicking on a web link and listening to on-demand Internet radio programmes. He says that the cost of producing and globally distributing audio or video podcasts is nearly always less than traditional print, radio, CD video/audio, DVDs, and even other electronic media such as websites.

Other benefits include a large listener base, as tens of millions of MP3 players have been sold and nearly every computer made since 2001 can play MP3 (audio) and MP4 (video) files. Podcasting is also convenient as listeners can access 24/7 at their own convenience. Low production and distribution costs mean a highly targeted listening base can be addressed affordably, known as narrow casting.

Ball's article lists a number of applications for podcasting in the conventions and meetings industry:

* Meetings and events can be podcast (either audio or video) as a service to members unable to attend or as a promotion for those wishing to attend in the future.
* Podcasts can be an alternative or an addition to blast emails on important event announcements.
* Podcast interviews with key presenters posted at a conference website can create interest in an event.
* MP3 and MP4 files promoting events or providing content can easily be added to websites to add 'punch' or provide an alternative communication method.
* MP3 players (pre-loaded with conference or promotional content) will become cheap enough to be conference 'giveaways' or even promotional merchandise for trade-shows.
* Convention and visitor bureaux can send out promotional videos customised to each group – all by simply adding a link to a targeted blast email.

Further information can be found at: http://en.wikipedia.org/wiki/Podcasting

Web conferencing

Holding conferences over the web has become increasingly popular since the advent of broadband technology which enables the simultaneous transfer of one- or two-way voice, video and data over IP to take place. The technology allows unlimited online viewers or participants sharing a common computer screen interface, with added tools including chat rooms, polling, online Q &A and resources downloads including presentations, PDFs, case studies, research and other relevant items. The conference can be integrated with a live event for both face-to-face and online audiences, be it an online archive of a previous event, or a stand-alone live web conference with an online audience only.

A variation on the theme of web conferencing is known as 'webinars', short for virtual web seminars. Often pre-recorded, they present the user with a streamed video of a conference, additional key information like text or statistics to support a 'PowerPoint' presentation, or images used during the conference, and links to related websites. Events can either be joined live for interactivity or viewed afterwards on demand at a time that suits.

Webcasting

Webcasting is broadcasting over the Internet. It is the electronic distribution of audio and video over IP. Conference sessions and presentations can be broadcast in this way, either in real time as a live event or recorded and made available after the conference, either as free access or on a paid-for basis. Registration systems capture relevant information about viewers as well as preventing unauthorised access to content by requiring viewers to enter a password to view the content. The technology, therefore, extends the life of the conference and extends its reach, with the potential to attract a worldwide audience.

Wi-Fi

Wi-Fi is an abbreviation for 'wireless fidelity', although this full term is rarely used these days. Wi-Fi refers to the technology of *wireless* local area networks. A person with a Wi-Fi-enabled device such as a computer, mobile (or cell) phone or PDA can connect to the Internet when in proximity to an access point. The region covered by one or several access points is called a hotspot. Hotspots can range from a single room to many square miles of overlapping hotspots (e.g. Wireless Philadelphia – www.phila.gov/wireless, and other cities such as Amsterdam, Manchester, Seattle, San Francisco, which provide free Internet access across large urban areas).

When the technology was first commercialised there were many problems because consumers could not be sure that products from different suppliers would work together. The Wi-Fi Alliance began as a community to solve this issue and address the needs of the end user, and allow the technology to mature. The Alliance created the branding Wi-Fi CERTIFIED to show consumers that products are interoperable with other products displaying the same branding.

Conference venues and hotels are increasingly offering Wi-Fi facilities, although many currently charge a fee for this service provision. Wi-Fi has a range of applications in formal business meetings but is also a benefit for conference delegates during refreshment breaks or outside the conference sessions, enabling them to access the Internet and their email messages.

The disadvantages of Wi-Fi include its potential for interruption by other devices. Wi-Fi 'pollution', interference by other open access points in an area, can also be a problem in high-density areas such as office buildings with many Wi-Fi access points.

Trends in meetings technology

The rate of technology change is increasing, with meetings and tradeshow technology continuing to advance through the advent of better, cheaper and easier-to-use products. Corbin Ball is acknowledged internationally as one of the leading technology gurus for the sector and he identified a number of trends to watch for in 2012 (Ball 2011):

- *More free or low cost apps for events and tradeshows* – Web services and application programming interfaces (programming standards allowing easy data sharing among websites) allow greatly simplified sharing of data between websites. Consequently, many free or very low cost web tools have emerged to help meeting professionals do their job better. There are free online databases of meeting facilities; free exhibition floor plan/sales tools; a wide range of social media tools for promoting events; free HD video conference tools; free collaboration tools; thousands of free or very low cost mobile travel and other apps to help meeting professionals and attendees; and much more. These are just a few examples – there are many more to come.

- *Mobile technology crosses the chasm from the early adopter to the early majority for events* – Data from MPI's FutureWatch 2011 survey and others indicate that more than 80 per cent of meeting professionals use smartphones and other mobile devices in their jobs. Yet, relatively few planners (9 per cent) have used mobile applications for their own meetings. This is about to change. There will be very significant adoption of mobile apps for events in 2012 and 2013. If a meeting does not have a mobile app, the attendees will soon wonder why the meeting organisers are behind the times. There are hundreds of mobile companies and mobile apps targeting meeting professionals. Although there will likely be a shakeout similar to the dot.com deflation in the late 1990s, the companies that survive will change how we do business. There is a very strong business case for adopting mobile apps for your events including:

  - better real-time distribution of conference information
  - better location-aware/way-finding capabilities
  - event greening through paper reduction
  - better onsite networking
  - lower cost survey/polling options
  - enhanced branding
  - better attendee analytics
  - better CRM, advertising revenue generation and enhanced attendee experiences.

- Another driver increasing the use of mobile apps at events is the growth of applications targeted at meeting venues rather than the meeting planner. Meeting facilities managers will either resell (at low cost) or give the app customised to the event to meeting planners and attendees.

- *Do-it-yourself mobile event apps will proliferate* – One of the hottest areas of mobile development is in the low cost DIY arena. It is possible to create a fully featured, cross-platform business app (iPhone, Android, iPad and mobile web) with customised logos, colours and content using *www.BiznessApps.com* for as little as $39.95 per month. This website is very easy to use with video tutorials throughout. Although BiznessApps has an 'events' option among the dozens of business templates offered, there are several companies targeting events specifically with DIY products,

often at a fraction of the cost of a standard application built by mobile app pro-grammers. See also Case Study 10.2 below.

- *HTML5 will become the standard for many event mobile applications* – Hypertext Markup Language Version 5 is the latest version of the standard programming language for describing the contents and appearance of web pages. It provides many benefits for mobile app development over native apps and previous versions of HTML. It will drive down the cost and development time while increasing the flexibility for mobile app development for events. It will also make the DIY model easier to provide.

- *Conference recording and distribution is becoming cheaper, faster and more capable* – Conference recording has been around for decades starting in the days when audio cassettes of the presentations were mass-produced onsite and sold in the foyer. Recent technology advances have made it possible to quickly and relatively inexpensively distribute speaker video, audio and visuals over the web in real time and on demand afterwards.

- *Near field communication (NFC) will provide streamlined connectivity and services for events* – NFC is a short-range wireless connectivity standard to enable com-munication between devices when they are touched together. It is expected to become a widely used system for making payments by smartphone in the US. NFC has been widely used in Japan and parts of Europe for the past few years. The applications for events are significant allowing for very fast, secure and simplified means of:

  - electronic ticketing
  - electronic business card exchange
  - credit card payment
  - easy pick-up of conference literature, exhibition brochures, course notes, and other digital documents.

- *YouTube and other social publishing tools will be used increasingly to promote and manage meetings and to engage attendees.*

- *Social gaming tools will be used to engage face-to-face and virtual attendees at events* – Social gaming is being used to engage virtual and hybrid meeting attendees. Contests and challenges have been proved to engage people attending virtually. The Cisco GSX hybrid conference had 19,000 virtual attendees with one million views, 13,000 active players of the 'Threshold' interactive espionage immersive reality thriller, 8,000 participants in group chats and 9,500 playing GSX mini games.

- *iPads and tablets will provide a new medium for accessing data at events* – The iPad is the most recent of the long-running, game-changing innovations from Apple. This and other tablet devices represent new ways to access information. Lightweight, highly mobile, highly intuitive. The larger screens allow for bigger fonts, easier reada-bility and more real estate to display material in a page-like format. The navigation is intuitive: with your fingers instead of a keyboard and mouse. Tablets will increasingly be used at events for interactive conference programmes, course notes distributions, surveys, interactive exhibition floorplans, product displays, information kiosks, lead exchange, speaker Q&A, onsite blogging/social networking and more.

- *Free, easy-to-access Wi-Fi is increasingly expected by meeting planners* – Free basic Wi-Fi broadband Internet access is expected by planners in the meeting room, guest rooms and the lobby. However, this does not mean *unlimited* access. Internet bandwidth can be expensive and most venues cannot handle unexpected very large demands. If 500 event attendees pulled out their iPads to access HD video simultaneously, there are few venues that could handle this without making special arrangements. If a group needs dedicated bandwidth, a dedicated IP address or other Internet services, it is reasonable to charge for these. But basic, throttled access (with a minimum of 500 kb/second download – fast enough to access email and limited video streaming) should be free. Additionally, venues need to make logging onto the Wi-Fi network easier. Opening the browser and clicking 'OK' is all that should be required.

- *'Indoor positioning systems' will greatly assist in event and tradeshow way-finding and navigation* – Standard GPS does not work indoors. Standard Wi-Fi triangulation only gets to about 100 ft (30 m) accuracy – not good enough for precise tracking through an exhibition hall, venue or for person-to-person finding at an event. New technology promises to overcome these challenges by providing very precise positioning (as fine as 1 m) by tracking Wi-Fi-enabled smartphones.

Advances in speech recognition technology (such as the SIRI voice recognition on the Apple 4S mobile phone) offer several applications for the meetings and conventions sector, such as:

- Speech-to-text transcription allows for the immediate tagging of keywords, making the distribution of presentations and talks rapid and providing almost-instant written notes. Delegates no longer need to take notes themselves.
- New voice recognition technology can identify speakers and distinguish between them, which will mean that panel discussions should no longer present problems.

And yet, for all the advances and benefits that technology undoubtedly offers the conference and conventions industry, it is still possible to detect a certain ambivalence towards it from various quarters. This ambivalence is neatly summarised in a report (IMEX America 2011) on the Executive Meeting Forum held as part of IMEX America (Las Vegas, October 2011). The Forum was an invitation-only programme for senior, corporate executives who manage multinational meetings and events, as well as their senior procurement colleagues who support meetings programmes. One of the issues identified by Forum attendees was the 'tech gap', by generation, culture, learning type and products used. The report of the Forum describes:

The variety of technology and the experiences therein lead to meetings of under-whelmed and overwhelmed delegates. Generally, younger audiences seek technology-enriched interactions, but some delegates may not see the value of technology tools and/or feel overwhelmed by the number of tools/options they have to engage with.

There is clearly a need for greater training in technology options and tools, both in order to understand how and where to invest but also to be able to talk to the experts, rather than to become experts. The first part of a three-year study into 'The Future of Meetings' (MPI 2012b) undertaken by the International Centre for Research in Events, Tourism and Hospitality at Leeds Metropolitan University for Meeting Professionals International concludes that:

Undoubtedly, meeting professionals see technology as the biggest challenge and opportunity. It is dynamic, rapid, disruptive and supportive, requiring new skills and new knowledge for planners and more dialogue between developers and users. Planners need to be as educated as possible so that they can partner better with technology providers and better understand their audiences' preferences. The effectiveness of techonology usage in meetings is defined by how well the technology used matches the business needs and audiences' technology capabilities.

CASE STUDY 10.2 App keeps knee specialists on their toes

Delegates to a 2011 international conference in Rome were given a free app of presentations. A spokesperson for AIM Group International, the organisers of the 6th International Congress on Modern Trends and Perspectives in Total Hip and Knee Arthroplasties, said:

The increased popularity of smartphones and tablets provides the ability to radically transform conferences and events: the flow of information, the immediate availability of scientific reports, the communications transmitted in real time to all the delegates – all of this especially helps to strengthen the cultural and professional exchange inherent in the purpose behind scientific congresses and medical meetings.

Hundreds of the world's leading orthopaedics experts came together for the congress, which was held at the Auditorium Parco della Musica in Rome. Each presentation was instantly downloadable and available to anyone with an iPad or iPhone. Delegates were able to see the content on their smartphone or tablet, and then keep and store the presentations of all speakers at the conference.

Article in *Association Meetings International* magazine (September 2011) – www.meetpie.com – reproduced with permission.

Virtual, face-to-face or hybrid?

The technology for virtual conferencing continues to evolve and improve at a rapid rate. Earlier in this chapter we examined the key technologies available and their applications. This section looks at whether virtual conferences and meetings will, in time, replace the need for face-to-face events, or whether the real future lies with hybrid events.

Campbell (2000) contends that:

> the weight of argument and evidence suggests that precisely because technology is invading our lives, then so is there an increased requirement for human contact and inter-personal chemistry. In other words, touchy-feely events will always matter, and perhaps even more so. Some suggest that motivational and morale-boosting get-togethers will, in fact, grow in importance, for precisely the reason that technology exacerbates the sense of working in isolation.

Corbin Ball, conference technology expert and professional speaker (www.corbinball.com), shares his experiences of both virtual and face-to-face conferences in an article 'Face-to-Face Vs. Web Meetings – What Should I Use When?' (Ball 2006a). He suggests that face-to-face (F2F) meetings have:

- *Focus* – F2F can accomplish many goals including: information exchange (learning), collaboration, commerce, interaction and more.
- *Strengths* – F2F has many strong points – as the saying goes 'There is no such thing as a virtual beer':
  - *Richer experience* – There is no better way of getting to know a person than by meeting them in person. There are so many nuances we tune into instinctively when we are meeting someone, or see them on the platform, that simply cannot be transmitted on the web. These subtleties in communication in a speaking/training situation assist in learning. As a speaker, to be able to see the whites of people's eyes, to hear their questions, to observe how attentive they are is invaluable in adjusting my presentation to keep them with me and enhance the learning process.
  - *Networking, brainstorming, interactivity* – F2F has other strengths as well. There is the opportunity to network, brainstorm, to break people into small groups, and much more that will enhance learning and increase the fun. Often much of the learning at a meeting happens in the hallways outside the room or during the social functions. Virtual meetings simply can't compete in this realm.
  - *More conducive learning environment* – As people are away from the distractions of their office (except for the mobile or cell phone), they can focus better on the learning environment.

- *Length* – Presentations can last for 10 minutes or workshops for two days or longer. As long as you keep people engaged, and keep them fed and happy, people will stick to the tasks in hand.
- *Weaknesses* – Time and travel costs/hassle are two of the biggest weaknesses of live meetings.

Ball then assesses virtual meetings in the same way, with particular reference to web conferences:

- *Focus* – Virtual meetings focus primarily on one issue: information exchange – the ability to collaborate, brainstorm, etc. is significantly limited.
- *Strengths* – The major strengths are the opposite of weaknesses of F2F – they are cheap, easy to set up, and easy to get to as they happen at your computer:

  - *Less travel hassle*
  - *Lower cost* – Up to 90 per cent less expensive if the total costs of F2F are considered (travel costs, time out of the office, room/AV rental, catering, marketing)
  - *Shorter time to market* – Web conferencing can have a much shorter time to market. Web conferences can be set up to happen almost instantly
  - *Global access* – People can meet immediately from around the world – all that is needed is a computer and a good connection to the Internet
  - *Interactivity tools* – Several interactive tools are built into many of the web conferencing products: the ability to ask questions, annotate slides, create ad hoc surveys/polls with the results appearing immediately on the screen are just some of the options. Desktop sharing, application sharing, audience chat, audience feedback to ask the speaker to speed up or slow down are others. The tools are needed to keep the audience's attention
  - *Archive capabilities* – These allow the conference to be recorded and played back at a later time
  - *More structure* – So more likely to follow a structure (i.e. follow the slides) and less likely to overrun time-wise.

- *Time* – Virtual meetings should almost never last more than 45 minutes. After that, you will lose people. There are simply too many distractions at the desktop. Viewers may be reading their email, people are walking by, and a host of other disruptions – and the speaker never knows. It is imperative for the speaker, even to keep attention for 45 minutes, to be well organised, enthusiastic and articulate, and he or she must use the interactivity tools.
- *Weaknesses* – The flip side of F2F meetings: they are less interactive and with a less sensory-rich learning experience.

Ball concludes his article:

When television and VCRs came out, pundits predicted the end of the movie industry. They were wrong – the film industry is as strong as ever as people like to get together in groups and they like the rich sensory environment. We are gregarious animals and grouping is what we tend to do. Very similarly, when videoconferencing and web conferencing emerged, some predicted the end of F2F meetings. This will never happen for the same reason. We like to get together and there are social exchanges that just can't be replicated over the web. Planners should think of virtual meeting tools not as a threat but as additional tools in their toolbox, to be used effectively to bring people together.

A 2010 study by Cornell Center for Hospitality Research, entitled 'The Future of Meetings: The Case for Face-to-Face' (Duffy and McEuen 2010), examines the complex issues surrounding the format of group meetings and events against a backcloth of an explosion in virtual meeting technology. The study notes that meetings can be completely virtual, completely face-to-face, or a hybrid of the two, with leading companies using all three formats. The challenge for meeting planners is to decide which format is most effective for important business outcomes. Rather than rely on personal preferences or currently popular approaches, the study recommends that the decision in respect of meeting type is a strategic one that should rest on specific, scientific criteria. These science-based criteria help executives determine when face-to-face is the most effective approach to large group meetings and events. This decision is important because face-to-face meetings require the greatest investment of all meeting types, and thus carry the greatest expectations for a strong return on investment. The study concludes that face-to-face is most likely to be the best format in the following three business situations:

- to capture attention, particularly when you want to initiate something new or different;
- to inspire a positive emotional climate, as a way to catalyse collaboration, innovation and performance; and
- to build human networks and relationships, realising that information can increasingly be shared virtually whereas the greater value is in people networks and relationships.

Commenting on the virtual v. face-to-face debate, UK trade body Eventia says (in 'The Summer Eventia 2010' conference programme):

Our industry is at a tipping point in the understanding and adoption of technology. Embracing the digital media age and appreciating its role within the fast-evolving media mix and then being able to harness that to engage audiences is more crucial now than ever before. The much-discussed hypothesis of whether 'virtual' will ever replace 'live' events is irrelevant. There is a place for both in a healthy, symbiotic business relationship.

The 'British Meetings and Events Industry Survey 2011–12' found that 16.5 per cent of association meeting planners were using virtual meetings in addition to face-to-face meetings, while 13.4 per cent were using them instead of face-to-face meetings. Among corporate planners, the figures were 20.6 per cent and 12.0 per cent respectively.

In the period since Campbell and Ball were airing their views, a new phrase has entered the meetings industry lexicon: the hybrid event. Hybrid events combine digital formats with the live event experience to create, it is hoped, the best of all worlds. However, when the worlds of digital and live marketing meet, the resultant hybrid event presents both challenges and opportunities for event organisers who may struggle to understand the options available. An article by Richard John (2012), industry trainer/writer, succinctly summarises the key challenges and opportunities:

> For beginners, the new technology can be daunting, but essentially it's about considering what social media can be included in all phases of an event. Before the date, platforms such as Facebook, Twitter and LinkedIn offer invitation opportunities. Additionally, the use of event apps offers a mobile dimension. The same technology can be used during the event, with interactive event walls and online communities. There are new websites, such as Pinterest, and it is easy for a program such as Videobuilder to be used as a portal for relevant videos on sites such as YouTube and Vimeo. Special aggregators like Friendfeed.com and Tumblr.com bundle the contents of different platforms. This is a relatively new area, that of 'content curation'. And applications such as QR codes can be used to drive visitors to microsites and link to downloadable presentations. In the next couple of years, expect to see the development of augmented reality software; viewing an item through the camera of your smartphone will provide a combination of real and virtual scenario.
>
> After the event, the increasing capacity of the Internet, plus the development of 4G, will allow for swift dissemination of video presentations and the ongoing curation of a wealth of expert knowledge, all delivered seamlessly to a screen near you.
>
> This new form of communication also requires the mastering of new skills. Organisers need to understand a large element of time should be spent exploring the digital universe, in order to find out where the potential audiences are lurking. For the less techno-savvy that could be a challenge, but it can mean exploring blogs, forums, webinars, websites, networks, in fact any platform the target group is present.

John quotes MPI (2012b) and Vok Dams (2011) research into hybrid events which reveals that new rules are required. For example,

> the online element needs careful design, building on the lessons learned from a decade of e-learning; skilled facilitation (will be needed) for getting delegates involved who can't be present physically; and then ensuring the effective dissemination of all this newly created, and curated, content.

John concludes his article by quoting MPI (2012b) research ('The Future of Meetings') among planners suggesting that, *'ultimately, all events will become hybrid because technology will be a part of every conference that we produce'*. This may prove to be a slight overstatement as there will always be some events which, for reasons of confidentiality or perhaps exclusivity, do not wish to broadcast their content to a wider audience.

Fisher, in an article entitled 'Fellow Traveller' (Fisher 2012), reviewing 25 years spent in the meetings and incentives industry, writes:

> *In 25 years a lot of the detail has changed, but the principles of event management remain the same. Despite the improvements in communications technology and logistical speed, a good 'event' is usually where people meet face-to-face and enjoy each other's company. Good business then follows. Contrary to the views of many futurists, there are no meetings on the Moon, we have not actually exchanged hot food for vitamin pills, we don't do virtual conferencing unless we are desperate to save money, we don't make the really big budget decisions purely based on downloaded data and reports, and we don't hire key people without meeting them. At some stage we have to engage with other humans on a physical and psychological level to make the most of the transaction.*

It is to be hoped, for the sake of society, that the benefits of face-to-face meetings do, indeed, continue to be accepted and embraced by the next generation and generations beyond. But it also makes total sense to combine face-to-face with the opportunities that technology offers to generate a much wider audience and to facilitate the dissemination of ideas, knowledge and expertise globally. Hybrid does, indeed, seem to make this a reality.

Corporate social responsibility

For many years there have been minority pressure groups attempting to focus the world's attention on the ethical, commercial and environmental practices of major corporations, particularly when such practices have been shown to cause harm to developing countries. The promotion of baby milk products in place of breast feeding in West Africa, the decimation of the rainforest causing flooding and irretrievable damage to fragile ecologies, the use of child labour in Asian countries to manufacture sports goods for western countries, investments in corrupt regimes and exploitative businesses, are just a few examples of issues highlighted by these pressure groups. But, until the last few years, the work of these groups has caused little more than occasional embarrassment to the offending corporations.

Now this is changing as companies appreciate the commercial and employment benefits of adopting socially responsible policies and practices. Davidson and Rogers (2006) suggest that companies are increasingly seeking to:

> engage with their stakeholders and deal with potentially contentious issues pro-actively, instead of waiting until campaigners' accusations lead to disastrous press coverage. Now, more companies than ever are engaged in integrating CSR (corporate social responsibility) into all aspects of their business, encouraged by a growing body of evidence that CSR has a positive impact on businesses' economic performance.

Companies are realising that all areas of their operations are under the microscope and that they are required to demonstrate their credentials as good corporate citizens. In addition to corporate citizenship, Davidson and Rogers (2006) list a variety of terms relating to CSR including business ethics, corporate accountability and sustainability. They quote a definition for CSR used by the US-based organisation Business for Social Responsibility as:

> achieving commercial success in ways that honour ethical values and respect people, communities, and the natural environment.

They describe how:

> in Europe, CSR has moved to a prominent place in both the business and policy agenda. The European Commission has placed CSR at the core of Europe's competition strategy, and has issued a Green Paper on CSR and a subsequent communication outlining the Commission's definition of CSR and steps that companies, governments, and civil society can undertake to refine their commitments to it.

The Corporate Responsibility Officer Association (CROA) surveyed 300 companies about their CSR practices in 2011. It found that 72 per cent of companies now have a formal CSR programme, up from 62 per cent in 2010. Moreover, 60 per cent of companies have dedicated CSR budgets, about half of which are over US$500,000 a year. In its March 2012 report entitled 'The State of the Corporate Responsibility Profession' (USCCBCL 2012), Stephen Jordan, Executive Director of the US Chamber of Commerce Business Civic Leadership Center, asserts that CSR programmes can contribute to corporate strategy by providing a kind of moral rallying-point:

> Individual companies are increasingly conscious that their values are a strategic asset, the core of their brands, and a substantial factor in defining and knitting their employees together into cohesive teams. Values help to safeguard companies against

scandals, provide a sense of common purpose among employees, and frame how companies approach complex problems.

However, the CROA study found that only 35 per cent of companies are able to measure the impact of CSR programmes on profitability, and 51 per cent cannot measure its impact on competitive positioning.

With specific reference to the conventions, meetings and hospitality sector, a study into CSR by the International Centre for Research in Events, Tourism and Hospitality at Leeds Metropolitan University on behalf of Meeting Professionals International (MPI), one of MPI's Thought Leadership projects, concludes that CSR practices are '*over-complicated, under-regulated but on the money*' (MPI 2012a). The findings are only the first part of a landmark three-year study into the impacts, trends and drivers of CSR in the sector. James Musgrave, author of the first report entitled 'January 2012: The State of Corporate Social Responsibility', explains that, following a review of CSR worldwide:

> *Some interesting outcomes emerge: with over 300 codes of practice, businesses cannot be blamed for being confused. But there is a strong business case for companies to build CSR into their work. Responsibility makes business sense as well as meeting moral and ethical obligations.*

The MPI/Leeds Metropolitan University study of 1,100 businesses involved in the meetings and hospitality sector found that:

- 9 out of 10 meeting industry businesses are now actively engaging in some aspect of CSR;
- the adoption of CSR policies and practices has increased the businesses' credibility and trustworthiness to key clients and provided market differentiation;
- CSR is a means for distributing wealth throughout the surrounding economy;
- having a CSR policy has increased the businesses' recruitment pool, making them more attractive to potential future employees and improving the calibre of applicants;
- CSR has contributed to urban development.

However, the study also discovered that the value of formalised CSR accreditation is not recognised, and the proliferation of standards and guides is causing confusion. Some interviewees felt that there were issues around definitions and a lack of understanding of what corporate responsibility actually is. There is a danger that this mis-communication could mean that the right solutions for business will not be found.

According to the MPI (2012a) study, public perception, growing knowledge, competitors and improved business performance will drive CSR, all resulting in increased employee satisfaction and more reliable and sustainable supply chain partnerships. The study identified the following key drivers:

- *Knowledge* – Diverse business issues will require CSR education and training. CSR will grow from checklist to organisational strategy.
- *Resources* – Finite resources will be repositioned and managed through long-term supply chain management and high-commitment HR strategies.
- *Consumer* – Socially aware and ethically demanding consumers will expect transparency of economic and social reporting.
- *Regulations* – Diverse regulations will impact the triple bottom line and increase credibility and the adoption of international standards.
- *Competition* – Innovation in CSR-differentiated products and investment opportunities will thrive in the sustainable global marketplace.

The MPI study will conclude in 2014 and reports from the various stages will be accessible on the MPI website (www.mpiweb.org/csr).

As the drive for greater transparency grows, all industries and organisations, public as well as private, will be increasingly obliged to demonstrate their ethical, environmental and social credentials. All stakeholders in the conference industry, from airlines, hotels and venues to intermediaries and the delegates themselves, will need to examine their own commitment to CSR. CSR is certainly here to stay and both sides of the conference industry need to understand its implications and seize the opportunities it offers.

The future of meetings, conferences and conventions

Aside from the myriad developments in technology and the impact of CSR, there are other major trends influencing the ways in which meetings, conferences and conventions will be promoted, planned and managed. Some of these are with us already but may not yet be fully embraced in all corners of the world. Others are still at more of an embryonic stage but seem likely to have a substantial influence and impact in the years ahead. This section examines some of these key developments.

Strategic meetings management programmes

Strategic Meetings Management provides direction to guide the strategy, operations and tactical activities of meetings and events in order to improve business processes, quality, and return on investment (ROI), and reduce costs, risks and inefficiencies.

An MPI (2005) paper ('Defining a Strategic Meetings Management Program: How Meetings Drive Business in Partnership-Focused Companies' – the fourth paper under the banner of MPI's Global Corporate Circle of Excellence (GCCOE)), looked at the global drivers of strategic meetings management, including trust, transparency, cross-functional teams, technology, consolidation and management styles. It also outline the Partnership Model of doing business, with trust, accountability, respect, sharing of information, process improvement and alignment with organisational goals as key elements.

The paper emphasised the creation and delivery of value within a strategic meetings management programme, with reference to an organisation's unique vision, mission, landscape and culture.

The paper stated that companies' needs for Strategic Meetings Management Programmes evolved from current global trends in business, both external and internal, to what might be called a customer economy. In a customer economy, an organisation or department must provide added-value solutions, not just a commodity or service, because the customer (whether an internal customer or an external one) has more options to replace that commodity or service than ever before. While cost may be a driver, provision of value is a differentiator. Businesses are refocusing on value, strategy and structural realignments to produce the most efficient supply chains.

The meetings industry, in turn, has reached a 'tipping point' in its evolution. Through the corporate trend toward Strategic Meetings Management Programmes, the industry will ultimately differentiate based on value, or it will become a commodity that competes on price alone.

A Strategic Meetings Management Programme has many vital components and objectives, all defined and dictated by a company's culture (see below for MPI's list of key components). Beyond acknowledging the components and objectives, however, savvy planners identify the Programme's key drivers in their organisations (the unique management styles, processes, content and messaging most important to the company) and realise that the successful implementation of such a Programme must involve key internal and external stakeholders. For some, marketing and brand management concerns may drive the meetings programme; for others, finance, operations and procurement may be the integral drivers.

The MPI (2005) paper suggested that a Strategic Meetings Management Programme should have the following objectives and key components:

Objectives

- Maximise quality and service at an affordable price by consolidating best practice processes.
- Manage cost without sacrificing quality and service.
- Consolidate the 'buy' for vendor (supplier) categories that serve meeting management.
- Streamline the meetings management supply chain for greater efficiencies.
- Create a customised operational and service model that fits the company landscape and culture, including appropriate and efficient levels of collaboration among internal and external stakeholders.
- Be conversant in the language of business (especially the language of internal stakeholders).
- Enhance the importance of partnership through focus on organisational strategy and culture.

- Address global drivers of business change in order to identify future goals and timeline milestones that are critical to success.

Key components

There should be a co-ordinated approach to meeting management, with clear policies and strategies covering the following actions:

- Mandate meetings (guidelines) through the meetings programme.
- Approach consolidation through centralised processes for purchasing, data tracking and reporting.
- Collaborate with stakeholders for customised best practices.
- Obtain senior leader support for meetings policy including administration, finance, procurement, branding, accounts payable, senior leadership.
- Communicate policy, best practices and efficient supply chain processes across the programme.

The first textbook on SMMP was published in 2011. The book's editor, Kevin Iwamoto (2011), suggests that an SMMP can:

- align with an organisation's strategic goals and vision;
- increase visibility of its meetings spend;
- save money and bolster control over expenditure;
- improve process efficiencies;
- raise service levels to meetings attendees;
- boost leverage with suppliers;
- mitigate risk.

He explains that:

> While an SMMP can help you with all these goals, there is often resistance within an organisation, with bias toward already established ways of planning and managing events, as well as any home-grown program of managing meetings activities and spend. In many cases, such as in a decentralized environment, multiple planners (some untrained) source for venues manually in very inefficient ways; use their own favoured suppliers; pay for services in a variety of ways (including personal cards); sign contracts worth thousands of dollars; and fail to track valuable meetings data that can be used to improve control and elevate buying power.

He concludes:

> There is a better way – strategic meetings management – a holistic, centralized, automated, and more efficient way of managing all of a firm's meetings and events activities and spend.

StarCite Inc., producers of technology platforms for the meetings and events sector (and now linked with Active Network), have published a paper entitled '7 Step Guide to Initiate a Strategic Meetings Management Program' (Starcite 2012), which suggests that there is no one way to design, develop and implement an SMMP. Such programmes can be started in phases or deployed in one go, depending on the needs and requirements of the organisation. The steps include selecting a project leader and core team, ensuring senior management buy-in, carrying out a situation assessment to determine the scope of the programme, setting goals and priorities, determining appropriate technology solutions, undertaking a strategic value analysis and writing a business case, and creating an action/implementation plan and timeline.

Cvent, US developers of meetings technology programmes, announced (August 2011) the addition of new globalisation features to their Strategic Meetings Management technology (Conworld.net 2011). The new globalisation features allow meeting managers to:

- set a default account currency to consistently roll-up financial data while allowing users to work in their own local currency when drafting requests for proposals (RFPs), attendee registration sites, and event budgets;
- boost online registration by building one event registration site in multiple languages, enabling meeting attendees to register and receive communications in their native languages;
- capture attendee travel details, regardless of the booking system used or country of origin, through additional integrations with all major global distribution systems (GDS);
- run reports on meeting activities as well as spend by country and region for detailed analysis and analytics on their organisation's global meeting programme;
- search detailed profiles and send RFPs to more than 150,000 meeting venues based on regional criteria through the Cvent Supplier Network.

Also in August 2011 the GBTA Foundation, the research and education arm of the Global Business Travel Association, in partnership with the Strategic Meetings Management Taskforce and StarCite Inc., announced the launch of the Strategic Meetings Management (SMM) Maturity Index. The SMM Maturity Index aims to enable companies to track the developmental progress of their SMM programmes and provides a prescriptive report of recommendations for further improvement. It will help companies to gauge the progress of their SMMP across 13 categories including: Strategy, Data Analysis and Reporting, Policy, Approval, Technology, Sourcing/Procurement, and more. Recognising that each SMMP is as unique as the organisation which implements it, the SMM Maturity Index takes differing approaches into consideration and is based on best-in-class models. Users complete an online questionnaire about their SMM programmes, taking into account parameters like company size and using preloaded benchmarks.

'Meeting Architecture'

There is growing interest in, and support for, the concept of 'Meeting Architecture', first launched in 2008 by the Meeting Support Institute and formalised through the publication of 'Meeting Architecture: A Manifesto' by Belgium-based Maarten Vanneste (2009). There is a sense in which this follows on from strategic meetings management. The Manifesto's seven clauses are shown in Figure 10.1.

Meeting Architecture is not new. There are meeting planners in organisations and meeting planning agencies who are experts at designing meetings that deliver excellent value for stakeholders, but these are self-taught exceptions and not the rule, claims Vanneste. He suggests that '*the main focus of the industry today* [2009] *is on hospitality and logistics, rather than the value creation process that happens inside the meeting*'. The Meeting Architecture Manifesto, and now perhaps Movement, aims to move the primary focus away from hospitality and logistics towards

> *designing, executing and measuring objective-based meeting contents and formats that have a purposeful impact on participants. By designing meetings to support Learning, Networking and Motivation objectives, participant action will, as a consequence, provide more value for stakeholders.*

In order to bring about this major change in focus, Vanneste proposed:

> *The establishment of the 'Project Meeting Architecture' (international, not-for-profit) in order to plan for the longer-term development and implementation of this new meeting management discipline and as the first step towards the vision of transforming meetings into a much more effective means of achieving stakeholder objectives. Major project tasks include:*
>
> - *To perform an extensive needs analysis for Meeting Architecture skills, including an assessment of market maturity and estimate a demand curve for the services of Meeting Architecture professionals.*
> - *To investigate alternative pathways and make a plan for the implementation of Meeting Architecture skills through alliances with meeting industry associations, universities and other stakeholders, providing compelling value propositions for each of them to join in a significant and long-term collaborative effort.*
> - *To secure funding for the further development of Meeting Architecture, including a curriculum to be implemented through university and industry educational programmes.*
> - *To develop the concept of Meeting Architecture through conceptual models and practical case studies.*

Project Meeting Architecture has an international steering committee (2011).

Meeting Architecture is a term now accepted and commonly used at a global level, and the concept is gaining a central position in the meetings industry's discussions about its future direction and development. There are also clear synergies between the objectives of Meeting Architecture and those outlined earlier in this chapter, namely the importance of broadening the existing focus on the economic benefits of meetings and events to promote the wider benefits of what meetings achieve such as knowledge exchange, innovation and professional advancement.

The Meeting Architecture – The Manifesto

I. Meetings have the potential to create significantly greater value for stakeholders through better design of content and format

II. Meetings provide value for stakeholders through the actions of the participants, and meetings are, therefore, designed to reinforce or change participant behaviour

III. Meeting Architecture is the discipline of identifying objectives, designing, executing and assessing the results of the meeting experience, its content, format and context, in order to facilitate the desired reinforcement or change in participant behaviour and thus provide greater value for stakeholders

IV. The Meeting Architect does not create the meeting on his/her own. Meetings logistics professionals are specialists who make sure that all aspects of operations and logistics are perfect and delivered at the lowest achievable cost. They are equally important and their professional skills need to be further developed

V. In order to realise the full potential of Meeting Architecture, everyone involved in the industry needs to work together, putting the common interests of the industry before the interests of individual associations or other stakeholders. Only by sharing and collaborating can we create significant global impact

VI. We need recognised and consistent education at university level as well as professional development by industry organisations in order to realise the full potential of Meeting Architecture

VII. We believe it is necessary to set a two-year industry-wide project with a mission to provide the conceptual, organisational and financial foundations for the long-term implementation of Meeting Architecture as a recognised meeting management discipline.

FIGURE 10.1 The Meeting Architecture: the Manifesto

Convention 2020 Study: key findings

The Convention 2020 Study is a major international study of the meetings industry looking at key trends, changes and developments over the period up to 2020. The Study is co-ordinated by Fast Future Research (2010) and the methodology was an in-depth online questionnaire completed by meetings sector buyers and suppliers globally – over 1,000 people contributed to the first survey questionnaire. The initial tranche of findings was released at the IMEX–Frankfurt tradeshow (May 2011) and a summary of the key issues is given below. For full details visit: www.convention-2020.com

Factors influencing the decision to attend live events such as conferences and exhibitions in 2020

The following factors were identified, in ranking order:

- quality of networking (75 per cent);
- seeing very latest sector developments (69 per cent);
- guaranteed opportunity to meet key people (68 per cent);
- high quality speakers (66 per cent);
- high quality educational content (65 per cent);
- find out what competitors are doing (53 per cent);
- identifying new prospects (50 per cent);
- value for money pricing (43 per cent);
- latest industry buzz/gossip (39 per cent);
- interesting foreign location (39 per cent);
- high-tech participative sessions (38 per cent);
- personalised education (37 per cent).

Size and variety of events in 2020

While less than half of respondents (49 per cent) expected that, by 2020, there would be fewer but larger conferences and exhibitions covering wide topics, industry sectors or 'communities of interest' (with less choice of which events to attend but much more choice within the events themselves), 79 per cent of respondents anticipated that there would be a greater choice of many more smaller, highly specialised conferences, exhibitions and meetings, with much more competition from events wanting delegates to attend.

Pricing models

Some 77 per cent of respondents thought that, by 2020, conferences and exhibitions would have to offer strong price incentives (e.g. free attendance, subsidised travel to 'buyers', sponsors to pay for key senior delegates to be present) in order to attract the right kind of participants. 60 per cent of respondents believed that participants will pay according to the returns they obtain from attending e.g. sales appointments booked, individual education sessions attended. Organisers will have to guarantee quantifiable 'returns on investment' – simply paying a flat fee to attend or exhibit will decrease in frequency.

Experiential focus

In 2020, conferences and exhibitions will include far greater opportunities to sample and purchase products and services than they do at the moment (76 per cent of respondents), and there will be vastly more business opportunities than there are today. Adelaide Convention Centre is cited as an example of an event venue which regularly creates experiences for its clients (e.g. buyers are invited to cookery classes led by the Centre's chefs and to wine tasting sessions to experience South Australia's array of fine wines).

Event agency priorities and strategies

The report draws comparisons between 2011 priorities and necessary 2015 strategies for event agencies. In 2011 the priorities were seen as:

- Attract new customers (75 per cent).
- Maintain the existing customer base (68 per cent).
- Maximize delegate satisfaction (60 per cent).

By 2015 the key strategies envisaged for event agencies are:

- Develop solutions which help clients capture and re-use the knowledge generated at events (62 per cent).
- Look more like management consultancies – providing a range of additional consulting and research services (61 per cent).
- Focus on developing a deep understanding of client business strategies and priorities (58 per cent).

Destination priorities and strategies

Similar priorities and strategies for event destinations are outlined in the Study. The destination priorities in 2011 are:

- Find differentiators in the face of intense competition (69 per cent).
- Use web/social media more to promote the destination (67 per cent).
- Prioritise key events, industries and associations to target (56 per cent).

Destination strategies in 2015 are expected to focus on:

- Show ROI for event owners/delegates (63 per cent).
- Show longer term contribution to economic development (61 per cent).
- More extensive data mining (57 per cent).

Venue priorities and strategies

Priorities for venues in 2011 were seen to be:

- Provide free broadband wireless access (64 per cent).
- Create lower cost operating models (64 per cent).
- Give more flexible service offerings to meet customer demand (63 per cent).

2015 venue strategies are expected to include:

- Offering a full AV package (63 per cent).
- Offering a full meeting planning service to help attract events (55 per cent).
- Full e-solution to event organisers (55 per cent).

Association event priorities and strategies

The priorities in 2011 for the organisers of association events were:

- Demonstrate event benefits to potential delegates (65 per cent).
- Differentiate events in the face of increased competition (58 per cent).
- Identify benefits/proof of value for sponsors and exhibitors (58 per cent).

Event management strategies in 2015 will include:

- Greater focus on capturing the knowledge generated at an event (58 per cent).
- Stronger focus on personalisation and maximising individual learning (56 per cent).
- Increased emphasis on the overall 'meeting architecture' to ensure delivery against objectives (53 per cent).

The Study also summarises several 'alternative business event models 2015', especially:

- Presentations streamed live to the web (67 per cent).
- All sessions available on a pay-per-view basis after the event (63 per cent).
- Sponsorship based on level of interest or actual business generated (55 per cent).

Technology, customisation, knowledge

Some 77 per cent of respondents felt that, by 2020, all conferences and exhibitions will offer a totally personalised experience, tailor-made to delegates' needs, and offering whatever technological tools are required to make the event fully interactive so that delegates can engage with and influence the content of the event.

About 70 per cent of respondents anticipated that the personal comfort of attendees will be much more important to organisers than today. Individuals will be able to obtain personalised menus at meals, there will be many options for entertainment and relaxation e.g. customised seating. Organisers will make far better use of information about individual attendees than they do today.

And 93 per cent of respondents expected that, by 2020, everything that happens at events will be measured and stored as useful data for organisers and participants to use in real time, including sessions that individuals attend, interactions between attendees, appointments that are made and the educational and business interests that individuals express (before, during and after the event).

Convention 2020 Conclusions

- Demand will hold up.
- Innovation required in formats, business models, capability and technology.
- Focus on 'enabling business'.
- Personalisation is key.
- 'Total sustainability' agenda.

Meeting formats and generations Y and Z

In an article entitled 'The Future of the Meetings Industry' reproduced in Conworld.net (now GMI Portal) Shuli Golovinski (2012), CEO of Newtonstrand Innovations, outlined changes to the format of meetings that he envisages, driven in part by the need to cater for participation by younger generations, Generation Y (born between 1981 and 1999) and then Generation Z (Millennials). He suggests that:

> Events 1.0 were our first type of meeting or congress with industry speakers presenting to the audience – the whole education format was thoroughly planned out for the event. This used to be exactly what was needed for a previous generation who wanted to sit and listen to the education planned for their participation. You can compare this to when the Internet was introduced (Web 1.0) with a large amount of information readily available for us to learn from.
>
> Events 1.0 developed into Events 2.0 where we introduced to more delegate networking and interaction, supporting the educational programme. Compare this to Web 2.0 with the introduction of social media, blogging and interaction.

Events 3.0 recognises the need for changes in our current meetings format to support the younger attendees just coming into our industry. They already want to be active participants, contribute to the programme and decide for themselves who they want to meet and network with.

He gives some practical examples of what such changes might entail:

Think about typical networking and coffee breaks during breakout sessions at a conference. Although they allow people to network with each other, they are not long enough to allow attendees to have significant exchanges. Of course we already have events and exhibitions with pre-scheduled meetings and hosted buyer programmes where delegates can arrange meetings with suppliers, but there is a need to move on to a more structured networking format at all events. Attendees should be able to choose who they want to meet with before an event (whether supplier or industry colleague) and then have a structured networking time with a pre-set meeting during the event.

Take another example of the need for change whilst looking back at Events 1.0 with industry speakers presenting their knowledge and ideas to participants. This has progressed to some extent with the introduction of interactive voting and audience participation tools. However, to satisfy the needs of the younger generation, we need them to get involved and take an active participation in education. An 'Open-Stage' at an event will allow all delegates the chance to book a speaking slot in advance and present an industry topic of their choice.

A three-year study into 'The Future of Meetings' by MPI (2012b) and being undertaken by the International Centre for Research in Events, Tourism and Hospitality at Leeds Metropolitan University confirms that some of the changes recommended by Shuli Golovinski are already being implemented by meeting professionals. It says that meeting professionals are:

Rethinking traditional conferences with keynote presentations and seated audiences in light of new innovations, which claim active learning as a way to attract delegates, foster collaboration and address the concepts that delegates find most interesting. Peer-driven unconferences and open-space meetings demonstrate the extent to which participants control their own experiences, because most adults are capable of finding out what they need, rather than someone else determining what they need.

The study also suggests that a key challenge will be to:

Cater to multi-generational delegates who have diverse value drivers and seek diverse benefits from their meetings. Gen Y, with its WIIFM: (What's in it for me?) attitude, will seek opportunities for professional development, personalisation, concise content and visible technology; older generations will value social opportunities, knowledge sharing and accessibility.

Content is king but . . .

Today it is common to hear the mantra 'Content is King', describing the overriding importance of the educational programme in contemporary conferences. Unless the content is topical, controversial perhaps, thought-provoking, and relevant, delegates will not attend, no matter how strong the social programme or how attractive the destination. And this is how it should be, although some balance and perspective were provided in an article by Kim Myrhe (2011), Managing Director of George P Johnson EMEA, written for the 'British Meetings and Events Industry Survey 2011–12'. He writes:

> *But as we have moved on a bit from these particularly difficult economic times, it seemed like the pendulum was swinging back to where delegates may now attend business events in nice surroundings with quality accommodation and even hospitality – so long as while they are enjoying these nice surroundings they receive a healthy dose of relevant content.*
>
> *This is as it should be. A business delegate's time is valuable and attending events can be costly in terms of time and money – clearly we need to deliver business value by providing relevant content.*
>
> *But we should not overlook that the real value of events is that they bring people together in a live experience – and it's that live event experience that delegates really value. If it was only about relevant content, delegates could stay at home and surf the Internet.*

Martin Sirk, CEO of the International Congress and Convention Association (ICCA), writing in *Association Meetings International* magazine (Sirk 2011), stressed the need for finding smarter ways of making international congresses more relevant and handling effectively the abundance of information that is made available on a daily basis:

> *It will come as no surprise that we will need much better interpretative IT systems that help us make more sense of the avalanche of new information. And, crucially, we will have to get much smarter about making our international congresses more relevant. We must find ways to connect researchers across their narrow professional furrows, place vast amounts of relevant data in the palms of delegates' hands and link congress centres to laboratories and medical surgery theatres. This is going to mean a radical re-think for many associations about how they design their major meetings. Get it right and they will find themselves at the forefront of this new phase in the Information Revolution. Get it wrong, and they will become ever more irrelevant.*

MPI's (2012b) 'The Future of Meetings' study stresses the important opportunity afforded by 'structuring' information. It says:

> The desire for information quickly and easily will result in shorter, more strategic, targeted and information-rich meetings. And while rapidity may shorten meetings, information overload could provide opportunity for meeting planners to deliver content more effectively over time. Structuring information might be the USP (unique selling proposition) that will help meetings differentiate themselves from other sources.

The study also suggests that content value is reducing as digitisation and ease of access put a much lower cost on actual content. Meeting planners will need to find new models to monetise content and customise their pricing and increase perceived value. New specialisms such as knowledge structuring and embedding information could emerge and there will be a need to view knowledge as know-how and to integrate experiential learning into content design. For further details of 'The Future of Meetings' study visit www.mpiweb.org/fom.

In conclusion

An optimistic forecast

The author makes no claim to have covered all of the topical issues facing the conference and conventions industry in this chapter or even in this book. Reference has been made to a number of important issues elsewhere in this book – the need to continue improving the industry's statistical base, the importance of enhancing education and training and CPD programmes, the need to attract and retain staff with the right personal qualities and skills, for example – but space has precluded adequate coverage of other key issues.

Readers must, and will, draw their own conclusions on whether this great conference industry faces future expansion or contraction. In the author's view, and in the opinion of many leading figures in the industry, the importance of face-to-face contact and personal networking will continue to sustain the conference and meetings industry. People are social, gregarious creatures by nature, and conferences and conventions are a wonderful way of bringing people together in beneficial interaction, and for communicating and sharing experiences through inspirational presentations, educational workshops and memorable social programmes.

To those working in this dynamic industry, buyers and suppliers, it offers variety, stimulation, scope for creativity and imagination, travel, fulfilment, excitement, enjoyment, constant challenges, the chance to build friendships around the world, and so much more. Few other industries can offer as much. Surely, none can offer more. Industry journalist Rob Spalding, writing in *Association Meetings International* magazine (Spalding 2002), sums it up well when he writes about the *'sense of warmth, the heart, and the personality of the meetings phenomenon'*.

He refers to the

> *skill and devotion, the generosity of sharing and the loyalty of service of those who make meetings that makes the profession so unique. Oh yes, and that meetings have saved the world from self-destruction once or twice.*

The Congress of Vienna marked the beginning of a long period of peace and stability for Europe in the nineteeth century. Conferences and conventions have the potential for ensuring a permanent peace for the world throughout the twenty-first century and beyond, as they provide the framework for discussion rather than conflict, for uniting rather than dividing communities and nations, and for encouraging the sharing of ideas and information for the benefit of all mankind. Whether 'conference' will still be the most appropriate word to describe what the industry will become in this millennium is another matter, and perhaps a keynote topic for a twenty-first-century congress!

SUMMARY

- The conference, conventions and business events sector is working hard to position, or perhaps reposition, itself as the deliverer of vital economic, business and community development benefits, and downplay its links with leisure tourism and hospitality.
- The application of new multimedia technologies is revolutionising communication systems and learning methods, and enhancing the ways in which delegates communicate before, during and after an event.
- The advent of web-based and electronic communications tools has reduced the need for people to meet face-to-face for certain types of business event. However, the live event experience is still expected to play a vital role for the foreseeable future, with technology making possible the combined virtual and face-to-face event to offer the best of all worlds.
- Companies and organisations are now much more aware of the ethical and environmental dimensions to their events and of the importance of conducting business and planning meetings in ways that show genuine corporate social responsibility.
- The organisation of conferences and conventions is adopting a much more strategic approach than hitherto, and facing up to the challenge of promoting the wider benefits of what meetings achieve, such as knowledge exchange, innovation and professional advancement.

- The ways in which meetings content is provided also face a sea change as new generations of attendees influence the programme design, contribute actively to the events themselves, and approach events with new and different expectations from their predecessors.

REVIEW AND DISCUSSION QUESTIONS

1 Television, computers and the Internet have had a dramatic effect on society and on the lives of individual people. Television, in particular, has been accused of creating a generation of 'couch potatoes'. Texting and email have reduced the need to speak to other human beings. Computer games have replaced the outdoor games and 'playtime' familiar to previous generations. Is the home, therefore, likely to become the conference venue of the future as we all become 'virtual' delegates? Or are people's social and gregarious instincts strong enough to ensure that face-to-face communication remains the pre-eminent form of human interaction? Outline the arguments for and against both scenarios, and attempt an assessment of where future growth will lie.

2 With reference to the concept of the 'content' of meetings and events, discuss the most common objectives for meetings, and review the formats that are regularly used in the presentation of educational content. What do you envisage will be the key changes and developments in the next few years?

3 'We need to focus on and promote more effectively what meetings and conventions accomplish and downplay our traditional emphasis on the hotels and venues that have been filled while the event has taken place.' Critically assess such a change of approach.

REFERENCES

Ball, C. (2005) *Selecting the Right Meeting Planning Technology: A Step-by-Step Guide*, available at www.corbinball.com (accessed 13 August 2012)

—— (2006a) 'Face-to-Face Vs. Web Meetings: What Should I Use When?', available at www.corbinball.com (accessed 13 August 2012)

—— (2006b) 'Podcasting', *Meetings & Incentive Travel* magazine (October), available at www.meetpie.com

—— (2011) '12+ Meetings Technology Trends to Watch for 2012', available at www.corbinball.com (accessed 13 August 2012)

Campbell, D. (2000) 'Market-driven Venues Adapt to Meetings Needs', *Catering Magazine*, Issue 15 (December)

Conworld.net (2011) 'Cvent Unveils New Features for Global Strategic Meetings Management Programs', www.conworld.net/index.php/Suppliers/cvent-unveils-new-features-for-global-strategic-meetings-management-programs.html (August) (accessed 12 September 2012)

Davidson, R. and Rogers, T. (2006) *Marketing Destinations and Venues for Conferences, Conventions and Business Events*, Butterworth-Heinemann

Duffy, C. and McEuen, M. B. (2010) 'The Future of Meetings: The Case for Face-to-Face', Cornell Center for Hospitality Research, available at www.hotelschool.cornell.edu (accessed 13 August 2012)

Fast Future Research (2010) 'Convention 2020', a study on behalf of a number of industry organisations, available at www.convention-2020.com (accessed 13 August 2012)

Fisher, J. (2012) 'Fellow Traveller', *Meetings & Incentive Travel* magazine (March), available at www.meetpie.com

Garofani, Inge (2012) 'BECA Redefining and Refocusing', available at www.Conworld.net/index (Conworld.net now trades as GMI Portal) (accessed 3 March 2012)

Golovinski, S. (2012) 'The Future of the Meetings Industry', (April), available at www.gmiportal.com (accessed 13 August 2012)

IMEX America (2011) *Executive Meeting Forum Report,* IMEX America (October), available at www.imex-america.com (accessed 13 August 2012)

Iwamoto, K. (2011) *Strategic Meetings Management Handbook: From Theory to Practice*, Easton Studio Press

Jago, L. and Deery, M. (2010) *Delivering Innovation, Knowledge and Performance: The Role of Business Events*, Business Events Council of Australia, available at www.businessevents council.org.au (accessed 13 August 2012)

JMIC (2008) *Understanding the Value of the Meetings Industry*, Joint Meetings Industry Council, available at www.themeetingsindustry.org (accessed 13 August 2012)

John, R. (2012) 'Get Your Hybrid Motor Running', *Conference News* magazine (May), available at view.digipage.net/?id = cn052012&page = 23 (accessed 13 August 2012)

MPI (2005) *Defining a Strategic Meetings Management Program: How Meetings Drive Business in Partnership-Focused Companies*, Meeting Professionals International, available at www.mpiweb.org

—— (2012a) *January 2012: The State of CSR*, Meeting Professionals International, the first paper in a 3-year study, available at www.mpiweb.org/csr (accessed 13 August 2012)

—— (2012b) *The Future of Meetings: A Top-Line Analysis of the Industry's Opportunities and Potential*, Meeting Professionals International (January), available at www.mpiweb.org (accessed 13 August 2012)

Myrhe, K. 'Why you can't beat the experience', in CAT, *British Meetings and Events Industry Survey 2011–12*, CAT Publications, available at www.meetpie.com

Peter, L. (2012) 'Real-world Beaming: The Risk of Avatar and Robot Crime', *BBC News Magazine* (11 May) available at www.bbc.co.uk/news/world-europe-17905533 (accessed 13 August 2012)

Sirk, M. (2011) 'It Takes a Lot to Confound Me, but . . . ', *Association Meetings International* magazine (November), available at www.meetpie.com

Spalding, R. (2002) 'Packaged At Last!' *Association Meetings International* magazine (September) available at www.meetpie.com

Starcite (2012) *7 Step Guide to Initiate a Strategic Meetings Management Program*, available at www.starcite.com (accessed 13 August 2012)

USCCBCL (2012) *The State of the Corporate Responsibility Profession*, US Chamber of Commerce Business Civic Leadership and the Corporate Responsibility Officer Association (March)

Vanneste, M. (2009) 'Meeting Architecture: A Manifesto', available at www.meetingarchitecture.org (accessed 13 August 2012)

Vok Dams (2011) *Hybrid Events: Innovation Trend in Live Marketing*, Vok Dams Consulting, available at http://issuu.com/vokdams/docs/11–07–13-studie-hybrid-events_int (accessed 13 August 2012)

FURTHER READING

Fryatt, J., Garriga, R., Janssen, R., John, R. and Smith, S. J. (2012) *The Strategic Value of Virtual Meetings and Events*, Meeting Professionals International, available at www.mpiweb.org

Upton, G. (2012) *Strategic meetings management programmes*, Hotel Booking Agents Association, available at http://www.hbaa.org.uk

Vining, S. (2011) *The Future of the Meetings Industry: Why Certain Conference Innovators Are Winning*, The National Conference Center, available at http://bit.ly/qWmjdV (accessed 13 August 2012)

—— (2012) *Technology's Secret Potential to Empower Participants and Make Meetings Better*, The National Conference Center, available at http://bit.ly/TechnologyWP (accessed 13 August 2012)

Meetings and events industry lexicon

The following is a slightly abridged version of an Industry Lexicon produced by event and communications agency, Grass Roots (www.grassroots-events. co.uk), and reproduced with permission. It also contains one or two additions by the author.

24-Hour Hold A term used to describe the type of reservation made on function space within a venue (hotel, convention centre, etc.). An event organiser who has 24-hour hold on a space has exclusive use and access to that space for a period of 24 hours, usually 12.01 am – 12.00 pm

24-Hour Rate Inclusive meeting rate usually includes: room hire of main meeting room, tea/coffee, mineral water, cordials and mints throughout the meeting, lunch, dinner, breakfast and overnight hotel accommodation. Some venues may also include some equipment, for example OHP, screen, flipchart

Acceleration Clause A provision sometimes used in contracts to accelerate deposit payment schedule or to demand full prepayment of master account in the event of a default or lack of credit by the organisation. May also apply in other situations, such as assignments. Sometimes used in a hotel to accelerate deposit payment schedule or to demand full prepayment of master account in the event of a default by organisation

Accommodation Any seat, berth, room or service provided and/or sold to a guest, attendee or passenger

Accompanying Person Guest or spouse of a traveller/guest/event attendee

Account Sheet
1. Form used to keep track of number of rooms sold and/or still available. See Tally Sheet
2. Designates equipment, materials and teaching aids used in sound and visual presentation

Act of God An extraordinary natural event such as extreme weather, flood, hurricanes, tornadoes, earthquake or similar natural disaster that cannot be reasonably foreseen or prevented over which a contracting party has no reasonable control, making performance of the contract illegal, impracticable or impossible, thus the parties have no legal responsibility to continue performance of the contract. See also Force Majeure

Active Language The language being used by the speaker

Addendum Document used in advance of a contract being raised which outlines expected preferential terms and conditions

Adjoining Rooms Hotel rooms which, while next to each other, have no connecting doors

ADR (Average Daily Room Rate) Statistical unit used to measure a hotel's pricing scale. Figure derived by dividing actual daily revenue by the total number of available rooms

Advance Deposit Amount of money paid to secure a room, facility or service in advance

Advance Purchase Rate Price for a product or service purchased or guaranteed a specified number of days prior to arrival or use

Advance Registration Registration for meeting activity made prior to opening day

Agenda Subjects to be discussed at a meeting. Document that outlines flow of a meeting or the overall schedule of an event

Air Freight Materials shipped via aircraft

Airfreight Forwarder An airfreight company that transports freight via scheduled airlines. Forwarders do not operate their own aircraft

Air Wall Walls or light movable panels used for dividing areas or concealing an area

Alcohol Licence An official licence to sell and/or serve alcoholic beverages. There are three basic types of licences:
1. On-Sale: alcohol sold and must be consumed on the premises (bar or banquet room)
2. Off-Sale: alcohol is sold unopened and must be consumed off the premises (off-licence)
3. Beer and Wine: not authorised to sell spirits. Alcohol licences are based on the physical premises. If you are holding an event at a venue without an alcohol licence, you must obtain a temporary permit

All Risks Insurance Insurance against loss of or damage to property arising from any fortuitous cause except those that are specifically excluded. An insurance contract which provides All-Risks Insurance is an All-Risks policy

All Space Hold All function space at a facility is reserved for one client

All-Suite Describing a hotel in which all bedrooms have a separate living room and/or kitchen facilities

Alteration A change made by the client after any part of the production process has begun. Usually billed as an extra charge

Ambassador Programme A programme developed by a conference destination, and occasionally a convention centre, to recruit, train and support academic, professional

and business people from a particular city or destination to bid for congresses with which they are professionally linked on behalf of that destination. Also known as Local Host Programme

Amendment Changes to a booking e.g. in name, descriptive data or validity

Amenities Complimentary items in sleeping rooms such as shower caps, shampoo, shoe shine mitt, etc. provided by facility for guests

Ancillary Activities All event-related support services within a facility that generate revenue

Appetiser Any small, bite-size food served before a meal to whet and excite the palate. Used synonymously with the term Hors d'Oeuvres, though this term more aptly describes finger food, whereas appetiser can also apply to a first course served at table

Arrival Manifest An itemised list of anticipated dates and times of arrival of group members

Arrival Pattern Anticipated dates and times of arrival of group members

Arrival Time Time or approximate time guests plan to arrive at a facility

At-A-Glance Programme Condensed, quick reference version of an event's programme

Atrium A large open space in a building, usually topped by a glass roof, sometimes containing elaborate landscaping and ponds. A popular style of hotel lobby

Attendance Total number of people at an event

Attendee Individual guest at a meeting or event. Also the American term for a delegate

Attrition Percentage (%) of room inventory which can be released in line with specified dates in advance of actual event dates. The difference between the actual number of sleeping rooms picked up (or food and beverage covers or revenue projections) and the number or formulas agreed to in the terms of the facility's contract. Usually there is an allowable shortfall before damages are assessed

Attrition Clause Contract wording that outlines potential damages or fees that a party may be required to pay in the event that it does not fulfil minimum commitments in the contract

Audience Polling Technology that enables voting and then collects and displays the results

Audio Conference A conference using only voice transmissions between two or more sites

Audio-Visual Aids Audio and visual support for events, usually taking the form of film, slides, overhead projection, flip charts, sound equipment and blackboards

Audit A methodical examination and review of records pertaining to an event. For instance, an independent verification of attendance figures submitted by an exhibition's producers

Audition A tryout performance before producers, directors, casting directors or others for the purpose of obtaining a part in a production or a booking as a speaker

Auditorium Room for gathering an audience for speeches, concerts, etc. Often used to name entire facilities, though properly applied only to the seated portion of the facility in which the audience is assembled

Authorised Signatory A person who is authorised to legally bind an individual or organisation to contract, to sign cheques on behalf of an organisation, or charge to an organisation's master account

AV (Audio-Visual) The equipment required to make your event be seen and heard. This can be from the most basic screen and microphones, to those of a higher specification and include the use of lighting and stage sets

Availability The current inventory of seats, rooms, cabins, etc. that can be sold or reserved

Available Rooms In a hotel, the number of rooms actually available for use on a given day, eliminating rooms not available due to damage, repairs, and so forth

Average Daily Rate (ADR) Statistical unit used to measure a hotel's pricing scale. Figure derived by dividing actual daily revenue by the total number of available rooms

Average Room Rate Mathematical average of a series of sleeping room rates

AVI (Audio Video Interleave) The file format used by video for Windows, one of three video technologies used on PCs (the others are MPEG and QuickTime)

B&B Bed and breakfast

Back of House Support and service areas usually used by staff only and not seen by guests of a hotel

Back Office Describing business activities, such as accounting, that usually take place out of the view of customers

Back Projector The image is projected from the opposite side of the screen to the audience

Back-of-Room Sales The act/process of selling books, tapes and other products at the back of the room, usually immediately after a speech

Back-Up Facility Substitute facility that will serve as a viable alternative if the original facility becomes unavailable or inadequate for its intended purpose

Badge Identifying tag worn by meeting participants, sometimes called a name tag

Banquet Event Order (BEO) A document providing complete and precise instructions to a hotel for the running of a banquet, meeting, or other event to be held in the hotel. Also called a function sheet

Banquet Set-Up Seating arrangements where typically a grouping of round tables is set in such a way as to facilitate the serving of food, most often a hexagonal or square pattern

Bed Night In the hotel industry, a measurement of occupancy. One person for one night

Bed Nights The aggregated number of nights over which the total number of bookings made by a client at a specific hotel takes place in one year

Bid Document A document assembled by a destination, venue, PCO or others to tender for hosting or planning an organisation's conference or congress. May be in paper format, electronic or web-based

Billback Invoice for service(s) purchased

Billing Instructions Notice as to how charges for an event should be handled and to whom invoices should be addressed

Blacked Out Not available

Blackout Dates, Blackout Periods Dates on which hotels and conference, training facilities are not available

Block

1. Total number of sleeping rooms reserved for an event
2. A number of rooms, seats or space reserved in advance for a group
3. To assign space

Blocked Space Sleeping rooms, exhibition, event or other function space reserved for future use by an individual or organisation

Boardroom Set-Up Seating arrangement in which rectangle or oval shaped tables are set up with chairs on both sides and ends

Breakdown

1. The process of dismantling/clearing and cleaning a meeting/conference room after a function
2. To itemise estimates, invoices and the like

Break-Out Room A smaller room, near a large meeting room, for use when a larger group breaks into sections

Break-Out Sessions Small group sessions, within the meeting, formed to discuss specific subjects. Multiple sessions typically occur concurrently

Buffet A serve-yourself meal featuring several choices in each course

Business Casual A style of dress that is less formal than the standard office attire of suit and tie or dress

Business Centre An area in hotel or event venue offering various office facilities and services

By The Bottle Alcohol served and charged by the full bottle

By The Drink Alcohol served and charged for by the number of drinks served

By The Person A fixed price per attendee; covers all consumption of food and beverage at a function, within a given time frame; usually includes beverages, snacks or hors d'oeuvres. In some cases, beverages are purchased by the person, while food is ordered by the piece

By The Piece Food purchased by the individual piece, usually for a reception

Cabaret Set-Up Room arrangement with round tables with chairs and a stage

Call For Papers An invitation to submit topic ideas for the conference programme. Document containing detailed instructions for submission of papers for assessment and selection by a review committee, often referred to as Abstract forms

Campus Housing Dormitory or other university/college sleeping accommodation

Cancellation Clause

1. Provision in a contract which outlines penalties if cancellation occurs, for both parties for failure to comply with the terms of the agreement

2. Entertainment: provision within artist's contract which allows artist to cancel within a specified period of time prior to play date

Cancellation or Interruption Insurance Insurance that protects an event organiser against financial loss or expenses incurred when contractually specific periods necessitate cancelling or relocating an event, or cause a reduction in attendance

Cancellation Penalty An amount deducted by a supplier from a refund of prepaid funds when a reservation is cancelled in line with specified dates in advance of actual event dates

Cancellation/No-Show Percentage The number of rooms that did not materialise (either cancelled or no-showed on the planned date of arrival) calculated as a percentage of the total number of rooms initially booked

Capacity Maximum number of people allowed in any given area

Card-Not-Present Transaction Payment with a credit card when the customer and merchant are not in the same physical location, such as by mail, fax, or through a website

Cash Bar Private room bar set-up where guests pay for drinks individually

Caterer
1. A food service vendor, often used to describe a vendor who specialises in banquets and theme parties
2. An exclusive food and beverage contractor within a facility

Centralised Commissions A system in which a supplier, such as a hotel chain, sends commission payments from a central office, rather than having individual properties pay commissions separately

Centrepiece Decoration for the centre of a banquet table

Chain A group of hotels, or other businesses, sharing a common name and ownership

Check-In A procedure whereby a hotel guest is registered as having arrived. Check-In may require the presentation of payment, reservations, or other documentation or identification

Check-In Time In hotels, the earliest time at which a room will be available

Check-Out The term used when a guest leaves a hotel and pays – or signs the bill. Many hotels offer Express Check-Out which means the bill will be settled automatically with the traveller's charge card and a statement sent to the guest by post

Check-Out Time In hotels, the latest time a guest may leave without being charged for another night's lodging

Chef's Table The opportunity to sample a menu in advance of the event, usually in the company of the chef. Also refers to a food event held in the kitchen where attendees interact with the chef and kitchen staff

Chevron Set-Up Seating arrangement in which chairs are arranged in rows slanted in a V shape and separated by a centre aisle. They face the head table or speaker. See also Herringbone Set-Up

Citywide Event An event that requires the use of a convention centre or event complex, as well as multiple hotels in the host city

Classroom Set-Up Seating arrangement in which rows of tables with chairs face the front of a room and each person has a space for writing

Client Rate A special rate offered to a specific client in return for pre-agreed bednight volumes. Usually lower than the corporate rate

Climate Neutral Climate Neutral products or services reduce and offset the greenhouse gases generated at each stage of their life-cycle on a cradle-to-cradle basis: the sourcing of their materials, their manufacturing or production, their distribution, use, and ultimate end-of-life disposition

Closed Dates Dates on which travel, hotel rooms or meeting rooms are unavailable due to prior sale or booking

Closing Session The final session of an event in which the subjects which have been discussed are summarised and possible conclusions reached and announced

Commission A percentage of a sale price paid to a third party as payment for making a sale

Commission Cap The maximum amount a supplier will pay as commission regardless of the actual price of the service(s) or the standard commission rate

Commission Split An agreed division of commission income between two entities

Commissionable Denoting the portion of total cost on which commission is payable

Comp Rooms Complimentary room(s) which a facility provides without charge based on the number of rooms picked up and occupied by a group

Complete Meeting Package An all-inclusive plan offered by hotels and conference centres; includes lodging, all meals and support services

Complimentary (Comp – *slang*) Complimentary concessions provided by supplier in relation to the overall volume contracted e.g. one upgrade or free room per 50 booked

Complimentary Ratio The number of rooms provided at no cost based on the number of occupied rooms

Complimentary Registration Waiver of registration fees

Complimentary Room A sleeping room or function room provided to an individual organisation at no cost

Computer Card (Registration) Plastic card used in place of room key

Computerised Registration Automated registration records

Concierge
1. Facility staff who provide special services such as tickets to local events, transportation, and tour arrangements
2. Designated area in facility providing special amenities and services to guests

Concierge Level In a hotel, a separate floor providing a higher level of service and security for a premium price. Also called Concierge Floor

Concurrent Sessions Sessions scheduled at the same time

Conference
1. Participatory meeting designed for discussion, fact-finding, problem solving and consultation
2. An event used by any organisation to meet and exchange views, convey a message, open a debate or give publicity to some area of opinion on a specific issue. No tradition, continuity or timing is required to convene a conference. Conferences are usually of short duration with specific objectives, and are generally on a smaller scale than congresses or conventions

Conference Centre A hotel-like property designed specifically for hosting conventions, exhibitions and meetings, normally without bedroom space

Conference Handbook A manual which provides information about a conference. Contents would include descriptions of programmes, information on participants, agendas, schedules of events, speaker notes and logistical information

Conference Report An official summary of conference events

Conference Set-Up Venues will request preferred set-up which could include:
1. Banquet seating in round tables, 10 or 12 per table
2. Cabaret round tables with chairs set at the rear half of each table, facing front
3. Classroom seating is set out in rows but behind long tables
4. Theatre-style seating is set out in rows, usually with an aisle down the middle
5. U-shape horseshoe shape typically for boardroom meetings

Confirmation Number An alphanumeric code used to identify and document the confirmation of a booking

Congress
1. The regular coming together of large groups of individuals, generally to discuss a particular subject. A congress will often last several days and have several simultaneous sessions
2. European term for convention

Connecting Rooms Hotel rooms which are next to each other and have a connecting door, in addition to the doors which give out onto the hallway

Consecutive Interpretation Oral translation of several phrases or entire speeches from one language to another. Speaker pauses between phrases to allow for interpretation

Continental Buffet Buffet consisting of pastries, juices and hot beverages

Contingency Plan An alternative plan that may replace the original plan when circumstances change

Control Room A room in the hall where the operators and most of the control equipment are located

Convention Gathering of delegates, representatives, and members of a membership or industry organisation convened for a common purpose. Common features include educational sessions, committee meetings, social functions, and meetings to conduct the governance business of the organisation. Conventions are typically recurring events with specific, established timing

Corkage The charge placed on beer, alcohol and wine brought into the facility but purchased elsewhere. The charge sometimes includes glassware, ice and mixers

Corporate Hospitality Entertainment provided by an organisation for marketing or motivational purposes

Corporate Rate
1. A lower rate negotiated by a specific corporation for the use of its employees, guests and retained consultants
2. A rate extended by a hotel to all business travellers

Corporate Travel Manager Corporate travel managers are tasked with a range of responsibilities including strategy, setting corporate travel policy, managing and overseeing all travel by corporate employees on company business, sourcing and negotiation of suppliers, communications, operations, technology, traveller security and health, meetings management and car fleet management

Cost of Sales The cost of goods plus the expenses involved in selling and delivering the product or service

Cost Plus Basic charge for a service plus the mark-up or margin to ensure margin and profit for service provider

Count
1. The total number of individuals in attendance at a function for a given period
2. Total number of exhibitors for a given period

Cover Table setting for one person

Cover Charge A fee, usually a flat amount per person, charged to patrons to cover the cost of music and entertainment

Covers Actual number of meals served at a function

Crisis Management Process by which an organisation deals with a major unpredictable event that threatens to harm the organisation, its stakeholders, or the general public

CRS (Computer Reservation System) A computerised system used to store and retrieve information and conduct transactions relating to air travel

CSR (Corporate Social Responsibility) The social, environmental and economic ways in which a company conducts its business. Usually companies will have codes of conduct relating to one or more of the following elements: environmental, community, suppliers/marketplace and employee/workplace

Currency Restriction Any rule or law imposed by a country to regulate the flow of currency into or out of its territory

Custom Menu Menu specifically created for a client

Cut-Off Date Date when a non-guaranteed reservation must be filled or it may be cancelled

CVB (Convention and Visitors Bureau) An organisation responsible for the promotion of a town, city, country, area or region to potential visitors, especially convention organisers

Dais Raised platform in a room or hall on which a speaker's lectern or table for VIPs is situated

Damage Clause Part of a contract dealing with procedures, penalties and rights of the party causing damages

Day Rate
1. In hotels, the fee charged for a stay of limited duration, typically during daylight hours
2. A fee charged for the use of a facility during a 24-hour period

DB&B Dinner, Bed and Breakfast

DDR Day Delegate Rate

De-Brief Post-event review of all aspects of an event to identify learnings for the future and capture ROI/ROO

Definite Booking Space reservations confirmed in writing

Delegate Individual guest at a meeting or event, may also be referred to as an attendee

Delegate Badges Delegate badges come in different shapes and sizes depending on what they need to be used for. Whether it is to show name, company name and country or to record attendance at workshops through mag-stripe swipe or scan technology. They can be magnetic, slip into a plastic wallet on the end of a lanyard or a simple pin

Delegate Management Team Staffed by highly skilled individuals providing high levels of customer care. Deal with all event enquiries and special requirements. Also manage the registration system

Delegate Registration Process by which participants are registered to attend an event e.g. online through a website or paper-based form

Demographics Socio-economic characteristics of delegates, such as age, sex, status. These help to build a profile of the group

Departure Date Date when majority of meeting participants check out of a facility

Deposit Partial payment to secure product or service. May be fully or partially refundable if the meeting/accommodation requirements are cancelled with enough advance notice

Designer's Remote A portable extension of the lighting desk which may be plugged in at various positions around the auditorium allowing the lighting staves to be set up and modified very rapidly

Destination Management Company (DMC) A company that specialises in the organisation and logistics of meetings and events in a specific location, for groups originating from elsewhere. Also called Ground Agents

Dimmer Rack A self-contained portable unit containing a number of lighting dimmers complete with their own mains and circuit distribution

Direct Access System or programme that gives the user the capability of tapping directly into a vendor's computer system to get last-minute information about seat or product availability

Directional Signage Event-specific signs to enable a delegate to locate where a meeting or function is taking place. This is in addition to hotel signage which is often not sufficient

Double Booking
1. Reserving space for two groups to use the same space at the same time and neither can be fully accommodated as contracted
2. An organisation reserving space in more than one venue for the same event

Double Occupancy Rate The rate charged when two people will occupy a room, suite, apartment, etc. For example, a hotel might charge an individual £100 per night for a room (single occupancy) but charge two people only £130 for double occupancy of the same room

Double Room A room designed to be shared by two people. It may have one double (or larger) bed, two twin beds, or two double (or larger) beds. Rooms with double beds are sometimes called a double double

Downgrade To move to a lower grade or quality of services or accommodation

Drape A soft cloth used to mask stage sets

Dress Code Required or suggested acceptable manner or style of dress for an occasion or event

Dry Run Rehearsal or trial run-through of programme

Dual Set-Up Arrangement of duplicate set-ups in two or more different locations

Dumbwaiter A small, hand-operated elevator system used to transport food and dishes from one level to another, as between kitchen and dining room

Duty Fee levied on imported and exported goods

DVD (Digital Version Disc) DVD has the same physical dimensions of a CD – however, it can hold much more information

Early Arrival
1. Guest arrival before confirmed reservation date and/or time
2. Arrival prior to arrival of the majority of the group

Early Registration Registration received before a pre-defined date, usually offering a lower fee

Early-Out A guest who checks out of a hotel one or more days earlier than his or her scheduled departure date. Also called an under-stay or unexpected departure

Economy Hotel A hotel offering few amenities. The phrase 'budget hotel' is also heard

EFT (Electronic Funds Transfer) A computer-based financial transaction

Electronic Whiteboard A system of controlling multimedia presentations by displaying computer-generated images onto white board. The board copies all information written or taped onto it, and saves, publishes or prints out the notes

Emergency Action Plan Procedures about how to react and respond to an emergency situation, such as medical emergencies, fire and acts of terrorism

Emergency Medical Plan A formalised plan of action for handling on-site emergencies from basic first aid to fire or serious injury

En Suite In the hotel industry, a phrase indicating that an amenity or feature is in the room itself or immediately adjacent

English Breakfast A breakfast of cereal, juice, eggs, meats, breads or beverages

ETA Estimated time of arrival

ETD Estimated date of departure

E-Ticket An electronic ticket used to represent the purchase of a seat on a passenger airline. This form of airline ticket rapidly replaced the old paper tickets and became mandatory for IATA members as of 1 June 2008

Event Order A document providing complete and precise instructions to a hotel for the running of a banquet, meeting, or other event to be held in the hotel. Also called a banquet event order or resume sheet

Extended Stay A hotel stay of more than seven days

F&B Food and beverage

Fam Trip Short for familiarisation trip, which is a marketing programme designed by supplier(s) to acquaint event planners with a specific destination

Final Billing Final reconciled cost of the event completed to contract terms

Final Programme Document containing the definitive conference and social programme, circulated immediately prior to a conference or distributed at the commencement of the event

Final Report Conclusive summary of conference events

Finger Food Food at a reception that does not require a knife, fork or spoon

Flats Solid masking or panels, sometimes called flatage

Flatware Utensils used in a place setting (e.g. knife, fork, spoon)

Floodlight A floodlight has a reflector to control the beam and has a wide angle of distribution

FOC Free of Charge

FOH (Front of House) Public areas of a theatre. Lighting FOH refers to lighting positions within the auditorium

Folio The written record

Follow Spot A narrow angle focusing hard edge spotlight used to follow the moving artist or presenter

Force Majeure An unexpected or uncontrollable event (e.g. war, labour strike, extreme weather, or other disruptive circumstances) or effect that cannot be reasonably anticipated or controlled

Foyer Public area in hotel or hall for assembly or registration

Front Desk
1. Hotel registration area
2. The centre of event facility activities, including registration and cashier services

Front Office The office situated in the hotel lobby, the main functions of which are:
1. Control and sale of bedrooms
2. Providing key, mail and information service for guests

3. Keeping guest accounts, rendering bills and receiving payments

4. Providing information to other departments

Front Projection The image is projected onto the screen from the same side as the audience

Function Board Announcements on facility board or video screen listing the day's events. Also known as directory or reader boards

Function Book In a hotel or conference centre, the official record that controls room assignments for meetings and other events

Function Sheet A document providing complete and precise instructions to a hotel for the running of a banquet, meeting, or other event to be held in the hotel. Also called a banquet event order or resume sheet

Function Space Space in facility where private functions or events can be held

Gala Dinner Primary social function of an event, usually in the evening, including entertainment or speeches after a formal meal

GDS (Global Distribution System) A computer reservation system that travel agents use to book airline seats, hotels, car hire, etc.

GMT (Greenwich Mean Time) A time against which hours are measured around the world. It is also known as Standard Clock Time (SCT). Behind the scenes all airlines operate their schedules in GMT – often called Zulu time

GoPAR Gross Operating Profit per Available Room

Graphic Equaliser Frequency control at predetermined frequencies that can be boosted or cut to enhance a particular sound or cut out frequencies that feedback (howl), thus increasing the overall level of gain (loudness) in the system

Gratuities Discretionary payment commonly known as a 'tip' in recognition for outstanding service

Ground Arrangements Services covering the land portion of a trip, such as lodging, visits to museums, sightseeing tours, and transfers between airport and hotel

Ground Operator A company that provides land services such as sightseeing tours, transfers from airport to hotel, limos, taxis, and so on

Ground Transport/Transportation Any method of transport other than air. Trains, coaches, taxis, monorails, trams, buses and ferries are all ways of moving around the airport or between the airport and the city

Group Arrivals/Departures Information included in the specifications guide for an event that outlines approximate dates and times at which groups of event attendees can be expected to arrive at a facility (venue) for check-in or check-out. This is intended to give the facility notice in order to prepare for front desk staffing

Group Booking Reservation for a block of rooms specifically for a group

Group Desk The department or counter of a hotel, or other supplier, that handles group reservations

Group Rate The fare or room rate offered to a group of travellers

Guaranteed Late Arrival Guest room that is guaranteed by credit card or advance payment if arrival is later than hotel's deadline (often 4 pm or 6 pm)

Guaranteed Payment A hotel reservation secured by the guest's agreement to pay for the room whether he or she uses it or not

Guaranteed Reservation A reservation that will be held all night, whether or not the party arrives on time. Generally, the buyer pays for the privilege by guaranteeing payment whether or not the reservation is used

Guest Programme Educational and/or social events planned for spouses and guests of event participants (also called a Partner Programme)

Hand-Measured Pouring The dispensing of alcoholic beverages using shot glasses, jiggers, or other measuring tools, as opposed to free pouring

HBA Hotel Booking Agent

HD High Definition is a new digital format. It was designed from DigiBeta but HD is not compatible with any of the five Betacam formats. The main advantage of HD is its superior quality. It has become a replacement for 8 mm film used on film sets as it is a cheaper and more viable option

Headquarters Hotel Facility, as the centre of operations where registration, general sessions, and conference office staff are located

Health and Safety Risk Assessment Policy by which we assess and manage any risk associated with an event

Herringbone Set-Up Seating arrangement in which chairs are arranged in rows slanted in a V shape and separated by a centre aisle. They face the head table or speaker. See also Chevron Set-Up

High Season The season of the year when travel to an area peaks and rates are at their highest

Hold Time In the hospitality industry, the hour at which hotel rooms that have been reserved but not guaranteed are released for general sale, usually 4 pm or 6 pm

Hollow Circle Set-Up Seating arrangement of tables and/or chairs all facing each other in a single circle

Hollow Square Set-Up A seating arrangement for meetings in which tables or chairs are arranged in a square (or rectangle) with an open space in the centre

Honorarium Payment made to a speaker or expert in recognition of their contribution to an event

Horseshoe Set-Up A seating arrangement for meetings in which tables or chairs are arranged in a U shape

Hospitality Suite A hotel room, or suite, reserved by a company or group in which to greet customers or others. Typically, refreshments are served

Host Bar Private room bar set-up where drinks are paid for by a sponsor

Hotel Representative A booking agent or agency for hotels

Hotel Voucher A pre-paid coupon that can be exchanged at certain hotels for a night's lodging

House A synonym for hotel commonly used within the industry. Examples are full house, house count, house income, house bank and house charge

House Brand Any brand of alcohol served when a customer requests a drink by its generic name (e.g. gin and tonic, scotch and soda). The least expensive brand served, as opposed to more expensive brands

House Count Number of sleeping rooms actually occupied during a particular night

House Limit In a hotel or other establishment, the maximum extent to which credit will be extended before payment is requested. In restaurants and bars, the maximum number of alcoholic beverages that will be served to a single customer

House Wine Moderately priced wines carried by the facility

Housekeeping The department of a hotel charged with cleaning and maintaining rooms and public spaces

Housekeeping Announcements Announcements about schedule changes, locations of functions, and similar programme information

Housekeeping Instructions Special directions to a facility's housekeeping department from an event organiser that apply to that event and its attendees. Can include information such as the best time frame for refreshing sleeping rooms

Housing Curtain Also known as housing tabs. A set of curtains used to hide the stage set until the start of the presentation or performance. More usually used in theatre than conference

Housing Management The sourcing of bedrooms, management of that inventory and all associated contracted terms and conditions

Hybrid Event An event combining live/face-to-face format with a digital/virtual format

Incentive Event A reward event intended to showcase persons who meet or exceed sales or production goals

Incentive House A company that runs incentive programmes, often including travel programmes, for other companies

Incentive Meeting Reward meeting, usually of high quality, in payment for achieving goals

Incentive Travel Travel that is given to employees as a reward for outstanding performance

Incentive Travel Company Company which designs and handles some or all elements of incentive travel programmes

Incidentals Small items or miscellaneous expenditures. For example, in a hotel costs other than room and tax, billed to guest's account such as phone, room service, etc.

Inclusive Rate The amount charged inclusive of all taxes and service charges

In-Out Dates Dates on which a guest arrives and departs

In-Room Messaging System that allows hotel guests to receive electronic mail and faxes on their room televisions

Insurance Specialist cover to insure conferences, events or the guest against losses due to accidents, personal injury claims, cancellations, etc.

Interactive Response A system which enables the audience to respond to prepared questions by means of a multifunction keypad. Responses are fed to a computer which tabulates them and can display the results graphically or in text form on a projection screen

International Event An event that draws a national and international audience. Typically 15 per cent or more of attendees reside outside of the host country

Interpretation The process of explaining or translating

Interpretation in Relay Oral translation utilising two interpreters. Because the first interpreter is not master of the second language, another makes the final interpretation to the audience

Interpreter's Booth/Stand A soundproof cubicle in which the interpreter works

Inventory A detailed list of all the items in stock e.g. total number of bedrooms contracted

Invitation Programme A provisional programme sometimes incorporating a call for papers. The programme gives details of venue, participants, agenda, accommodation, etc.

Involuntary Upgrade Supplier moves guest to higher grade service/facility at no charge

ISO International quality standard

ITT Invitation to Tender (more usually called RFI or RFP)

JI (Joining instructions) The final piece of communication sent in advance of the travel trip to the participant confirming all travel arrangements

Jigger A 1-ounce measure used in making alcoholic drinks

Keynote Address A session that opens or highlights the show, meeting or event

Keynote Speaker Speaker who sets forth the theme of the meeting

King Room A hotel room with a king-size bed suitable for one or two persons

Lanyard A cord or string worn around the neck, typically includes a clip that is used to attach a name badge

Laser Pointer A hand-held unit used to pinpoint areas of the screen using a laser light source

Last-Room Availability
1. A feature of a CRS/booking system allowing up-to-the-minute information on the number of rooms available at a hotel
2. A hotel guarantees provision of an agreed room type e.g. double for single occupancy, at the agreed rate regardless of whether they have bookings for the same room type at a higher rate. When negotiating an annual hotel programme there is usually a premium added to the negotiated nightly rate to secure this guarantee for the life of the contract

Late Registration A booking that is received after the stated deadline, usually incurring a penalty fee

Lead Time The amount or period of time before the announcement of an event and its occurrence, or between the notification that a task must be undertaken and the time at which it must be completed

Lectern A stand used for resting scripts on

Letter of Agreement Document outlining proposed services, space, or products which becomes binding upon written approval by both parties

Liability Insurance An insurance policy that protects you in the event that there is bodily injury or property damage to other people. The liability can be because of negligence or a failure to live up to promises made under a contract

Lighting Bridge A lighting position within the auditorium ceiling

Limited Consumption Bar Host establishes the maximum to be spent at an open bar. Bar is closed or converted to cash when limit is reached

Live Communications The strategy, design, delivery and measurement of live events which may involve messaging/content development, creative, logistics and production support

Livery The uniform worn by some employees, such as chauffeurs and doormen

Loading A term used when delegates are being moved into an area or vehicle as a group

Low Season The time of year when travel to a destination is at its lowest and prices decline

Mag-Stripe (Magnetic Strip) A lead retrieval system using a magnetic strip on either the back of paper badge (similar to some airline tickets) or on plastic badges similar to credit cards

Major Arrival Information included in the specifications guide for an event that notes approximate dates and times at which large numbers of event attendees can be expected to arrive at a facility for check-in. This is intended to give the facility notice in order to prepare for front desk staffing

Major Departure Information included in the specifications guide for an event that notes approximate dates and times at which large numbers of event attendees can be expected to check out of the facility. This is intended to give the facility notice in order to prepare front desk staffing

Management Contract An arrangement whereby a hotel's owner contracts with a separate company to run the hotel

Masking Flatage or drapes used to form a screen surround

Master Account/Bill Set up by a hotel/venue to which authorised charges can be applied and payment reconciled post-event. A record of transactions during an event, may include room, tax, incidentals food and beverage, audio-visual equipment, decor, etc.

Master Key One key that will open function and guest rooms

MC (Master of Ceremonies) Person who acts as the official host for an event and presides over the programme. Usually presents performers and/or speakers, talks to the audience, and generally keeps the event moving

Meeting An event where the primary activity of the participants is to attend educational sessions, participate in discussions, social functions or attend other organised events.

Meeting Point Meeting place in venue for individual appointments of delegates

Menu Pricing A pricing plan that lets the organisation see an itemised list of fees for goods and services

MICE Meetings, Incentives, Conferences/Congresses, and Exhibitions (also Events). An internationally used term for the business events industry

Minibar A hotel room amenity consisting of a small, stocked refrigerator containing beverages and snacks which are inventoried daily and paid for as they are used

MIS Management Information System

Moderator Person who presides over panel discussions and forums

MOU Memo of understanding

Movable Wall Walls or light movable panels used for dividing areas or concealing an area

Move-Out Dates set for dismantling

MPEG (Motion Picture Experts Group) There are multiple types of MPEG files, the common ones being MP3, an audio format that gives CD quality sound due to clever compression techniques. There is also MPG: an abbreviation of MPEG-1 or MPEG-2 video files. MPEG-4, the compression commonly used in picture phones

Multi-Screen The use of two or more screens at the same time. Also called multivision

Multi-Track Conference A conference with parallel programme sessions where participants have the choice to follow one or the other road or to jump from one track to the other for the duration of the event

Name Card Card placed on a banquet or event table, inscribed with the name of the person designated to sit at that place

Net Amount The amount due to the supplier after commissions have been deducted

Net Rate Non-commissionable rate

No-Show Reservation made, but not kept. Any person, group or exhibitor who fails to appear to claim accommodation, meeting space, exhibit space or ordered service

Occupancy Rate
1. In the hotel industry, the percentage of total number of available sleeping rooms actually occupied. Derived by dividing the total number of rooms occupied during a given time period (night, week, year) by the total number of rooms available for occupancy during that same period
2. Measurement of building use, usually expressed as an annual percentage rate comparing potential facility capacity to actual usage

Off Premise Catering Foods usually prepared in a central kitchen and transported for service to an off-site location

Official Banquet Formally seated evening dinner which is normally included in the registration fee and at which speeches are made

Off-Season A period of the year when demand for a destination decreases and prices go down

OHP Overhead Projector

On-Site Documentation Documents used to communicate with the participants and on-site staff. These may include:

- *Welcome Packs*: collation of documents to inform the participants of activities
- *Dietary Cards*: cards which inform staff of participants' dietary, allergy or medical requirements
- *Name Badges*
- *Hospitality Desk Log Book*: book used to document any issues and actions taken while on-site
- *Cash Allowance Sheets*: documents any cash outlaid for audit purposes
- *Gratuities Form*: documents any gratuities outlaid for audit purposes
- *POE (programme of events)*: an overview given to participants on-site so they know the activities during their stay

Open Bar Private room bar set-up where drinks are paid by a sponsor

Open Seating/Open Sitting Seats or tables are not assigned and will be occupied on a first-come basis

Option Date Date by which payment must be made to secure a reservation

Overbooking The practice of taking more reservations than there are seats/rooms, etc. in the expectation that no shows will bring the number of reservations actually used below maximum occupancy

Participant Evaluation Form This gives the delegates a chance to feed back on all aspects of the event. It is distributed to participants on the final evening of the event or given directly to them at another convenient time toward the end of the event

PAX Term used for number of people e.g. 10 PAX is 10 people

Payment Collection The invoicing and collection of payments from individuals e.g. for registration to an event or individual activities on an event. This will be completed via a secure online tool or manually via invoice

PCO Professional Conference (or Congress) Organiser

PDQ Pre-departure questionnaire. Sent to participants in advance of a travel trip to check details e.g. dietary requirements, etc.

Peak Night Referring to the night during an event when most rooms are occupied by those in attendance

Peak Season The season of the year when travel to an area peaks and rates are at their highest

Penthouse The top floor of a hotel

Per Diem Allowance for food and beverage for the day, normally allocated to on-site staff only

Pick Up Room bookings used against stock

Pillow Gift An in-room amenity left in the evening while an event is underway, that the attendee will discover upon returning to the room. Can be gifts from sponsors, etc.

Porterage The use of a concierge to deliver bags/goods within a hotel

Positive Space Seating or rooms that can actually be occupied, as opposed to space reserved on a standby or if-available basis

Post-Event Report The industry-preferred term for a report of the details and activities of an event. A collection of post-event reports over time will provide the complete history of an event

Pre- and Post-Event Organised outing taking place before (pre) or after (post) an event for both attendees and accompanying persons

Pre-Function Space Area adjacent to the main event location. Often used for receptions prior to a meal or coffee breaks during an event

Priority Rating System System of assigning points to exhibiting companies to determine which firms will be allowed to select first their booth/stand space for the next event

Production Supply of audio-visual services to support delivery of events e.g. dry-hire kit, staging, lighting, etc.

Production Company A company that presents special effects and theatrical acts. This type of company may contract to put on an entire event or only parts of one. They sometimes hire speakers as part of their contract

Pro-Forma Invoice Raised based on an estimated cost in order to pay a deposit to a supplier

Queen Room Room with one queen-size bed suitable for one or two persons

Quick Set Function room set-up that saves room turnover time, limits the number of event rooms required, and avoids additional charges for changing room set-up

QuickTime Developed by Apple Computers, QuickTime is a method of storing sound, graphics and movie files. If you see a MOV file on the Web or on a CD-ROM, you'll know it's a QuickTime file

Rack Rate The published rates of a hotel room, printed on the hotel's brochures and on show in reception – these are the prices a hotel charges for a room before any discount has been taken into account. Sometimes set artificially high and used to calculate a variety of discounts

Radio Mic A microphone that does not require a cable, useful where the artist or microphone has to move around. For example, an audience question microphone

Rates Charge agreed in relation to the provision of goals or services. In relation to hotels, the following terms may apply:
- Best agreement between the agency and supplier to offer the best available rate
- Corporate agreed rate between client and supplier
- DDR: day delegate rate
- First offer: first rate offered by supplier, from which negotiation takes place
- Group discounted rate based on volume committed
- Rack cost of a hotel room before taking into account any discount
- Room only rate for hotel room only
- 24-hour rate which encompasses all services agreed in 24-hour period

Reader Board At a facility, a listing, either printed or on a video screen, of the day's events including times and locations

Ready Room Area set aside for speakers to meet, relax, test AV, or prepare prior to or between speeches

Real-Time Events happening that particular moment. Immediate

Refresh To clean room after or between meetings, refilling water pitchers, changing glassware, and other general housekeeping

Refreshment Break Time between sessions where coffee and/or other refreshments are served

Refund Policies Rules and regulations which determine allowable reasons and timelines under which fees for meeting or event will be refunded in whole or in part

Registration Desks Used for larger groups for speed and efficiency. For smaller groups, this could then turn into a Hospitality Desk

Release

1. Signed form giving permission to use a person's name, picture, or statement (often in an advertisement)
2. Form signed by presenter allowing recording of presentation
3. To release space, as in returning unsold air reservations, cruise cabins, or hotel rooms to the supplier that originally allotted them
4. Document provided by management to permit removal of goods from exhibition during event hours

Release Date Date beyond which a supplier is free to sell seats, unused sleeping rooms or function space to others

Rental Charges Cost of hiring a piece of equipment or function space for a specified period of time

Rental Contract Contract stating terms and conditions for rental of exhibition venue or for individual booth/stand within a venue

Request for Information (RFI) A preliminary step to a request for proposal (RFP), in which a company solicits a number of potential vendors for information about their products and services

Request for Proposal (RFP) A formal request by a company, containing detailed specifications, to a potential vendor asking for a bid on satisfying those specifications

Resume Sheet A document providing complete and precise instructions to a hotel for the running of a banquet, meeting, or other event to be held in the hotel. Also called a banquet event order

Retention Rate

1. The percentage of exhibitors or attendees that return to an event from one year to the next
2. The percentage of an organisation's membership or company's employees that remain with the organisation or company from one year to another

Revenue Management System A sophisticated computer-based pricing system that vendors use to adjust prices based on anticipated demand. Also referred to as Yield Management

Revision List Summarised list of changes and updates to be made to a function sheet

RevPAR Revenue Per Available Room. A performance measurement commonly used in the hotel industry. It is calculated by dividing a hotel's net rooms revenue (i.e. after discounts, meals and tax) by the total number of available rooms in the same period, or by multiplying a hotel's average daily room rate (ADR) by its occupancy rate

RFI Request for Information

RFID Radio Frequency Identification – a means of tracking 'footfall' around a venue

RFP Request for Proposal

Roadshow A multi-venue event

ROI (Return on Investment) Net Profit divided by Net Worth. A financial ratio indicating the degree of profitability

Roll-In Foods and/or beverages preset on rolling tables and then moved into function room at designated time

Roll-In Meal Light buffet meal on a cart

Room Block In a hotel, a number of rooms set aside or reserved for a group

Room Capacity Number of people that can function safely and comfortably in a room

Room Commitment Rooms to be held open each night of the event, specified by room type (single, double, etc.)

Room Deposit Money that must be paid in advance in order for a hotel to guarantee to hold a room

Room Gifts A gift from the client company to the delegate put in their room before the delegate has arrived or whilst the delegate is out, so it is received as a surprise. It is usually done on the gala dinner night

Room Nights Number of rooms blocked or occupied multiplied by number of nights each room is reserved or occupied

Room Rate The amount charged for the occupancy of a room

Room Set-Up Layout of tables, chairs, other furniture and equipment for functions

Room Turnover Amount of time needed to tear down and reset a function room

Rooming List A roster of guests and their lodging needs presented to a hotel by a group prior to a meeting. A list that is provided to the hotel for names to put against the room block being held. It should include any medical notes, etc. relevant to room requirements e.g. no feather pillows. It is also the list required from the hotel to check they have a room for everyone on the correct dates

Safety Curtain Also known as the 'iron'. This is an iron or steel shutter door that cuts off the stage from the auditorium in the event of an emergency

Second Tier City A city where the space limitations of the convention centre, the hotels, or the air lift, make the city more appropriate for smaller meetings and events

Security Deposit A deposit made to assure credit usually returned after the event if no damage occurs

Security Service Service providing security arrangements, such as checking delegates' credentials, searching hand luggage, protecting equipment and patrolling congress and exhibition areas

Service Bar A counter from which alcoholic beverages are served that is located outside a function room, usually in an area not visible to guests

Service Charge A mandatory and automatic amount added to standard food and drink charges, usually used to defray the cost of labour, such as housemen, servers, technicians, etc. and of which the facility receives a portion of the charge. In return, the guest is relieved of the responsibility for tipping

Service Compris Literally 'service included', that is, there is no need for an additional tip

Service Non Compris Literally 'service not included', that is, an additional tip is expected

Set The pieces of scenery combined on stage to create the setting

Set-Up
1. Way in which a function room is arranged
2. Erecting displays, installation, or articles in their assembled condition

Set-Up Time The period necessary for the preparation of the conference and exhibition venue before the arrival of delegates and exhibitors

Shell Scheme European booth/stand system, usually includes raised floor, back and side walls, plus fascia

Shoulder Season An abbreviated season that falls between the high and low seasons and offers fares and rates between those of the other seasons

Show Breaking Time specified for the close of the exhibition and the start of demolishing

Shuttle Service
1. A short-run conveyance, sometimes provided free of charge, operating on a frequent schedule, usually between two points, such as between venues, a hotel and the airport, the airport and a car rental agency, etc.
2. Transportation for participants, usually by coach or people carrier, provided on a continuous basis for a certain time period

Simultaneous Translation (ST) Language interpretation used for large multi-lingual events

Single Supplement A charge added to a per-person occupancy rate that is based on an assumption of double occupancy, as in a hotel

Site Inspection Visit to a hotel/venue to inspect suitability and complete an audit before contracting. A site inspection questionnaire is used to prompt response and a site inspection report is completed immediately post-visit

SLA (Service Level Agreement) Usually an adjunct document to a vendor contract. An agreement reached between two parties for the delivery of a service that is measurable

SMERF An acronym used mainly in North America to describe organisations and organisation conventions that are not primarily work-related i.e. Social, Military, Educational, Religious, Fraternal types of events

Social Media Social media is part of the Web 2.0 revolution, the use of web-based channels and mobile technologies to turn communication into interactive dialogue

Social Programme Programme of organised functions, not directly related to the main subject of an event

Soft Opening Time when a property is open for business, prior to the grand opening. All services/facilities may not be complete or available

Sommelier Wine steward, responsible for the opening, decanting and serving of wine in a restaurant

Speakers' Lounge Area set aside for speakers to meet, relax, or prepare prior to or between speeches

Special Needs Any physical or mental consideration that requires special alternatives to ensure travellers' access, safety and comfort and to accommodate those individual needs. Special needs can include food allergies, wheelchair access, signing interpreters, etc.

Sponsor
1. Person(s) or company(-ies) underwriting all or part of the costs of an event. Sponsors may or may not participate in any of the profit from the event
2. An individual who assumes all or part of the financial responsibility for an event. A commercial sponsor that provides financial backing for an aspect of an event and who, in return, receives visibility, advertising or other remuneration in lieu of cash

Sponsored Bar Private room bar set-up where drinks are paid for by a venue

Sponsorship Donated financial or material support, usually in exchange for recognition. Paid opportunity for an entity or an exhibitor to increase its visibility at the event

Spot Rate Rate available on the day of booking

Spouse Programme Educational and/or social events planned for spouses and guests of meeting participants

Square Set-Up Seating arrangement in which double or triple-wide tables are set up with chairs placed around all sides

Statement of Account Statement of income and expenses following the end of an event

Stock Allocation Inventory of rooms

Sub Bass Very low frequency sound that can be felt rather than heard. Important for music, however, not required for speech

Subvention Grant of money, especially from a government. The word is used to describe various types of financial and in-kind support used by destinations (and sometimes venues) to bid for and attract conventions and other events

Sub-Woofer A loudspeaker and enclosure designed to reproduce sub bass

Supplement An additional charge or payment, as a single supplement

Surcharge An additional charge levied for the provision of certain additional features or because of special or extenuating circumstances. For example, fuel surcharge

Sustainability Business approach of balancing economic interests against social and environmental concerns

Tally Sheet Form used to keep track of number of rooms sold and/or still available

Team Building Event used to motivate, educate or train participants, usually in an informal manner

Tear Down Dates set for dismantling

Teaser Piece of communication used in advance of an event to motivate recipients to improve performance in order to achieve attendance or to inspire them to attend, if optional e.g. this may take the form of a plan of regular teasers over a sales period

Teleconference Type of meeting which brings together three or more people in two or more locations through telecommunications

Theatre Set-Up In a meeting, a configuration in which seats are arranged in rows, facing front, as in a theatre

Theme Restaurant A restaurant designed around a particular sport, era, style of music, or entertainment industry personality. Such establishments are typically designed in a theatrical fashion, with as much attention paid to decor and memorabilia as to the food

Tier A row or bank of seats rising in increments to provide improved sight lines for an audience

Total Meeting Room Days Total number of event rooms in a facility multiplied by the number of opportunities to lease the space. Commonly 365 days is used as the multiplier

Total Room Day Inventory Total number of leasable square feet within a facility multiplied by the number of days in the year

Transfer
1. Process of moving equipment and/or people from one point to another
2. Transportation between terminals and hotels

Travel Advisory A formal warning advising caution in travelling to specific countries due to political unrest, natural disaster, or other cause

Travel Insurance An insurance against accidents that occur in the course of travel to or from an event

Try Out Room Room where speakers can check their presentations, slides, overheads, etc.

Turndown Service In hotels, the practice of folding back the blanket and sheet of the bed in the evening, sometimes accompanied by putting a mint on the pillow or a cordial on the night stand

Vendor In the travel industry, any supplier of travel products or services

Venue Sourcing Research and contracting of hotels/venues to fulfil event requirements

Video Data Projector Allows a computer/video image to be enlarged for viewing

VIP Very important person

Voluntary Upgrade Individual moves to higher priced class of service or accommodation for additional fare

Walk-Through
1. Review of meeting details
2. Site inspection
3. Inspection of function room prior to function
4. Inspection of trade show floor prior to opening

Water Stations Tables with pitchers of water and glasses for self-service

Webcast An event that broadcasts the audio and/or video portion of a keynote presentation or other educational sessions over the web in real-time or on-demand

Webconferencing Web browser-based videoconferencing

Welcome Pack Delegates are given this on their arrival at the hotel/venue. It is most commonly given out at the Hospitality Desk but can also be put in the delegate rooms. It usually contains a welcome letter, programme of events, activity confirmation details, dietary confirmation details and can include a departure notice for short events

Welcome Reception An opening event where welcome drinks and often food are served

Wi-Fi Wi-Fi is an abbreviation for 'wireless fidelity', although this full term is rarely used these days. Wi-Fi refers to the technology of wireless local area networks. A person with a Wi-Fi-enabled device such as a computer, mobile (or cell) phone, or PDA can connect to the Internet when in proximity to an access point

Working Programme Timetable of conference content

Workshop
1. Meeting of several persons for intensive discussion. The workshop concept has been developed to compensate for diverging views in a particular discipline or on a particular subject
2. Informal and public session of free discussion organised to take place between formal plenary sessions of a congress or of a conference, either on a subject chosen by the participants themselves or on a special problem suggested by the organisers
3. Training session in which participants, often through exercises, develop skills and knowledge in a given field

Yield Management The practice of adjusting price up or down in response to demand in order to control yield (revenue). The process is usually computerised

Yield Management System A sophisticated computer-based pricing system that vendors use to adjust prices based on anticipated demand. Also referred to as Revenue Management

Index

Aberdeen
   Aberdeen Exhibition and Conference
     Centre 7
   Energy Cities Alliance (The) 115
Abu Dhabi 115, 319
Accor 117
Adelaide 115
   Convention Centre 6, 380
agencies 64–78, 107, 127–130, 195, 380
AIM (Accredited in Meetings) 61
AIME 12, 194
AIPC (International Association of
     Convention Centres) 5, 277, 324–325
Alice Springs Convention Centre 6
ambassador, conference ambassador
     programmes 136, 151–157
American Society of Association Executives
     (ASAE) 325
APEX (Accepted Practices Exchange) 22,
     160, 271, 274, 327
apps 254, 319, 362, 363, 365, 369
association management company 49
Association Internationale des Villes
     Francophones de Congrès (AIVFC)
     326
Association of Australian Convention
     Bureaux (AACB) 341–342
Association of British Professional
     Conference Organisers (ABPCO) 5,
     342–344
associations, professional 49, 79
Atlantic City 5

beaming 359
Beijing (China National Convention Center)
     237–242
Belfast Waterfront Hall 7
Belmont Square Conference Centre 62
BestCities Global Alliance 115
bidding 55–59, 107, 135–136, 157–160
Birmingham
   International Convention Centre 7,
     62
   Meet Birmingham digital bidding system
     159–160
   National Indoor Arena 8
Bournemouth International Centre 7
branding 110–119, 203
Brazilian Association of Event Organisers
     (ABEOC) 344
Bremen, Stadthalle 62
Brisbane
   Brisbane Convention and Exhibition
     Centre 6
   Brisbane City Hall 62
   Brisbane Destination Management Plan
     101–102
Britain for Events campaign 354
British Standard 8901 269–270
Brussels Fund for Scientific Conferences
     (The) 104–105
budgeting 46, 186–191
Buenos Aires 84–87
Business Events Council of Australia
     (BECA) 354–355

business tourism 25–30
business travel agency 75
Business Value of Meetings (BVOM)
    212–213
buyers
    corporate buyers 43–48
    association 48–59
    public sector 59–60
    entrepreneurial/commercial 60
    hosted 88–89
buying patterns 45, 50–51

Cairns Convention Centre 6
Calgary 115
Canada 21, 22, 25, 258–260, 261, 268–269,
    276–282
Canadian Tourism Human Resources Council
    291, 292, 296
Canberra National Convention Centre 6
Cardiff
    ambassador programme/corporate
        champions initiative 156–157
Cardiff International Arena 7
    City Hall 62
    Wales Millennium Centre 7
careers in the conference industry 300–302,
    304–320
Celtic Manor Resort (The) 246–249
Certification in Meetings Management (CMM)
    294
Certified Destination Management Executive
    (CDME) 296–297
Certified Event Management Professional
    (CEMP) 299
Certified in Exhibition Management (CEM)
    299
Certified Meeting Professional (CMP) 295–296
Chartridge Conference Centre 62
China National Convention Center 237–242
Cleveland 5
competency standards 291–292
Confederation of Latin American Congress
        Organizing Entities and Related
        Activities (COCAL) 5, 326
conference (definition of) 22, 24
conference ambassador programmes 136,
    151–157
Conference Centres of Excellence 116–117

conference management and production
    206–208
conference production company 66
congress (definition of) 22
consultancies 78, 80
continuing professional development (CPD)
    24, 290, 293–300
Conventa 87–94, 274–275
Convention (definition of) 22
Convention 2020 Study 379–382
convention and visitor bureau (CVB) 4–5, 64,
    112, 119–127, 187–188
Convention Industry Council 5, 22, 160, 190,
    271, 275, 296, 327, 336, 339
Copenhagen Sustainable Meetings Protocol
    270
Cornell Center for Hospitality Research 368
corporate events/hospitality 25, 46, 74–75
corporate social responsibility (CSR) 56, 70,
    185, 266, 267, 370–373
customer relationship management (CRM) 45,
    106–110, 241, 249
Cvent 193, 206, 376
Cyprus Tourism Organisation 163–164

Daejeon 115
Darwin Convention Centre 6
Daytona Beach Area CVB 102, 103
delegate profile 47–48, 49–50
Denmark 258, 260, 262, 272–273
    Copenhagen Sustainable Meetings
        Protocol 270
    Danish Sustainable Events Initiative 273
Denver 5, 273
destination types 63–64
destination marketing organisation (DMO) 64,
    112, 119–127
destination management company (DMC) 65,
    72–74, 107, 123
Destination Marketing Association
        International (DMAI) 5, 296–297,
        327–328
Detroit 5
discretionary (business tourism) 25
Durban
    Future Convention Cities Initiative 115
    International Convention Centre 62,
        262

East Midlands Conference Centre 62
economic impact 77–78, 255–263
Edinburgh International Conference Centre 7
EIBTM 12, 20–21, 194
EMBOK (events management body of
    knowledge) 290–291
Energy Cities Alliance (The) 115
environmental impacts 267–276
European Association of Event Centres
    (EVVC) 328
European Cities Marketing (ECM) 297–298,
    328–329
European Federation of the Associations of
    Professional Congress Organisers
    (EFAPCO) 329
event evaluation 208–214
event management company 67–68, 107,
    17–129, 195, 380
Event Organisers Sector Supplement 272–273
Event ROI Institute (The) 210–211, 213–214
Eventia 5, 24, 67, 344–345, 368
events management international competency
    standards 291
ExCel 7
exhibition organiser 75–78
exhibitions, economic impact 77–78
experiential marketing agency 67–68, 81–84
    (case study)

face-to-face events 366–370
familiarisation visits 107, 142–143, 148–151
Finland 272
fragmentation 349–350
France 21
Future Convention Cities Initiative 115, 266
future of meetings 373–385

Generation Y 266, 382–384
Generation Z 382–384
German Convention Bureau 125
Glasgow 110
    Scottish Exhibition and Conference
        Centre 7
    Scotland Means Business workshop
        149–151
    The Glasgow Model 165–167
Global Business Travel Association (GBTA)
    330–331, 376

globalisation 12–19
Grass Roots 84–87, 391
green tourism 30, 266

Harrogate International Centre 7
Hellenic Association of Professional Congress
    Organizers (HAPCO) 346
Highgate House 242–246
Historic Conference Centres of Europe
    117
Hobart – Federation Concert Hall and
    Convention Centre 6
Holiday Inn 117
Holland's Pre-Financing and Guarantee Fund
    162–163
Hong Kong Convention and Exhibition Centre
    62
hotel transient occupancy tax 121–122
hybrid events 185, 366–370
Hyderabad 115

Iceland 272
i-Meet.com 349
IMEX 12, 125, 194, 214, 318, 354, 364
incentive travel 21, 25, 27, 29, 68–72
INCON 130, 148
Inspection visits (of venues) 193, 195–198,
    230–232
International Association of Conference
    Centres 331
International Association of Exhibitions and
    Events (IAEE) 5, 331–332
International Association of Professional
    Congress Organisers (IAPCO) 5, 160,
    183, 228, 293–294, 332–335
International Confex 192, 194
International Congress and Convention
    Association (ICCA) 5, 12–15, 20, 53–54,
    55–59, 152–153, 335–337
International Congress of Ophthalmology
    356
International Pharmaceutical Congress
    Advisory Association (IPCAA) 337
International Special Events Society (ISES)
    338
Isle of Man, The Villa Marina 7
ISO20121 270–271
IT&CMA 194

Japan 154, 253
job titles 44
Joint Meetings Industry Council (JMIC) 5, 22,
    334, 338–339, 352–354, 355

Kenes Group (The) 214–217

Lancaster University 62
lead times 46, 51
LEED (Leadership in Energy and
    Environmental Design) 35, 273, 277,
    279
Leeds Arena 7
Leeds Metropolitan University 300, 365,
    372–373, 383–384
leisure tourism 27–28
Liverpool, Arena and Convention Centre 7,
    263
Llandudno, Venue Cymru 7
London
    ExCel 7
    Future Convention Cities Initiative 115
Louisville 5
Los Angeles 5

Malaysia Convention and Exhibition Bureau
    125–126
Manchester
    Bridgewater Hall 8
    Manchester Central 7, 263
    Nynex Arena 8
market intelligence 19–21
marketing
    definition 99
    destination marketing organisation 64, 112,
        119–127
    event marketing 202–206
    market segmentation 102–104
    marketing mix 104–106
    planning 100–102
    principles 98–106
    relationship marketing 106–110
    web marketing 143–148
media, trade 79, 194
meeting (definition of) 23
Meeting architecture 183, 217, 377–378
Meeting Professionals International (MPI)
    5, 21, 212, 214, 258, 267, 268–269,

291–292, 294, 339, 362, 365, 369–370,
    372–373, 373–375, 383–384, 385
Meetings & Events Australia (MEA) 5,
    347–348
Meetings and Business Events Competency
    Standards (MBECS) 291–292, 296
Meetings Industry Association (MIA) 5, 61,
    319, 346–347
Melbourne 2, 13
    AIME 12, 194
    Club Melbourne 155
Melbourne Exhibition and Convention Centre
    6, 62
Mexico 21, 25, 261
MICE 21–22
Multipliers 256–257

National Meetings Week 354
national tourism organisations 80,
    124–127
near field communication (NFC) 363
negotiating
    with clients 235–236
    with venues 198–200
Netherlands Board of Tourism 162–163
NewcastleGateshead
    Convention Bureau 182, 187
Newcastle Arena 8
    The Sage 7
Norway 272

Orlando Convention Center 62

partner programmes 52
per diem 60
performance improvement agency 68–72
Perth
    Convention and Exhibition Centre 6
    Energy Cities Alliance (The) 115
PEST analysis 101
podcasting 359–360
procurement 45, 47, 127, 128, 137, 206,
    281, 374
production company, conference 66
Professional Convention Management
    Association (PCMA) 5, 298–299,
    339–340

professional conference/congress organiser
    (PCO) 49, 59, 65–66, 73, 107, 181–183
    core PCO 59
professional development 29
Professional in Destination Management
    (PDM) 296–297
Programme planning 200–201

Qatar National Convention Centre 32–37
QHotels 104–105
qualifications 24, 292–293

request for proposal (RFP) 127, 157–158
return on investment (ROI) 31, 45, 47, 175,
    181, 208–214
return on objectives (ROO) 47, 208–214
REVPAR 232–235
risk assessment 186
Rome 365
rotation 51–52, 53–54, 55

salary levels 302–303
São Paulo Convention and Visitors Bureau
    130–137
Science Alliance 115
Scotland Means Business workshop
    149–151
search engine optimisation (SEO) 144,
    145–146, 204
Seoul 13
    Convention Bureau social media campaign
        168–171
    Future Convention Cities Initiative 115
Sheffield Arena 8
showrounds (of venues) 230–232
SMERF 48
social impacts/legacies 263–267
social media 54, 76, 129, 130, 142, 146–148,
    168–171, 204, 205, 208, 218–225
    (Blue Paper), 281–282
Society of Incentive and Travel Executives
    (Site) 68, 72, 339, 340
Southern African Association for the
    Conference Industry (SAACI) 5,
    348–349
Southport Theatre and Floral Hall 7
St Louis 5
StarCite 193, 206, 376

Starwood Hotels 118
strategic meetings management programmes
    (SMMP) 47, 183, 373–376
subvention 105, 123, 143, 160–167
suppliers 60–78
sustainability 93, 267–276
Sustainable Tourism Cooperative Research
    Centre 21
Sweden 272
Sydney 8–10, 356
    Business Events Sydney 157, 263–264
    Future Convention Cities Initiative 115
    Sydney Convention and Exhibition Centre
        6

technology trends 356–365
teleconferencing 357–358
tendering 137, 157–160
terminology 2, 21–23, 233, 334
Telford, The International Centre 7
Thailand 194, 267
    Convention and Exhibition Bureau
        126–127, 271
Thistle Hotels 117
Toronto 115
Toulouse 115
Tourism Satellite Account 20–21, 258
trade associations 79
travel management company 75
TRO 81–84

Union of International Associations (UIA) 12,
    16–19, 53–54, 340–341
Unique Venues 116
United Kingdom 8, 21, 28, 47
University of Strathclyde 62
University of Warwick 62
USA 21, 25, 44, 60, 260

Vancouver 115, 267
    Vancouver Convention Centre 276–282
venue, conference (definition of) 25, 62
venue finding agency 65–66, 195
venue inspections 195–198, 230–232
venue preferences 46, 52
venue sourcing/selection 192–198
venue types 61–63
videoconferencing 358–359

Vienna
   Congress of, 3–4, 386
   Convention Bureau 164–165, 273
Vilnius Convention Bureau branding
   113–114
virtual events 185, 366–370
VisitEngland 124–125
VisitScotland Business Tourism Unit 149–151
Vok Dams 369

webcasting 254, 361
web conferencing 360, 366–368

web marketing 143–148, 204
Westminster Collection (The) 117
Wi-Fi 208, 224, 361, 364
World Federation of Societies of Intensive
   and Critical Care Medicine 172–175
World PCO Alliance (The) 130
World Tourism Organisation (WTO) 20

yield management 232–235

THE LEARNING CENTRE
EALING, HAMMERSMITH AND WEST LONDON COLLEGE
GLIDDON ROAD
LONDON W14 9BL